Get the eBook FREE!

(PDF, ePub, Kindle, and liveBook all included)

We believe that once you buy a book from us, you should be able to read it in any format we have available. To get electronic versions of this book at no additional cost to you, purchase and then register this book at the Manning website.

Go to https://www.manning.com/freebook and follow the instructions to complete your pBook registration.

That's it!
Thanks from Manning!

Learn Generative AI with PyTorch

MARK LIU

FOREWORD BY SARAH SANDERS

MANNING
SHELTER ISLAND

For online information and ordering of this and other Manning books, please visit www.manning.com. The publisher offers discounts on this book when ordered in quantity.

For more information, please contact

    Special Sales Department
    Manning Publications Co.
    20 Baldwin Road
    PO Box 761
    Shelter Island, NY 11964
    Email: orders@manning.com

Manning Publications Co.
20 Baldwin Road
PO Box 761
Shelter Island, NY 11964

Development editor:	Rebecca Johnson
Technical editors:	Emmanuel Maggiori and Wee Hyong Tok
Review editor:	Dunja Nikitović
Production editor:	Andy Marinkovich
Copy editor:	Kari Lucke
Proofreader:	Jason Everett
Technical proofreader:	Kostas Passadis
Typesetter:	Tamara Švelić Sabljić
Cover designer:	Marija Tudor

ISBN 9781633436466
Printed in the United States of America

To all AI enthusiasts!

contents

foreword

I first met Mark at the PNC Innovation Summit at the University of Kentucky, at which we were both presenters. His topic was *How Machines Learn.* From our very first encounter, I was struck by Mark's ability to explain complex concepts in an engaging and easy-to-understand manner. His knack for breaking down intricate ideas into digestible, relatable terms was truly impressive, and it's a gift that he now shares through his latest book, *Learn Generative AI with PyTorch.*

At Native AI, where I am cofounder and chief operating officer, we are tasked with generating predictive synthetic data that is both highly accurate and robust. Mark's exploration of techniques like temperature and top-K sampling to control the precision of AI-generated text is cutting-edge. These methods are essential for tailoring natural language processing outputs to specific use cases, a topic that will continue to grow in importance and business value.

Learn Generative AI with PyTorch is a comprehensive guide that not only introduces readers to the fascinating world of generative AI but also equips them with practical skills to build and implement their own models. Mark's use of PyTorch as the framework of choice is a testament to its flexibility and power in developing advanced AI models. From long short-term memory models to variational autoencoders, generative adversarial networks, and Transformers, this book covers an impressive breadth of topics.

Mark's book is an invaluable resource for anyone looking to dive into generative AI, whether they are beginners seeking to understand the basics or experienced practitioners aiming to expand their knowledge and skills. His ability to make complex topics accessible and engaging ensures that readers will come away with a solid understanding and the confidence to apply what they've learned.

I am honored to write the foreword for this exceptional book and am excited for the many readers who will benefit from Mark's expertise. *Learn Generative AI with PyTorch* is sure to inspire and educate, paving the way for future innovations in the field of generative AI.

—SARAH SANDERS, COFOUNDER AND COO, NATIVEAI

preface

My fascination with generative AI began a few years ago when I first saw models converting horse images into zebra images and Transformers producing lifelike text. This book is born out of my journey in building and understanding these models from scratch. It's the book I wish I had during my experiments with various generative models. It begins with simple models, helping readers build foundational deep learning skills before advancing to more complex challenges. I chose PyTorch for its dynamic computational graph and clear syntax after experimenting with TensorFlow.

All generative models in this book are deep neural networks. The book starts with a comprehensive deep learning project in PyTorch, ideal for those new to the field. Each chapter is carefully structured to build upon the previous one. You'll first learn to create basic content, such as shapes, numbers, and images using generative adversarial networks with straightforward architectures. As you progress, the complexity increases, culminating in building state-of-the-art models such as Transformers to generate text and music and diffusion models to generate high-resolution images.

On the surface, this book provides an exploration of various generative AI models. At a deeper level, the technological journey reflects how our mind works and the essence of what it means to be human. The prominence of deep neural networks in these generative models is a testament to our quest to understand and replicate the complex processes of human learning. Generative AI models, drawing inspiration from the marvels of evolutionary biology that shaped our brains, learn from the vast amount of data they encounter, much like we humans learn from the stimuli around us.

The implications of generative AI extend far beyond its practical applications. As we stand at the forefront of this technological revolution, we are compelled to re-evaluate our understanding of consciousness, life, and the very nature of human existence. The parallels between machine learning and human learning are striking. Just as generative

AI operates through neural networks inspired by the human brain, our thoughts, emotions, and behaviors are the outputs of the neural networks within our body. Thus, the study of generative AI transcends technological boundaries, becoming an exploration of the human condition and the mechanisms that underlie our consciousness. The study of generative AI leads us to a profound speculation: Are humans, in essence, sophisticated generative AI models?

In that sense, generative AI is not just a tool: it is a mirror reflecting our deepest existential questions. As we continue to develop and interact with these technologies, we are not only shaping the future of *artificial intelligence* but also deepening our understanding of *human intelligence*. Ultimately, the exploration of generative AI is an exploration of ourselves, a journey into the heart of consciousness and the essence of life, challenging us to redefine what it means to be conscious, to be alive, and to be human.

acknowledgments

Many people have helped to make this book a reality. Jonathan Gennick, my acquisition editor at Manning, played a crucial role in identifying the topics readers are eager to learn and in structuring the chapters to facilitate learning. A special thanks goes to my developmental editor, Rebecca Johnson, whose relentless pursuit of perfection significantly improved the book. She encouraged me to explain complex concepts in a clear and understandable manner.

My gratitude also extends to my technical editor, Emmanuel Maggiori, author of *Smart Until It's Dumb* (Applied Maths Ltd., 2023). Every time I got carried away in my writing about AI's wondrous potential, Emmanuel was always quick to point out its limitations. While my favorite quote is, "Any sufficiently advanced technology is indistinguishable from magic" by Arthur C. Clarke, Emmanuel's perspective on AI can be summed up by the title of his book. This clash of viewpoints, I believe, provides our readers with a more balanced perspective.

Thank you to all the reviewers: Abhilash Babu, Ankit Virmani, Arpit Singh, Christopher Kottmyer, David Cronkite, Eduardo Rienzi, Erim Erturk, Francis Osei Annin, Georg Piwonka, Holger Voges, Ian Long, Japneet Singh, Karrtik Iyer, Kollin Trujillo, Michael Petrey, Mirerfan Gheibi, Nathan Crocker, Neeraj Gupta, Neha Shetty, Palak Mathur, Peter Henstock, Piergiorgio Faraglia, Rajat Kant Goel, Ramaa Vissa, Ravi Kiran Bamidi, Richard Tobias, Ruud Gijsen, Slavomir Furman, Sumit Pal, Thiago Britto Borges, Tony Holdroyd, Ursin Stauss, Vamsi Srinivas Parasa, Viju Kothuvatiparambil, and Walter Alexander Mata López, your suggestions helped make this a better book.

I also wish to thank the production team at Manning Publications for helping me bring this project to completion.

Finally, I want to express my deepest gratitude to my wife, Ivey Zhang, and my son, Andrew Liu, for their unwavering support throughout this journey.

about this book

Learn Generative AI with PyTorch aims to guide you through the creation of various content (shapes, numbers, images, text, and music) from scratch. It begins with simple models, helping readers build foundational deep learning skills before advancing to more complex challenges. All generative models in this book are deep neural networks. The book starts with a comprehensive deep learning project in PyTorch, ideal for those new to the field. Each chapter is carefully structured to build upon the previous one. You'll first create basic content like shapes, numbers, and images using generative adversarial networks with straightforward architectures. As you progress, the complexity increases, culminating in building state-of-the-art models like Transformers and diffusion models.

Who should read this book?

Learn Generative AI with PyTorch is designed for machine learning enthusiasts and data scientists in various business fields who possess intermediate Python programming skills. This book aims to teach generative AI techniques for creating novel and innovative content, such as images, text, patterns, numbers, shapes, and audio, to enhance both their employers' businesses and their own careers. While many free learning materials are available online covering individual topics, this book consolidates everything into a clear, easy-to-follow, and up-to-date format, making it an invaluable resource for anyone aspiring to become an expert in generative AI.

I assume the readers have a solid grasp of Python. You should be familiar with variable types, Python functions and classes, and the installation of third-party Python libraries and packages. If you need to brush up on these skills, the free online Python tutorial provided by W3Schools is a great resource (https://www.w3schools.com/python/).

You also should have a basic understanding of machine learning, particularly neural networks and deep learning. If not, a good book for this purpose is *Deep Learning with PyTorch* by Stevens, Antiga, and Viehmann (2020), also published by Manning Publications. Appendix B of this book provides a review of key concepts such as loss functions, activation functions, and optimizers, which are essential for developing and training deep neural networks. However, this appendix is not meant to be a comprehensive tutorial on these topics.

How this book is organized: a roadmap

This book has 16 chapters, organized into four parts. Part I introduces you to generative AI and deep learning with PyTorch.

- Chapter 1 explains what generative AI is and the rationale behind selecting PyTorch over other AI frameworks like TensorFlow for building generative models in this book.
- Chapter 2 uses PyTorch to create deep neural networks to perform binary and multicategory classifications so that you become well-versed in deep learning and classification tasks. The intention is to get you ready for the upcoming chapters, where you use deep neural networks in PyTorch to create various generative models.
- Chapter 3 introduces you to generative adversarial networks (GANs). You learn to use GANs to generate shapes and sequences of numbers with certain patterns.

Part II covers image generation.

- Chapter 4 discusses how to build and train GANs to generate high-resolution color images. In particular, you'll learn to use convolutional neural networks to capture spatial features in images. You'll also learn to use transposed convolutional layers to upsample and generate high-resolution feature maps in images.
- Chapter 5 details two ways to select characteristics in generated images. The first method involves selecting specific vectors in the latent space. The second method uses a conditional GAN, where you build and train a GAN with labeled data.
- Chapter 6 teaches you how to use a CycleGAN to translate images between two domains such as images with black hair and images with blond hair or horse images and zebra images.
- Chapter 7 explains how to generate high-resolution images using another generative model: autoencoders and their variant, variational autoencoders.

Part III dives into natural language processing and text generation.

- Chapter 8 discusses text generation with a recurrent neural network. Along the way, you learn how tokenization and word embedding work. You'll also learn to generate text autoregressively with the trained model and how to use temperature and top-K sampling to control the creativity of the generated text.

- Chapter 9 builds a Transformer from scratch, based on the paper "Attention Is All You Need," to translate between any two languages. You'll implement line by line the multihead attention mechanism and an encoder-decoder Transformer.
- Chapter 10 trains the Transformer you built in chapter 9 with more than 47,000 pairs of English-to-French translations. You'll learn to translate common English phrases to French with the trained model.
- Chapter 11 builds GPT-2XL, the largest version of GPT-2, from scratch. After that, you'll learn how to extract the pretrained weights from Hugging Face and load them to your own GPT-2 model to generate text.
- Chapter 12 constructs a scaled-down version of the GPT model with approximately 5 million parameters so that you can train it on a regular computer. You'll use three novels by Ernest Hemingway as the training data. The trained model can generate text in Hemingway style.

Part IV discusses some practical applications of the generative models in the book and the most recent developments in the field of generative AI.

- Chapter 13 builds and trains a MuseGAN to generate music. MuseGAN treats a piece of music as a multidimensional object akin to an image. The generator produces a complete piece of music and submits it to the critic for evaluation. The generator then modifies the music based on the critic's feedback until it closely resembles real music from the training dataset.
- Chapter 14 takes a different approach to AI music creation. Instead of treating a piece of music as a multidimensional object, you treat it as a sequence of musical events. You'll then apply techniques from text generation to predict the next element in a sequence.
- Chapter 15 introduces you to diffusion models, which form the foundation of all leading text-to-image Transformers (such as DALL-E 2 or Imagen). You'll build and train a diffusion model to generate high-resolution flower images.
- Chapter 16 ends the book with a project in which you use the LangChain library to combine pretrained large language models with Wolfram Alpha and Wikipedia APIs to create a zero-shot know-it-all personal assistant.

Appendix A discusses how to install PyTorch on your computer, with or without a compute unified device architecture-enabled GPU. Appendix B provides information on what background you need in order to proceed with projects in this book and some basic concepts in deep learning such as loss functions, activation functions, and optimizers.

About the code

This book contains many examples of source code both in numbered listings and in line with normal text. In both cases, source code is formatted in a `fixed-width font like this` to separate it from ordinary text. Sometimes code is also **in bold** to highlight code that has changed from previous steps in the chapter, such as when a new feature adds to an existing line of code.

In many cases, the original source code has been reformatted; we've added line breaks and reworked indentation to accommodate the available page space in the book. In rare cases, even this was not enough, and listings include line-continuation markers (➥). Additionally, comments in the source code have often been removed from the listings when the code is described in the text. Code annotations accompany many of the listings, highlighting important concepts.

You can get executable snippets of code from the liveBook (online) version of this book at https://livebook.manning.com/book/learn-generative-ai-with-pytorch. All Python programs in this book are available for download from the Manning website at www.manning.com and from the book's GitHub repository at https://github.com/markhliu/DGAI. The programs are organized by chapters with each chapter in a single Jupyter Notebook file. See appendix A on how to install Python, PyTorch, and Jupyter Notebook on your computer.

liveBook discussion forum

Purchase of *Learn Generative AI with PyTorch* includes free access to liveBook, Manning's online reading platform. Using liveBook's exclusive discussion features, you can attach comments to the book globally or to specific sections or paragraphs. It's a snap to make notes for yourself, ask and answer technical questions, and receive help from the author and other users. To access the forum, go to https://livebook .manning.com/book/learn-generative-ai-with-pytorch/discussion. You can also learn more about Manning's forums and the rules of conduct at https://livebook.manning .com/discussion.

Manning's commitment to our readers is to provide a venue where a meaningful dialogue between individual readers and between readers and the author can take place. It is not a commitment to any specific amount of participation on the part of the author, whose contribution to the forum remains voluntary (and unpaid). We suggest you try asking the author some challenging questions lest their interest stray! The forum and the archives of previous discussions will be accessible from the publisher's website for as long as the book is in print.

about the author

DR. MARK LIU is a tenured finance professor and the (founding) director of the Master of Science in Finance program at the University of Kentucky. He is the author of two books: *Make Python Talk* (No Starch Press, 2021) and *Machine Learning, Animated* (CRC Press, 2023). Mark has more than 20 years of coding experience. He obtained his PhD in finance from Boston College. Mark has published his research in top finance journals such as the *Journal of Financial Economics*, the *Journal of Financial and Quantitative Analysis*, and the *Journal of Corporate Finance*.

about the cover illustration

The figure on the cover of *Learn Generative AI with PyTorch,* captioned "L'Agent de la rue de Jerusalem," or "The Jerusalem Street Agent," is taken from a book by Louis Curmer published in 1841. Each illustration is finely drawn and colored by hand.

In those days, it was easy to identify where people lived and what their trade or station in life was just by their dress. Manning celebrates the inventiveness and initiative of the computer business with book covers based on the rich diversity of regional culture centuries ago, brought back to life by pictures from collections such as this one.

Part 1

Introduction to generative AI

What is generative AI? How is it different from its nongenerative counterparts, discriminative models? Why do we choose PyTorch as the AI framework in this book?

In this part, we answer these questions. In addition, all generative AI models in this book are deep neural networks. Therefore, you'll learn how to use PyTorch to create deep neural networks to perform binary and multicategory classifications so that you become well versed in deep learning and classification tasks. The intention is to get you ready for the upcoming chapters, where you use deep neural networks in PyTorch to create various generative models. You'll also learn to use PyTorch to build and train generative adversarial networks to generate shapes and sequences of numbers.

What is generative AI and why PyTorch?

This chapter covers

- Generative AI vs. nongenerative AI
- Why PyTorch is ideal for deep learning and generative AI
- The concept of Generative Adversarial Networks
- The benefits of the attention mechanism and Transformers
- Advantages of creating generative AI models from scratch

Generative AI has significantly affected the global landscape, capturing widespread attention and becoming a focal point since the advent of ChatGPT in November 2022. This technological advancement has revolutionized numerous aspects of everyday life, ushering in a new era in technology and inspiring a host of startups to explore the extensive possibilities offered by various generative models.

Consider the advancements made by Midjourney, a pioneering company, which now creates high-resolution, realistic images from brief text inputs. Similarly, Freshworks, a software company, has accelerated application development dramatically, reducing the time required from an average of 10 weeks to mere days, a feat achieved through the capabilities of ChatGPT (see the *Forbes* article "10 Amazing Real-World Examples of How Companies Are Using ChatGPT in 2023," by Bernard Barr, 2023, https://mng.bz/Bgx0). To add a case in point, elements of this very introduction have been enhanced by generative AI, demonstrating its ability to refine content to be more engaging.

> **NOTE**   What better way to explain generative AI than letting generative AI do itself? I asked ChatGPT to rewrite an early draft of this introduction in a "more engaging manner" before finalizing it.

The repercussions of this technological advancement extend far beyond these examples. Industries are experiencing significant disruption due to the advanced capabilities of generative AI. This technology now produces essays comparable to those written by humans, composes music reminiscent of classical compositions, and rapidly generates complex legal documents, tasks that typically require considerable human effort and time. Following the release of ChatGPT, CheggMate, an educational platform, witnessed a significant decrease in its stock value. Furthermore, the Writers Guild of America, during a recent strike, reached a consensus to put guardrails around AI's encroachment on scriptwriting and editing (see the *WIRED* article "Hollywood Writers Reached an AI Deal That Will Rewrite History," by Will Bedingfield, 2023, https://mng.bz/1ajj).

> **NOTE**   CheggMate charges college students to have their questions answered by human specialists. Many of these jobs can now be done by ChatGPT or similar tools at a fraction of the costs.

This raises several questions: What is generative AI, and how does it differ from other AI technologies? Why is it causing such widespread disruption across various sectors? What is the underlying mechanism of generative AI, and why is it important to understand?

This book offers an in-depth exploration of generative AI, a groundbreaking technology reshaping numerous industries through its efficient and rapid content creation capabilities. Specifically, you'll learn to use state-of-the-art generative models to create various forms of content: shapes, numbers, images, text, and audio. Further, instead of treating these models as black boxes, you'll learn to create them from scratch so that you have a deep understanding of the inner workings of generative AI. In the words of physicist Richard Feynman, "What I cannot create, I do not understand."

All these models are based on deep neural networks, and you'll use Python and PyTorch to build, train, and use these models. We chose Python for its user-friendly syntax, cross-platform compatibility, and wide community support. We also chose PyTorch over other frameworks like TensorFlow for its ease of use and adaptability to various model architectures. Python is widely regarded as the primary tool for machine learning (ML), and PyTorch has become increasingly popular in the field of AI. Therefore, using Python and PyTorch allows you to follow the new developments in generative AI. Because PyTorch allows for graphics processing unit (GPU) training acceleration, you'll train these models in a matter of minutes or hours and witness generative AI in action!

1.1 Introducing generative AI and PyTorch

This section explains what generative AI is and how it's different from its nongenerative counterparts: discriminative models. Generative AI is a category of technologies with the remarkable capacity to produce diverse forms of new content, including text, images, audio, video, source code, and intricate patterns. Generative AI crafts entirely new worlds of novel and innovative content; ChatGPT is a notable example. In contrast, discriminative modeling predominantly concerns itself with the task of recognizing and categorizing pre-existing content.

1.1.1 What is generative AI?

Generative AI is a type of artificial intelligence that creates new content, such as text, images, or music, by learning patterns from existing data. It differs from discriminative models, which specialize in discerning disparities among distinct data instances and learning the boundary between classes. Figure 1.1 illustrates the difference between these two modeling methods. For instance, when confronted with an array of images featuring dogs and cats, a discriminative model determines whether each image portrays a dog or a cat by capturing a few key features that distinguish one from the other (e.g., cats have small noses and pointy ears). As the top half of the figure shows, a discriminative model takes data as inputs and produces probabilities of different labels, which we denote by Prob(dog) and Prob(cat). We can then label the inputs based on the highest predicted probabilities.

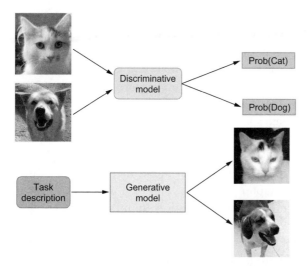

Figure 1.1 A comparison of generative models versus discriminative models. A discriminative model (top half of the figure) takes data as inputs and produces probabilities of different labels, which we denote by Prob(dog) and Prob(cat). In contrast, a generative model (bottom half) acquires an in-depth understanding of the defining characteristics of these images to synthesize new images representing dogs and cats.

In contrast, generative models exhibit a unique ability to generate novel instances of data. In the context of our dog and cat example, a generative model acquires an in-depth understanding of the defining characteristics of these images to synthesize new images representing dogs and cats. As the bottom half of figure 1.1 shows, a generative model takes task descriptions (such as varying values in a latent space that result in different characteristics in the generated image, which we will discuss in detail in chapters 4 to 6) as inputs and produces entirely new images of dogs and cats.

From a statistical perspective, when presented with data examples with features X, which describe the input and various corresponding labels Y, discriminative models undertake the responsibility of predicting conditional probabilities, specifically the probability prob(Y|X). Conversely, generative models attempt to learn the joint probability distribution of the input features X and the target variable Y, denoted as prob (X, Y). Armed with this knowledge, they sample from the distribution to conjure fresh instances of X.

There are different types of generative models depending on the specific forms of content you want to create. In this book, we focus primarily on two prominent technologies: Generative Adversarial Networks (GANs) and Transformers (although we'll also cover variational autoencoders and diffusion models). The word "adversarial" in GANs refers to the fact that the two neural networks compete against each other in a zero-sum game framework: the generative network tries to create data instances indistinguishable from real samples, while the discriminative network tries to identify the generated samples from real ones. The competition between the two networks leads to the improvement of both, eventually enabling the generator to create highly realistic data. Transformers are deep neural networks that can efficiently solve sequence-to-sequence prediction tasks, and we'll explain them in more detail later in this chapter.

GANs, celebrated for their ease of implementation and versatility, empower individuals with even rudimentary knowledge of deep learning to construct their generative models from the ground up. These versatile models can give rise to a plethora of creations, from geometric shapes and intricate patterns, as exemplified in chapter 3 of this book, to high-quality color images like human faces, which you'll learn to generate in chapter 4. Furthermore, GANs exhibit the ability to transform image content, seamlessly morphing a human face image with blond hair into one with black hair, a phenomenon discussed in chapter 6. Notably, they extend their creative prowess to the field of music generation, producing realistic-sounding musical compositions, as demonstrated in chapter 13.

In contrast to shape, number, or image generation, the art of text generation poses formidable challenges, chiefly due to the sequential nature of textual information, where the order and arrangement of individual characters and words hold significant meaning. To confront this complexity, we turn to Transformers, deep neural networks designed to proficiently address sequence-to-sequence prediction tasks. Unlike their predecessors, such as recurrent neural networks (RNNs) or convolutional neural networks (CNNs), Transformers excel in capturing intricate, long-range dependencies inherent in both input and output sequences. Notably, their capacity for parallel training (a distributed training method in which a model is trained on multiple devices simultaneously) has substantially reduced training times, making it possible for us to train Transformers on vast amounts of data.

The revolutionary architecture of Transformers underpins the emergence of large language models (LLMs; deep neural networks with a massive number of parameters and trained on large datasets), including ChatGPT, BERT, DALL-E, and T5. This transformative architecture serves as the bedrock of the recent surge in AI advancement, ushered in by the introduction of ChatGPT and other generative pretrained Transformer (GPT) models.

In the subsequent sections, we dive into the comprehensive inner workings of these two pioneering technologies: their underlying mechanisms and the myriad possibilities they unlock.

1.1.2 The Python programming language

I assume you have a working knowledge of Python. To follow the content in the book, you need to know the Python basics such as functions, classes, lists, dictionaries, and so on. If not, there are plenty of free resources online to get you started. Follow the instructions in appendix A to install Python. After that, create a virtual environment for this book and install Jupyter Notebook as the computing environment for projects in this book.

Python has established itself as the leading programming language globally since the latter part of 2018, as documented by *The Economist* (see the article "Python Is Becoming the World's Most Popular Coding Language" by the Data Team at *The Economist*, 2018, https://mng.bz/2gj0). Python is not only free for everyone to use but also allows other users to create and tweak libraries. Python has a massive community-driven ecosystem, so you can easily find resources and assistance from fellow Python enthusiasts. Plus, Python programmers love to share their code, so instead of reinventing the wheel, you can import premade libraries and share your own with the Python community.

No matter if you're on Windows, Mac, or Linux, Python's got you covered. It's a cross-platform language, although the process of installing software and libraries might vary a bit depending on your operating system—but don't worry; I'll show you how to do it in appendix A. Once everything's set up, Python code behaves the same across different systems.

Python is an expressive language that's suitable for general application development. Its syntax is easy to grasp, making it straightforward for AI enthusiasts to understand and work with. If you run into any problems with the Python libraries mentioned in this book, you can search Python forums or visit sites like Stack Overflow (https://stackoverflow.com/questions/tagged/python) for answers. And if all else fails, don't hesitate to reach out to me for assistance.

Lastly, Python offers a large collection of libraries that make creating generative models easy (relative to other languages such as C++ or R). In this journey, we'll exclusively use PyTorch as our AI framework, and I'll explain why we pick it over competitors like TensorFlow shortly.

1.1.3   Using PyTorch as our AI framework

Now that we have settled on using Python as the programming language for this book, we'll choose a suitable AI framework for generative modeling. The two most popular AI frameworks in Python are PyTorch and TensorFlow. In this book, we use PyTorch over TensorFlow for its ease of use, and I strongly encourage you to do the same.

PyTorch is an open-source ML library developed by Meta's AI Research lab. Built on the Python programming language and the Torch library, PyTorch aims to offer a flexible and intuitive platform for creating and training deep learning models. Torch, the predecessor of PyTorch, was an ML library for building deep neural networks in C with a Lua wrapper, but its development was discontinued. PyTorch was designed to meet the needs of researchers and developers by providing a more user-friendly and adaptable framework for deep learning projects.

A computational graph is a fundamental concept in deep learning that plays a crucial role in the efficient computation of complex mathematical operations, especially those involving multidimensional arrays or tensors. A computational graph is a directed graph where the nodes represent mathematical operations, and the edges represent data that flow between these operations. One of the key uses of computational graphs is the calculation of partial derivatives when implementing backpropagation and gradient descent algorithms. The graph structure allows for the efficient calculation of gradients required to update the model parameters during training. PyTorch creates and modifies the graph on the fly, which is called a dynamic computational graph. This makes it more adaptable to varying model architectures and simplifies debugging. Further, just like TensorFlow, PyTorch provides accelerated computation through GPU training, which can significantly reduce training time compared to central processing unit (CPU) training.

PyTorch's design aligns well with the Python programming language. Its syntax is concise and easy to understand, making it accessible to both newcomers and experienced developers. Researchers and developers alike appreciate PyTorch for its flexibility. It empowers them to experiment with novel ideas quickly, thanks to its dynamic computational graph and simple interface. This flexibility is crucial in the rapidly evolving fields of generative AI. PyTorch also has a rapidly growing community that actively contributes to its development. This results in an extensive ecosystem of libraries, tools, and resources for developers.

PyTorch excels in transfer learning, a technique where pretrained models designed for a general task are fine-tuned for specific tasks. Researchers and practitioners can easily utilize pretrained models, saving time and computational resources. This feature is especially important in the age of pretrained LLMs and allows us to adopt LLMs for downstream tasks such as classification, text summarization, and text generation.

PyTorch is compatible with other Python libraries, such as NumPy and Matplotlib. This interoperability allows data scientists and engineers to seamlessly integrate

PyTorch into their existing workflows, enhancing productivity. PyTorch is also known for its commitment to community-driven development. It evolves rapidly, with regular updates and enhancements based on real-world usage and user feedback, ensuring that it remains at the cutting edge of AI research and development.

Appendix A provides detailed instructions on how to install PyTorch on your computer. Follow the instructions to install PyTorch in the virtual environment for this book. In case you don't have a Compute Unified Device Architecture (CUDA)-enabled GPU installed on your computer, all programs in this book are compatible with CPU training as well. Better yet, I'll provide the trained models on the book's GitHub repository https://github.com/markhliu/DGAI so you can see the trained models in action (in case the trained model is too large, I'll provide them on my personal website https://gattonweb.uky.edu/faculty/lium/). In chapter 2, you'll dive deep into PyTorch. You'll first learn the data structure in PyTorch, Tensor, which holds numbers and matrices and provides functions to conduct operations. You'll then learn to perform an end-to-end deep learning project using PyTorch. Specifically, you'll create a neural network in PyTorch and use clothing item images and the corresponding labels to train the network. Once done, you use the trained model to classify clothing items into 10 different label types. The project will get you ready to use PyTorch to build and train various generative models in later chapters.

1.2 GANs

This section first provides a high-level overview of how GANs work. We then use the generation of anime face images as an example to show you the inner workings of GANs. Finally, we'll discuss the practical uses of GANs.

1.2.1 A high-level overview of GANs

GANs represent a category of generative models initially proposed by Ian Goodfellow and his collaborators in 2014 ("Generative Adversarial Nets," https://arxiv.org/abs/1406.2661). GANs have become extremely popular in recent years because they are easy to build and train, and they can generate a wide variety of content. As you'll see from the illustrating example in the next subsection, GANs employ a dual-network architecture comprising a generative model tasked with capturing the underlying data distribution to generate content and a discriminative model that serves to estimate the likelihood that a given sample originates from the authentic training dataset (considered as "real") rather than being a product of the generative model (considered as "fake"). The primary objective of the model is to produce new data instances that closely resemble those in the training dataset. The nature of the data generated by GANs is contingent upon the composition of the training dataset. For example, if the training data consists of grayscale images of clothing items, the synthesized images will closely resemble such clothing items. Conversely, if the training dataset comprises color images of human faces, the generated images will also resemble human faces.

Take a look at figure 1.2—the architecture of our GAN and its components. To train the model, both real samples from the training dataset (as shown at the top of figure 1.2) and fake samples created by the generator (left) are presented to the discriminator (middle). The principal aim of the generator is to create data instances that are virtually indistinguishable from the examples found within the training dataset. Conversely, the discriminator strives to distinguish fake samples generated by the generator from real samples. These two networks engage in a continual competitive process similar to a cat-and-mouse game, trying to outperform each other iteratively.

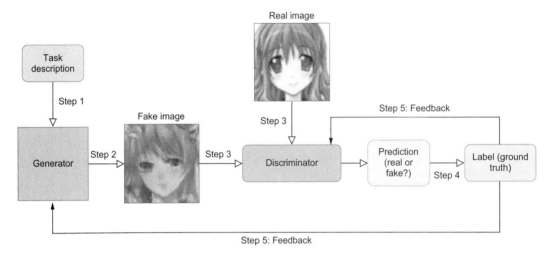

Figure 1.2   GANs architecture and its components. GANs employ a dual-network architecture comprising a generative model (left) tasked with capturing the underlying data distribution and a discriminative model (center) that serves to estimate the likelihood that a given sample originates from the authentic training dataset (considered as "real") rather than being a product of the generative model (considered as "fake").

The training process of the GAN model involves multiple iterations. In each iteration, the generator takes some form of task description (step 1) and uses it to create fake images (step 2). The fake images, along with real images from the training set, are presented to the discriminator (step 3). The discriminator tries to classify each sample as either real or fake. It then compares the classification with the actual labels, the ground truth (step 4). Both the discriminator and the generator receive feedback (step 5) from the classification and improve their capabilities: while the discriminator adapts its ability to identify fake samples, the generator learns to enhance its capacity to generate convincing samples to fool the discriminator. As training advances, an equilibrium is reached when neither network can further improve. At this point, the generator becomes capable of producing data instances that are practically indistinguishable from real samples.

To understand exactly how GANs work, let's look at an illustrating example.

1.2.2   An illustrating example: Generating anime faces

Picture this: you're a passionate anime enthusiast, and you're on a thrilling quest to create your very own anime faces using a powerful tool known as a deep convolutional GAN (or DCGAN for short; don't worry, we'll dive deeper into this in chapter 4).

If you look at the top middle of figure 1.2, you'll spot a picture that reads "Real Image." We'll use 63,632 colorful images of anime faces as our training dataset. And if you flip to figure 1.3, you'll see 32 examples from our training set. These special images play a crucial role as they form half of the inputs to our discriminator network.

Figure 1.3   Examples from the anime faces training dataset

The left of figure 1.2 is the generator network. To generate different images every time, the generator takes as input a vector Z from the latent space. We could think of this vector as a "task description." During training, we draw different Z vectors from the latent space, so the network generates different images every time. These fake images are the other half of the inputs to the discriminator network.

> **NOTE**   By altering the values in the vector Z, we generate different outputs. In chapter 5, you'll learn how to select the vector Z to generate images with certain characteristics (e.g., male or female features).

But here's the twist: before we teach our two networks the art of creation and detection, the images produced by the generator are, well, gibberish! They look nothing like the realistic anime faces you see in figure 1.3. In fact, they resemble nothing more than static on a TV screen (you'll witness this firsthand in chapter 4).

We train the model for multiple iterations. In each iteration, we present a group of images created by the generator, along with a group of anime face images from our training set to the discriminator. We ask the discriminator to predict whether each image is created by the generator (fake) or from the training set (real).

You may wonder: How do the discriminator and the generator learn during each iteration of training? Once the predictions are made, the discriminator doesn't just sit back; it learns from its prediction blunders for each image. With this newfound knowledge, it fine-tunes its parameters, shaping itself to make better predictions in the next round. The generator isn't idle either. It takes notes from its image generation process and the discriminator's prediction outcomes. With that knowledge in hand, it adjusts its own network parameters, striving to create increasingly lifelike images in the next iteration. The goal? To reduce the odds of the discriminator sniffing out its fakes.

As we journey through these iterations, a remarkable transformation takes place. The generator network evolves, producing anime faces that grow more and more realistic, akin to those in our training collection. Meanwhile, the discriminator network hones its skills, becoming a seasoned detective when it comes to spotting fakes. It's a captivating dance between creation and detection.

Gradually, a magical moment arrives. An equilibrium, or perfect balance, is achieved. The images created by the generator become so astonishingly real that they are indistinguishable from the genuine anime faces in our training archives. At this point, the discriminator is so confused that it assigns a 50% chance of authenticity to every image, whether it's from our training set or was crafted by the generator.

Finally, behold some examples of the artwork of the generator, as shown in figure 1.4: they do look indistinguishable from those in our training set.

Figure 1.4   Generated anime face images by the trained generator in DCGAN

1.2.3   *Why should you care about GANs?*

GANs are easy to implement and versatile: you'll learn to generate geometric shapes, intricate patterns, high-resolution images, and realistic-sounding music in this book alone.

The practical use of GANs doesn't stop at generating realistic data. GANs can also translate attributes in one image domain to another. As you'll see in chapter 6, you can train a CycleGAN (a type of generative model in the GAN family) to convert blond hair to black hair in human face images. The same trained model can also convert black hair to blond hair. Figure 1.5 shows four rows of images. The first row is the original images with blond hair. The trained CycleGAN converts them to images with black hair (second row). The last two rows are the original images with black hair and the converted image with blond hair, respectively.

Original images with blond hair:

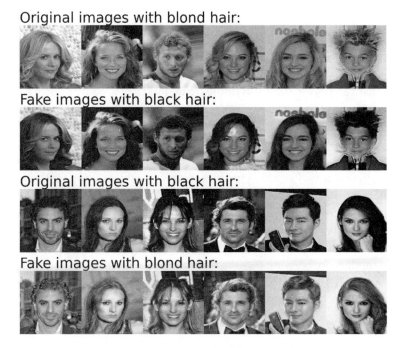

Fake images with black hair:

Original images with black hair:

Fake images with blond hair:

Figure 1.5   Changing hair color with CycleGAN. If we feed images with blond hair (first row) to a trained CycleGAN model, the model converts blond hair to black hair in these images (second row). The same trained model can also convert black hair (third row) to blond hair (bottom row).

Think about all the amazing skills you'll pick up from training GANs—they're not just cool; they're super practical too! Let's say you run an online clothing store with a "Make to Order" strategy (which allows users to customize their purchases before manufacturing). Your website showcases tons of unique designs for customers to pick from, but here's the catch: you only make the clothes once someone places an order. Creating high-quality images of these clothes can be quite expensive since you have to produce the items and then photograph them.

GANs to the rescue! You don't need a massive collection of manufactured clothing items and their images; instead, you can use something like CycleGAN to transform features from one set of images into another, creating a whole new array of styles. This is just one nifty way to use GANs. The possibilities are endless because these models are super versatile and can handle all sorts of data—making them a game-changer for practical applications.

1.3   Transformers

Transformers are deep neural networks that excel at sequence-to-sequence prediction problems, such as taking an input sentence and predicting the most likely next words. This section introduces you to the key innovation in Transformers: the self-attention mechanism. We'll then discuss the Transformer architecture and different types of Transformers. Finally, we'll discuss some recent developments in Transformers, such as multimodal models (Transformers whose inputs include not only text but also other data types such as audio and images) and pretrained LLMs (models trained on large textual data that can perform various downstream tasks).

Before the Transformer architecture was invented in 2017 by a group of Google researchers (Vaswani et al., "Attention Is All You Need," https://arxiv.org/abs/1706.03762), natural language processing (NLP) and other sequence-to-sequence prediction tasks were primarily handled by RNNs. However, RNNs struggle with retaining information about earlier elements in a sequence, which hampers their ability to capture long-term dependencies. Even advanced RNN variants like long short-term memory (LSTM) networks, which can handle longer-range dependencies, fall short when it comes to extremely long-range dependencies.

More importantly, RNNs (including LSTMs) process inputs sequentially, which means these models process one element at a time, in sequence, instead of looking at the entire sequence simultaneously. The fact that RNNs conduct computation along the symbol positions of the input and output sequences prevents parallel training, which makes training slow. This, in turn, makes it impossible to train the models on huge datasets.

The key innovation of Transformers is the self-attention mechanism, which excels at capturing long-term dependencies in a sequence. Further, since the inputs are not handled sequentially in the model, Transformers can be trained in parallel, which greatly reduces the training time. More importantly, parallel training makes it possible to train Transformers on large amounts of data, which makes LLMs intelligent and knowledgeable (based on their ability to process and generate human-like text, understand context, and perform a variety of language tasks). This has led to the rise of LLMs such as ChatGPT and the recent AI boom.

1.3.1   The attention mechanism

The attention mechanism assigns weights on how an element is related to all elements in a sequence (including the element itself). The higher the weight, the more closely the two elements are related. These weights are learned from large sets of training data in the training process. Therefore, a trained LLM such as ChatGPT can figure out the relationship between any two words in a sentence, hence making sense of the human language.

You may wonder: How does the attention mechanism assign scores to elements in a sequence to capture the long-term dependencies? The attention weights are calculated by first passing the inputs through three neural network layers to obtain query Q, key K, and value V (which we'll explain in detail in chapter 9). The method of using query, key, and value to calculate attention comes from retrieval systems. For example, you may go to a public library to search for a book. You can type in, say, "machine learning in finance" in the library's search engine. In this case, the query Q is "machine learning in finance." The keys K are the book titles, book descriptions, and so on. The library's retrieval system will recommend a list of books (values V) based on the similarities between the query and the keys. Naturally, books with the phrases "machine learning" or "finance" or both in titles or descriptions come up on top while books with neither phrase in the title or description will show up at the bottom of the list because these books will be assigned a low matching score.

In chapters 9 and 10, you'll learn the details of the attention mechanism—better yet, you'll implement the attention mechanism from scratch to build and train a Transformer to successfully translate English to French.

1.3.2 The Transformer architecture

Transformers were first proposed when designing models for machine language translation (e.g., English to German or English to French). Figure 1.6 is a diagram of the Transformer architecture. The left side is the encoder, and the right side is the decoder. In chapters 9 and 10, you'll learn to construct a Transformer from scratch to train the model to translate English to French, and we'll explain figure 1.6 in greater detail then.

The encoder in the Transformer "learns" the meaning of the input sequence (e.g., the English phrase "How are you?") and converts it into vectors that represent this meaning before passing the vectors to the decoder. The decoder constructs the output (e.g., the French translation of an English phrase) by predicting one word at a time, based on previous words in the sequence and the output from the encoder. The trained model can translate common English phrases into French.

There are three types of Transformers: encoder-only Transformers, decoder-only Transformers, and encoder-decoder Transformers. An encoder-only Transformer has no decoder and is capable of converting a sequence into an abstract representation for various downstream tasks such as sentiment analysis, named entity recognition, and text generation. For example, BERT is an encoder-only Transformer. A decoder-only Transformer has only a decoder but no encoder, and it's well suited for text generation, language modeling, and creative writing. GPT-2 (the predecessor of ChatGPT) and ChatGPT are both decoder-only Transformers. In chapter 11, you'll learn to create GPT-2 from scratch and then extract the trained model weights from Hugging Face (an AI community that hosts and collaborates on ML models, datasets, and applications). You'll load the weights to your GPT-2 model and start generating coherent text.

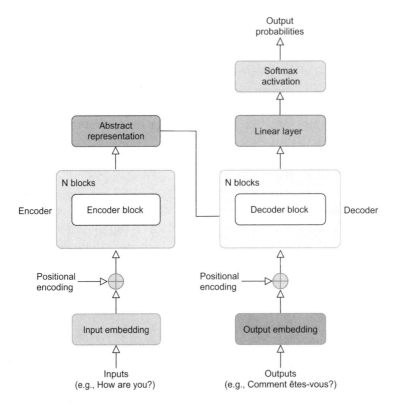

Figure 1.6   The Transformer architecture. The encoder in the Transformer (left side of the diagram) learns the meaning of the input sequence (e.g., the English phrase "How are you?") and converts it into an abstract representation that captures its meaning before passing it to the decoder (right side of the diagram). The decoder constructs the output (e.g., the French translation of the English phrase) by predicting one word at a time, based on previous words in the sequence and the abstract representation from the encoder.

Encoder-decoder Transformers are needed for complicated tasks such as multimodal models that can handle text-to-image generation or speech recognition. Encoder-decoder Transformers combine the strengths of both encoders and decoders. Encoders are efficient in processing and understanding input data, while decoders excel in generating output. This combination allows the model to effectively understand complex inputs (like text or speech) and generate intricate outputs (like images or transcribed text).

1.3.3 *Multimodal Transformers and pretrained LLMs*

Recent developments in generative AI give rise to various multimodal models: Transformers that can use not only text but also other data types, such as audio and images, as inputs. Text-to-image Transformers are one such example. DALL-E 2, Imagen, and Stable Diffusion are all text-to-image models, and they have garnered much media attention due to their ability to generate high-resolution images from textual prompts. Text-to-image Transformers incorporate the principles of diffusion models, which involve a series of transformations to gradually increase the complexity of data. Therefore, we first need to understand diffusion models before we discuss text-to-image Transformers.

Imagine you want to generate high-resolution flower images by using a diffusion-based model. You'll first obtain a training set of high-quality flower images. You then ask the model to gradually add noise to the flower images (the so-called diffusion process) until they become completely random noise. You then train the model to progressively remove noise from these noisy images to generate new data samples. The diffusion process is illustrated in figure 1.7. The left column contains four original flower images. As we move to the right, some noise is added to the images in each step, until at the right column, the four images are pure random noise.

Figure 1.7 **The diffusion model adds more and more noise to the images and learns to reconstruct them. The left column contains four original flower images. As we move to the right, some noise is added to the images in each time step, until at the right column, the four images are pure random noise. We then use these images to train a diffusion-based model to progressively remove noise from noisy images to generate new data samples.**

You may be wondering: How are text-to-image Transformers related to diffusion models? Text-to-image Transformers take a text prompt as input and generate images that correspond to that textual description. The text prompt serves as a form of conditioning, and the model uses a series of neural network layers to transform that textual description into an image. Like diffusion models, text-to-image Transformers use a hierarchical architecture with multiple layers, each progressively adding more detail to the generated image. The core concept of iteratively refining the output is similar in both diffusion models and text-to-image Transformers, as we'll explain in chapter 15.

Diffusion models have now become more popular due to their ability to provide stable training and generate high-quality images, and they have outperformed other generative models such as GANs and variational autoencoders. In chapter 15, you'll first learn to train a simple diffusion model using the Oxford Flower dataset. You'll also learn the basic idea behind multimodal Transformers and write a Python program to ask OpenAI's DALL-E 2 to generate images through a text prompt. For example, when I entered "an astronaut in a space suit riding a unicorn" as the prompt, DALL-E 2 generated the image shown in figure 1.8.

Figure 1.8   Image generated by DALL-E 2 with text prompt "an astronaut in a space suit riding a unicorn"

In chapter 16, you'll learn how to access pretrained LLMs such as ChatGPT, GPT4, and DALL-E 2. These models are trained on large textual data and have learned general knowledge from the data. Hence, they can perform various downstream tasks such as text generation, sentiment analysis, question answering, and named entity recognition. Since pretrained LLMs were trained on information a few months ago, they cannot provide information on events and developments in the last one or two months, let alone real-time information such as weather conditions, flight status, or stock prices. We'll use LangChain (a Python library designed for building applications with LLMs, providing tools for prompt management, LLM chaining, and output parsing) to chain together LLMs with the Wolfram Alpha and Wikipedia APIs to create a know-it-all personal assistant.

1.4   *Why build generative models from scratch?*

The goal of this book is to show you how to build and train all generative models from scratch. This way, you'll have a thorough understanding of the inner workings of these models and can make better use of them. Creating something from scratch is the best way to understand it. You'll accomplish this goal for GANs: all models, including DCGAN and CycleGAN, are built from the ground up and trained using well-curated data in the public domain.

For Transformers, you'll build and train all models from scratch except for LLMs. This exception is due to the vast amount of data and the supercomputing facilities needed to train certain LLMs. However, you'll make serious progress in this direction. Specifically, you'll implement in chapters 9 and 10 the original groundbreaking 2017 paper "Attention Is All You Need" line by line with English-to-French translation as an example (the same Transformer can be trained on other datasets such as Chinese to English or English to German translations). You'll also build a small-size decoder-only Transformer and train it using several of Ernest Hemingway's novels, including *The Old Man and the Sea*. The trained model can generate text in Hemingway style. ChatGPT and GPT-4 are too large and complicated to build and train from scratch for our purposes, but you'll peek into their predecessor, GPT-2, and learn to build it from scratch. You'll also extract the trained weights from Hugging Face and load them up to the GPT-2 model you built and start to generate realistic text that can pass as human-written.

In this sense, the book is taking a more fundamental approach than most books. Instead of treating generative AI models as a black box, readers have a chance to look under the hood and examine in detail the inner workings of these models. The goal is for you to have a deeper understanding of generative models. This, in turn, can potentially help you build better and more responsible generative AI for the following reasons.

First, having a deep understanding of the architecture of generative models helps readers make better practical uses of these models. For example, in chapter 5, you'll learn how to select characteristics in generated images such as male or female features and with or without eyeglasses. By building a conditional GAN from the ground up, you understand that certain features of the generated images are determined by the random noise vector, Z, in the latent space. Therefore, you can choose different values of Z as inputs to the trained model to generate the desired characteristics (such as male or female features). This type of attribute selection is hard to do without understanding the design of the model.

For Transformers, knowing the architecture (and what encoders and decoders do) gives you the ability to create and train Transformers to generate the types of content you are interested in (say, Jane Austin–style novels or Mozart-style music). This understanding also helps you with pretrained LLMs. For example, while it is hard to train GPT-2 from scratch with its 1.5 billion parameters, you can add an additional layer to the model and fine-tune it for other downstream tasks such as text classification, sentiment analysis, and question-answering.

Second, a deep understanding of generative AI helps readers have an unbiased assessment of the dangers of AI. While the extraordinary powers of generative AI have benefitted us in our daily lives and work, it also has the potential to create great harm. Elon Musk went so far as saying that "there's some chance that it goes wrong and destroys humanity" (see the article by Julia Mueller in *The Hill*, 2023, "Musk: There's a Chance AI 'Goes Wrong and Destroys Humanity,'" https://mng.bz/Aaxz). More and more people in academics and in the tech industry are worried about the dangers posed by AI in general and generative AI in particular. Generative AI, especially LLMs, can lead to unintended consequences, as many pioneers in the tech profession have warned (see, e.g., Stuart Russell, 2023, "How to Stop Runaway AI," https://mng.bz/ZVzP). It's not a coincidence that merely five months after the release of ChatGPT, many tech industry experts and entrepreneurs, including Steve Wozniak, Tristan Harris, Yoshua Bengio, and Sam Altman, signed an open letter calling for a pause in training any AI system that's more powerful than GPT-4 for at least six months (see the article by Connie Loizos in *TechCrunch*, "1,100+ Notable Signatories Just Signed an Open Letter Asking 'All AI Labs to Immediately Pause for at Least 6 Months,'" https://mng.bz/RNEK). A thorough understanding of the architecture of generative models helps us provide a deep and unbiased evaluation of the benefits and potential dangers of AI.

Summary

- Generative AI is a type of technology with the capacity to produce diverse forms of new content, including texts, images, code, music, audio, and video.
- Discriminative models specialize in assigning labels while generative models generate new instances of data.
- PyTorch, with its dynamic computational graphs and the ability for GPU training, is well suited for deep learning and generative modeling.
- GANs are a type of generative modeling method consisting of two neural networks: a generator and a discriminator. The goal of the generator is to create realistic data samples to maximize the chance that the discriminator thinks they are real. The goal of the discriminator is to correctly identify fake samples from real ones.
- Transformers are deep neural networks that use the attention mechanism to identify long-term dependencies among elements in a sequence. The original Transformer has an encoder and a decoder. When it's used for English-to-French translation, for example, the encoder converts the English sentence into an abstract representation before passing it to the decoder. The decoder generates the French translation one word at a time, based on the encoder's output and the previously generated words.

Deep learning with PyTorch 2

This chapter covers

- PyTorch tensors and basic operations
- Preparing data for deep learning in PyTorch
- Building and training deep neural networks with PyTorch
- Conducting binary and multicategory classifications with deep learning
- Creating a validation set to decide training stop points

In this book, we'll use deep neural networks to generate a wide range of content, including text, images, shapes, music, and more. I assume you already have a foundational understanding of machine learning (ML) and, in particular, artificial neural networks. In this chapter, I'll refresh your memory on essential concepts such as loss functions, activation functions, optimizers, and learning rates, which are crucial for developing and training deep neural networks. If you find any gaps in your understanding of these topics, I strongly encourage you to address them before proceeding with the projects in this book. Appendix B provides a summary of the basic skills and concepts needed, including the architecture and training of artificial neural networks.

NOTE There are plenty of great ML books out there for you to choose from. Examples include *Hands-on Machine Learning with Scikit-Learn, Keras, and Tensor-Flow* (2019, O'Reilly) and *Machine Learning, Animated* (2023, CRC Press). Both books use TensorFlow to create neural networks. If you prefer a book that uses PyTorch, I recommend *Deep Learning with PyTorch* (2020, Manning Publications).

Generative AI models are frequently confronted with the task of either binary or multicategory classification. For instance, in generative adversarial networks (GANs), the discriminator undertakes the essential role of a binary classifier, its purpose being to distinguish between the fake samples created by the generator from real samples from the training set. Similarly, in the context of text generation models, whether in recurrent neural networks or Transformers, the overarching objective is to predict the subsequent character or word from an extensive array of possibilities (essentially a multicategory classification task).

In this chapter, you'll learn how to use PyTorch to create deep neural networks to perform binary and multicategory classifications so that you become well-versed in deep learning and classification tasks.

Specifically, you'll engage in an end-to-end deep learning project in PyTorch, on a quest to classify grayscale images of clothing items into different categories such as coats, bags, sneakers, shirts, and so on. The intention is to prepare you for the creation of deep neural networks, capable of performing both binary and multicategory classification tasks in PyTorch. This, in turn, will get you ready for the upcoming chapters, where you use deep neural networks in PyTorch to create various generative models.

To train generative AI models, we harness a diverse range of data formats such as raw text, audio files, image pixels, and arrays of numbers. Deep neural networks created in PyTorch cannot take these forms of data directly as inputs. Instead, we must first convert them into a format that the neural networks understand and accept. Specifically, you'll convert various forms of raw data into PyTorch tensors (fundamental data structures used to represent and manipulate data) before feeding them to generative AI models. Therefore, in this chapter, you'll also learn the basics of data types, how to create various forms of PyTorch tensors, and how to use them in deep learning.

Knowing how to perform classification tasks has many practical applications in our society. Classifications are widely used in healthcare for diagnostic purposes, such as identifying whether a patient has a particular disease (e.g., positive or negative for a specific cancer based on medical imaging or test results). They play a vital role in many business tasks (stock recommendations, credit card fraud detection, and so on). Classification tasks are also integral to many systems and services that we use daily such as spam detection and facial recognition.

2.1 *Data types in PyTorch*

We'll use datasets from a wide range of sources and formats in this book, and the first step in deep learning is to transform the inputs into arrays of numbers.

In this section, you'll learn how PyTorch converts different formats of data into algebraic structures known as *tensors*. Tensors can be represented as multidimensional arrays of numbers, similar to NumPy arrays but with several key differences, chief among them the ability of GPU accelerated training. There are different types of tensors depending on their end use, and you'll learn how to create different types of tensors and when to use each type. We'll discuss the data structure in PyTorch in this section by using the heights of the 46 U.S. presidents as our running example.

Refer to the instructions in appendix A to create a virtual environment and install PyTorch and Jupyter Notebook on your computer. Open the Jupyter Notebook app within the virtual environment and run the following line of code in a new cell:

```
!pip install matplotlib
```

This command will install the Matplotlib library on your computer, enabling you to plot images in Python.

2.1.1 *Creating PyTorch tensors*

When training deep neural networks, we feed the models with arrays of numbers as inputs. Depending on what a generative model is trying to create, these numbers have different types. For example, when generating images, the inputs are raw pixels in the form of integers between 0 and 255, but we'll convert them to floating-point numbers between –1 and 1; when generating text, there is a "vocabulary" akin to a dictionary, and the input is a sequence of integers telling you which entry in the dictionary the word corresponds to.

> **NOTE** The code for this chapter, as well as other chapters in this book, is available at the book's GitHub repository: https://github.com/markhliu/DGAI.

Imagine you want to use PyTorch to calculate the average height of the 46 U.S. presidents. We can first collect the heights of the 46 U.S. presidents in centimeters and store them in a Python list:

```
heights = [189, 170, 189, 163, 183, 171, 185,
           168, 173, 183, 173, 173, 175, 178,
           183, 193, 178, 173, 174, 183, 183,
           180, 168, 180, 170, 178, 182, 180,
           183, 178, 182, 188, 175, 179, 183,
           193, 182, 183, 177, 185, 188, 188,
           182, 185, 191, 183]
```

The numbers are in chronological order: the first value in the list, 189, indicates that the first U.S. president, George Washington, was 189 centimeters tall. The last value shows that Joe Biden's height is 183 centimeters. We can convert a Python list into a PyTorch tensor by using the `tensor()` method in PyTorch:

```
import torch

heights_tensor = torch.tensor(heights,
        dtype=torch.float64)
```

Converts a Python list
to a PyTorch tensor

Specifies the data type
in the PyTorch tensor

We specify the data type using the `dtype` argument in the `tensor()` method. The default data type in PyTorch tensors is `float32`, a 32-bit floating-point number. In the preceding code cell, we converted the data type to `float64`, double-precision floating-point numbers. `float64` provides more precise results than `float32`, but it takes longer to compute. There is a tradeoff between precision and computational costs. Which data type to use depends on the task at hand.

Table 2.1 lists different data types and the corresponding PyTorch tensor types. These include integers and floating-point numbers with different precisions. Integers can also be either signed or unsigned.

Table 2.1   Data and tensor types in PyTorch

PyTorch tensor type	dtype argument in `tensor()`	Data type
FloatTensor	torch.float32 or torch.float	32-bit floating point
HalfTensor	torch.float16 or torch.half	16-bit floating point
DoubleTensor	torch.float64 or torch.double	64-bit floating point
CharTensor	torch.int8	8-bit integer (signed)
ByteTensor	torch.uint8	8-bit integer (unsigned)
ShortTensor	torch.int16 or torch.short	16-bit integer (signed)
IntTensor	torch.int32 or torch.int	32-bit integer (signed)
LongTensor	torch.int64 or torch.long	64-bit integer (signed)

You can create a tensor with a certain data type in one of the two ways. The first way is to use the PyTorch class as specified in the first column of table 2.1. The second way is to use the `torch.tensor()` method and specify the data type using the `dtype` argument (the value of the argument is listed in the second column of table 2.1). For example, to convert the Python list [1, 2, 3] into a PyTorch tensor with 32-bit integers in it, you can use two methods in the following listing.

Listing 2.1   Two ways of specifying tensor types

```
t1=torch.IntTensor([1, 2, 3])
t2=torch.tensor([1, 2, 3],
          dtype=torch.int)
print(t1)
print(t2)
```

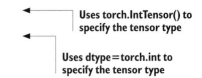

Uses torch.IntTensor() to specify the tensor type

Uses dtype=torch.int to specify the tensor type

This leads to the following output:

```
tensor([1, 2, 3], dtype=torch.int32)
tensor([1, 2, 3], dtype=torch.int32)
```

> **Exercise 2.1**
>
> Use two different methods to convert the Python list `[5, 8, 10]` into a PyTorch tensor with 64-bit floating-point numbers in it. Consult the third row in table 2.1 for this question.

Many times, you need to create a PyTorch tensor with values 0 everywhere. For example, in GANs, we create a tensor of zeros as the labels for fake samples, as you'll see in chapter 3. The `zeros()` method in PyTorch generates a tensor of zeros with a certain shape. In PyTorch, a tensor is an n-dimensional array, and its shape is a tuple representing the size along each of its dimensions. The following lines of code generate a tensor of zeros with two rows and three columns:

```
tensor1 = torch.zeros(2, 3)
print(tensor1)
```

The output is as follows:

```
tensor([[0., 0., 0.],
        [0., 0., 0.]])
```

The tensor has a shape of (2, 3), which means the tensor is a 2D array; there are two elements in the first dimension and three elements in the second dimension. Here, we didn't specify the data type, and the output has the default data type of `float32`.

From time to time, you need to create a PyTorch tensor with values 1 everywhere. For example, in GANs, we create a tensor of ones as the labels for real samples. Here we use the `ones()` method to create a 3D tensor with values 1 everywhere:

```
tensor2 = torch.ones(1,4,5)
print(tensor2)
```

The output is

```
tensor([[[1., 1., 1., 1., 1.],
         [1., 1., 1., 1., 1.],
         [1., 1., 1., 1., 1.],
         [1., 1., 1., 1., 1.]]])
```

We have generated a 3D PyTorch tensor. The shape of the tensor is (1, 4, 5).

> **Exercise 2.2**
>
> Create a 3D PyTorch tensor with values 0 in it. Make the shape of the tensor (2, 3, 4).

You can also use a NumPy array instead of a Python list in the tensor constructor:

```
import numpy as np

nparr=np.array(range(10))
pt_tensor=torch.tensor(nparr, dtype=torch.int)
print(pt_tensor)
```

The output is

```
tensor([0, 1, 2, 3, 4, 5, 6, 7, 8, 9], dtype=torch.int32)
```

2.1.2   *Index and slice PyTorch tensors*

We use square brackets ([ ]) to index and slice PyTorch tensors, as we do with Python lists. Indexing and slicing allow us to operate on one or more elements in a tensor, instead of on all elements. To continue our example of the heights of the 46 U.S. presidents, if we want to assess the height of the third president, Thomas Jefferson, we can do the following:

```
height = heights_tensor[2]
print(height)
```

This leads to an output of

```
tensor(189., dtype=torch.float64)
```

The output shows that the height of Thomas Jefferson was 189 centimeters.

   We can use negative indexing to count from the back of the tensor. For example, to find the height of Donald Trump, who is the second to last president in the list, we use index –2:

```
height = heights_tensor[-2]
print(height)
```

The output is

```
tensor(191., dtype=torch.float64)
```

The output shows that Trump's height is 191 centimeters.

   What if we want to know the heights of five recent presidents in the tensor `heights_tensor`? We can obtain a slice of the tensor:

```
five_heights = heights_tensor[-5:]
print(five_heights)
```

The colon (:) is used to separate the starting and end index. If no starting index is provided, the default is 0; if no end index is provided, you include the very last element in the tensor (as we did in the preceding code cell). Negative indexing means you count from the back. The output is

```
tensor([188., 182., 185., 191., 183.], dtype=torch.float64)
```

The results show that the five recent presidents in the tensor (Clinton, Bush, Obama, Trump, and Biden) are 188, 182, 185, 191, and 183 centimeters tall, respectively.

Exercise 2.3

Use slicing to obtain the heights of the first five U.S. presidents in the tensor `heights_tensor`.

2.1.3   *PyTorch tensor shapes*

PyTorch tensors have an attribute *shape*, which tells us the dimensions of a tensor. It's important to know the shapes of PyTorch tensors because mismatched shapes will lead to errors when we operate on them. For example, if we want to find out the shape of the tensor `heights_tensor`, we can do this:

```
print(heights_tensor.shape)
```

The output is

```
torch.Size([46])
```

This tells us that `heights_tensor` is a 1D tensor with 46 values in it.

You can also change the shape of a PyTorch tensor. To learn how, let's first convert the heights from centimeters to feet. Since a foot is about 30.48 centimeters, we can accomplish this by dividing the tensor by 30.48:

```
heights_in_feet = heights_tensor / 30.48
print(heights_in_feet)
```

This leads to the following output (I omitted some values to save space; the complete output is in the book's GitHub repository):

```
tensor([6.2008, 5.5774, 6.2008, 5.3478, 6.0039, 5.6102, 6.0696, …
        6.0039], dtype=torch.float64)
```

The new tensor, `heights_in_feet`, stores the heights in feet. For example, the last value in the tensor shows that Joe Biden is 6.0039 feet tall.

We can use the `cat()` method in PyTorch to concatenate the two tensors:

```
heights_2_measures = torch.cat(
    [heights_tensor,heights_in_feet], dim=0)
print(heights_2_measures.shape)
```

The `dim` argument is used in various tensor operations to specify the dimension along which the operation is to be performed. In the preceding code cell, `dim=0` means we concatenate the two tensors along the first dimension. This leads to the following output:

```
torch.Size([92])
```

The resulting tensor is 1D with 92 values, with some values in centimeters and others in feet. Therefore, we need to reshape it into two rows and 46 columns so that the first row represents heights in centimeters and the second in feet:

```
heights_reshaped = heights_2_measures.reshape(2, 46)
```

The new tensor, `heights_reshaped`, is 2D with a shape of (2, 46). We can index and slice multidimensional tensors using square brackets as well. For example, to print out the height of Trump in feet, we can do this:

```
print(heights_reshaped[1,-2])
```

This leads to a result of

```
tensor(6.2664, dtype=torch.float64)
```

The command `heights_reshaped[1,-2]` tells Python to look for the value in the second row and the second to last column, which returns Trump's height in feet, 6.2664.

> **TIP**   The number of indexes needed to refer to scalar values within the tensor is the same as the dimensionality of the tensor. That's why we used only one index to locate values in the 1D tensor `heights_tensor` but we used two indexes to locate values in the 2D tensor `heights_reshaped`.

Exercise 2.4

Use indexing to obtain the height of Joe Biden in the tensor `heights_reshaped` in centimeters.

2.1.4   *Mathematical operations on PyTorch tensors*

We can conduct mathematical operations on PyTorch tensors by using different methods such as `mean()`, `median()`, `sum()`, `max()`, and so on. For example, to find the median height of the 46 presidents in centimeters, we can do this:

```
print(torch.median(heights_reshaped[0,:]))
```

The code snippet `heights_reshaped[0,:]` returns the first row and all columns in the tensor `heights_reshaped`. The preceding line of code returns the median value in the first row, and this leads to an output of

```
tensor(182., dtype=torch.float64)
```

This means the median height of U.S. presidents is 182 centimeters.

To find the average height in both rows, we can use the `dim=1` argument in the `mean()` method:

```
print(torch.mean(heights_reshaped,dim=1))
```

The `dim=1` argument indicates that the averages are calculated by collapsing columns (the dimension indexed 1), effectively obtaining averages along the dimension indexed 0 (rows). The output is

```
tensor([180.0652,    5.9077], dtype=torch.float64)
```

The results show that the average values in the two rows are 180.0652 centimeters and 5.9077 feet.

To find out the tallest president, we can do this:

```
values, indices = torch.max(heights_reshaped, dim=1)
print(values)
print(indices)
```

The output is

```
tensor([193.0000,    6.3320], dtype=torch.float64)
tensor([15, 15])
```

The `torch.max()` method returns two tensors: a tensor `values` with the tallest president's height (in centimeters and in feet), and a tensor `indices` with the indexes of the president with the maximum height. The results show that the 16th president (Lincoln) is the tallest, at 193 centimeters, or 6.332 feet.

Exercise 2.5

Use the `torch.min()` method to find out the index and height of the shortest U.S. president.

2.2 An end-to-end deep learning project with PyTorch

In the next few sections, you'll work through an example deep learning project with PyTorch, learning to classify grayscale images of clothing items into 1 of the 10 types. In this section, we'll first provide a high-level overview of the steps involved. We then discuss how to obtain training data for this project and how to preprocess the data.

2.2.1 Deep learning in PyTorch: A high-level overview

Our job in this project is to create and train a deep neural network in PyTorch to classify grayscale images of clothing items. Figure 2.1 provides a diagram of the steps involved.

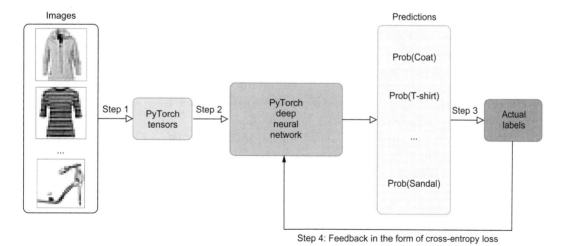

Figure 2.1 The steps involved in training a deep learning model

First, we'll obtain a dataset of grayscale clothing images, as shown on the left of figure 2.1. The images are in raw pixels, and we'll convert them to PyTorch tensors in the form of float numbers (step 1). Each image comes with a label.

We'll then create a deep neural network in PyTorch, as shown in the center of figure 2.1. Some neural networks in this book involve convolutional neural networks (CNNs). For this simple classification problem, we'll use dense layers only for the moment.

We'll select a loss function for multicategory classification, and cross-entropy loss is commonly used for this task. Cross-entropy loss measures the difference between the predicted probability distribution and the true distribution of the labels. We'll use the Adam optimizer (a variant of the gradient descent algorithm) to update the network's weights during training. We set the learning rate to 0.001. The learning rate controls how much the model's weights are adjusted with respect to the loss gradient during training.

Optimizers in ML

Optimizers in ML are algorithms that update model parameters based on gradient information to minimize the loss function. Stochastic Gradient Descent (SGD) is the most fundamental optimizer, utilizing straightforward updates based on the loss gradient. Adam, the most popular optimizer, is known for its efficiency and out-of-the-box performance, as it combines the strengths of the Adaptive Gradient Algorithm (AdaGrad) and Root Mean Square Propagation (RMSProp). Despite their differences, all optimizers aim to iteratively adjust parameters to minimize the loss function, each creating a unique optimization path to reach this goal.

We'll divide the training data into a train set and a validation set. In ML, we usually use the validation set to provide an unbiased evaluation of the model and to select the best hyperparameters such as the learning rate, number of epochs of training, and so on. The validation set can also be used to avoid overfitting the model in which the model works well in the training set but poorly on unseen data. An epoch is when all the training data is used to train the model once and only once.

During training, you'll iterate through the training data. During forward passes, you feed images through the network to obtain predictions (step 2) and compute the loss by comparing the predicted labels with the actual labels (step 3; see the right side of figure 2.1). You'll then backpropagate the gradient through the network to update the weights. This is where the learning happens (step 4), as shown at the bottom of figure 2.1.

You'll use the validation set to determine when we should stop training. We calculate the loss in the validation set. If the model stops improving after a fixed number of epochs, we consider the model trained. We then evaluate the trained model on the test set to assess its performance in classifying images into different labels.

Now that you have a high-level overview of how deep learning in PyTorch works, let's dive into the end-to-end project!

2.2.2 *Preprocessing data*

We'll be using the Fashion Modified National Institute of Standards and Technology (MNIST) dataset in this project. Along the way, you'll learn how to use the `datasets` and `transforms` packages in the Torchvision library, as well as the `Dataloader` packages in PyTorch that will help you for the rest of the book. You'll use these tools to preprocess data throughout the book. The Torchvision library provides tools for image processing, including popular datasets, model architectures, and common image transformations for deep learning applications.

We first import needed libraries and instantiate a `Compose()` class in the `transforms` package to transform raw images to PyTorch tensors.

Listing 2.2 Transforming raw image data to PyTorch tensors

```
import torch
import torch.nn as nn
import torchvision
import torchvision.transforms as T

torch.manual_seed(42)
transform=T.Compose([
    T.ToTensor(),
    T.Normalize([0.5],[0.5])])
```

Composes several transforms together

Converts image pixels to PyTorch tensors

Normalizes the values to the range [–1, 1]

We use the `manual_seed()` method in PyTorch to fix the random state so that results are reproducible. The *transforms* package in Torchvision can help create a series of transformations to preprocess images. The `ToTensor()` class converts image data (in either Python Imaging Library (PIL) image formats or NumPy arrays) into PyTorch tensors. In particular, the image data are integers ranging from 0 to 255, and the `ToTensor()` class converts them to float tensors with values in the range of 0.0 and 1.0.

The `Normalize()` class normalizes tensor images with mean and standard deviation for *n* channels. The Fashion MNIST data are grayscale images of clothing items so there is only one color channel. Later in this book, we'll deal with images of three different color channels (red, green, and blue). In the preceding code cell, `Normalize([0.5],[0.5])` means that we subtract 0.5 from the data and divide the difference by 0.5. The resulting image data range from –1 to 1. Normalizing the input data to the range [–1, 1] allows gradient descent to operate more efficiently by maintaining more uniform step sizes across dimensions. This helps in faster convergence during training, and you'll do this often in this book.

> **NOTE** The code in listing 2.2 only defines the data transformation process. It doesn't perform the actual transformation, which happens in the next code cell.

Next, we use the *datasets* package in Torchvision to download the dataset to a folder on your computer and perform the transformation:

```
train_set=torchvision.datasets.FashionMNIST(
    root=".",
    train=True,
    download=True,
    transform=transform)
test_set=torchvision.datasets.FashionMNIST(root=".",
    train=False,download=True,transform=transform)
```

Which dataset to download

Where to save the data

The training or test dataset

Whether or not to download the data to your computer

Performs data transformation

You can print out the first sample in the training set:

```
print(train_set[0])
```

The first sample consists of a tensor with 784 values and a label 9. The 784 numbers represent a 28 by 28 grayscale image (28 × 28 = 784), and the label 9 means it's an ankle boot. You may be wondering: How do you know the label 9 indicates an ankle boot? There are 10 different types of clothing items. The labels in the dataset are numbered from 0 to 9. You can search online and find the text labels for the 10 categories (for example, I got the text labels here https://github.com/pranay414/Fashion-MNIST -Pytorch). The list `text_labels` contains the 10 text labels corresponding to the numerical labels 0 to 9. For example, if an item has a numerical label of 0 in the dataset, the corresponding text label is "t-shirt." The list `text_labels` is defined as follows:

```
text_labels=['t-shirt', 'trouser', 'pullover', 'dress', 'coat',
             'sandal', 'shirt', 'sneaker', 'bag', 'ankle boot']
```

We can plot the data to visualize the clothing items in the dataset.

Listing 2.3   Visualizing the clothing items

```
!pip install matplotlib
import matplotlib.pyplot as plt

plt.figure(dpi=300,figsize=(8,4))
for i in range(24):
    ax=plt.subplot(3, 8, i + 1)
    img=train_set[i][0]
    img=img/2+0.5
    img=img.reshape(28, 28)
    plt.imshow(img,
            cmap="binary")
    plt.axis('off')
    plt.title(text_labels[train_set[i][1]],
        fontsize=8)
plt.show()
```

Where to place the image

Obtains the i-th image from the training data

Converts the values from [–1,1] to [0,1]

Reshapes the image to 28 by 28

Adds text label to each image

The plot in figure 2.2 shows 24 clothing items such as coats, pullovers, sandals, and so on.

Figure 2.2   Grayscale images of clothing items in the Fashion MNIST dataset.

You'll learn how to create deep neural networks with PyTorch to perform binary and multicategory classification problems in the next two sections.

2.3   *Binary classification*

In this section, we'll first create batches of data for training. We then build a deep neural network in PyTorch for this purpose and train the model using the data. Finally, we'll use the trained model to make predictions and test how accurate the predictions are. The steps involved with binary and multicategory classifications are similar, with a few notable exceptions that I'll highlight later.

2.3.1   *Creating batches*

We'll create a training set and a test set that contain only two types of clothing items: t-shirts and ankle boots. (Later in this chapter when we discuss multicategory classification, you'll also learn to create a validation set to determine when to stop training.) The following code cell accomplishes that goal:

```
binary_train_set=[x for x in train_set if x[1] in [0,9]]
binary_test_set=[x for x in test_set if x[1] in [0,9]]
```

We only keep samples with numerical labels 0 and 9 to create a binary classification problem with a balanced training set. Next, we create batches for training the deep neural network.

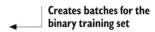

Listing 2.4   Creating batches for training and testing

```
batch_size=64
binary_train_loader=torch.utils.data.DataLoader(        ◄─── Creates batches for the
    binary_train_set,                                        binary training set
```

```
    batch_size=batch_size,
    shuffle=True)
binary_test_loader=torch.utils.data.DataLoader(
    binary_test_set,
    batch_size=batch_size,shuffle=True)
```

Number of samples
in each batch

Shuffles the observations
when batching

Creates batches for
the binary test set

The `DataLoader` class in the PyTorch *utils* package helps create data iterators in batches. We set the batch size to 64. We created two data loaders in listing 2.4: a training set and a test set for binary classification. We shuffle the observations when creating batches to avoid correlations among the original dataset: the training is more stable if different labels are evenly distributed in the data loader.

2.3.2 Building and training a binary classification model

We'll first create a binary classification model. We then train the model by using the images of t-shirts and ankle boots. Once it's trained, we'll see if the model can tell t-shirts from ankle boots. We use PyTorch to create the following neural network by using the Pytorch `nn.Sequential` class (in later chapters, you'll also learn to use the `nn.Module` class to create PyTorch neural networks).

Listing 2.5 Creating a binary classification model

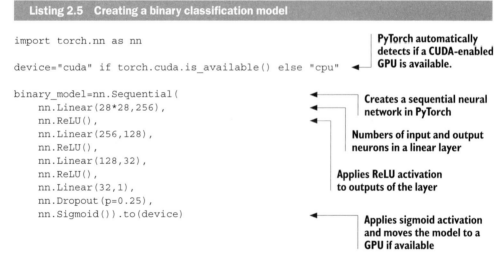

```
import torch.nn as nn

device="cuda" if torch.cuda.is_available() else "cpu"

binary_model=nn.Sequential(
    nn.Linear(28*28,256),
    nn.ReLU(),
    nn.Linear(256,128),
    nn.ReLU(),
    nn.Linear(128,32),
    nn.ReLU(),
    nn.Linear(32,1),
    nn.Dropout(p=0.25),
    nn.Sigmoid()).to(device)
```

PyTorch automatically
detects if a CUDA-enabled
GPU is available.

Creates a sequential neural
network in PyTorch

Numbers of input and output
neurons in a linear layer

Applies ReLU activation
to outputs of the layer

Applies sigmoid activation
and moves the model to a
GPU if available

The `Linear()` class in PyTorch creates a linear transformation of the incoming data. This effectively creates a dense layer in the neural network. The input shape is 784 because we'll later flatten the 2D image to a 1D vector with $28 \times 28 = 784$ values in it. We flatten the 2D image into a 1D tensor because dense layers only take 1D inputs. In later chapters, you'll see that you don't need to flatten images when you use convolutional layers. There are three hidden layers in the network, with 256, 128, and 32 neurons in them, respectively. The numbers 256, 128, and 32 are chosen somewhat arbitrarily: changing them to, say, 300, 200, and 50 won't affect the training process.

We apply the rectified linear unit (ReLU) activation function on the three hidden layers. The ReLU activation function decides whether a neuron should be turned on based on the weighted sum. These functions introduce nonlinearity to the output of a neuron so that the network can learn nonlinear relations between inputs and outputs. ReLU is your go-to activation function with very few exceptions, and you'll encounter a few other activation functions in later chapters.

The output of the last layer of the model contains a single value, and we use the sigmoid activation function to squeeze the number to the range [0, 1] so that it can be interpreted as the probability that the object is an ankle boot. With the complementary probability, the object is a t-shirt.

Here we set the learning rate and define the optimizer and the loss function:

```
lr=0.001
optimizer=torch.optim.Adam(binary_model.parameters(),lr=lr)
loss_fn=nn.BCELoss()
```

We set the learning rate to 0.001. What learning rate to set is an empirical question, and the answer comes with experience. It can also be determined by using hyperparameter tuning using a validation set. Most optimizers in PyTorch use a default learning rate of 0.001. The Adam optimizer is a variant of the gradient descent algorithm, which is used to determine how much to adjust the model parameters in each training step. The Adam optimizer was first introduced in 2014 by Diederik Kingma and Jimmy Ba.[1] In the traditional gradient descent algorithm, only gradients in the current iteration are considered. The Adam optimizer, in contrast, takes into consideration gradients in previous iterations as well.

We use nn.BCELoss(), which is the binary cross-entropy loss function. Loss functions measure how well an ML model performs. The training of a model involves adjusting parameters to minimize the loss function. The binary cross-entropy loss function is widely used in ML, particularly in binary classification problems. It measures the performance of a classification model whose output is a probability value between 0 and 1. The cross-entropy loss increases as the predicted probability diverges from the actual label.

We train the neural network we just created as shown in the following listing.

Listing 2.6 Training a binary classification model

```
for i in range(50):                          ←————  Trains for 50 epochs
    tloss=0
    for imgs,labels in binary_train_loader:  ←————  Iterates through all batches
        imgs=imgs.reshape(-1,28*28)
        imgs=imgs.to(device)                 ←————  Flattens the image before moving the tensor to GPU
        labels=torch.FloatTensor(\
            [x if x==0 else 1 for x in labels])  ←————  Converts labels to 0 and 1
```

```
        labels=labels.reshape(-1,1).to(device)
        preds=binary_model(imgs)
        loss=loss_fn(preds,labels)              ◀──── Calculates the loss
        optimizer.zero_grad()
        loss.backward()                         ◀──── Backpropagation
        optimizer.step()
        tloss+=loss.detach()
    tloss=tloss/n
    print(f"at epoch {i}, loss is {tloss}")
```

In training deep learning models in PyTorch, `loss.backward()` computes the gradient of the loss with respect to each model parameter, enabling backpropagation, while `optimizer.step()` updates the model parameters based on these computed gradients to minimize the loss. We train the model for 50 epochs for simplicity (an epoch is when the training data is used to train the model once). In the next section, you'll use a validation set and an early stopping class to determine how many epochs to train. In binary classifications, we label the targets as 0s and 1s. Since we have kept only t-shirts and ankle boots with labels 0 and 9, respectively, we converted them to 0 and 1 in listing 2.6. As a result, the labels for the two categories of clothing items are 0 and 1, respectively.

This training takes a few minutes if you use GPU training. It takes longer if you use CPU training, but the training time should be less than an hour.

2.3.3   *Testing the binary classification model*

The prediction from the trained binary classification model is a number between 0 and 1. We'll use the `torch.where()` method to convert the predictions into 0s and 1s: if the predicted probability is less than 0.5, we label the prediction as 0; otherwise, we label the prediction as 1. We then compare these predictions with the actual labels to calculate the accuracy of the predictions. In the following listing, we use the trained model to make predictions on the test dataset.

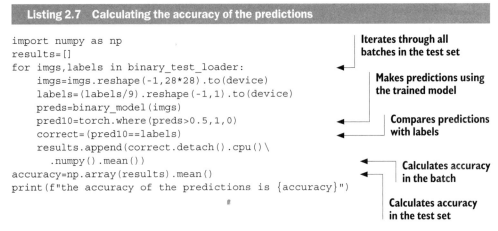

Listing 2.7   Calculating the accuracy of the predictions

```
import numpy as np
results=[]
                                                         Iterates through all
                                                         batches in the test set
for imgs,labels in binary_test_loader:          ◀────
    imgs=imgs.reshape(-1,28*28).to(device)
                                                         Makes predictions using
    labels=(labels/9).reshape(-1,1).to(device)          the trained model
    preds=binary_model(imgs)
    pred10=torch.where(preds>0.5,1,0)           ◀────    Compares predictions
    correct=(pred10==labels)                    ◀────    with labels
    results.append(correct.detach().cpu()\
      .numpy().mean())
                                                         Calculates accuracy
accuracy=np.array(results).mean()               ◀────    in the batch
print(f"the accuracy of the predictions is {accuracy}")
                                                         Calculates accuracy
                                                         in the test set
```

We iterate through all batches of data in the test set. The trained model produces a probability that the image is an ankle boot. We then convert the probability into 0 or

1 based on the cutoff value of 0.5, by using the `torch.where()` method. The predictions are either 0 (i.e., a t-shirt) or 1 (an ankle boot) after the conversion. We compare the predictions with the actual labels and see how many times the model gets it right. Results show that the accuracy of the predictions is 87.84% in the test set.

2.4 Multicategory classification

In this section, we'll build a deep neural network in PyTorch to classify the clothing items into one of the 10 categories. We'll then train the model with the Fashion MNIST dataset. Finally, we'll use the trained model to make predictions and see how accurate they are. We first create a validation set and define an early stopping class so that we can determine when to stop training.

2.4.1 Validation set and early stopping

When we build and train a deep neural network, there are many hyperparameters that we can choose (such as the learning rate and the number of epochs to train). These hyperparameters affect the performance of the model. To find the best hyperparameters, we can create a validation set to test the performance of the model with different hyperparameters.

To give you an example, we'll create a validation set in the multicategory classification to determine the optimal number of epochs to train. The reason we do this in the validation set instead of the training set is to avoid overfitting, when a model performs well in the training set but poorly in out-of-the-sample tests (i.e., on unseen data).

Here we divide 60,000 observations of the training dataset into a train set and a validation set:

```
train_set,val_set=torch.utils.data.random_split(\
    train_set,[50000,10000])
```

The original train set now becomes two sets: the new train set with 50,000 observations and a validation set with the remaining 10,000 observations.

We use the `DataLoader` class in the PyTorch *utils* package to convert the train, validation, and test sets into three data iterators in batches:

```
train_loader=torch.utils.data.DataLoader(
    train_set,
    batch_size=batch_size,
    shuffle=True)
val_loader=torch.utils.data.DataLoader(
    val_set,
    batch_size=batch_size,
    shuffle=True)
test_loader=torch.utils.data.DataLoader(
    test_set,
    batch_size=batch_size,
    shuffle=True)
```

Next, we define an `EarlyStop()` class and create an instance of the class.

Listing 2.8   The `EarlyStop()` class to determine when to stop training

```
class EarlyStop:
    def __init__(self, patience=10):
        self.patience = patience
        self.steps = 0
        self.min_loss = float('inf')
    def stop(self, val_loss):
        if val_loss < self.min_loss:
            self.min_loss = val_loss
            self.steps = 0
        elif val_loss >= self.min_loss:
            self.steps += 1
        if self.steps >= self.patience:
            return True
        else:
            return False
stopper=EarlyStop()
```

Sets the default value of patience to 10

Defines the stop() method

If a new minimum loss is reached, updates the value of min_loss

Counts how many epochs since the last minimum loss

The `EarlyStop()` class determines if the loss in the validation set has stopped improving in the last `patience=10` epochs. We set the default value of `patience` argument to 10, but you can choose a different value when you instantiate the class. The value of `patience` measures how many epochs you want to train since the last time the model reached the minimum loss. The `stop()` method keeps a record of the minimum loss and the number of epochs since the minimum loss and compares the number to the value of `patience`. The method returns a value of `True` if the number of epochs since the minimum loss is greater than the value of `patience`.

2.4.2 Building and training a multicategory classification model

The Fashion MNIST dataset contains 10 different categories of clothing items. Therefore, we create a multicategory classification model to classify them. Next, you'll learn how to create such a model and train it. You'll also learn how to make predictions using the trained model and assess the accuracy of the predictions. We use PyTorch to create the neural network for multicategory classification in the following listing.

Listing 2.9   Creating a multicategory classification model

```
model=nn.Sequential(
    nn.Linear(28*28,256),
    nn.ReLU(),
    nn.Linear(256,128),
    nn.ReLU(),
    nn.Linear(128,64),
    nn.ReLU(),
    nn.Linear(64,10)
    ).to(device)
```

There are 10 neurons in the output layer.

Does not apply softmax activation on the output

Compared to the binary classification model we created in the last section, we have made a few changes here. First, the output now has 10 values in it, representing the 10 different types of clothing items in the dataset. Second, we have changed the number of neurons in the last hidden layer from 32 to 64. A rule of thumb in creating deep neural networks is to gradually increase or decrease the number of neurons from one layer to the next. Since the number of output neurons has increased from 1 (in binary classification) to 10 (in multicategory classification), we change the number of neurons from 32 to 64 in the second to last layer to match the increase. However, there is nothing special about the number 64: if you use, say, 100 neurons in the second to last layer, you'll get similar results.

We'll use the PyTorch `nn.CrossEntropyLoss()` class as our loss function, which combines `nn.LogSoftmax()` and `nn.NLLLoss()` in one single class. See the documentation here for details: https://mng.bz/pxd2. In particular, the documentation states, "This criterion computes the cross entropy loss between input logits and target." This explains why we didn't apply the softmax activation in the proceeding listing. In the book's GitHub repository, I have demonstrated that if we use `nn.LogSoftmax()` in the model and use `nn.NLLLoss()` as the loss function, we obtain identical results.

As a result, the `nn.CrossEntropyLoss()` class will apply the softmax activation function on the output to squeeze the 10 numbers into the range [0, 1] before the logarithm operation. The preferred activation function on the output is sigmoid in binary classifications and softmax in multicategory classifications. Further, the 10 numbers after softmax activation add up to 1, which can be interpreted as the probabilities corresponding to the 10 types of clothing items. We'll use the same learning rate and optimizer as those in the binary classification in the last section.

```
lr=0.001
optimizer=torch.optim.Adam(model.parameters(),lr=lr)
loss_fn=nn.CrossEntropyLoss()
```

We define the `train_epoch()` as follows:

```
def train_epoch():
    tloss=0
    for n,(imgs,labels) in enumerate(train_loader):
        imgs=imgs.reshape(-1,28*28).to(device)
        labels=labels.reshape(-1,).to(device)
        preds=model(imgs)
        loss=loss_fn(preds,labels)
        optimizer.zero_grad()
        loss.backward()
        optimizer.step()
        tloss+=loss.detach()
    return tloss/n
```

The function trains the model for one epoch. The code is similar to what we have seen in the binary classification, except that the labels are from 0 to 9, instead of two numbers (0 and 1).

We also define a `val_epoch()` function:

```
def val_epoch():
    vloss=0
    for n,(imgs,labels) in enumerate(val_loader):
        imgs=imgs.reshape(-1,28*28).to(device)
```

```
        labels=labels.reshape(-1,).to(device)
        preds=model(imgs)
        loss=loss_fn(preds,labels)
        vloss+=loss.detach()
    return vloss/n
```

The function uses the model to make predictions on images in the validation set and calculate the average loss per batch of data.

We now train the multicategory classifier:

```
for i in range(1,101):
    tloss=train_epoch()
    vloss=val_epoch()
    print(f"at epoch {i}, tloss is {tloss}, vloss is {vloss}")
    if stopper.stop(vloss)==True:
        break
```

We train a maximum of 100 epochs. In each epoch, we first train the model using the training set. We then calculate the average loss per batch in the validation set. We use the EarlyStop() class to determine if the training should stop by looking at the loss in the validation set. The training stops if the loss hasn't improved in the last 10 epochs. After 19 epochs, the training stops.

The training takes about 5 minutes if you use GPU training, which is longer than the training process in binary classification since we have more observations in the training set now (10 clothing items instead of just 2).

The output from the model is a vector of 10 numbers. We use torch.argmax() to assign each observation a label based on the highest probability. We then compare the predicted label with the actual label. To illustrate how the prediction works, let's look at the predictions on the first five images in the test set.

Listing 2.10   Testing the trained model on five images

```
plt.figure(dpi=300,figsize=(5,1))
for i in range(5):
    ax=plt.subplot(1,5, i + 1)          ◄──── Plots the first five
    img=test_set[i][0]                         images in the test set
    label=test_set[i][1]                       with their labels
    img=img/2+0.5
    img=img.reshape(28, 28)             ◄──── Obtains the
    plt.imshow(img, cmap="binary")             i-th image and
    plt.axis('off')                            label in the
    plt.title(text_labels[label]+f"; {label}", fontsize=8)    test set
plt.show()
for i in range(5):
    img,label = test_set[i]
    img=img.reshape(-1,28*28).to(device)    ◄──── Predicts using
    pred=model(img)                                the trained
    index_pred=torch.argmax(pred,dim=1)    ◄──── model
    idx=index_pred.item()                  ◄──── Uses the torch
    print(f"the label is {label}; the prediction is {idx}")    .argmax()
```

Prints out the actual label
and the predicted label   method to
                                             obtain the
                                             predicted label

We plot the first five clothing items in the test set in a 1 × 5 grid. We then use the trained model to make a prediction on each clothing item. The prediction is a tensor with 10 values. The `torch.argmax()` method returns the position of the highest probability in the tensor, and we use it as the predicted label. Finally, we print out both the actual label and the predicted label to compare and see if the predictions are correct. After running the previous code listing, you should see the image in figure 2.3.

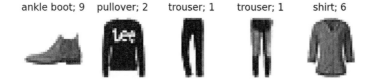

Figure 2.3 **The first five clothing items in the test dataset and their respective labels. Each clothing item has a text label and a numerical label between 0 and 9.**

Figure 2.3 shows that the first five clothing items in the test set are ankle boot, pullover, trouser, trouser, and shirt, respectively, with numerical labels 9, 2, 1, 1, and 6.

The output after running the code in listing 2.10 is as follows:

```
the label is 9; the prediction is 9
the label is 2; the prediction is 2
the label is 1; the prediction is 1
the label is 1; the prediction is 1
the label is 6; the prediction is 6
```

The preceding output shows that the model has made correct predictions on all five clothing items.

Fixing the random state in PyTorch

The `torch.manual_seed()` method fixes the random state so the results are the same when you rerun your programs. However, you may get different results from those reported in this chapter even if you use the same random seed. This happens because different hardware and different versions of PyTorch handle floating point operations slightly differently. See, for example, the explanations at https://mng.bz/RNva. The difference is generally minor, though, so no need to be alarmed.

Next, we calculate the accuracy of the predictions on the whole test dataset.

Listing 2.11 Testing the trained multicategory classification model

```
results=[]

for imgs,labels in test_loader:              Iterates through all
    imgs=imgs.reshape(-1,28*28).to(device)   batches in the test set
    labels=(labels).reshape(-1,).to(device)
    preds=model(imgs)                         Predicts using the
                                              trained model
```

```
pred10=torch.argmax(preds,dim=1)
correct=(pred10==labels)
results.append(correct.detach().cpu().numpy().mean())

accuracy=np.array(results).mean()
print(f"the accuracy of the predictions is {accuracy}")
```

◀ Converts probabilities to a predicted label

◀ Compares the predicted label with the actual label

◀ Calculates accuracy in the test set

The output is

```
the accuracy of the predictions is 0.8819665605095541
```

We iterate through all clothing items in the test set and use the trained model to make predictions. We then compare the predictions with the actual labels. The accuracy is about 88% in the out-of-sample test. Given that a random guess has an accuracy of about 10%, 88% accuracy is fairly high. This indicates that we have built and trained two successful deep learning models in PyTorch! You'll use these skills quite often later in this book. For example, in chapter 3, the discriminator network you'll construct is essentially a binary classification model, similar to what you have created in this chapter.

Summary

- In PyTorch, we use tensors to hold various forms of input data so we can feed them to deep learning models.
- You can index and slice PyTorch tensors, reshape them, and conduct mathematical operations on them.
- Deep learning is a type of ML method that uses deep artificial neural networks to learn the relation between input and output data.
- The ReLU activation function decides whether a neuron should be turned on based on the weighted sum. It introduces nonlinearity to the output of a neuron.
- Loss functions measure how well an ML model performs. The training of a model involves adjusting parameters to minimize the loss function.
- Binary classification is an ML model to classify observations into one of two categories.
- Multicategory classification is an ML model to classify observations into one of multiple categories.

Generative adversarial networks: Shape and number generation

This chapter covers

- Building generator and discriminator networks in generative adversarial networks from scratch
- Using GANs to generate data points to form shapes (e.g., exponential growth curve)
- Generating integer sequences that are all multiples of 5
- Training, saving, loading, and using GANs
- Evaluating GAN performance and determining training stop points

Close to half of the generative models in this book belong to a category called generative adversarial networks (GANs). The method was first proposed by Ian Goodfellow and his coauthors in 2014.[1] GANs, celebrated for their ease of implementation and versatility, empower individuals with even rudimentary knowledge of deep learning to construct their models from the ground up. The word "adversarial" in

---

[1] Goodfellow et al, 2014, "Generative Adversarial Nets." https://arxiv.org/abs/1406.2661.

GAN refers to the fact that the two neural networks compete against each other in a zero-sum game framework. The generative network tries to create data instances indistinguishable from real samples. In contrast, the discriminative network tries to identify the generated samples from real ones. These versatile models can generate various content formats, from geometric shapes and sequences of numbers to high-resolution color images and even realistic-sounding musical compositions.

In this chapter, we'll briefly review the theory behind GANs. Then, I'll show you how to implement that knowledge in PyTorch. You'll learn to build your first GAN from scratch so that all the details are demystified. To make the example relatable, imagine you put $1 in a savings account that pays 8% a year. You want to find out the balance in your account based on the number of years you have invested. The true relation is an exponential growth curve. You'll learn to use GANs to generate data samples—pairs of values (x, y) that form such an exponential growth curve, with a mathematical relation $y = 1.08^x$. Armed with this skill, you'll be able to generate data to mimic any shape: sine, cosine, quadratic, and so on.

In the second project in this chapter, you'll learn how to use GANs to generate a sequence of numbers that are all multiples of 5. But you can change the pattern to multiples of 2, 3, 7, or other patterns. Along the way, you'll learn how to create a generator network and a discriminator network from scratch. You'll learn how to train, save, and use GANs. Further, you'll also learn to assess the performance of GANs either by visualizing samples generated by the generator network or by measuring the divergence between the generated sample distribution and the real data distribution.

Imagine that you need data to train a machine learning (ML) model to predict the relation between pairs of values (x, y). However, the training dataset is costly and time-consuming for human beings to prepare by hand. GANs can be well-suited to generate data in such cases: while the generated values of x and y generally conform to a mathematical relation, there is also noise in the generated data. The noise can be useful for preventing overfitting when the generated data is used to train the ML model.

The primary goal of this chapter is not necessarily to generate novel content with the most practical use. Instead, my objective is to teach you how to train and use GANs to create various formats of content from scratch. Along the way, you will gain a solid understanding of the inner workings of GANs. This foundation will allow us to concentrate on other, more advanced, aspects of GANs in later chapters when generating other content such as high-resolution images or realistic-sounding music (e.g., convolutional neural networks or how to represent a piece of music as a multidimensional object).

3.1   *Steps involved in training GANs*

In chapter 1, you gained a high-level overview of the theories behind GANs. In this section, I'll provide a summary of the steps involved in training GANs in general and in creating data points to form an exponential growth curve in particular.

Let's return to our previous example: you plan to invest in a savings account that pays 8% annual interest. You put \$1 in the account today and want to know how much money you'll have in the account in the future.

The amount in your account in the future, y, depends on how long you invest in the savings account. Let's denote the number of years you invest by x, which can be a number, say, between 0 and 50. For example, if you invest for 1 year, the balance is \$1.08; if you invest for 2 years, the balance is $1.08^2 = \$1.17$. To generalize, the relationship between x and y is $y = 1.08^x$. The function depicts an exponential growth curve. Note here that x can be a whole number such as 1 or 2, as well as a decimal number such as 1.14 or 2.35 and the formula still works.

Training GANs to generate data points that conform to a specific mathematical relation, like the preceding example, is a multistep process. In your case, you want to generate data points (x, y) such that $y = 1.08^x$. Figure 3.1 provides a diagram of the architecture of GANs and the steps involved in generating an exponential growth curve. When you generate other content such as a sequence of integers, images, or music, you follow similar steps, as you'll see in the second project in this chapter, as well as in other GAN models later in this book.

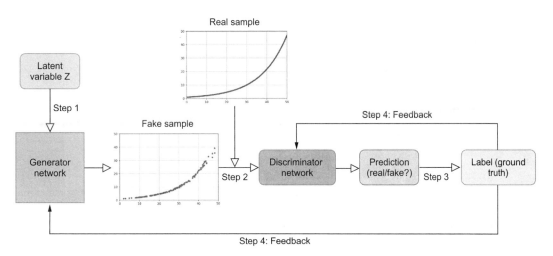

Figure 3.1   The steps involved in training GANs to generate an exponential growth curve and the dual-network architecture in GANs. The generator obtains a random noise vector Z from the latent space (top left) to create a fake sample and presents it to the discriminator (middle). The discriminator classifies a sample as real (from the training set) or fake (created by the generator). The predictions are compared to the ground truth and both the discriminator and the generator learn from the predictions. After many iterations of training, the generator learns to create shapes that are indistinguishable from real samples.

Before we start, we need to obtain a training dataset to train GANs. In our running example, we'll generate a dataset of (x, y) pairs using the mathematical relation $y = 1.08^x$. We use the savings account example so that the numbers are relatable. The techniques you learn in this chapter can be applied to other shapes: sine, cosine, U-shape, and so on. You can choose a range of x values (say, 0 to 50) and calculate the corresponding y values. Since we usually train models in batches of data in deep learning, the number of observations in your training dataset is usually set to a multiple of the batch size. A real sample is located at the top of figure 3.1, which has an exponential growth curve shape.

Once you have the training set ready, you need to create two networks in GANs: a generator and a discriminator. The generator, located at the bottom left of figure 3.1, takes a random noise vector Z as the input and generates data points (step 1 of our training loop). The random noise vector Z used by the generator is obtained from the latent space, which represents the range of possible outputs the GAN can produce and is central to the GAN's ability to generate diverse data samples. In chapter 5, we'll explore the latent space to select the attributes of the content created by the generator. The discriminator, located at the center of figure 3.1, evaluates whether a given data point (x, y) is real (from the training dataset) or fake (created by the generator); this is step 2 of our training loop.

The meaning of the latent space

The latent space in a GAN is a conceptual space where each point can be transformed into a realistic data instance by the generator. This space represents the range of possible outputs the GAN can produce and is central to the GAN's ability to generate varied and complex data. The latent space acquires its significance exclusively when it is employed in conjunction with the generative model. Within this context, one can interpolate between points in the latent space to affect the attributes of output, which we'll discuss in chapter 5.

To know how to adjust model parameters, we must choose the right loss functions. We need to define the loss functions for both the generator and discriminator. The loss function encourages the generator to generate data points that resemble data points from the training dataset, making the discriminator classify them as real. The loss function encourages the discriminator to correctly classify real and generated data points.

In each iteration of the training loop, we alternate between training the discriminator and the generator. During each training iteration, we sample a batch of real (x, y) data points from the training dataset and a batch of fake data points generated by the generator. When training the discriminator, we compare the predictions by the discriminative model, which is a probability that the sample is from the training set, with the ground truth, which is 1 if the sample is real and 0 if the sample is fake (shown at the right of figure 3.1); this constitutes half of step 3 in the training loop. We adjust the weights in the discriminator network slightly so that in the next iteration, the predicted probability moves closer to the ground truth (half of step 4 in our training loop).

When training the generator, we feed fake samples to the discriminative model and obtain a probability that the sample is real (the other half of step 3). We then adjust the weights in the generator network slightly so that in the next iteration, the predicted probability moves closer to 1 (since the generator wants to create samples to fool the discriminator into thinking they are real); this constitutes the other half of step 4. We repeat this process for many iterations, making the generator network create more realistic data points.

A natural question is when to stop training the GANs. For that, you evaluate the GAN's performance by generating a set of synthetic data points and comparing them to the real data points from the training dataset. In most cases, we use visualization techniques to assess how well the generated data conforms to the desired relation. However, in our running example, since we know the distribution of the training data, we can calculate the mean squared error (MSE) between the generated data and the true data distribution. We stop training GANs when the generated samples stop improving their qualities after a fixed number of rounds of training.

At this point, the model is considered trained. We then discard the discriminator and keep the generator. To create an exponential growth curve, we feed a random noise vector Z to the trained generator and obtain pairs of (x, y) to form the desired shape.

3.2 *Preparing training data*

In this section, you'll create the training dataset so that you can use it to train the GAN model later in this chapter. Specifically, you'll create pairs of data points (x, y) that conform to the exponential growth shape. You'll place them in batches so that they are ready to be fed to deep neural networks.

NOTE The code for this chapter, as well as other chapters in this book, is available at the book's GitHub repository: https://github.com/markhliu/DGAI.

3.2.1 *A training dataset that forms an exponential growth curve*

We'll create a dataset that contains many observations of data pairs, (x, y), where x is uniformly distributed in the interval [0, 50] and y is related to x based on the formula $y = 1.08^x$, as shown in the following listing.

Listing 3.1 Creating training data to form an exponential growth shape

```
import torch

torch.manual_seed(0)                                    Fixes the random state so
                                                        results are reproducible
observations = 2048
                                                        Creates a tensor with 2,048
train_data = torch.zeros((observations, 2))             rows and 2 columns

train_data[:,0]=50*torch.rand(observations)             Generates values of x
                                                        between 0 and 50

train_data[:,1]=1.08**train_data[:,0]                   Generates values of y based
                                                        on the relation y = 1.08ˣ
```

First, we create 2,048 values of x between 0 and 50 using the `torch.rand()` method. We use the `manual_seed()` method in PyTorch to fix the random state so that all results are reproducible. We first create a PyTorch tensor, `train_data`, with 2,048 rows and 2 columns. The values of x are placed in the first column in the tensor `train_data`. The `rand()` method in PyTorch generates random values between 0.0 and 1.0. By multiplying the value by 50, the resulting values of x are between 0.0 and 50.0. We then fill the second column of `train_data` with values of $y = 1.08^x$.

Exercise 3.1

Modify listing 3.1 so that the relation between x and y is y = sin(x) by using the `torch.sin()` function. Set the value of x between –5 and 5 by using this line of code: `train_data[:,0]=10*(torch.rand(observations)-0.5)`.

We plot the relation between x and y by using the Matplotlib library.

Listing 3.2   Visualizing the relation between x and y

```
import matplotlib.pyplot as plt

fig=plt.figure(dpi=100,figsize=(8,6))
plt.plot(train_data[:,0],train_data[:,1],".",c="r")      ◄──┐  Plots the relation
plt.xlabel("values of x",fontsize=15)                        │  between x and y
plt.ylabel("values of $y=1.08^x$",fontsize=15)           ◄──── Labels y-axis
plt.title("An exponential growth shape",fontsize=20)     ◄──┐
plt.show()                                                   │  Creates a title
                                                             │  for the plot
```

You will see an exponential growth curve shape after running listing 3.2, which is similar to the top graph in figure 3.1.

Exercise 3.2

Modify listing 3.2 to plot the relation between x and y = sin(x) based on your changes in exercise 3.1. Make sure you change the y-axis label and the title in the plot to reflect the changes you made.

3.2.2   *Preparing the training dataset*

We'll place the data samples you just created into batches so that we can feed them to the discriminator network. We use the `DataLoader()` class in PyTorch to wrap an iterable around the training dataset so that we can easily access the samples during training, like so:

```
from torch.utils.data import DataLoader

batch_size=128
train_loader=DataLoader(
    train_data,
    batch_size=batch_size,
    shuffle=True)
```

Make sure you select the total number of observations and the batch size so that all batches have the same number of samples in them. We chose 2,048 observations with a batch size of 128. As a result, we have 2,048/128 = 16 batches. The shuffle=True argument in DataLoader() shuffles the observations randomly before dividing them into batches.

> **NOTE** Shuffling makes sure that the data samples are evenly distributed and observations within a batch are not correlated, which, in turn, stabilizes training. In this specific example, shuffling ensures that values of x fall randomly between 0 and 50, instead of clustering in a certain range, say, between 0 and 5.

You can access a batch of data by using the next() and iter() methods, like so:

```
batch0=next(iter(train_loader))
print(batch0)
```

You will see 128 pairs of numbers (x, y), where the value of x falls randomly between 0 and 50. Further, the values of x and y in each pair conform to the relation $y = 1.08^x$.

3.3 *Creating GANs*

Now that the training dataset is ready, we'll create a discriminator network and a generator network. The discriminator network is a binary classifier, which is very similar to the binary classifier for clothing items we have created and trained in chapter 2. Here, the discriminator's job is to classify the samples into either real or fake. The generator network, on the other hand, tries to create data points (x, y) that are indistinguishable from those in the training set so that the discriminator will classify them as real.

3.3.1 *The discriminator network*

We use PyTorch to create a discriminator neural network. We'll use fully connected (dense) layers with ReLU activations. We'll also use dropout layers to prevent overfitting. We create a sequential deep neural network in PyTorch to represent the discriminator, as shown in the following listing.

Listing 3.3 Creating a discriminator network

```
import torch.nn as nn

device="cuda" if torch.cuda.is_available() else "cpu"   ◄──
```
Automatically checks if CUDA-enabled GPU is available.

```
D=nn.Sequential(
    nn.Linear(2,256),
    nn.ReLU(),
    nn.Dropout(0.3),
    nn.Linear(256,128),
    nn.ReLU(),
    nn.Dropout(0.3),
    nn.Linear(128,64),
    nn.ReLU(),
    nn.Dropout(0.3),
    nn.Linear(64,1),
    nn.Sigmoid()).to(device)
```

The number of input features in the first layer is 2, matching the number of elements in each data instance, which has two values, x and y.

The dropout layer prevents overfitting.

The number of output features in the last layer is 1 so that we can squeeze it into a value between 0 and 1.

Make sure that in the first layer, the input shape is 2 because, in our sample, each data instance has two values in it: x and y. The number of inputs in the first layer should always match with the size of the input data. Also, make sure that the number of output features is 1 in the last layer: the output of the discriminator network is a single value. We use the sigmoid activation function to squeeze the output to the range [0, 1] so that it can be interpreted as the probability, p, that the sample is real. With the complementary probability, $1 - p$, the sample is fake. This is very similar to what we have done in chapter 2 when a binary classifier attempts to identify a piece of clothing item as either an ankle boot or a t-shirt.

The hidden layers have 256, 128, and 64 neurons in them, respectively. There is nothing magical about these numbers, and you can easily change them and have similar results as long as they are in a reasonable range. If the number of neurons in hidden layers is too large, it may lead to overfitting of the model; if the number is too small, it may lead to underfitting. The number of neurons can be optimized separately using a validation set through hyperparameter tuning.

Dropout layers randomly deactivate (or "drop out") a certain percentage of neurons in the layer to which they are applied. This means that these neurons do not participate in forward or backward passes during training. Overfitting occurs when a model learns not only the underlying patterns in the training data but also the noise and random fluctuations, leading to poor performance on unseen data. Dropout layers are an effective way to prevent overfitting.[2]

3.3.2   *The generator network*

The generator's job is to create a pair of numbers (x, y) so that it can pass the screening of the discriminator. That is, the generator is trying to create a pair of numbers to maximize the probability that the discriminator thinks that the numbers are from the training dataset (i.e., they conform to the relation $y = 1.08^x$). We create the neural network in the following listing to represent the generator.

---

[2] Nitish Srivastava, Geoffrey Hinton, Alex Krizhevsky, Ilya Sutskever, and Ruslan Salakhutdinov, 2014, "Dropout: A Simple Way to Prevent Neural Networks from Overfitting." *Journal of Machine Learning Research* 15 (56): 1929–1958.

Listing 3.4 Creating a generator network

```
G=nn.Sequential(
    nn.Linear(2,16),
    nn.ReLU(),
    nn.Linear(16,32),
    nn.ReLU(),
    nn.Linear(32,2)).to(device)
```

◄─── The number of input features in the first layer is 2, the same as the dimension of the random noise vector from the latent space.

◄─── The number of output features in the last layer is 2, the same as the dimension of the data sample, which contains two values (x, y).

We feed a random noise vector from a 2D latent space, (z_1, z_2), to the generator. The generator then generates a pair of values (x, y), based on the input from the latent space. Here we use a 2D latent space, but changing the dimension to other numbers such as 5 or 10 wouldn't affect our results.

3.3.3 *Loss functions, optimizers, and early stopping*

Since the discriminator network is essentially performing a binary classification task (identifying a data sample as real or fake), we use binary cross-entropy loss, the preferred loss function in binary classifications, for the discriminator network. The discriminator is trying to maximize the accuracy of the binary classification: identify a real sample as real and a fake sample as fake. The weights in the discriminator network are updated based on the gradient of the loss function with respect to the weights.

The generator is trying to minimize the probability that the fake sample is being identified as fake. Therefore, we'll also use binary cross-entropy loss for the generator network: the generator updates its network weights so that the generated samples will be classified as real by the discriminator in a binary classification problem.

As we have done in chapter 2, we use the Adam optimizer as the gradient descent algorithm. We set the learning rate to 0.0005. Let's code those steps in by using PyTorch:

```
loss_fn=nn.BCELoss()
lr=0.0005
optimD=torch.optim.Adam(D.parameters(),lr=lr)
optimG=torch.optim.Adam(G.parameters(),lr=lr)
```

One question remains before we get to the actual training: How many epochs should we train the GANs? How do we know the model is well trained so that the generator is ready to create samples that can mimic the exponential growth curve shape? If you recall, in chapter 2, we split the training set further into a train set and a validation set. We then used the loss in the validation set to determine whether the parameters had converged so that we could stop training. However, GANs are trained using a different approach compared to traditional supervised learning models (such as the classification models you have seen in chapter 2). Since the quality of the generated samples improves throughout training, the discriminator's task becomes more and more difficult (in a way, the discriminator in GANs is making predictions on a moving target).

The loss from the discriminator network is not a good indicator of the quality of the model.

One common method to measure the performance of GANs is through visual inspection. Humans can assess the quality and realism of generated data instances by simply looking at them. This is a qualitative approach but can be very informative. But in our simple case, since we know the exact distribution of the training dataset, we'll look at the MSE of the generated samples relative to samples in the training set and use it as a measure of the performance of the generator. Let's code that in:

```
mse=nn.MSELoss()                                          ◀──── Uses MSE as the criterion
                                                                 to measure performance
def performance(fake_samples):
    real=1.08**fake_samples[:,0]          ◀──── Finds out the true distribution
    mseloss=mse(fake_samples[:,1],real)   ◀───┐
    return mseloss                            │  Compares the generated
                                                 distribution with the true
                                                 distribution and calculates MSE
```

We'll stop training the model if the performance of the generator doesn't improve in, say, 1,000 epochs. Therefore, we define an early stopping class, as we did in chapter 2, to decide when to stop training the model.

Listing 3.5   An early stopping class to decide when to stop training

```
class EarlyStop:                                          ┌─ Sets the default value
    def __init__(self, patience=1000):          ◀─────────┘  of patience to 1000
        self.patience = patience
        self.steps = 0                                       Defines the stop()
        self.min_gdif = float('inf')                         method
    def stop(self, gdif):                         ◀────────┘
        if gdif < self.min_gdif:            ◀───┐  If a new minimum difference between
            self.min_gdif = gdif                │  the generated distribution and true
            self.steps = 0                      │  distribution is reached, updates the
        elif gdif >= self.min_gdif:             │  value of min_gdif.
            self.steps += 1
        if self.steps >= self.patience:    ◀───┐  Stops training if the model stops
            return True                         │  improving for 1,000 epochs
        else:
            return False

stopper=EarlyStop()
```

With that, we have all the components we need to train our GANs, which we'll do in the next section.

3.4   *Training and using GANs for shape generation*

Now that we have the training data and two networks, we'll train the model. After that, we'll discard the discriminator and use the generator to generate data points to form an exponential growth curve shape.

3.4.1   *The training of GANs*

We first create labels for real samples and fake samples, respectively. Specifically, we'll label all real samples as 1s and all fake samples as 0s. During the training process, the discriminator compares its own predictions with the labels to receive feedback so that it can adjust model parameters to make better predictions in the next iteration.

Here, we define two tensors, real_labels and fake_labels:

```
real_labels=torch.ones((batch_size,1))
real_labels=real_labels.to(device)

fake_labels=torch.zeros((batch_size,1))
fake_labels=fake_labels.to(device)
```

The tensor real_labels is 2D with a shape of (batch_size,   1)—that is, 128 rows and 1 column. We use 128 rows because we'll feed a batch of 128 real samples to the discriminator network to obtain 128 predictions. Similarly, the tensor fake_labels is 2D with a shape of (batch_size,   1). We'll feed a batch of 128 fake samples to the discriminator network to obtain 128 predictions and compare them with the ground truth: 128 labels of 0s. We move the two tensors to the GPU for fast training if your computer has a CUDA-enabled GPU.

To train the GANs, we define a few functions so that the training loop looks organized. The first function, train_D_on_real(), trains the discriminator network with a batch of real samples.

Listing 3.6   Defining a `train_D_on_real()` function

```
def train_D_on_real(real_samples):
    real_samples=real_samples.to(device)
    optimD.zero_grad()
    out_D=D(real_samples)                      Makes predictions
    loss_D=loss_fn(out_D,real_labels)          on real samples
    loss_D.backward()                          ◄─── Calculates loss
    optimD.step()
    return loss_D
```

Makes predictions on real samples

Calculates loss

Backpropagation (i.e., updates model weights in the discriminator network so predictions are more accurate in the next iteration)

The function train_D_on_real() first moves the real samples to GPU if the computer has a CUDA-enabled GPU. The discriminator network, D, makes predictions on the batch of samples. The model then compares the discriminator's predictions, out_D, with the ground truth, real_labels, and calculates the loss of the predictions accordingly. The backward() method calculates the gradients of the loss function with respect to model parameters. The step() method adjusts the model parameters (that is, backpropagation). The zero_grad() method means that we explicitly set the gradients to 0 before backpropagation. Otherwise, the accumulated gradients instead of the incremental gradients are used on every backward() call.

> **TIP**   We call the `zero_grad()` method before updating model weights when training each batch of data. We explicitly set the gradients to 0 before backpropagation to use incremental gradients instead of the accumulated gradients on every `backward()` call.

The second function, `train_D_on_fake()`, trains the discriminator network with a batch of fake samples.

Listing 3.7   Defining the `train_D_on_fake()` function

```
def train_D_on_fake():
    noise=torch.randn((batch_size,2))
    noise=noise.to(device)
    fake_samples=G(noise)                          Generates a batch
    optimD.zero_grad()                             of fake samples
    out_D=D(fake_samples)                          Makes predictions
    loss_D=loss_fn(out_D,fake_labels)              on the fake samples
    loss_D.backward()
    optimD.step()                                  Calculates loss
    return loss_D
                                                   Backpropagation
```

The function `train_D_on_fake()` first feeds a batch of random noise vectors from the latent space to the generator to obtain a batch of fake samples. The function then presents the fake samples to the discriminator to obtain predictions. The function compares the discriminator's predictions, `out_D`, with the ground truth, `fake_labels`, and calculates the loss of the predictions accordingly. Finally, it adjusts the model parameters based on the gradients of the loss function with respect to model weights.

> **NOTE**   We use the terms *weights* and *parameters* interchangeably. Strictly speaking, model parameters also include bias terms, but we use the term *model weights* loosely to include model biases. Similarly, we use the terms *adjusting weights*, *adjusting parameters*, and *backpropagation* interchangeably.

The third function, `train_G()`, trains the generator network with a batch of fake samples.

Listing 3.8   Defining the `train_G()` function

```
def train_G():
    noise=torch.randn((batch_size,2))              Creates a batch
    noise=noise.to(device)                         of fake samples
    optimG.zero_grad()
    fake_samples=G(noise)                          Presents the fake samples
    out_G=D(fake_samples)                          to the discriminator to
    loss_G=loss_fn(out_G,real_labels)              obtain predictions
    loss_G.backward()
                                                   Calculates the loss based on
                                                   whether G has succeeded
```

```
optimG.step()
return loss_G, fake_samples
```

Backpropagation (i.e., updates weights in the generator network so the generated samples are more realistic in the next iteration)

To train the generator, we first feed a batch of random noise vectors from the latent space to the generator to obtain a batch of fake samples. We then present the fake samples to the discriminator network to obtain a batch of predictions. We compare the discriminator's predictions with `real_labels`, a tensor of 1s, and calculate the loss. It's important that we use a tensor of 1s, not a tensor of 0s, as the labels, because the objective of the generator is to fool the discriminator into thinking that fake samples are real. Finally, we adjust the model parameters based on the gradients of the loss function with respect to model weights so that in the next iteration, the generator can create more realistic samples.

NOTE We use the tensor `real_labels` (a tensor of 1s) instead of `fake_labels` (a tensor of 0s) when calculating loss and assessing the generator network because the generator wants the discriminator to predict fake samples as real.

Finally, we define a function, `test_epoch()`, which prints out the losses for the discriminator and the generator periodically. Further, it plots the data points generated by the generator and compares them to those in the training set. The function `test_epoch()` is shown in the following listing.

Listing 3.9　Defining the `test_epoch()` function

```
import os
os.makedirs("files", exist_ok=True)                          Creates a folder to hold files

def test_epoch(epoch,gloss,dloss,n,fake_samples):
    if epoch==0 or (epoch+1)%25==0:
        g=gloss.item()/n                                     Periodically
        d=dloss.item()/n                                     prints out
        print(f"at epoch {epoch+1}, G loss: {g}, D loss {d}")  losses
        fake=fake_samples.detach().cpu().numpy()
        plt.figure(dpi=200)
        plt.plot(fake[:,0],fake[:,1],"*",c="g",              Plots the generated
            label="generated samples")                       points as asterisks (*)
        plt.plot(train_data[:,0],train_data[:,1],".",c="r",
            alpha=0.1,label="real samples")                  Plots training
        plt.title(f"epoch {epoch+1}")                        data as dots (.)
        plt.xlim(0,50)
        plt.ylim(0,50)
        plt.legend()
        plt.savefig(f"files/p{epoch+1}.png")
        plt.show()
```

After every 25 epochs, the function prints out the average losses for the generator and the discriminator in the epoch. Further, it plots a batch of fake data points generated by the generator (in asterisks) and compares them to the data points in the training set (in dots). The plot is saved as an image in your local folder /files/.

Now we are ready to train the model. We iterate through all batches in the training dataset. For each batch of data, we first train the discriminator using the real samples. After that, the generator creates a batch of fake samples, and we use them to train the discriminator again. Finally, we let the generator create a batch of fake samples again, but this time, we use them to train the generator instead. We train the model until the early stopping condition is satisfied, as shown in the following listing.

Listing 3.10 Training GANs to generate an exponential growth curve

```
for epoch in range(10000):                                      Starts training loops
    gloss=0
    dloss=0
    for n, real_samples in enumerate(train_loader):             Iterates through all batches
        loss_D=train_D_on_real(real_samples)                    in the training dataset
        dloss+=loss_D
        loss_D=train_D_on_fake()
        dloss+=loss_D
        loss_G,fake_samples=train_G()                           Shows generated
        gloss+=loss_G                                           samples periodically
    test_epoch(epoch,gloss,dloss,n,fake_samples)
    gdif=performance(fake_samples).item()                       Determines if training
    if stopper.stop(gdif)==True:                                should stop
        break
```

The training takes a few minutes if you are using GPU training. Otherwise, it may take 20 to 30 minutes, depending on the hardware configuration on your computer. Alternatively, you can download the trained model from the book's GitHub repository: https://github.com/markhliu/DGAI.

After 25 epochs of training, the generated data are scattered around the point (0,0) and don't form any meaningful shape (an epoch is when all training data is used for training once). After 200 epochs of training, the data points start to form an exponential growth curve shape, even though many points are far away from the dotted curve, which is formed by points from the training set. After 1,025 epochs, the generated points fit closely with the exponential growth curve. Figure 3.2 provides subplots of the output from six different epochs. Our GANs work really well: the generator is able to generate data points to form the desired shape.

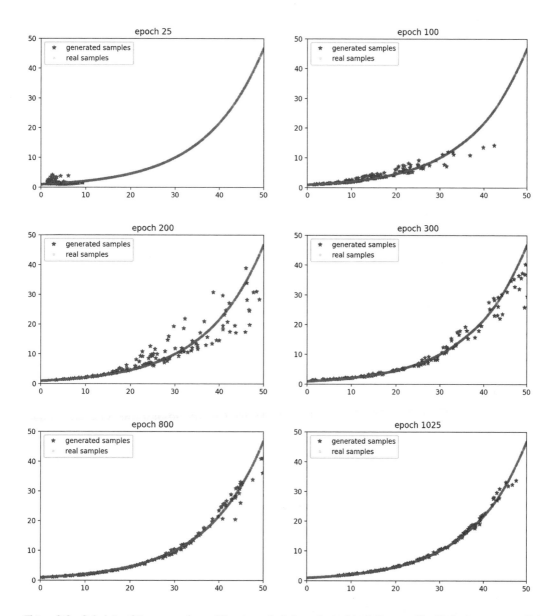

Figure 3.2 Subplots of the comparison of the generated shape (asterisks in the graph) with the true exponential growth curve shape (dots in the graph) at different stages of the training process. At epoch 25, the generated samples don't form any meaningful shape. At epoch 200, the samples start to look like an exponential growth curve shape. At epoch 1025, the generated samples align closely with the exponential growth curve.

3.4.2   *Saving and using the trained generator*

Now that the GANs are trained, we'll discard the discriminator network, as we always do in GANs, and save the trained generator network in the local folder, as follows:

```
import os
os.makedirs("files", exist_ok=True)
scripted = torch.jit.script(G)
scripted.save('files/exponential.pt')
```

The `torch.jit.script()` method scripts a function or a `nn.Module` class as Torch-Script code using the TorchScript compiler. We use the method to script our trained generator network and save it as a file, `exponential.pt`, on your computer.

   To use the generator, we don't even need to define the model. We simply load up the saved file and use it to generate data points as follows:

```
new_G=torch.jit.load('files/exponential.pt',
                     map_location=device)
new_G.eval()
```

The trained generator is now loaded to your device, which is either CPU or CUDA depending on if you have a CUDA-enabled GPU on your computer. The `map_location=device` argument in `torch.jit.load()` specifies where to load the generator. We can now use the trained generator to generate a batch of data points:

```
noise=torch.randn((batch_size,2)).to(device)
new_data=new_G(noise)
```

Here, we first obtain a batch of random noise vectors from the latent space. We then feed them to the generator to produce the fake data. We can plot the generated data:

```
fig=plt.figure(dpi=100)
plt.plot(new_data.detach().cpu().numpy()[:,0],
  new_data.detach().cpu().numpy()[:,1],"*",c="g",
        label="generated samples")
plt.plot(train_data[:,0],train_data[:,1],".",c="r",
        alpha=0.1,label="real samples")
plt.title("Inverted-U Shape Generated by GANs")
plt.xlim(0,50)
plt.ylim(0,50)
plt.legend()
plt.show()
```

Plots the generated data samples as asterisks

Plots the training data as dots

You should see a plot similar to the last subplot in figure 3.2: the generated data samples closely resemble an exponential growth curve.

   Congratulations! You have created and trained your very first GANs. Armed with this skill, you can easily change the code so that the generated data matches other shapes such as sine, cosine, U-shape, and so on.

> ### Exercise 3.3
> Modify the programs in the first project so that the generator generates data samples to form a sine shape between x = –5 and x = 5. When you plot the data samples, set the value of y between –1.2 and 1.2.

3.5 *Generating numbers with patterns*

In this second project, you'll build and train GANs to generate a sequence of 10 integers between 0 and 99, all of them multiples of 5. The main steps involved are similar to those to generate an exponential growth curve, with the exception that the training set is not data points with two values (x, y). Instead, the training dataset is a sequence of integers that are all multiples of 5 between 0 and 99.

In this section, you'll first learn to convert the training data into a format that neural networks understand: one-hot variables. Further, you'll convert one-hot variables back to an integer between 0 and 99, so it's easy for human beings to understand. Hence you are essentially translating data between human-readable and model-ready formats. After that, you'll create a discriminator and a generator and train the GANs. You'll also use early stopping to determine when the training is finished. You then discard the discriminator and use the trained generator to create a sequence of integers with the pattern you want.

3.5.1 *What are one-hot variables?*

One-hot encoding is a technique used in ML and data preprocessing to represent categorical data as binary vectors. Categorical data consists of categories or labels, such as colors, types of animals, or cities, which are not inherently numeric. ML algorithms typically work with numerical data, so converting categorical data into a numerical format is necessary.

Imagine you are working with a categorical feature—for example, the color of a house that can take values "red," "green," and "blue." With one-hot encoding, each category is represented as a binary vector. You'll create three binary columns, one for each category. The color "red" is one-hot encoded as [1, 0, 0], "green" as [0, 1, 0], and "blue" as [0, 0, 1]. Doing so preserves the categorical information without introducing any ordinal relationship between the categories. Each category is treated as independent.

Here we define a `onehot_encoder()` function to convert an integer to a one-hot variable:

```
import torch
def onehot_encoder(position,depth):
    onehot=torch.zeros((depth,))
    onehot[position]=1
    return onehot
```

The function takes two arguments: the first argument, `position`, is the index at which the value is turned on as 1, and the second argument, `depth`, is the length of the one-hot variable. For example, if we print out the value of `onehot_encoder(1,5)`, it will look like this:

```
print(onehot_encoder(1,5))
```

The result is

```
tensor([0., 1., 0., 0., 0.])
```

The result shows a five-value tensor with the second place (the index value of which is 1) turned on as 1 and the rest turned off as 0s.

Now that you understand how one-hot encoding works, you can convert any integer between 0 and 99 to a one-hot variable:

```
def int_to_onehot(number):
    onehot=onehot_encoder(number,100)
    return onehot
```

Let's use the function to convert the number 75 to a 100-value tensor:

```
onehot75=int_to_onehot(75)
print(onehot75)
```

The output is

```
tensor([0., 0., 0., 0., 0., 0., 0., 0., 0., 0., 0., 0., 0., 0., 0., 0.,
0., 0., 0., 0., 0., 0., 0., 0., 0., 0., 0., 0., 0., 0., 0., 0.,
0., 0., 0., 0., 0., 0., 0., 0., 0., 0., 0., 0., 0., 0., 0., 0.,
0., 0., 0., 0., 0., 0., 0., 0., 0., 0., 0., 0., 0., 0., 0.,
0., 0., 1., 0., 0., 0., 0., 0., 0., 0., 0., 0., 0., 0., 0., 0.,
0., 0., 0., 0., 0., 0., 0., 0., 0.])
```

The result is a 100-value tensor with the 76th place (the index value of which is 75) turned on as 1 and all other positions turned off as 0s.

To function `int_to_onehot()` converts an integer into a one-hot variable. In a way, the function is translating human-readable language into model-ready language.

Next, we want to translate model-ready language back to human-readable language. Suppose we have a one-hot variable: How can we convert it into an integer that humans understand? The following function `onehot_to_int()` accomplishes that goal:

```
def onehot_to_int(onehot):
    num=torch.argmax(onehot)
    return num.item()
```

The function `onehot_to_int()` takes the argument `onehot` and converts it into an integer based on which position has the highest value.

Let's test the function to see what happens if we use the tensor `onehot75` we just created as the input:

```
print(onehot_to_int(onehot75))
```

The output is

```
75
```

The result shows that the function converts the one-hot variable to an integer 75, which is the right answer. So we know that the functions are defined properly.

Next, we'll build and train GANs to generate multiples of 5.

3.5.2 GANs to generate numbers with patterns

Our goal is to build and train a model so that the generator can generate a sequence of 10 integers, all multiples of 5. We first prepare the training data and then convert them to model-ready numbers in batches. Finally, we use the trained generator to generate the patterns we want.

For simplicity, we'll generate a sequence of 10 integers between 0 and 99. We'll then convert the sequence into 10 model-ready numbers.

The following function generates a sequence of 10 integers, all multiples of 5:

```
def gen_sequence():
    indices = torch.randint(0, 20, (10,))
    values = indices*5
    return values
```

We first use the `randint()` method in PyTorch to generate 10 numbers between 0 and 19. We then multiply them by 5 and convert them to PyTorch tensors. This creates 10 integers that are all multiples of 5.

Let's try to generate a sequence of training data:

```
sequence=gen_sequence()
print(sequence)
```

The output is

```
tensor([60, 95, 50, 55, 25, 40, 70,  5,  0, 55])
```

The values in the preceding output are all multiples of 5.

Next, we convert each number to a one-hot variable so that we can feed them to the neural network later:

```
import numpy as np

def gen_batch():
    sequence=gen_sequence()
    batch=[int_to_onehot(i).numpy() for i in sequence]
    batch=np.array(batch)
    return torch.tensor(batch)
batch=gen_batch()
```

Creates a sequence of 10 numbers, all multiples of 5

Converts each integer to a 100-value one-hot variable

The preceding function `gen_batch()` creates a batch of data so that we can feed them to the neural network for training purposes.

We also define a function `data_to_num()` to convert one-hot variables to a sequence of integers so that humans can understand the output:

```
def data_to_num(data):
    num=torch.argmax(data,dim=-1)
    return num
numbers=data_to_num(batch)
```

Converts vectors to integers based on the largest values in a 100-value vector

Applies the function on an example

The dim=-1 argument in the torch.argmax() function means we are trying to find the position (i.e., index) of the largest value in the last dimension: that is, among the 100-value one-hot vector, which position has the highest value.

Next, we'll create two neural networks: one for the discriminator D and one for the generator G. We'll build GANs to generate the desired pattern of numbers. Similar to what we did earlier in this chapter, we create a discriminator network, which is a binary classifier that distinguishes fake samples from real samples. We also create a generator network to generate a sequence of 10 numbers. Here is the discriminator neural network:

```
from torch import nn
D=nn.Sequential(
    nn.Linear(100,1),
    nn.Sigmoid()).to(device)
```

Since we'll convert integers into 100-value one-hot variables, we use 100 as the input size in the first Linear layer in the model. The last Linear layer has just one output feature in it, and we use the sigmoid activation function to squeeze the output to the range [0, 1] so it can be interpreted as the probability, p, that the sample is real. With the complementary probability 1 − p, the sample is fake.

The generator's job is to create a sequence of numbers so that they can pass as real in front of the discriminator D. That is, G is trying to create a sequence of numbers to maximize the probability that D thinks that the numbers are from the training dataset.

We create the following neural network to represent the generator G:

```
G=nn.Sequential(
    nn.Linear(100,100),
    nn.ReLU()).to(device)
```

We'll feed random noise vectors from a 100-dimensional latent space to the generator. The generator then creates a tensor of 100 values based on the input. Note here that we use the ReLU activation function at the last layer so that the output is nonnegative. Since we are trying to generate 100 values of 0 or 1, nonnegative values are appropriate here.

As in the first project, we use the Adam optimizer for both the discriminator and the generator, with a learning rate of 0.0005:

```
loss_fn=nn.BCELoss()
lr=0.0005
optimD=torch.optim.Adam(D.parameters(),lr=lr)
optimG=torch.optim.Adam(G.parameters(),lr=lr)
```

Now that we have the training data and two networks, we'll train the model. After that, we'll discard the discriminator and use the generator to generate a sequence of 10 integers.

3.5.3 *Training the GANs to generate numbers with patterns*

The training process for this project is very similar to that in our first project in which you generated an exponential growth shape.

We define a function `train_D_G()`, which is a combination of the three functions `train_D_on_real()`, `train_D_on_fake()`, and `train_G()` that we have defined for the first project. The function `train_D_G()` is in the Jupyter Notebook for this chapter in the book's GitHub repository: https://github.com/markhliu/DGAI. Take a look at the function `train_D_G()` so you can see what minor changes we have made compared to the three functions we defined for the first project.

We use the same early stopping class that we defined for the first project so we know when to stop training. However, we have modified the `patience` argument to 800 when we instantiate the class, as shown in the following listing.

Listing 3.11 Training GANs to generate multiples of 5

```
stopper=EarlyStop(800)                                    ◄─┐ Creates an instance of
                                                            │ the early stopping class
mse=nn.MSELoss()
real_labels=torch.ones((10,1)).to(device)
fake_labels=torch.zeros((10,1)).to(device)
def distance(generated_data):                             ◄─┐ Defines a distance() function
    nums=data_to_num(generated_data)                        │ to calculate the loss in the
    remainders=nums%5                                        │ generated numbers
    ten_zeros=torch.zeros((10,1)).to(device)
    mseloss=mse(remainders,ten_zeros)
    return mseloss

for i in range(10000):
    gloss=0
    dloss=0
    generated_data=train_D_G(D,G,loss_fn,optimD,optimG)    ◄─┐ Trains the GANs
    dis=distance(generated_data)                             │ for one epoch
    if stopper.stop(dis)==True:
        break
    if i % 50 == 0:                                        ◄─┐ Prints out the generated
        print(data_to_num(generated_data))                   │ sequence of integers after
                                                             │ every 50 epochs
```

We have also defined a `distance()` function to measure the difference between the training set and the generated data samples: it calculates the MSE of the remainder of each generated number when divided by 5. The measure is 0 when all generated numbers are multiples of 5.

If you run the preceding code cell, you'll see the following output:

```
tensor([14, 34, 19, 89, 44,  5, 58,  6, 41, 87], device='cuda:0')
...
tensor([ 0, 80, 65,  0,  0, 10, 80, 75, 75, 75], device='cuda:0')
tensor([25, 30,  0,  0, 65, 20, 80, 20, 80, 20], device='cuda:0')
tensor([65, 95, 10, 65, 75, 20, 20, 20, 65, 75], device='cuda:0')
```

In each iteration, we generate a batch of 10 numbers. We first train the discriminator D using real samples. After that, the generator creates a batch of fake samples, and we use them to train the discriminator D again. Finally, we let the generator create a batch of fake samples again, but we use them to train the generator G instead. We stop training if the generator network stops improving after 800 epochs since the last time the minimum loss was achieved. After every 50 epochs, we print out the sequence of 10 numbers created by the generator so you can tell if they are indeed all multiples of 5.

The output during the training process is as shown previously. In the first few hundred epochs, the generator still produces numbers that are not multiples of 5. But after 900 epochs, all the numbers generated are multiples of 5. The training process takes just a minute or so with GPU training. It takes less than 10 minutes if you use CPU training. Alternatively, you can download the trained model from the book's GitHub repository: https://github.com/markhliu/DGAI.

3.5.4   *Saving and using the trained model*

We'll discard the discriminator and save the trained generator in the local folder:

```
import os
os.makedirs("files", exist_ok=True)
scripted = torch.jit.script(G)
scripted.save('files/num_gen.pt')
```

We have now saved the generator to the local folder. To use the generator, we simply load up the model and use it to generate a sequence of integers:

```
new_G=torch.jit.load('files/num_gen.pt',
                     map_location=device)          ◀──  Loads the saved generator
new_G.eval()
noise=torch.randn((10,100)).to(device)             ◀──  Obtains random
new_data=new_G(noise)                                    noise vectors
print(data_to_num(new_data))          ◀────┐
                                            │  Feeds the random noise vectors
                                               to the trained model to generate
                                               a sequence of integers
```

The output is as follows:

```
tensor([40, 25, 65, 25, 20, 25, 95, 10, 10, 65], device='cuda:0')
```

The generated numbers are all multiples of 5.

You can easily change the code to generate other patterns, such as odd numbers, even numbers, multiples of 3, and so on.

Exercise 3.4

Modify the programs in the second project so that the generator generates a sequence of ten integers that are all multiples of 3.

Now that you know how GANs work, you'll be able to extend the idea behind GANs to other formats in later chapters, including high-resolution images and realistic-sounding music.

Summary

- GANs consist of two networks: a discriminator to distinguish fake samples from real samples and a generator to create samples that are indistinguishable from those in the training set.
- The steps involved in GANs are preparing training data, creating a discriminator and a generator, training the model and deciding when to stop training, and finally, discarding the discriminator and using the trained generator to create new samples.
- The content generated by GANs depends on the training data. When the training dataset contains data pairs (x, y) that form an exponential growth curve, the generated samples are also data pairs that mimic such a shape. When the training dataset has sequences of numbers that are all multiples of 5, the generated samples are also sequences of numbers, with multiples of 5 in them.
- GANs are versatile and capable of generating many different formats of content.

Part 2

Image generation

Part II dives deep into image generation.

In chapter 4, you'll learn to build and train generative adversarial networks to generate high-resolution color images. In particular, you'll learn to use convolutional neural networks to capture spatial features in images. You'll also learn to use transposed convolutional layers to upsample and generate high-resolution feature maps in images. In chapter 5, you'll learn two ways to select characteristics in the generated images. In chapter 6, you'll learn to build and train a Cycle-GAN to translate images between two domains such as images with black hair and images with blond hair or horse images and zebra images. In chapter 7, you'll learn to create images using another generative model: autoencoders and their variant, variational autoencoders.

Image generation
with generative
adversarial networks

4

This chapter covers

- Designing a generator by mirroring steps in the discriminator network
- How a 2D convolutional operation works on an image
- How a 2D transposed convolutional operation inserts gaps between the output values and generates feature maps of a higher resolution
- Building and training generative adversarial networks to generate grayscale and color images

You have successfully generated an exponential growth curve and a sequence of integers that are all multiples of 5 in chapter 3. Now that you understand how generative adversarial networks (GANs) work, you are ready to apply the same skills to generate many other forms of content, such as high-resolution color images and realistic-sounding music. However, this may be easier said than done (you know what they say: the devil is in the details). For example, exactly how can we make the generator conjure up realistic images out of thin air? That's the question we're going to tackle in this chapter.

A common approach for the generator to create images from scratch is to mirror steps in the discriminator network. In the first project in this chapter, your goal is to create grayscale images of clothing items such as coats, shirts, sandals, and so on. You learn to mirror the layers in the discriminator network when designing a generator network. In this project, only dense layers are used in both the generator and discriminator networks. Each neuron in a dense layer is connected to every neuron in the previous and next layer. For this reason, dense layers are also called fully connected layers.

In the second project in this chapter, your goal is to create high-resolution color images of anime faces. Like in the first project, the generator mirrors the steps in the discriminator network to conjure up images. However, high-resolution color images in this project contain many more pixels than the low-resolution grayscale images in the first project. If we use dense layers only, the number of parameters in the model increases enormously. This, in turn, makes learning slow and ineffective. We, therefore, turn to convolutional neural networks (CNNs). In CNNs, each neuron in a layer is connected only to a small region of the input. This local connectivity reduces the number of parameters, making the network more efficient. CNNs require fewer parameters than fully connected networks of similar size, leading to faster training times and lower computational costs. CNNs are also generally more effective at capturing spatial hierarchies in image data because they treat images as multidimensional objects instead of 1D vectors.

To prepare you for the second project, we'll show you how convolutional operations work and how they downsample the input images and extract spatial features in them. You'll also learn concepts such as filter size, stride, and zero-padding and how they affect the degree of downsampling in CNNs. While the discriminator network uses convolutional layers, the generator mirrors these layers by using transposed convolutional layers (also known as deconvolution or upsampling layers). You'll learn how transposed convolutional layers are used for upsampling to generate high-resolution feature maps.

To summarize, you'll learn how to mirror the steps in the discriminator network to create images from scratch in this chapter. In addition, you'll learn how convolutional layers and transposed convolutional layers work. After this chapter, you'll use convolutional layers and transposed convolutional layers to create high-resolution images in other settings later in this book (such as in feature transfers when training a CycleGAN to convert blond hair to black hair or in a variational autoencoder [VAE] to generate high-resolution human face images).

4.1 GANs to generate grayscale images of clothing items

Our goal in the first project is to train a model to generate grayscale images of clothing items such as sandals, t-shirts, coats, and bags.

When you use GANs to generate images, you'll always start by obtaining training data. You'll then create a discriminator network from scratch. You'll mirror steps in the discriminator network when creating a generator network. Finally, you'll train the GANs and use the trained model for image generation. Let's see how that works with a simple project that creates grayscale images of clothing items.

4.1.1   *Training samples and the discriminator*

The steps involved with preparing the training data are similar to what we have done in chapter 2, with a few exceptions that I'll highlight later. To save time, I'll skip the steps you have seen before in chapter 2 and refer you to the book's GitHub repository. Follow the steps in the Jupyter Notebook for this chapter in the book's GitHub repository (https://github.com/markhliu/DGAI) so that you create a data iterator with batches.

There are 60,000 images in the training set. In chapter 2, we split the training set further into a train set and a validation set. We used the loss in the validation set to determine whether the parameters had converged so that we could stop training. However, GANs are trained using a different approach compared to traditional supervised learning models (such as the classification models you have seen in chapter 2). Since the quality of the generated samples improves throughout training, the discriminator's task becomes more and more difficult. The loss from the discriminator network is not a good indicator of the quality of the model. The usual way of measuring the performance of GANs is through visual inspection to assess the quality and realism of generated images. We can potentially compare the quality of generated samples with training samples and use methods such as the Inception Score to evaluate the performance of GANs (See, for example, "Pros and Cons of GAN Evaluation Measures," by Ali Borji, 2018, for a survey on various GAN evaluation methods; https://arxiv.org/abs/1802.03446). However, researchers have documented the weaknesses of these measures ("A Note on the Inception Score," by Shane Barratt and Rishi Sharma, 2018, demonstrates that the inception score fails to provide useful guidance when comparing models; https://arxiv .org/abs/1801.01973). In this chapter, we'll use visual inspections to check the quality of generated samples periodically and determine when to stop training.

The discriminator network is a binary classifier, which is similar to the binary classifier for clothing items we discussed in chapter 2. Here the discriminator's job is to classify the samples into either real or fake.

We use PyTorch to create the following discriminator neural network D:

```
import torch
import torch.nn as nn

device="cuda" if torch.cuda.is_available() else "cpu"
D=nn.Sequential(
    nn.Linear(784, 1024),
    nn.ReLU(),
    nn.Dropout(0.3),
    nn.Linear(1024, 512),
    nn.ReLU(),
    nn.Dropout(0.3),
    nn.Linear(512, 256),
    nn.ReLU(),
    nn.Dropout(0.3),
    nn.Linear(256, 1),
    nn.Sigmoid()).to(device)
```

The first fully connected layer has 784 inputs and 1,024 outputs.

The last fully connected layer has 256 inputs and 1 output.

The input size is 784 because each grayscale image has a size of 28 × 28 pixels in the training set. Because dense layers take only 1D inputs, we flatten the images before feeding them to the model. The output layer has just one neuron in it: the output of the discriminator D is a single value. We use the sigmoid activation function to squeeze the output to the range [0, 1] so that it can be interpreted as the probability, p, that the sample is real. With complementary probability 1 − p, the sample is fake.

Exercise 4.1

Modify the discriminator D so that the numbers of outputs in the first three layers are 1,000, 500, and 200 instead of 1,024, 512, and 256. Make sure the number of outputs in a layer matches the number of inputs in the next layer.

4.1.2 A generator to create grayscale images

While the discriminator network is fairly easy to create, how to create a generator so that it can conjure up realistic images is a different matter. A common approach is to mirror the layers used in the discriminator network to create a generator, as shown in the following listing.

Listing 4.1   Designing a generator by mirroring layers in the discriminator

```
G=nn.Sequential(
    nn.Linear(100, 256),
    nn.ReLU(),
    nn.Linear(256, 512),
    nn.ReLU(),
    nn.Linear(512, 1024),
    nn.ReLU(),
    nn.Linear(1024, 784),
    nn.Tanh()).to(device)
```

The first layer in the generator is symmetric to the last layer in the discriminator.

The second layer in the generator is symmetric to the second to last layer in the discriminator (numbers of inputs and outputs have switched positions).

The third layer in the generator is symmetric to the third to last layer in the discriminator.

The last layer in the generator is symmetric to the first layer in the discriminator.

Uses Tanh() activation so the output is between −1 and 1, the same as values in images

Figure 4.1 provides a diagram of the architecture of generator and discriminator networks in the GAN to generate grayscale images of clothing items. As shown in the top right corner of figure 4.1, a flattened grayscale image from the training set, which contains 28 × 28 = 784 pixels, goes through four dense layers sequentially in the discriminator network, and the output is the probability that the image is real. To create an image, the generator uses the same four dense layers but in reverse order: it obtains a 100-value random noise vector from the latent space (bottom left in figure 4.1) and feeds the vector through the four dense layers. In each layer, the numbers of *inputs* and *outputs* in the discriminator are reversed and used as the numbers of *outputs* and *inputs* in the generator. Finally, the generator comes up with a 784-value tensor, which can be reshaped into a 28 × 28 grayscale image (top left).

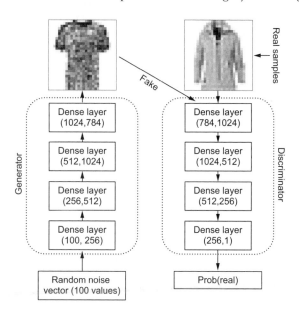

Figure 4.1 Designing a generator network to create clothing items by mirroring the layers in the discriminator network. The right side of the diagram shows the discriminator network, which contains four dense layers. To design a generator that can conjure up clothing items from thin air, we mirror the layers in the discriminator network. Specifically, as shown on the left half of the figure, the generator has four similar dense layers in it but in reverse order: the first layer in the generator mirrors the last layer in the discriminator, the second layer in the generator mirrors the second to last layer in the discriminator, and so on. Further, in each of the top three layers, the numbers of inputs and outputs in the discriminator are reversed and used as the numbers of outputs and inputs in the generator.

The left side of figure 4.1 is the generator network, while the right side is the discriminator network. If you compare the two networks, you'll notice how the generator mirrors the layers used in the discriminator. Specifically, the generator has four similar dense layers in it but in reverse order: the first layer in the generator mirrors the last layer in the discriminator, the second layer in the generator mirrors the second to last layer in the discriminator, and so on. The number of outputs of the generator is 784, with values between -1 and 1 after the `Tanh()` activation, and this matches the input to the discriminator network.

Exercise 4.2

Modify the generator G so that the numbers of outputs in the first three layers are 1,000, 500, and 200 instead of 1,024, 512, and 256. Make sure that the modified generator mirrors the layers used in the modified discriminator in exercise 4.1.

As in GAN models we have seen in chapter 3, the loss function is the binary cross-entropy loss since the discriminator D is performing a binary classification problem. We'll use the Adam optimizer for both the discriminator and the generator, with a learning rate of 0.0001:

```
loss_fn=nn.BCELoss()
lr=0.0001
optimD=torch.optim.Adam(D.parameters(),lr=lr)
optimG=torch.optim.Adam(G.parameters(),lr=lr)
```

Next, we'll train the GANs we just created by using the clothing item images in the training dataset.

4.1.3 *Training GANs to generate images of clothing items*

The training process is similar to what we have done in chapter 3 when training GANs to generate an exponential growth curve or to generate a sequence of numbers that are all multiples of 5.

Unlike in chapter 3, we'll solely rely on visual inspections to determine whether the model is well-trained. For that purpose, we define a `see_output()` function to visualize the fake images created by the generator periodically.

> **NOTE**   Interested readers can check this GitHub repository to learn how to implement the inception score in PyTorch to evaluate GANs: https://github .com/sbarratt/inception-score-pytorch. However, the repository doesn't recommend using the inception score to evaluate generative models due to its ineffectiveness.

Listing 4.2   Defining a function to visualize the generated clothing items

```
import matplotlib.pyplot as plt

def see_output():
    noise=torch.randn(32,100).to(device=device)
    fake_samples=G(noise).cpu().detach()          ◀——— Generates 32 fake images
    plt.figure(dpi=100,figsize=(20,10))
    for i in range(32):
        ax=plt.subplot(4, 8, i + 1)               ◀——— Plots them in a 4 × 8 grid
        img=(fake_samples[i]/2+0.5).reshape(28, 28)
        plt.imshow(img)                           ◀——— Shows the ith image
```

```
        plt.xticks([])
        plt.yticks([])
    plt.show()
see_output()
```
◄────── Calls the see_output() function to visualize the generated images before training

If you run the preceding code cell, you'll see 32 images that look like snowflake statics on a TV screen, as shown in figure 4.2. They don't look like clothing items at all because we haven't trained the generator yet.

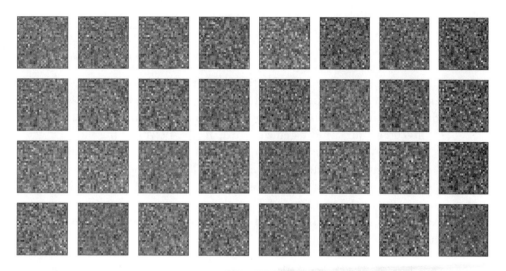

Figure 4.2 Output from the GAN model to generate clothing items before training. Since the model is not trained, the generated images are nothing like the images in the training set.

To train the GAN model, we define a few functions: train_D_on_real(), train_D_on_fake(), and train_G(). They are similar to those defined in chapter 3. Go to the Jupypter Notebook for this chapter in the book's GitHub repository and see what minor modifications we have made.

Now we are ready to train the model. We iterate through all batches in the training dataset. For each batch of data, we first train the discriminator using the real samples. After that, the generator creates a batch of fake samples, and we use them to train the discriminator again. Finally, we let the generator create a batch of fake samples again, but this time, we use them to train the generator instead. We train the model for 50 epochs, as shown in the following listing.

Listing 4.3 Training GANs for clothing item generation

```
for i in range(50):
    gloss=0
    dloss=0
    for n, (real_samples,_) in enumerate(train_loader):
```

```
        loss_D=train_D_on_real(real_samples)
        dloss+=loss_D
        loss_D=train_D_on_fake()
        dloss+=loss_D
        loss_G=train_G()
        gloss+=loss_G
    gloss=gloss/n
    dloss=dloss/n
    if i % 10 == 9:
        print(f"at epoch {i+1}, dloss: {dloss}, gloss {gloss}")
        see_output()
```

Trains the discriminator using real samples

Trains the discriminator using fake samples

Trains the generator

Visualizes generated samples after every 10 epochs

The training takes about 10 minutes if you are using GPU training. Otherwise, it may take an hour or so, depending on the hardware configuration on your computer. Or you can download the trained model from my website: https://gattonweb.uky.edu/faculty/lium/gai/fashion_gen.zip. Unzip it after downloading.

After every 10 epochs of training, you can visualize the generated clothing items, as shown in figure 4.3. After just 10 epochs of training, the model can already generate clothing items that clearly can pass as real: you can tell what they are. The first three items in the first row in figure 4.3 are clearly a coat, a dress, and a pair of trousers, for example. As training progresses, the quality of the generated images becomes better and better.

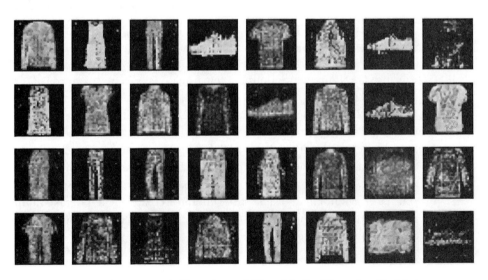

Figure 4.3   Clothing items generated by an image GAN model after 10 epochs of training

As we do in all GANs, we discard the discriminator and save the trained generator to generate samples later:

```
scripted = torch.jit.script(G)
scripted.save('files/fashion_gen.pt')
```

We have now saved the generator in the local folder. To use the generator, we load up the model:

```
new_G=torch.jit.load('files/fashion_gen.pt',
                     map_location=device)
new_G.eval()
```

The generator is now loaded. We can use it to generate clothing items:

```
noise=torch.randn(32,100).to(device=device)
fake_samples=new_G(noise).cpu().detach()
for i in range(32):
    ax = plt.subplot(4, 8, i + 1)
    plt.imshow((fake_samples[i]/2+0.5).reshape(28, 28))
    plt.xticks([])
    plt.yticks([])
plt.subplots_adjust(hspace=-0.6)
plt.show()
```

The generated clothing items are shown in figure 4.4. As you can see, the clothing items are fairly close to those in the training set.

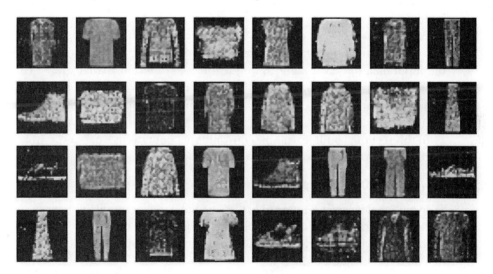

Figure 4.4   Clothing items generated by a trained image GAN model (after 50 epochs)

Now that you have learned how to create grayscale images by using GANs, you'll learn how to generate high-resolution color images by using deep convolutional GAN (DCGAN) in the remaining sections of this chapter.

4.2   Convolutional layers

To create high-resolution color images, we need more sophisticated techniques than simple fully connected neural networks. Specifically, we'll use CNNs, which are particularly effective for processing data with a grid-like topology, such as images. They are distinct from fully connected (dense) layers in a couple of ways. First, in CNNs, each neuron in a layer is connected only to a small region of the input. This is based on the understanding that in image data, local groups of pixels are more likely to be related to each other. This local connectivity reduces the number of parameters, making the network more efficient. Second, CNNs use the concept of shared weights—the same weights are used across different regions of the input. This is akin to sliding a filter across the entire input space. This filter detects specific features (e.g., edges or textures) regardless of their position in the input, leading to the property of translation invariance.

Due to their structure, CNNs are more efficient for image processing. They require fewer parameters than fully connected networks of similar size, leading to faster training times and lower computational costs. They are also generally more effective at capturing spatial hierarchies in image data.

Convolutional layers and transposed convolutional layers are two fundamental building blocks in CNNs, commonly used in image processing and computer vision tasks. They have different purposes and characteristics: convolutional layers are used for feature extraction. They apply a set of learnable filters (also known as kernels) to the input data to detect patterns and features at different spatial scales. These layers are essential for capturing hierarchical representations of the input data. In contrast, transposed convolutional layers are used for upsampling or generating high-resolution feature maps.

In this section, you'll learn how convolutional operations work and how kernel size, stride, and zero-padding affect convolutional operations.

4.2.1   How do convolutional operations work?

Convolutional layers use filters to extract spatial patterns on the input data. A convolutional layer is capable of automatically detecting a large number of patterns and associating them with the target label. Therefore, convolutional layers are commonly used in image classification tasks.

Convolutional operations involve applying a filter to an input image to produce a feature map. This process involves using element-wise multiplication of the filter with the input image and summing the results. The weights in the filter are the same as the filter moves on the input image to scan different areas. Figure 4.5 shows a numerical example of how convolutional operations work. The left column is the input image, and the second column is a filter (a 2×2 matrix). Convolutional operations (the third column) involve sliding the filter over the input image, multiplying corresponding elements, and summing them up (the last column).

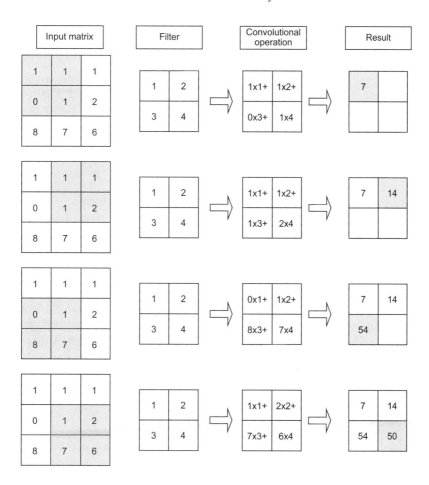

Figure 4.5 A numerical example of how convolutional operations work, with stride equal to 1 and no padding

To gain a deep understanding of exactly how convolutional operations work, let's implement the convolutional operations in PyTorch in parallel so that you can verify the numbers as shown in figure 4.5. First, let's create a PyTorch tensor to represent the input image in the figure:

```
img = torch.Tensor([[1,1,1],
                    [0,1,2],
                    [8,7,6]]).reshape(1,1,3,3)
```

> The four values in the shape of the image, (1, 1, 3, 3), are the number of images in the batch, number of color channels, image height, and image width, respectively.

The image is reshaped so that it has a dimension of (1, 1, 3, 3), indicating that there is just one observation in the batch, and the image has just one color channel. The height and the width of the image are both 3 pixels.

Let's represent the 2×2 filter, as shown in the second column of figure 4.5, by creating a 2D convolutional layer in PyTorch:

```
conv=nn.Conv2d(in_channels=1,
               out_channels=1,
               kernel_size=2,
               stride=1)
sd=conv.state_dict()
print(sd)
```

Initiates a 2D convolutional layer

Extracts the randomly initialized weights and bias in the layer

A 2D convolutional layer takes several arguments. The `in_channels` argument is the number of channels in the input image. This value is 1 for grayscale images and 3 for color images since color images have three color channels (red, green, and blue [RGB]). The `out_channels` is the number of channels after the convolutional layer, which can take any number based on how many features you want to extract from the image. The `kernel_size` argument controls the size of the kernel; for example, `kernel_size=3` means the filter has a shape of 3×3, and `kernel_size=4` means the filter has a shape of 4×4. We set the kernel size to 2 so the filter has a shape of 2×2.

A 2D convolutional layer also has several optional arguments. The `stride` argument specifies how many pixels to move to the right or down each time the filter moves along the input image. The `stride` argument has a default value of 1. A higher value of stride leads to more downsampling of the image. The `padding` argument means how many rows of zeros to add to four sides of the input image, with a default value of 0. The `bias` argument indicates whether to add a learnable bias as the parameter, with a default value of `True`.

The preceding 2D convolutional layer has one input channel, one output channel, with a kernel size of 2×2, and a stride of 1. When the convolutional layer is created, the weights and the bias in it are randomly initialized. You will see the following output as the weights and the bias of this convolutional layer:

```
OrderedDict([('weight', tensor([[[[ 0.3823,  0.4150],
          [-0.1171,  0.4593]]]])), ('bias', tensor([-0.1096]))])
```

To make our example easier to follow, we'll replace the weights and the bias with whole numbers:

```
weights={'weight':torch.tensor([[[[1,2],
    [3,4]]]]), 'bias':torch.tensor([0])}
for k in sd:
    with torch.no_grad():
        sd[k].copy_(weights[k])
print(conv.state_dict())
```

Handpicks weights and bias

Replaces the weights and bias in the convolutional layer with our handpicked numbers

Prints out the new weights and bias in the convolutional layer

Since we are not learning the parameters in the convolutional layer, `torch.no_grad()` is used to disable gradient calculation, which reduces memory consumption and speeds up computations. Now the convolutional layer has weights and the bias that we have chosen. They also match the numbers in figure 4.5. The output from the preceding code cell is:

```
OrderedDict([('weight', tensor([[[[1., 2.],
          [3., 4.]]]])), ('bias', tensor([0.]))])
```

If we apply the preceding convolutional layer on the 3×3 image we mentioned, what is the output? Let's find out:

```
output = conv(img)
print(output)
```

The output is

```
tensor([[[[ 7., 14.],
          [54., 50.]]]], grad_fn=<ConvolutionBackward0>)
```

The output has a shape of $(1, 1, 2, 2)$, with four values in it: 7, 14, 54, and 50. These numbers match those in figure 4.5.

But how exactly does the convolutional layer generate this output through the filter? We'll explain in detail next.

The input image is a 3×3 matrix, and the filter is a 2×2 matrix. When the filter scans over the image, it first covers the four pixels in the top left corner of the image, which have values `[[1, 1], [0, 1]]`, as shown in the first row in Figure 4.5. The filter has values `[[1,2],[3,4]]`. The convolution operation finds the sum of the element-wise multiplication of the two tensors (in this case, one tensor is the filter and the other is the covered area). In other words, the convolution operation performs element-wise multiplication in each of the four cells and then adds up the values in the four cells. Therefore, the output from scanning the top left corner is

$$1 \times 1 \times 1 \times 2 + 0 \times 3 + 1 \times 4 = 7.$$

This explains why the top left corner of the output has a value of 7. Similarly, when the filter is applied to the top right corner of the image, the covered area is `[[1,1], [1,2]]`. The output is therefore:

$$1 \times 1 + 1 \times 2 + 1 \times 3 + 2 \times 4 = 14.$$

This explains why the top right corner of the output has a value of 14.

Exercise 4.3

What are the values in the covered area when the filter is applied to the bottom right corner of the image? Explain why the bottom right corner of the output has a value of 50.

4.2.2   *How do stride and padding affect convolutional operations?*

Stride and zero padding are two important concepts in the context of convolutional operations. They play a crucial role in determining the dimensions of the output feature map and the way the filter interacts with the input data.

Stride refers to the number of pixels by which the filter moves across the input image. When the stride is 1, the filter moves 1 pixel at a time. A larger stride means the filter jumps over more pixels as it slides over the image. Increasing the stride reduces the spatial dimensions of the output feature map.

Zero padding involves adding layers of zeros around the border of the input image before applying the convolutional operation. Zero padding allows control over the spatial dimensions of the output feature map. Without padding, the dimensions of the output will be smaller than the input. By adding padding, you can preserve the dimensions of the input.

Let's use an example to show how stride and padding work. The following code cell redefines the 2D convolutional layer:

```
conv=nn.Conv2d(in_channels=1,
            out_channels=1,
            kernel_size=2,
            stride=2,
            padding=1)
sd=conv.state_dict()
for k in sd:
    with torch.no_grad():
        sd[k].copy_(weights[k])
output = conv(img)
print(output)
```

Changes the stride from 1 to 2

Changes the padding from 0 to 1

The output is

```
tensor([[[[ 4.,   7.],
        [32., 50.]]]], grad_fn=<ConvolutionBackward0>)
```

The `padding=1` argument adds one row of 0s around the input image, so the padded image now has a size of 5×5 instead of 3×3.

When the filter scans over the padded image, it first covers the top left corner, which has values `[[0, 0], [0, 1]]`. The filter has values `[[1,2],[3,4]]`. Therefore, the output from scanning the top left corner is:

$$0 \times 1 + 0 \times 2 + 0 \times 3 + 1 \times 4 = 4$$

This explains why the top left corner of the output has a value of 4. Similarly, when the filter slides two pixels down to the bottom left corner of the image, the covered area is `[[0,0],[0,8]]`. The output is therefore:

$$0 \times 1 + 0 \times 2 + 0 \times 3 + 8 \times 4 = 32$$

This explains why the bottom left corner of the output has a value of 32.

4.3   *Transposed convolution and batch normalization*

Transposed convolutional layers are also known as deconvolution or upsampling Layers. They are used for upsampling or generating high-resolution feature maps. They are often employed in generative models like GANs and VAEs.

Transposed convolutional layers apply a filter to the input data, but unlike standard convolution, they increase the spatial dimensions by inserting gaps between the output values, which effectively "upscales" the feature maps. This process generates feature maps of a higher resolution. Transposed convolutional layers help increase the spatial resolution, which is useful in image generation.

Strides can be used in transposed convolution layers to control the amount of upsampling. The greater the value of the stride, the more upsampling the transposed convolution layer has on the input data.

Two-dimensional batch normalization is a technique used in neural networks, particularly CNNs, to stabilize and speed up the training process. It addresses several problems, including saturation, vanishing gradients, and exploding gradients, which are common challenges in deep learning. In this section, you'll look at some examples so you have a deeper understanding of how it works. You'll use it when creating GANs to generate high-resolution color images in the next section.

> ### Vanishing and exploding gradients in deep learning
>
> The vanishing gradient problem occurs in deep neural networks when the gradients of the loss function with respect to the network parameters become exceedingly small during backpropagation. This results in very slow updates to the parameters, hindering the learning process, especially in the early layers of the network. Conversely, the exploding gradient problem happens when these gradients become excessively large, leading to unstable updates and causing the model parameters to oscillate or diverge to very large values. Both problems impede the effective training of deep neural networks.

4.3.1   *How do transposed convolutional layers work?*

Contrary to convolutional layers, transposed convolutional layers upsample and fill in gaps in an image to generate features and increase resolution by using kernels (i.e., filters). The output is usually larger than the input in a transposed convolutional layer. Therefore, transposed convolutional layers are essential tools when it comes to generating high-resolution images. To show you exactly how 2D transposed convolutional operations work, let's use a simple example and a figure. Suppose you have a very small 2×2 input image, as shown in the left column in figure 4.6.

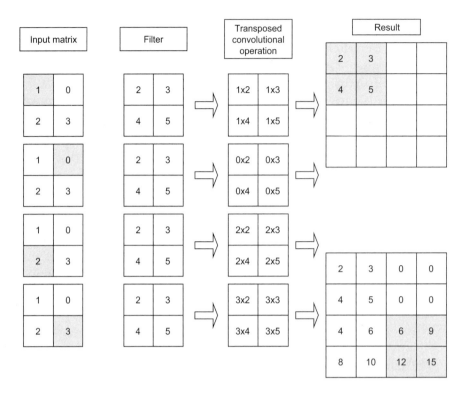

Figure 4.6   A numerical example of how transposed convolutional operations work

The input image has the following values in it:

```
img = torch.Tensor([[1,0],
                     [2,3]]).reshape(1,1,2,2)
```

You want to upsample the image so that it has a higher resolution. You can create a 2D transposed convolutional layer in PyTorch:

```
transconv=nn.ConvTranspose2d(in_channels=1,
        out_channels=1,
        kernel size=2,
        stride=2)
sd=transconv.state_dict()
weights={'weight':torch.tensor([[[[2,3],
   [4,5]]]]), 'bias':torch.tensor([0])}
for k in sd:
    with torch.no_grad():
        sd[k].copy_(weights[k])
```

A transposed convolutional layer with one input channel, one output channel, a kernel size of 2, and a stride of 2

Replaces the weights and bias in the transposed convolutional layer with handpicked values

This 2D transposed convolutional layer has one input channel, one output channel, with a kernel size of 2 × 2 and a stride of 2. The 2 × 2 filter is shown in the second column in figure 4.6. We replaced the randomly initialized weights and the bias in the layer with our handpicked whole numbers so it's easy to follow the calculations. The `state_dict()` method in the preceding code listing returns the parameters in a deep neural network.

When the transposed convolutional layer is applied to the 2 × 2 image we mentioned earlier, what is the output? Let's find out:

```
transoutput = transconv(img)
print(transoutput)
```

The output is

```
tensor([[[[ 2.,   3.,   0.,   0.],
          [ 4.,   5.,   0.,   0.],
          [ 4.,   6.,   6.,   9.],
          [ 8.,  10.,  12.,  15.]]]], grad_fn=<ConvolutionBackward0>)
```

The output has a shape of (1, 1, 4, 4), meaning we have upsampled a 2 × 2 image to a 4 × 4 image. How does the transposed convolutional layer generate the preceding output through the filter? We'll explain in detail next.

The image is a 2 × 2 matrix, and the filter is also a 2 × 2 matrix. When the filter is applied to the image, each element in the image multiplies with the filter and goes to the output. The top left value in the image is 1, and we multiply it with the values in the filter, `[[2, 3], [4, 5]]`, and this leads to the four values in the top left block of the output matrix `transoutput`, with values `[[2, 3], [4, 5]]`, as shown at the top right corner in figure 4.6. Similarly, the bottom left value in the image is 2, and we multiply it with the values in the filter, `[[2, 3], [4, 5]]`, and this leads to the four values in the bottom left block of the output matrix `transoutput`, `[[4, 6], [8, 10]]`.

Exercise 4.4

If an image has values `[[10, 10], [15, 20]]` in it, what is the output after you apply the 2D transposed convolutional layer `transconv` to the image? Assume `transconv` has values `[[2, 3], [4, 5]]` in it. Assume a kernel size of 2 and a stride size of 2.

4.3.2 Batch normalization

Two-dimensional batch normalization is a standard technique in modern deep learning frameworks and has become a crucial component for effectively training deep neural networks. You'll see it quite often later in this book.

In 2D batch normalization, normalization is performed independently for each feature channel by adjusting and scaling values in the channel so they have a mean of 0 and a variance of 1. A feature channel refers to one of the dimensions in a multidimensional tensor in CNNs used to represent different aspects or features of the input data. For example, they can represent color channels like red, green, or blue. The normalization ensures that the distribution of the inputs to layers deep in the network remains more stable during training. This stability arises because the normalization process reduces the internal covariate shift, which is the change in the distribution of network activations due to the update of weights in lower layers. It also helps to address the vanishing or exploding gradient problems by keeping the inputs in an appropriate range to prevent gradients from becoming too small (vanishing) or too large (exploding).[1]

Here's how the 2D batch normalization works: for each feature channel, we first calculate the mean and variance of all observations within the channel. We then normalize the values for each feature channel using the mean and variance obtained earlier (by subtracting the mean from each observation and then dividing the difference by the standard deviation). This ensures that the values in each channel have a mean of 0 and a standard deviation of 1 after normalization, which helps stabilize and speed up training. It also helps maintain stable gradients during backpropagation, which further aids in training deep neural networks.

Let's use a concrete example to show how the 2D batch normalization works.

Suppose that you have a three-channel input with a size of 64×64. You pass the input through a 2D convolutional layer with three output channels as follows:

```
torch.manual_seed(42)
img = torch.rand(1,3,64,64)
conv = nn.Conv2d(in_channels=3,
          out_channels=3,
          kernel_size=3,
          stride=1,
          padding=1)
out=conv(img)
print(out.shape)
```

Fixes the random state so results are reproducible

Creates a 3-channel input

Creates a 2D convolutional layer

Passes the input through the convolutional layer

The output from the preceding code cell is

```
torch.Size([1, 3, 64, 64])
```

We have created a three-channel input and passed it through a 2D convolutional layer with three output channels. The processed input has three channels with a size of 64×64 pixels.

Let's look at the mean and standard deviation of the pixels in each of the three output channels:

```
for i in range(3):
    print(f"mean in channel {i} is", out[:,i,:,:].mean().item())
    print(f"std in channel {i} is", out[:,i,:,:].std().item())
```

The output is

```
mean in channel 0 is -0.3766776919364929
std in channel 0 is 0.17841289937496185
mean in channel 1 is -0.3910464942455292
std in channel 1 is 0.16061744093894958
mean in channel 2 is 0.39275866746902466
std in channel 2 is 0.18207983672618866
```

---

[1] Sergey Ioffe, Christian Szegedy, 2015, "Batch Normalization: Accelerating Deep Network Training by Reducing Internal Covariate Shift." https://arxiv.org/abs/1502.03167.

The average values of the pixels in each output channel are not 0; the standard deviations of pixels in each output channel are not 1. Now, we perform a 2D batch normalization:

```
norm=nn.BatchNorm2d(3)
out2=norm(out)
print(out2.shape)
for i in range(3):
    print(f"mean in channel {i} is", out2[:,i,:,:].mean().item())
    print(f"std in channel {i} is", out2[:,i,:,:].std().item())
```

Then we have the following output:

```
torch.Size([1, 3, 64, 64])
mean in channel 0 is 6.984919309616089e-09
std in channel 0 is 0.9999650120735168
mean in channel 1 is -5.3085386753082275e-08
std in channel 1 is 0.9999282956123352
mean in channel 2 is 9.872019290924072e-08
std in channel 2 is 0.9999712705612183
```

The average values of pixels in each output channel are now practically 0 (or a very small number that is close to 0); the standard deviations of pixels in each output channel are now a number close to 1. That's what batch normalization does: it normalizes observations in each feature channel so that values in each feature channel have 0 mean and unit standard deviation.

4.4 Color images of anime faces

In this second project, you'll learn how to create high-resolution color images. The training steps in this project are similar to the first project, with the exception that the training data are color images of anime faces. Further, the discriminator and generator neural networks are more sophisticated. We'll use 2D convolutional and 2D transposed convolutional layers in the two networks.

4.4.1 Downloading anime faces

You can download the training data from Kaggle https://mng.bz/1a9R, which contains 63,632 color images of anime faces. You need to set up a free Kaggle account to log in first. Extract the data from the zip file and put them in a folder on your computer. For example, I placed everything in the zip file in /files/anime/ on my computer. As a result, all anime face images are in /files/anime/images/.

Define the path name so you can use it later to load the images in Pytorch:

```
anime_path = r"files/anime"
```

Change the name of the path depending on where you have saved the images on your computer. Note that the `ImageFolder()` class uses the directory name of the images to identify the class the images belong to. As a result, the final /images/ directory is not included in `anime_path` that we define earlier.

Next, we use the `ImageFolder()` class in Torchvision `datasets` package to load the dataset:

```
from torchvision import transforms as T
from torchvision.datasets import ImageFolder

transform = T.Compose([T.Resize((64, 64)),
    T.ToTensor(),
    T.Normalize([0.5, 0.5, 0.5], [0.5, 0.5, 0.5])])
train_data = ImageFolder(root=anime_path,
                         transform=transform)
```

Changes image size to 64 × 64

Converts images to PyTorch tensors

Normalizes image values to [-1, 1] in all three color channels

Loads the data and transforms images

We perform three different transformations when loading up the images from the local folder. First, we resize all images to 64 pixels in height and 64 pixels in width. Second, we convert the images to PyTorch tensors with values in the range [0, 1] by using the `ToTensor()` class. Finally, we use the `Normalize()` class to deduct 0.5 from the value and divide the difference by 0.5. As a result, the image data are now between –1 and 1.

We can now put the training data in batches:

```
from torch.utils.data import DataLoader

batch_size = 128
train_loader = DataLoader(dataset=train_data,
            batch_size=batch_size, shuffle=True)
```

The training dataset is now in batches, with a batch size of 128.

4.4.2 *Channels-first color images in PyTorch*

PyTorch uses a so-called channels-first approach when handling color images. This means the shape of images in PyTorch are (number_channels, height, width). In contrast, in other Python libraries such as TensorFlow or Matplotlib, a channels-last approach is used: a color image has a shape of (height, width, number_channels) instead.

Let's look at an example image in our dataset and print out the shape of the image:

```
image0, _ = train_data[0]
print(image0.shape)
```

The output is

```
torch.Size([3, 64, 64])
```

The shape of the first image is 3 × 64 × 64. This means the image has three color channels (RGB). The height and width of the image are both 64 pixels.

When we plot the images in Matplotlib, we need to convert them to channels-last by using the `permute()` method in PyTorch:

```
import matplotlib.pyplot as plt

plt.imshow(image0.permute(1,2,0)*0.5+0.5)
plt.show()
```

Note that we need to multiply the PyTorch tensor representing the image by 0.5 and then add 0.5 to it to convert the values from the range [−1, 1] to the range [0, 1]. You'll see a plot of an anime face after running the preceding code cell.

Next, we define a function `plot_images()` to visualize 32 images in four rows and eight columns:

```
def plot_images(imgs):                              ◄──── Defines a function to
    for i in range(32):                                   visualize 32 images
        ax = plt.subplot(4, 8, i + 1)           ◄────
        plt.imshow(imgs[i].permute(1,2,0)/2+0.5)
        plt.xticks([])                                Places them in a
        plt.yticks([])                                4 × 8 grid
    plt.subplots_adjust(hspace=-0.6)
    plt.show()
                                                      Obtains a batch
                                                      of images
imgs, _ = next(iter(train_loader))             ◄────
plot_images(imgs)                              ◄──── Calls the function to
                                                     visualize the images
```

You'll see a plot of 32 anime faces in a 4 × 8 grid after running the preceding code cell, as shown in figure 4.7.

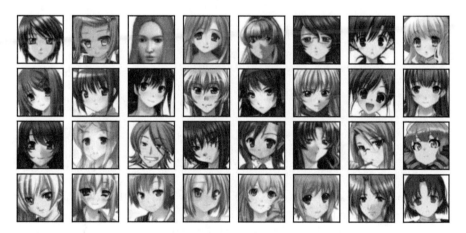

Figure 4.7   Examples from the anime faces training dataset

4.5   *Deep convolutional GAN*

In this section, you'll create a DCGAN model so that we can train it to generate anime face images. As usual, the GAN model consists of a discriminator network and a generator network. However, the networks are more sophisticated than the ones we have seen before: we'll use convolutional layers, transposed convolutional layers, and batch normalization layers in these networks.

We'll start with the discriminator network. After that, I'll explain how the generator network mirrors the layers in the discriminator network to conjure up realistic color images. You'll then train the model with the data you prepared earlier in this chapter and use the trained model to generate novel images of anime face images.

4.5.1   Building a DCGAN

As in previous GAN models we have seen, the discriminator is a binary classifier to classify samples into real or fake. However, different from the networks we have used so far, we'll use convolutional layers and batch normalizations. The high-resolution color images in this project have too many parameters, and if we use dense layers only, it's difficult to train the model effectively. The structure of the discriminator neural network is shown in the following listing.

Listing 4.4   A discriminator in DCGAN

```python
import torch.nn as nn
import torch

device = "cuda" if torch.cuda.is_available() else "cpu"

D = nn.Sequential(
    nn.Conv2d(3, 64, 4, 2, 1, bias=False),
    nn.LeakyReLU(0.2, inplace=True),
    nn.Conv2d(64, 128, 4, 2, 1, bias=False),
    nn.BatchNorm2d(128),
    nn.LeakyReLU(0.2, inplace=True),
    nn.Conv2d(128, 256, 4, 2, 1, bias=False),
    nn.BatchNorm2d(256),
    nn.LeakyReLU(0.2, inplace=True),
    nn.Conv2d(256, 512, 4, 2, 1, bias=False),
    nn.BatchNorm2d(512),
    nn.LeakyReLU(0.2, inplace=True),
    nn.Conv2d(512, 1, 4, 1, 0, bias=False),
    nn.Sigmoid(),
    nn.Flatten()).to(device)
```

Passes the image through a 2D convolutional layer

Applies the LeakyReLU activation on outputs of the first convolutional layer

Performs 2D batch normalization on outputs of the second convolutional layer

The output is a single value between 0 and 1, which can be interpreted as the probability that an image is real.

The input to the discriminator network is a color image with three color channels. The first 2D convolutional layer is Conv2d(3, 64, 4, 2, 1, bias=False): this means the input has three channels and the output has 64 channels; the kernel size is 4; the stride is 2; and the padding is 1. Each of the 2D convolutional layers in the network takes an image and applies filters to extract spatial features.

Starting from the second 2D convolutional layer, we apply 2D batch normalization (which I explained in the last section) and LeakyReLU activation (which I'll explain later) on the output. The LeakyReLU activation function is a modified version of ReLU. It allows the output to have a slope for values below zero. Specifically, the LeakyReLU function is defined as follows:

$$\text{LeakyReLU}(x) = \begin{cases} x, & \text{for } x > 0 \\ -\beta x, & \text{for } x \leq 0 \end{cases}$$

where β is a constant between 0 and 1. The LeakyReLU activation function is commonly used to address the sparse gradients problem (when most gradients become zero or near-zero). Training DCGANs is one such case. When the input to a neuron is negative, the output of ReLU is zero, and the neuron becomes inactive. LeakyReLU returns a small negative value, not zero, for negative inputs. This helps keep the neurons active and learning, maintaining a better gradient flow and leading to faster convergence of model parameters.

We'll use the same approach when building the generator for clothing item generation. We'll mirror the layers used in the discriminator in DCGAN to create a generator, as shown in the following listing.

Listing 4.5 Designing a generator in DCGAN

The first layer in the generator is modeled after the last layer in the discriminator.

The second layer in the generator is symmetric to the second to last layer in the discriminator (numbers of inputs and outputs have switched positions).

The last layer in the generator is symmetric to the first layer in the discriminator.

Uses the Tanh() activation to squeeze values in the output layer to the range [–1, 1] because the images in the training set have values between –1 and 1

```
G=nn.Sequential(
    nn.ConvTranspose2d(100, 512, 4, 1, 0, bias=False),
    nn.BatchNorm2d(512),
    nn.ReLU(inplace=True),
    nn.ConvTranspose2d(512, 256, 4, 2, 1, bias=False),
    nn.BatchNorm2d(256),
    nn.ReLU(inplace=True),
    nn.ConvTranspose2d(256, 128, 4, 2, 1, bias=False),
    nn.BatchNorm2d(128),
    nn.ReLU(inplace=True),
    nn.ConvTranspose2d(128, 64, 4, 2, 1, bias=False),
    nn.BatchNorm2d(64),
    nn.ReLU(inplace=True),
    nn.ConvTranspose2d(64, 3, 4, 2, 1, bias=False),
    nn.Tanh()).to(device)
```

As shown in figure 4.8, to create an image, the generator uses five 2D transposed convolutional layers: they are symmetric to the five 2D convolutional layers in the discriminator. For example, the last layer, `ConvTranspose2d(64, 3, 4, 2, 1, bias=False)`, is modeled after the first layer in the discriminator, `Conv2d(3, 64, 4, 2, 1, bias=False)`. The numbers of *input* and *output* channels in `Conv2d` are reversed and used as the numbers of *output* and *input* channels in `ConvTranspose2d`.

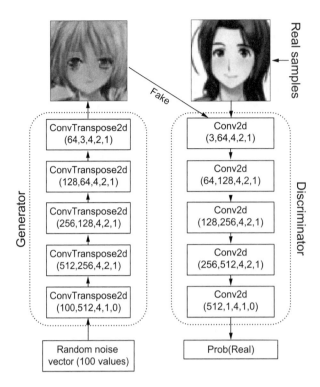

Figure 4.8   Designing a generator network in DCGAN to create anime faces by mirroring the layers in the discriminator network. The right side of the diagram shows the discriminator network, which contains five 2D convolutional layers. To design a generator that can conjure up anime faces out of thin air, we mirror the layers in the discriminator network. Specifically, as shown on the left half of the figure, the generator has five 2D transposed convolutional layers, symmetric to the 2D convolutional layers in the discriminator. Further, in each of the top four layers, the numbers of *input* and *output* channels in the discriminator are reversed and used as the numbers of *output* and *input* channels in the generator.

The number of input channels in the first 2D transposed convolutional layer is 100. This is because the generator obtains a 100-value random noise vector from the latent space (bottom left of figure 4.8) and feeds it to the generator. The number of output channels in the last 2D transposed convolutional layer in the generator is 3 because the output is an image with three color channels (RGB). We apply the Tanh activation function to the output of the generator to squeeze all values to the range [−1, 1] because the training images all have values between −1 and 1.

As usual, the loss function is binary cross-entropy loss. The discriminator is trying to maximize the accuracy of the binary classification: identify a real sample as real and a fake sample as fake. The generator, on the other hand, is trying to minimize the probability that the fake sample is being identified as fake.

We'll use the Adam optimizer for both the discriminator and the generator and set the learning rate to 0.0002:

```
loss_fn=nn.BCELoss()
lr = 0.0002
optimG = torch.optim.Adam(G.parameters(),
                          lr = lr, betas=(0.5, 0.999))
optimD = torch.optim.Adam(D.parameters(),
                          lr = lr, betas=(0.5, 0.999))
```

You have seen the Adam optimizer in chapter 2 but with default values of betas. Here, we select betas that are different from the default values. The betas in the Adam optimizer play crucial roles in stabilizing and speeding up the convergence of the training process. They do this by controlling how much emphasis is placed on recent versus past gradient information (beta1) and by adapting the learning rate based on the certainty of the gradient information (beta2). These parameters are typically fine-tuned based on the specific characteristics of the problem being solved.

4.5.2 *Training and using DCGAN*

The training process for DCGAN is similar to what we have done for other GAN models, such as those used in chapter 3 and earlier in this chapter. Since we don't know the true distribution of anime face images, we'll rely on visualization techniques to determine when the training is complete. Specifically, we define a `test_epoch()` function to visualize the anime faces created by the generator after each epoch of training:

```
def test_epoch():
    noise=torch.randn(32,100,1,1).\                    ◄── Obtains 32 random noise
        to(device=device)                                   vectors from the latent space
    fake_samples=G(noise).cpu().detach()    ◄── Generates 32 anime
                                                   face images
    for i in range(32):                     ◄──
        ax = plt.subplot(4, 8, i + 1)
        img=(fake_samples.cpu().detach()[i]/2+0.5).\   Plots the generated
            permute(1,2,0)                             images in a 4 × 8 grid
        plt.imshow(img)
        plt.xticks([])
        plt.yticks([])
    plt.subplots_adjust(hspace=-0.6)         Calls the function to
    plt.show()                               generate images before
test_epoch()                            ◄── training the model
```

If you run the preceding code cell, you'll see 32 images that look like snowflake statics on a TV screen. They don't look like anime faces at all because we haven't trained the generator yet.

We define three functions, `train_D_on_real()`, `train_D_on_fake()`, and `train_G()`, similar to those we used to train the GANs to generate grayscale images of clothing items earlier in this chapter. Go to the Jupyter Notebook for this chapter in the book's GitHub repository and familiarize yourself with the functions. They train the discriminator with real images. They then train the discriminator with fake images; finally, they train the generator.

Next, we train the model for 20 epochs:

```
for i in range(20):
    gloss=0
    dloss=0
    for n, (real_samples,_) in enumerate(train_loader):
        loss_D=train_D_on_real(real_samples)
        dloss+=loss_D
        loss_D=train_D_on_fake()
        dloss+=loss_D
        loss_G=train_G()
        gloss+=loss_G
    gloss=gloss/n
    dloss=dloss/n
    print(f"epoch {i+1}, dloss: {dloss}, gloss {gloss}")
    test_epoch()
```

The training takes about 20 minutes if you are using GPU training. Otherwise, it may take 2 to 3 hours, depending on the hardware configuration on your computer. Alternatively, you can download the trained model from my website: https://gattonweb .uky.edu/faculty/lium/gai/anime_gen.zip.

After every epoch of training, you can visualize the generated anime faces. After just one epoch of training, the model can already generate color images that look like anime faces, as shown in figure 4.9. As training progresses, the quality of the generated images becomes better and better.

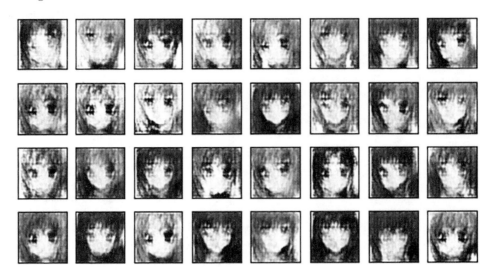

Figure 4.9   Generated images in DCGAN after one epoch of training

We'll discard the discriminator and save the trained generator in the local folder:

```
scripted = torch.jit.script(G)
scripted.save('files/anime_gen.pt')
```

To use the trained generator, we load up the model and use it to generate 32 images:

```
new_G=torch.jit.load('files/anime_gen.pt',
                        map_location=device)
new_G.eval()
noise=torch.randn(32,100,1,1).to(device)
fake_samples=new_G(noise).cpu().detach()
for i in range(32):
    ax = plt.subplot(4, 8, i + 1)
    img=(fake_samples.cpu().detach()[i]/2+0.5).permute(1,2,0)
    plt.imshow(img)
    plt.xticks([])
    plt.yticks([])
plt.subplots_adjust(hspace=-0.6)
plt.show()
```

The generated anime faces are shown in figure 4.10. The generated images bear a close resemblance to the ones in the training set shown in figure 4.7.

Figure 4.10 Generated anime face images by the trained generator in DCGAN

You may have noticed that the hair colors of the generated images are different: some are black, some are red, and some are blond. You may wonder: Can we tell the generator to create images with a certain characteristic, such as black hair or red hair? The answer is yes. You'll learn a couple of different methods to select characteristics in generated images in GANs in chapter 5.

Summary

- To conjure up realistic-looking images out of thin air, the generator mirrors layers used in the discriminator network.
- While it's feasible to generate grayscale images by using just fully connected layers, to generate high-resolution color images, we need to use CNNs.
- Two-dimensional convolutional layers are used for feature extraction. They apply a set of learnable filters (also known as kernels) to the input data to detect

patterns and features at different spatial scales. These layers are essential for capturing hierarchical representations of the input data.

- Two-dimensional transposed convolutional layers (also known as deconvolution or upsampling layers) are used for upsampling or generating high-resolution feature maps. They apply a filter to the input data. However, unlike standard convolution, they increase the spatial dimensions by inserting gaps between the output values, which effectively "upscales" the feature maps. This process generates feature maps of a higher resolution.

- Two-dimensional batch normalization is a technique commonly used in deep learning and neural networks to improve the training and performance of CNNs and other models that work with 2D data, such as images. It normalizes the values for each feature channel, so they have a mean of 0 and a standard deviation of 1, which helps stabilize and speed up training.

5

Selecting characteristics in generated images

This chapter covers

- Building a conditional generative adversarial network to generate images with certain attributes (human faces with or without eyeglasses, for example)
- Implementing Wasserstein distance and gradient penalty to improve image quality
- Selecting vectors associated with different features so that the trained GAN model generates images with certain characteristics (male or female faces, for example)
- Combining conditional GAN with vector selection to specify two attributes simultaneously (female faces without glasses or male faces with glasses, for example)

The anime faces we generated with deep convolutional GAN (DCGAN) in chapter 4 look realistic. However, you may have noticed that each generated image has different attributes such as hair color, eye color, and whether the head tilts toward the left or right. You may be wondering if there is a way to tweak the model so that the generated images have certain characteristics (such as with black hair and tilting toward the left). It turns out you can.

In this chapter, you'll learn two different ways of selecting characteristics in the generated images and their respective advantages and disadvantages. The first method involves selecting specific vectors in the latent space. Different vectors correspond to different characteristics—for example, one vector might result in a male face and another in a female face. The second method uses a conditional GAN (cGAN), which involves training the model on labeled data. This allows us to prompt the model to generate images with a specified label, each representing a distinct characteristic—like faces with or without eyeglasses.

In addition, you'll learn to combine the two methods so that you can select two independent attributes of the images at the same time. As a result, you can generate four different groups of images: males with glasses, males without glasses, females with glasses, and females without glasses. To make things more interesting, you can use a weighted average of the labels or a weighted average of the input vectors to generate images that transition from one attribute to another. For example, you can generate a series of images so that the eyeglasses gradually fade out on the same person's face (label arithmetic). Or you can generate a series of images so that the male features gradually fade out and a male face changes to a female face (vector arithmetic).

Being able to conduct either vector arithmetic or label arithmetic alone feels like science fiction, let alone performing the two simultaneously. The whole experience reminds us of the quote by Arthur C. Clarke (author of *2001: A Space Odyssey*), "Any sufficiently advanced technology is indistinguishable from magic."

Despite the realism of the anime faces generated in chapter 4, they were limited by low resolution. Training GAN models can be tricky and is often hampered by problems like small sample sizes or low-quality images. These challenges can prevent models from converging, resulting in poor image quality. To address this, we'll discuss and implement an improved training technique using the Wasserstein distance with gradient penalty in our cGAN. This enhancement results in more realistic human faces and noticeably better image quality compared to the previous chapter.

5.1   *The eyeglasses dataset*

We'll use the eyeglasses dataset in this chapter to train a cGAN model. In the next chapter, we'll also use this dataset to train a CycleGAN model in one of the exercises: to convert an image with eyeglasses to an image without eyeglasses and vice versa. In this section, you'll learn to download the dataset and preprocess images in it.

The Python programs in this chapter and the next are adapted from two excellent online open-source projects: the Kaggle project by Yashika Jain https://mng.bz/JNVQ and a GitHub repository by Aladdin Persson https://mng.bz/w5yg. I encourage you to look into these two projects while going through this chapter and the next.

5.1.1   *Downloading the eyeglasses dataset*

The eyeglasses dataset we use is from Kaggle. Log into Kaggle and go to the link https://mng.bz/q0oz to download the image folder and the two CSV files on the right: `train.csv` and `test.csv`. There are 5,000 images in the folder /faces-spring-2020/.

Once you have the data, place both the image folder and the two CSV files inside the folder /files/ on your computer.

Next, we'll sort the photos into two subfolders: one containing only images with eyeglasses and another one with images without eyeglasses.

First, let's look at the file train.csv:

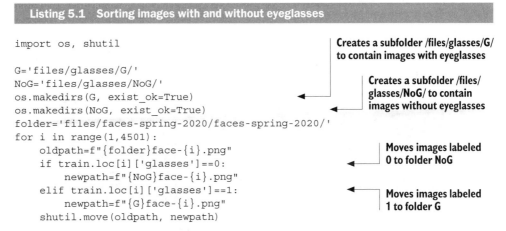

```
!pip install pandas
import pandas as pd

train=pd.read_csv('files/train.csv')
train.set_index('id', inplace=True)
```

Loads the data in the file train.
csv as a pandas DataFrame

Sets the values in the id column
as the indexes of observations

The previous code cell imports the file train.csv and sets the variable id as the index of each observation. The column glasses in the file has two values: 0 or 1, indicating whether the image has eyeglasses in it or not (0 means no glasses; 1 means with glasses).

Next, we separate the images into two different folders: one containing images with eyeglasses and one containing images without eyeglasses.

Listing 5.1 Sorting images with and without eyeglasses

```
import os, shutil

G='files/glasses/G/'
NoG='files/glasses/NoG/'
os.makedirs(G, exist_ok=True)
os.makedirs(NoG, exist_ok=True)
folder='files/faces-spring-2020/faces-spring-2020/'
for i in range(1,4501):
    oldpath=f"{folder}face-{i}.png"
    if train.loc[i]['glasses']==0:
        newpath=f"{NoG}face-{i}.png"
    elif train.loc[i]['glasses']==1:
        newpath=f"{G}face-{i}.png"
    shutil.move(oldpath, newpath)
```

Creates a subfolder /files/glasses/G/
to contain images with eyeglasses

Creates a subfolder /files/
glasses/NoG/ to contain
images without eyeglasses

Moves images labeled
0 to folder NoG

Moves images labeled
1 to folder G

In the preceding code cell, we first use the os library to create two subfolders / glasses/G/ and /glasses/NoG/ inside the folder /files/ on your computer. We then use the shutil library to move images to the two folders based on the label glasses in the file train.csv. Those labeled 1 are moved to folder G and those labeled 0 to folder NoG.

5.1.2 *Visualizing images in the eyeglasses dataset*

The classification column glasses in the file train.csv is not perfect. If you go to the subfolder G on your computer, for example, you'll see that most images have glasses, but about 10% have no glasses. Similarly, if you go to the subfolder NoG, you'll see that about 10% actually have glasses. You need to manually correct this by moving images from one folder to the other. This is important for our training later so you should manually move images in the two folders so that one contains only images with glasses and the other images without glasses. Welcome to the life of a data scientist: fixing data problems is part of daily routine! Let's first visualize some examples of images with eyeglasses.

Listing 5.2 Visualizing images with eyeglasses

```
import random
import matplotlib.pyplot as plt
from PIL import Image

imgs=os.listdir(G)
random.seed(42)
samples=random.sample(imgs,16)
fig=plt.figure(dpi=200, figsize=(8,2))
for i in range(16):
    ax = plt.subplot(2, 8, i + 1)
    img=Image.open(f"{G}{samples[i]}")
    plt.imshow(img)
    plt.xticks([])
    plt.yticks([])
plt.subplots_adjust(wspace=-0.01,hspace=-0.01)
plt.show()
```

Randomly selects 16 images from folder G

Displays the 16 images in a 2 × 8 grid

If you have manually corrected the mislabeling of images in folder G, you'll see 16 images with eyeglasses after running the code in listing 5.2. The output is shown in figure 5.1.

Figure 5.1 Sample images with eyeglasses in the training dataset

You can change G to NoG in listing 5.2 to visualize 16 sample images without eyeglasses in the dataset. The complete code is in the book's GitHub repository https://github .com/markhliu/DGAI. The output is shown in figure 5.2.

Figure 5.2 Sample images without eyeglasses in the training dataset

5.2   cGAN and Wasserstein distance

A cGAN is similar to the GAN models you have seen in chapters 3 and 4, with the exception that you attach a label to the input data. The labels correspond to different characteristics in the input data. Once the trained GAN model "learns" to associate a certain label with a characteristic, you can feed a random noise vector with a label to the model to generate output with the desired characteristic.[1]

GAN models often suffer from problems like mode collapse (the generator finds a certain type of output that is good at fooling the discriminator and then collapses its outputs to these few modes, ignoring other variations), vanishing gradients, and slow convergence. Wasserstein GAN (WGAN) introduces the Earth Mover's (or Wasserstein-1) distance as the loss function, offering a smoother gradient flow and more stable training. It mitigates problems like mode collapse.[2] We'll implement it in cGAN training in this chapter. Note that WGAN is a concept independent of cGAN: It uses the Wasserstein distance to improve the training process and can be applied to any GAN model (such as the ones we created in chapters 3 and 4). We'll combine both concepts in one setting to save space.

> **Other ways to stabilize GAN training**
>
> The problems with training GAN models are most common when generating high-resolution images. The model architecture is usually complex, with many neural layers. Other than WGAN, progressive GAN is another way to stabilize training. Progressive GANs enhance the stability of GAN training by breaking down the complex task of high-resolution image generation into manageable steps, allowing for more controlled and effective learning. For details, see "Progressive Growing of GANs for Improved Quality, Stability, and Variation." by Karas et al., https://arxiv.org/abs/1710.10196.

5.2.1   WGAN with gradient penalty

WGAN is a technique used to improve the training stability and performance of GAN models. Regular GANs (such as the ones you have seen in Chapters 3 and 4) have two components—a generator and a discriminator. The generator creates fake data, while the discriminator evaluates whether the data is real or fake. Training involves a competitive zero-sum game in which the generator tries to fool the discriminator, and the discriminator tries to accurately classify real and fake data instances.

Researchers have proposed to use Wasserstein distance (a measure of dissimilarity between two distributions) instead of the binary cross-entropy as the loss function to stabilize training with a gradient penalty term.[3] The technique offers a smoother gradi-

---

[1] Mehdi Mirza, Simon Osindero, 2014, "Conditional Generative Adversarial Nets." https://arxiv.org/abs/1411.1784.

[2] Martin Arjovsky, Soumith Chintala, and Léon Bottou, 2017, "Wasserstein GAN." https://arxiv.org/abs/1701.07875.

[3] Martin Arjovsky, Soumith Chintala, and Leon Bottou, 2017, "Wasserstein GAN." https://arxiv.org/abs/1701.07875; and Ishaan Gulrajani, Faruk Ahmed, Martin Arjovsky, Vincent Dumoulin, and Aaron Courville, 2017, "Improved Training of Wasserstein GANs." https://arxiv.org/abs/1704.00028.

ent flow and mitigates problems like mode collapse. Figure 5.3 provides a diagram of WGAN. As you can see on the right side of the figure, the losses associated with the real and fake images are Wasserstein loss instead of the regular binary cross-entropy loss.

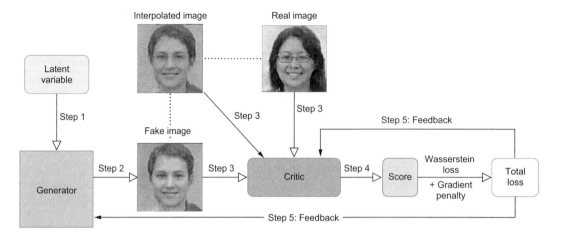

Figure 5.3   WGAN with gradient penalty. The discriminator network in WGAN (which we call the critic) rates input images: it tries to assign a score of $-\infty$ to a fake image (bottom left) and a score of ∞ to the real image (top middle). Further, an interpolated image of the real and fake images (top left) is presented to the critic, and the gradient penalty with respect to the critic's rating on the interpolated image is added to the total loss in the training process.

Further, for the Wasserstein distance to work correctly, the discriminator (called the critic in WGANs) must be 1-Lipschitz continuous, meaning the gradient norms of the critic's function must be at most 1 everywhere. The original WGAN paper proposed weight clipping to enforce the Lipschitz constraint.

To address weight clipping problems, the gradient penalty is added to the loss function to enforce the Lipschitz constraint more effectively. To implement WGAN with gradient penalty, we first randomly sample points along the straight line between real and generated data points (as indicated by the interpolated image in the top left of figure 5.3). Since both real and fake images have labels attached to them, the interpolated image also has a label attached to it, which is the interpolated value of the two original labels. We then compute the gradient of the critic's output with respect to these sampled points. Finally, we add a penalty to the loss function proportional to the deviation of these gradient norms from 1 (the penalty term is called gradient penalty). That is, gradient penalty in WGANs is a technique to improve training stability and sample quality by enforcing the Lipschitz constraint more effectively, addressing the limitations of the original WGAN model.

5.2.2   cGANs

cGAN is an extension of the basic GAN framework. In a cGAN, both the generator and the discriminator (or the critic since we are implementing WGAN and cGAN in the same setting) are conditioned on some additional information. This could be anything, such as class labels, data from other modalities, or even textual descriptions. This conditioning is typically achieved by feeding this additional information into both the generator and discriminator. In our setting, we'll add class labels to the inputs to both the generator and the critic: we attach one label to images with eyeglasses and another label to images without eyeglasses. Figure 5.4 provides a diagram of the training process for cGANs.

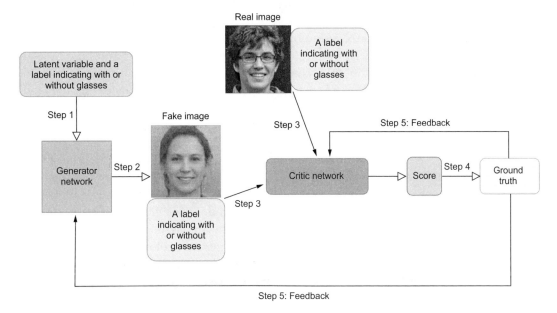

Figure 5.4 The training process for cGANs

As you can see at the top left of figure 5.4, in a cGAN, the generator receives both a random noise vector and the conditional information (a label indicating whether the image has eyeglasses or not) as input. It uses this information to generate data that not only looks real but also aligns with the conditional input.

The critic receives either real data from the training set or fake data generated by the generator, along with the conditional information (a label indicating whether the image has eyeglasses or not in our setting). Its task is to determine whether the given data is real or fake, taking the conditional information into account (does the generated image have eyeglasses in it?). In figure 5.4, we use the critic network instead of the discriminator network since we implement both cGAN and WGAN simultaneously, but the concept of cGAN applies to traditional GANs as well.

The main advantage of cGANs is their ability to select aspects of the generated data, making them more versatile and applicable in scenarios where the output needs to be directed or conditioned on certain input parameters. In our setting, we'll train the cGAN so that we have the ability to select whether the generated images have eyeglasses or not.

In summary, cGANs are a powerful extension of the basic GAN architecture, enabling targeted generation of synthetic data based on conditional inputs.

5.3 Create a cGAN

In this section, you'll learn to create a cGAN to generate human faces with or without eyeglasses. You'll also learn to implement the WGAN with gradient penalty to stabilize training.

The generator in cGANs uses not only random noise vectors but also conditional information such as labels as inputs to create images either with or without eyeglasses. Further, a critic network in WGANs is different from the discriminator network in traditional GANs. You'll also learn how to calculate the Wasserstein distance and the gradient penalty in this section.

5.3.1 A critic in cGAN

In cGANs, the discriminator is a binary classifier to identify the input as either real or fake, conditional on the label. In WGAN, we call the discriminator network the critic. The critic evaluates the input and gives a score between $-\infty$ and ∞. The higher the score, the more likely that the input is from the training set (that is, real).

Listing 5.3 creates the critic network. The architecture is somewhat similar to the discriminator network we used in chapter 4 when generating color images of anime faces. In particular, we use seven Conv2d layers in PyTorch to gradually downsample the input so that the output is a single value between $-\infty$ and ∞.

Listing 5.3 A critic network in cGAN with Wasserstein distance

```
class Critic(nn.Module):
    def __init__(self, img_channels, features):
        super().__init__()
        self.net = nn.Sequential(              ◀── The critic network has two
            nn.Conv2d(img_channels, features,       Conv2d layers plus five blocks.
                    kernel_size=4, stride=2, padding=1),
            nn.LeakyReLU(0.2),
            self.block(features, features * 2, 4, 2, 1),
            self.block(features * 2, features * 4, 4, 2, 1),
            self.block(features * 4, features * 8, 4, 2, 1),
            self.block(features * 8, features * 16, 4, 2, 1),
            self.block(features * 16, features * 32, 4, 2, 1),
            nn.Conv2d(features * 32, 1, kernel_size=4,
                    stride=2, padding=0))          ◀── The output has one feature,
    def block(self, in_channels, out_channels,         without activation.
            kernel_size, stride, padding):
        return nn.Sequential(                     ◀── Each block contains a
            nn.Conv2d(in_channels,out_channels,        Conv2d layer, an
                kernel_size,stride,padding,bias=False,),  InstanceNorm2d
            nn.InstanceNorm2d(out_channels, affine=True),  layer, with LeakyReLU
            nn.LeakyReLU(0.2))                          activation.
```

```
def forward(self, x):
    return self.net(x)
```

The input to the critic network is a color image with a shape of $5 \times 256 \times 256$. The first three channels are the color channels (colors red, green, and blue). The last two channels (the fourth and fifth channels) are label channels to tell the critic whether the image is with glasses or without glasses. We'll discuss the exact mechanism to accomplish this in the next section.

The critic network consists of seven Conv2d layers. In chapter 4, we discussed in depth how these layers work. They are used for feature extraction by applying a set of learnable filters on the input images to detect patterns and features at different spatial scales, effectively capturing hierarchical representations of the input data. The critic then evaluates the input images based on these representations. The five Conv2d layers in the middle are all followed by an InstanceNorm2d layer and a LeakyReLU activation; hence, we define a block() method to streamline the critic network. The InstanceNorm2d layer is similar to the BatchNorm2d layer we discussed in chapter 4, except that we normalize each individual instance in the batch independently.

Another key point is that the output is no longer a value between 0 and 1 since we don't use the sigmoid activation in the last layer in the critic network. Instead, the output is a value between $-\infty$ and ∞ since we use the Wasserstein distance with gradient penalty in our cGAN.

5.3.2 A generator in cGAN

In WGANs, the generator's job is to create data instances so that they can be evaluated at a high score by the critic. In cGANs, the generator must generate data instances with conditional information (with or without eyeglasses in our setting). Since we are implementing a cGAN with Wasserstein distance, we'll tell the generator what type of images we want to generate by attaching a label to the random noise vector. We'll discuss the exact mechanism in the next section.

We create the neural network shown in the following listing to represent the generator.

Listing 5.4 A generator in cGAN

```
class Generator(nn.Module):
    def __init__(self, noise_channels, img_channels, features):
        super(Generator, self).__init__()
        self.net = nn.Sequential(
            self.block(noise_channels, features *64, 4, 1, 0),
            self.block(features * 64, features * 32, 4, 2, 1),
            self.block(features * 32, features * 16, 4, 2, 1),
            self.block(features * 16, features * 8, 4, 2, 1),
            self.block(features * 8, features * 4, 4, 2, 1),
            self.block(features * 4, features * 2, 4, 2, 1),
            nn.ConvTranspose2d(
                features * 2, img_channels, kernel_size=4,
                stride=2, padding=1),
```

The generator consists of seven ConvTranspose2d layers.

```
            nn.Tanh())
    def block(self, in_channels, out_channels,
            kernel_size, stride, padding):
        return nn.Sequential(
            nn.ConvTranspose2d(in_channels,out_channels,
                kernel_size,stride,padding,bias=False,),
            nn.BatchNorm2d(out_channels),
            nn.ReLU(),)
    def forward(self, x):
        return self.net(x)
```

◄—— **Uses Tanh activation to squeeze values to the range [–1, 1], the same as images in the training set**

Each block consists of a ConvTranspose2d layer, a BatchNorm2d layer, and ReLU activation.

We'll feed a random noise vector from a 100-dimensional latent space to the generator as input. We'll also feed a 2-value one-hot encoded image label to the generator to tell it to generate an image either with or without eyeglasses. We'll concatenate the two pieces of information together to form a 102-dimensional input variable to the generator. The generator then generates a color image based on the input from the latent space and the labeling information.

The generator network consists of seven `ConvTranspose2d` layers, and the idea is to mirror the steps in the critic network to conjure up images, as we discussed in chapter 4. The first six `ConvTranspose2d` layers are all followed by a `BatchNorm2d` layer and a `ReLU` activation; hence, we define a `block()` method in the generator network to simplify the architecture. As we have done in chapter 4, we use the Tanh activation function at the output layer so the output pixels are all in the range of –1 and 1, the same as the images in the training set.

5.3.3   *Weight initialization and the gradient penalty function*

In deep learning, the weights in neural networks are randomly initialized. When the network architecture is complicated, and there are many hidden layers (which is the case in our setting), how weights are initialized is crucial.

We, therefore, define the following `weights_init()` function to initialize weights in both the generator and the critic networks:

```
def weights_init(m):
    classname = m.__class__.__name__
    if classname.find('Conv') != -1:
        nn.init.normal_(m.weight.data, 0.0, 0.02)
    elif classname.find('BatchNorm') != -1:
        nn.init.normal_(m.weight.data, 1.0, 0.02)
        nn.init.constant_(m.bias.data, 0)
```

The function initializes weights in `Conv2d` and `ConvTranspose2d` layers with values drawn from a normal distribution with a mean of 0 and a standard deviation of 0.02. It also initializes weights in `BatchNorm2d` layers with values drawn from a normal distribution with a mean of 1 and a standard deviation of 0.02. We choose a small standard deviation in weight initializations to avoid exploding gradients.

Next, we create a generator and a critic based on the `Generator()` and `Critic()` classes we defined in the last subsection. We then initialize the weights in them based on the `weights_init()` function defined earlier:

```
z_dim=100
img_channels=3
features=16
gen=Generator(z_dim+2,img_channels,features).to(device)
critic=Critic(img_channels+2,features).to(device)
weights_init(gen)
weights_init(critic)
```

As usual, we'll use the Adam optimizer for both the critic and the generator:

```
lr = 0.0001
opt_gen = torch.optim.Adam(gen.parameters(),
                           lr = lr, betas=(0.0, 0.9))
opt_critic = torch.optim.Adam(critic.parameters(),
                              lr = lr, betas=(0.0, 0.9))
```

The generator tries to create images that are indistinguishable from those in the training set with the given label. It presents the images to the critic to obtain high ratings on the generated images. The critic, on the other hand, tries to assign high ratings to real images and low ratings to fake images, conditional on the given label. Specifically, the loss function for the critic has three components:

$$\text{critic\_value(fake)} - \text{critic\_value(real)} + \text{weight} \times \text{GradientPenalty}$$

The first term, *critic_value(fake)*, says that if an image is fake, the critic's objective is to identify it as fake and give it a low evaluation. The second term, *– critic_value(real)*, indicates that if the image is real, the critic's objective is to identify it as real and give it a high evaluation. Further, the critic wants to minimize the gradient penalty term, *weight × GradientPenalty*, where *weight* is a constant to determine how much penalty we want to assign to deviations of the gradient norms from the value 1. The gradient penalty is calculated as shown in the following listing.

Listing 5.5 Calculating gradient penalty

```
def GP(critic, real, fake):
    B, C, H, W = real.shape
    alpha=torch.rand((B,1,1,1)).repeat(1,C,H,W).to(device)
    interpolated_images = real*alpha+fake*(1-alpha)     ◄  Creates an interpolated image of the real and the fake
    critic_scores = critic(interpolated_images)          ◄  Obtains the critic value with respect to the interpolated image
    gradient = torch.autograd.grad(
        inputs=interpolated_images,
        outputs=critic_scores,
        grad_outputs=torch.ones_like(critic_scores),
        create_graph=True,
        retain_graph=True)[0]                            ◄  Calculates the gradient of the critic value
    gradient = gradient.view(gradient.shape[0], -1)
    gradient_norm = gradient.norm(2, dim=1)
    gp = torch.mean((gradient_norm - 1) ** 2)            ◄  Gradient penalty is the squared deviation of the gradient norm from value 1.
    return gp
```

In the function GP(), we first create interpolated images of real ones and fake ones. This is done by randomly sampling points along the straight line between real and generated images. Imagine a slider: at one end is the real image, and at the other is the fake image. As you move the slider, you see a continuous blend from the real to the fake, with the interpolated images representing the stages in between.

We then present interpolated images to the critic network to obtain ratings on them and calculate the gradient of the critic's output with respect to the interpolated images. Finally, the gradient penalty is calculated as the squared deviation of the gradient norms from the target value of 1.

5.4   *Training the cGAN*

As we mentioned in the last section, we need to find a way to tell both the critic and the generator what the image label is so they know if the image has eyeglasses or not.

In this section, you'll first learn how to add labels to the inputs to the critic network and the inputs to the generator network so the generator knows what type of images to create while the critic can evaluate the images conditional on the labels. After that, you'll learn how to train the cGAN with Wasserstein distance.

5.4.1   *Adding labels to inputs*

We first preprocess the data and convert the images to torch tensors:

```
import torchvision.transforms as T
import torchvision

batch_size=16
imgsz=256
transform=T.Compose([
    T.Resize((imgsz,imgsz)),
    T.ToTensor(),
    T.Normalize([0.5,0.5,0.5],[0.5,0.5,0.5])])
data_set=torchvision.datasets.ImageFolder(
    root=r"files/glasses",
    transform=transform)
```

We set the batch size to 16 and the image size to 256 by 256 pixels. The pixel values are chosen so the generated images have higher resolutions than those in the last chapter (64 by 64 pixels). We choose a batch size of 16, smaller than the batch size in chapter 3, due to the larger image size. If the batch size is too large, your GPU (or even CPU) will run out of memory.

> **TIP** If you are using GPU training and your GPU has a small memory (say, 6GB), consider reducing the batch size to a smaller number than 16, such as 10 or 8, so that your GPU doesn't run out of memory. Alternatively, you can keep the batch size at 16 but switch to CPU training to address the GPU memory problem.

Next, we'll add labels to the training data. Since there are two types of images—images with eyeglasses and images without glasses—we'll create two one-hot image labels.

Images with glasses will have a one-hot label of [1, 0], and images without glasses will have a one-hot label of [0, 1].

The input to the generator is a 100-value random noise vector. We concatenate the one-hot label with the random noise vector and feed the 102-value input to the generator. The input to the critic network is a three-channel color image with a shape of 3 by 256 by 256 (PyTorch uses channel-first tensors to represent images). How do we attach a label with a shape of 1 by 2 to an image with a shape of 3 by 256 by 256? The solution is to add two channels to the input image so that the image shape changes from (3, 256, 256) to (5, 256, 256): the two additional channels are the one-hot labels. Specifically, if an image has eyeglasses in it, the fourth channel is filled with 1s and the fifth channel 0s; if the image has no eyeglasses in it, the fourth channel is filled with 0s and the fifth channel 1s.

Creating labels if there are more than two values in a characteristic

You can easily extend the cGAN model to characteristics with more than two values. For example, if you create a model to generate images with the different hair colors black, blond, and white, the image labels you feed to the generator can have values [1, 0, 0], [0, 1, 0], and [0, 0, 1], respectively. You can attach three channels to the input image before you feed it to the discriminator or critic. For example, if an image has black hair, the fourth channel is filled with 1s and the fifth and sixth channels 0s.

Additionally, in the eyeglasses example, since there are only two values in the label, you can potentially use values 0 and 1 to indicate images with and without glasses when you feed the label to the generator. You can attach one channel to the input image before you feed it to the critic: if an image has eyeglasses, the fourth channel is filled with 1s; if the image has no eyeglasses, the fourth channel is filled with 0s. I'll leave that as an exercise for you. The solution is provided in the book's GitHub repository: https://github.com/markhliu/DGAI.

We implement this change as shown in the following listing.

Listing 5.6 Attaching labels to input images

```
newdata=[]
for i,(img,label) in enumerate(data_set):
    onehot=torch.zeros((2))
    onehot[label]=1
    channels=torch.zeros((2,imgsz,imgsz))
    if label==0:
        channels[0,:,:]=1
    else:
        channels[1,:,:]=1
    img_and_label=torch.cat([img,channels],dim=0)
    newdata.append((img,label,onehot,img_and_label))
```

> **Creates two extra channels filled with 0s, each channel with a shape of 256 by 256, the same as the dimension of each channel in the input image**

> **If the original image label is 0, fills the fourth channel with 1s**

> **If the original image label is 1, fills the fifth channel with 1s**

> **Adds the fourth and fifth channels to the original image to form a five-channel labeled image**

TIP   Earlier when we load the images by using the `torchvision.datasets`
`.ImageFolder()` method from the folder /files/glasses, PyTorch assigns labels
to images in each subfolder in alphabetical order. Therefore, images in /files/
glasses/G/ are assigned a label of 0, and those in /files/glasses/NoG/, a label
of 1.

We first create an empty list `newdata` to hold images with labels. We create a PyTorch
tensor with a shape (2, 256, 256) to be attached to the original input image to form
a new image with a shape of (5, 256, 256). If the original image label is 0 (this means
images are from the folder /files/glasses/G/), we fill the fourth channel with 1s and
the fifth channel with 0s so that the critic knows it's an image with glasses. On the other
hand, if the original image label is 1 (this means images are from the folder /files/
glasses/NoG/), we fill the fourth channel with 0s and the fifth channel with 1s so that
the critic knows it's an image without glasses.

We create a data iterator with batches (to improve computational efficiency, memory
usage, and optimization dynamics in the training process) as follows:

```
data_loader=torch.utils.data.DataLoader(
    newdata,batch_size=batch_size,shuffle=True)
```

5.4.2 *Training the cGAN*

Now that we have the training data and two networks, we'll train the cGAN. We'll use
visual inspections to determine when the training should stop.

Once the model is trained, we'll discard the critic network and use the generator to
create images with a certain characteristic (with or without glasses, in our case).

We'll create a function to test periodically what the generated images look like.

Listing 5.7   Inspecting generated images

```
def plot_epoch(epoch):
    noise = torch.randn(32, z_dim, 1, 1)
    labels = torch.zeros(32, 2, 1, 1)
    labels[:,0,:,:]=1
    noise_and_labels=torch.cat([noise,labels],dim=1).to(device)
    fake=gen(noise_and_labels).cpu().detach()
    fig=plt.figure(figsize=(20,10),dpi=100)
    for i in range(32):
        ax = plt.subplot(4, 8, i + 1)
        img=(fake.cpu().detach()[i]/2+0.5).permute(1,2,0)
        plt.imshow(img)
        plt.xticks([])
        plt.yticks([])
    plt.subplots_adjust(hspace=-0.6)
    plt.savefig(f"files/glasses/G{epoch}.png")
    plt.show()
    noise = torch.randn(32, z_dim, 1, 1)
    labels = torch.zeros(32, 2, 1, 1)
    labels[:,1,:,:]=1
    … (code omitted)
```

Creates a one-hot label for images with glasses

Feeds the concatenated noise vector and label to the generator to create images with glasses

Plots the generated images with glasses

Creates a one-hot label for images without glasses

After each epoch of training, we'll ask the generator to create a set of images with glasses and a set of images without glasses. We then plot the images so that we can inspect them visually. To create images with glasses, we first create one-hot labels [1, 0] and attach them to the random noise vectors before feeding the concatenated vector to the generator network. The generator creates images with glasses since the label is [1, 0] instead of [0, 1]. We then plot the generated images in four rows and eight columns and save the subplots on your computer. The process of creating images without glasses is similar, except that we use the one-hot label [0, 1] instead of [1, 0]. I skipped part of the code in listing 5.7, but you can find it in the book's GitHub repository: https://github.com/markhliu/DGAI.

We define a `train_batch()` function to train the model with a batch of data.

Listing 5.8 Training the model with a batch of data

```
def train_batch(onehots,img_and_labels,epoch):
    real = img_and_labels.to(device)          ◄─┐ A batch of real images
    B = real.shape[0]                            │ with labels
    for _ in range(5):
        noise = torch.randn(B, z_dim, 1, 1)
        onehots=onehots.reshape(B,2,1,1)
        noise_and_labels=torch.cat([noise,onehots],dim=1).to(device)
        fake_img = gen(noise_and_labels).to(device)
        fakelabels=img_and_labels[:,3:,:,:].to(device)
        fake=torch.cat([fake_img,fakelabels],dim=1).to(device)  ◄─┐ A batch of
        critic_real = critic(real).reshape(-1)                     │ generated
        critic_fake = critic(fake).reshape(-1)                     │ images with
        gp = GP(critic, real, fake)                                │ labels
        loss_critic=(-(torch.mean(critic_real) -
            torch.mean(critic_fake)) + 10 * gp)   ◄─┐ The total loss for the critic
        critic.zero_grad()                           │ has three components: loss
        loss_critic.backward(retain_graph=True)      │ from evaluating real images,
        opt_critic.step()                            │ loss from evaluating fake
    gen_fake = critic(fake).reshape(-1)              │ images, and the gradient
    loss_gen = -torch.mean(gen_fake)   ◄─────────────┘ penalty loss.
    gen.zero_grad()
    loss_gen.backward()
    opt_gen.step()          ┌ Trains the generator with
    return loss_critic, loss_gen └ the Wasserstein loss
```

In the `train_batch()` function, we first train the critic with real images. We also ask the generator to create a batch of fake data with the given label. We then train the critic with fake images. In the `train_batch()` function, we also train the generator with a batch of fake data.

NOTE The loss for the critic has three components: loss from evaluating real images, loss from evaluating fake images, and the gradient penalty loss.

We now train the model for 100 epochs:

```
for epoch in range(1,101):
    closs=0
```

```
    gloss=0
    for _,_,onehots,img_and_labels in data_loader:
        loss_critic, loss_gen = train_batch(onehots,\
                            img_and_labels,epoch)
        closs+=loss_critic.detach()/len(data_loader)
        gloss+=loss_gen.detach()/len(data_loader)
    print(f"at epoch {epoch},\
    critic loss: {closs}, generator loss {gloss}")
    plot_epoch(epoch)
torch.save(gen.state_dict(),'files/cgan.pth')
```

> Iterates through all batches in the training dataset

> Trains the model with a batch of data

> Saves the weights in the trained generator

After each epoch of training, we print out the critic loss and the generator loss to ensure that the losses are in a reasonable range. We also generate 32 images of faces with glasses as well as 32 images without glasses by using the `plot_epoch()` function we defined earlier. We save the weights in the trained generator in the local folder after training is done so that later we can generate images using the trained model.

This training takes about 30 minutes if you are using GPU training. Otherwise, it may take several hours, depending on the hardware configuration on your computer. Alternatively, you can download the trained model from my website: https://gattonweb.uky .edu/faculty/lium/gai/cgan.zip. Unzip the file after downloading.

5.5   *Selecting characteristics in generated images*

There are at least two ways to generate images with a certain characteristic. The first is to attach a label to a random noise vector before feeding it to the trained cGAN model. Different labels lead to different characteristics in the generated image (in our case, whether the image has eyeglasses). The second way is to select the noise vector you feed to the trained model: while one vector leads to an image with a male face, another leads to an image with a female face. Note that the second way works even in a traditional GAN such as the ones we trained in chapter 4. It works in a cGAN as well.

Better yet, in this section, you'll learn to combine these two methods so you can select two characteristics simultaneously: an image of a male face with eyeglasses or a female face without eyeglasses, and so on.

There are pros and cons for each one of these two methods in selecting a certain characteristic in generated images. The first way, the cGAN, requires labeled data to train the model. Sometimes, labeled data is costly to curate. However, once you have successfully trained a cGAN, you can generate a wide range of images with a certain characteristic. In our case, you can generate many different images with eyeglasses (or without eyeglasses); each one is different from the other. The second way, handpicking a noise vector, doesn't need labeled data to train the model. However, each handpicked noise vector can only generate one image. If you want to generate many different images with the same characteristic as the cGAN, you'll need to handpick many different noise vectors ex ante.

5.5.1 *Selecting images with or without eyeglasses*

By attaching a label of either [1, 0] or [0, 1] to a random noise vector before you feed it to the trained cGAN model, you can select whether the generated image has eyeglasses.

First, we'll use the trained model to generate 32 images with glasses and plot them in a 4 × 8 grid. To make results reproducible, we'll fix the random state in PyTorch. Further, we'll use the same set of random noise vectors so that we look at the same set of faces.

We fix the random state at seed 0 and generate 32 images of faces with eyeglasses.

Listing 5.9   Generating images of human faces with eyeglasses

```
torch.manual_seed(0)

generator=Generator(z_dim+2,img_channels,features).to(device)
generator.load_state_dict(torch.load("files/cgan.pth",
    map_location=device))
generator.eval()

noise_g=torch.randn(32, z_dim, 1, 1)
labels_g=torch.zeros(32, 2, 1, 1)
labels_g[:,0,:,:]=1
noise_and_labels=torch.cat([noise_g,labels_g],dim=1).to(device)
fake=generator(noise_and_labels)
plt.figure(figsize=(20,10),dpi=50)
for i in range(32):
    ax = plt.subplot(4, 8, i + 1)
    img=(fake.cpu().detach()[i]/2+0.5).permute(1,2,0)
    plt.imshow(img.numpy())
    plt.xticks([])
    plt.yticks([])
plt.subplots_adjust(wspace=-0.08,hspace=-0.01)
plt.show()
```

Fixes the random state so results are reproducible

Loads up the trained weights

Generates a set of random noise vectors and saves it so we can select certain vectors from it to perform vector arithmetic

Creates a label to generate images with eyeglasses

We create another instance of the `Generator()` class and name it `generator`. We then load up the trained weights that we saved in the local folder in the last section (or you can download the weights from my website: https://mng.bz/75Z4). To generate 32 images of human faces with eyeglasses; we first draw 32 random noise vectors in the latent space. We'll also create a set of labels and name them `labels_g`, and they tell the generator to produce 32 images with eyeglasses.

If you run the program in listing 5.9, you'll see 32 images as shown in figure 5.5.

Figure 5.5   Images of human faces with eyeglasses that are generated by the trained cGAN model

First, all 32 images do have eyeglasses in them. This indicates that the trained cGAN model is able to generate images conditional on the provided labels. You may have noticed that some images have male features while others have female features. To prepare us for vector arithmetic in the next subsection, we'll select one random noise vector that leads to an image with male features and one that leads to female features. After inspecting the 32 images in figure 5.5, we select images with index values 0 and 14, like so:

```
z_male_g=noise_g[0]
z_female_g=noise_g[14]
```

To generate 32 images without eyeglasses, we first produce another set of random noise vectors and labels:

```
noise_ng = torch.randn(32, z_dim, 1, 1)
labels_ng = torch.zeros(32, 2, 1, 1)
labels_ng[:,1,:,:]=1
```

The new set of random noise vectors is named `noise_ng`, and the new set of labels `labels_ng`. Feed them to the generator and you should see 32 images without eyeglasses, as shown in figure 5.6.

None of the 32 faces in figure 5.6 has eyeglasses in it: the trained cGAN model can generate images contingent upon the given label. We select images with indexes 8 (male) and 31 (female) to prepare for vector arithmetic in the next subsection:

```
z_male_ng=noise_ng[8]
```

```
z_female_ng=noise_ng[31]
```

Figure 5.6 Images of human faces without eyeglasses that are generated by the trained cGAN model

Next, we'll use label interpolation to perform label arithmetic. Recall that the two labels, `noise_g` and `noise_ng`, instruct the trained cGAN model to create images with and without eyeglasses, respectively. What if we feed an interpolated label (a weighted average of the two labels [1, 0] and [0, 1]) to the model? What type of images will the trained generator produce? Let's find out.

Listing 5.10 Label arithmetic in cGAN

```
weights=[0,0.25,0.5,0.75,1]                                          Creates five weights
plt.figure(figsize=(20,4),dpi=300)
for i in range(5):
    ax = plt.subplot(1, 5, i + 1)
    # change the value of z
    label=weights[i]*labels_ng[0]+(1-weights[i])*labels_g[0]         Creates a
    noise_and_labels=torch.cat(                                      weighted
        [z_female_g.reshape(1, z_dim, 1, 1),                         average of the
         label.reshape(1, 2, 1, 1)],dim=1).to(device)               two labels
    fake=generator(noise_and_labels).cpu().detach()
    img=(fake[0]/2+0.5).permute(1,2,0)
    plt.imshow(img)                                                  Gives the new
    plt.xticks([])                                                   label to the
    plt.yticks([])                                                   trained model to
plt.subplots_adjust(wspace=-0.08,hspace=-0.01)                       create an image
plt.show()
```

We first create five weights (w): 0, 0.25, 0.5, 0.75, and 1, equally spaced between 0 and 1. Each of these five values of w is the weight we put on the no eyeglasses label `labels_ng`. The complementary weight is put on the eyeglasses label `labels_g`. The interpolated label therefore has a value of `w*labels_ng+(1-w)*labels_g`. We then feed the interpolated label to the trained model, along with the random noise vector z_female_g that we saved earlier. The five generated images, based on the five values of w, are plotted in a 1 × 5 grid, as shown in figure 5.7.

Figure 5.7   Label arithmetic in cGAN. We first create two labels: the no eyeglasses label labels_ng **and the eyeglasses label** labels_g**. These two labels instruct the trained generator to produce images with and without eyeglasses, respectively. We then create five interpolated labels, each as a weighted average of the original two labels:** w*labels_ng+(1-w)*labels_g**, where the weight** w **takes five different values, 0, 0.25, 0.5, 0.75, and 1. The five generated images based on the five interpolated labels are shown in the figure. The image on the far left has eyeglasses. As we move from the left to the right, the eyeglasses gradually fade away, until the image on the far right has no eyeglasses in it.**

When you look at the five generated images in figure 5.7 from the left to the right, you'll notice that the eyeglasses gradually fade away. The image on the left has eyeglasses while the image on the right has no eyeglasses. The three images in the middle show some signs of eyeglasses, but the eyeglasses are not as conspicuous as those in the first image.

Exercise 5.1

Since we used the random noise vector z_female_g in listing 5.10, the images in figure 5.7 have a female face. Change the noise vector to z_male_g in listing 5.10 and rerun the program; see what the images look like.

5.5.2   *Vector arithmetic in latent space*

You may have noticed that some generated human face images have male features while others have female features. You may wonder: Can we select male or female features in generated images? The answer is yes. We can achieve this by selecting noise vectors in the latent space.

In the last subsection, we have saved two random noise vectors, z_male_ng and z_female_ng, that lead to images of a male face and a female face, respectively. Next, we feed a weighted average of the two vectors (i.e., an interpolated vector) to the trained model and see what the generated images look like.

Listing 5.11   Vector arithmetic to select image characteristics

```
weights=[0,0.25,0.5,0.75,1]
plt.figure(figsize=(20,4),dpi=50)
for i in range(5):
```
← **Creates five weights**

```
ax = plt.subplot(1, 5, i + 1)
# change the value of z
z=weights[i]*z_female_ng+(1-weights[i])*z_male_ng
noise_and_labels=torch.cat(
    [z.reshape(1, z_dim, 1, 1),
     labels_ng[0].reshape(1, 2, 1, 1)],dim=1).to(device)
fake=generator(noise_and_labels).cpu().detach()
img=(fake[0]/2+0.5).permute(1,2,0)
plt.imshow(img)
plt.xticks([])
plt.yticks([])
plt.subplots_adjust(wspace=-0.08,hspace=-0.01)
plt.show()
```

Creates a weighted average of the two random noise vectors

Feeds the new random noise vector to the trained model to create an image

We have created five weights, 0, 0.25, 0.5, 0.75, and 1. We iterate through the five weights and create five weighted averages of the two random noise vectors, w*z_female_ng+(1-w)*z_male_ng. We then feed the five vectors, along with the label, labels_ng, to the trained model to obtain five images, as shown in figure 5.8.

Figure 5.8 Vector arithmetic in GAN. We first save two random noise vectors z_female_ng and z_male_ng. The two vectors lead to images of female and male faces, respectively. We then create five interpolated vectors, each as a weighted average of the original two vectors: w*z_female_ng+ (1-w)*z_male_ng, where the weight w takes five different values, 0, 0.25, 0.5, 0.75, and 1. The five generated images based on the five interpolated vectors are shown in the figure. The image on the far left has male features. As we move from the left to the right, the male features gradually fade away and the female features gradually appear, until the image on the far right shows a female face.

Vector arithmetic can transition from one instance of an image to another instance. Since we happen to have selected a male and a female image, when you look at the five generated images in figure 5.8 from the left to the right, you'll notice that male features gradually fade away and female features gradually appear. The first image shows an image with a male face while the last image shows an image with a female face.

Exercise 5.2

Since we used the label labels_ng in listing 5.11, the images in figure 5.8 have no eyeglasses in them. Change the label to labels_g in listing 5.11 and rerun the program to see what the images look like.

5.5.3 Selecting two characteristics simultaneously

So far, we have selected one characteristic at a time. By selecting the label, you have learned how to generate images with or without eyeglasses. By selecting a specific noise vector, you have learned how to select a specific instance of the generated image.

What if you want to select two characteristics (glasses and gender, for example) at the same time? There are four possible combinations of the two independent characteristics: male faces with glasses, male faces without glasses, female faces with glasses, and female faces without glasses. Next we'll generate an image of each type.

Listing 5.12   Selecting two characteristics simultaneously

```
plt.figure(figsize=(20,5),dpi=50)
for i in range(4):                                  ◄──────  Iterates through 0 to 3
    ax = plt.subplot(1, 4, i + 1)
    p=i//2                                          The value of p, which can be either 0
    q=i%2                                           or 1, selects the random noise vector
    z=z_female_g*p+z_male_g*(1-p)          ◄──┘     to generate a male or female face.
    label=labels_ng[0]*q+labels_g[0]*(1-q)   ◄──
    noise_and_labels=torch.cat(
        [z.reshape(1, z_dim, 1, 1),                 The value of q,
        label.reshape(1, 2, 1, 1)],dim=1).to(device)  ◄──  which can be
    fake=generator(noise_and_labels)                either 0 or 1,
    img=(fake.cpu().detach()[0]/2+0.5).permute(1,2,0)  selects the label
    plt.imshow(img.numpy())                         to determine
    plt.xticks([])                                  whether the
    plt.yticks([])                                  generated image
plt.subplots_adjust(wspace=-0.08,hspace=-0.01)      has eyeglasses in
plt.show()                                          it or not.
```

Combines the random noise vector with the label to select two characteristics

---

To generate four images to cover the four different cases, we need to use one of the noise vectors as the input: `z_female_g` or `z_male_g`. We also need to attach to the input a label, which can be either `labels_ng` or `labels_g`. To use one single program to cover all four cases, we iterate through four values of i, 0 to 3, and create two values, p and q, which are the integer quotient and the remainder of the value i divided by 2. Therefore, the values of p and q can be either 0 or 1. By setting the value of the random noise vector to `z_female_g*p+z_male_g*(1-p)`, we can select a random noise vector to generate either a male or female face. Similarly, by setting the value of the label to `labels_ng[0]*q+labels_g[0]*(1-q)`, we can select a label to determine whether the generated image has eyeglasses in it or not. Once we combine the random noise vector with the label and feed them to the trained model, we can select two characteristics simultaneously.

If you run the program in listing 5.12, you'll see four images as shown in figure 5.9.

Figure 5.9 Selecting two characteristics simultaneously in the generated image. We select a noise vector from the following two choices: z_female_ng and z_male_ng. We also select a label from the following two choices: labels_ng and labels_g. We then feed the noise vector and the label to the trained generator to create an image. Based on the values of the noise vector and the label, the trained model can create four types of images. By doing this, we effectively select two independent characteristics in the generated image: a male or a female face and whether the image has eyeglasses in it or not.

The four generated images in figure 5.9 have two independent characteristics: a male or a female face and whether the image has eyeglasses in it or not. The first image shows an image of a male face with glasses; the second image is a male face without glasses. The third image is a female face with glasses, while the last image shows a female face without glasses.

> ## Exercise 5.3
> We used the two random noise vectors z_female_g and z_male_g in listing 5.12. Change the two random noise vectors to z_female_ng and z_male_ng instead and rerun the program to see what the images look like.

Finally, we can conduct label arithmetic and vector arithmetic simultaneously. That is, we can feed an interpolated noise vector and an interpolated label to the trained cGAN model and see what the generated image looks like. You can achieve that by running the following code block:

```
plt.figure(figsize=(20,20),dpi=50)
for i in range(36):
    ax = plt.subplot(6,6, i + 1)
    p=i//6
    q=i%6
    z=z_female_ng*p/5+z_male_ng*(1-p/5)
    label=labels_ng[0]*q/5+labels_g[0]*(1-q/5)
    noise_and_labels=torch.cat(
        [z.reshape(1, z_dim, 1, 1),
         label.reshape(1, 2, 1, 1)],dim=1).to(device)
    fake=generator(noise_and_labels)
    img=(fake.cpu().detach()[0]/2+0.5).permute(1,2,0)
    plt.imshow(img.numpy())
    plt.xticks([])
    plt.yticks([])
```

```
plt.subplots_adjust(wspace=-0.08,hspace=-0.01)
plt.show()
```

The code is similar to that in listing 5.12, except that p and q each can take six different values: 0, 1, 2, 3, 4, and 5. The random noise vector, `z_female_ng*p/5+z_male_ng*(1-p/5)`, takes six different values based on the value of p. The label, `labels_ng[0]*q/5+labels_g[0]*(1-q/5)`, takes six different values based on the value of q. We therefore have 36 different combinations of images based on the interpolated noise vector and the interpolated label. If you run the previous program, you'll see 36 images as shown in figure 5.10.

Figure 5.10 Conducting vector arithmetic and label arithmetic simultaneously. The value of i changes from 0 to 35; p and q are the integer quotient and remainder, respectively, when i is divided by 6. Therefore, p and q each can take six different values: 0, 1, 2, 3, 4, and 5. The interpolated noise vector, `z_female_ng*p/5+z_male_ng*(1-p/5)`, and the interpolated label, `labels_ng[0]*q/5+labels_g[0]*(1-q/5)`, can each take six different values. In each row, when you go from left to right, the eyeglasses gradually fade away. In each column, when you go from top to bottom, the image changes gradually from a male face to a female face.

The are 36 images in figure 5.10. The interpolated noise vector is a weighted average of the two random noise vectors, `z_female_ng` and `z_male_ng`, which generate a female face and a male face, respectively. The label is a weighted average of the two labels, `labels_ng` and `labels_g`, which determine whether the generated image has eyeglasses in it or not. The trained model generates 36 different images based on the interpolated noise vector and the interpolated label. In each row, when you go from the left to the right, the eyeglasses gradually fade away. That is, we conduct label arithmetic in each row. In each column, when you go from the top to the bottom, the image changes gradually from a male face to a female face. That is, we conduct vector arithmetic in each column.

Exercise 5.4

In this project, there are two values in the label: one indicates eyeglasses and one indicates no eyeglasses. Therefore, we can use a binary value instead of one-hot variables as labels. Change the programs in this chapter and use values 1 and 0 (instead of [1, 0] and [0, 1]) to represent images with and without glasses. Attach 1 or 0 to the random noise vector so that you feed a 101-value vector to the generator. Attach one channel to the input image before you feed it to the critic: if an image has eyeglasses in it, the fourth channel is filled with 0s; if the image has no eyeglasses in it, the fourth channel is filled with 1s. Then create a generator and a critic; use the training dataset to train them. The solution is provided in the book's GitHub repository, along with solutions to the other three exercises in this chapter.

Now that you have witnessed what GAN models are capable of, you'll explore deeper in the next chapter by conducting style transfers with GANs. For example, you'll learn how to build a CycleGAN model and train it using celebrity face images so that you can convert blond hair to black hair or black hair to blond hair in these images. The exact same model can be trained on other datasets: for example, you can train it on the human face dataset you used in this chapter so that you can add or remove eyeglasses in human face images.

Summary

- By selecting a certain noise vector in the latent space and feeding it to the trained GAN model, we can select a certain characteristic in the generated image, such as whether the image has a male or female face in it.
- A cGAN is different from a traditional GAN. We train the model on labeled data and ask the trained model to generate data with a specific attribute. For example, one label tells the model to generate images of human faces with eyeglasses while another tells the model to create human faces without eyeglasses.
- After a cGAN is trained, we can use a series of weighted averages of the labels to generate images that transition from an image represented by one label to an image represented by another label—for example, a series of images in which

the eyeglasses gradually fade away on the same person's face. We call this label arithmetic.

- We can also use a series of weighted averages of two different noise vectors to create images that transition from one attribute to another—for example, a series of images in which the male features gradually fade away, and female features gradually appear. We call this vector arithmetic.

- Wasserstein GAN (WGAN) is a technique used to improve the training stability and performance of GAN models by using Wasserstein distance instead of the binary cross-entropy as the loss function. Further, for the Wasserstein distance to work correctly, the critic in WGANs must be 1-Lipschitz continuous, meaning the gradient norms of the critic's function must be at most 1 everywhere. The gradient penalty in WGANs adds a regularization term to the loss function to enforce the Lipschitz constraint more effectively.

CycleGAN: Converting blond hair to black hair

6

This chapter covers

- The idea behind CycleGAN and cycle consistency loss
- Building a CycleGAN model to translate images from one domain to another
- Training a CycleGAN by using any dataset with two domains of images
- Converting black hair to blond hair and vice versa

The generative adversarial networks (GAN) models we have discussed in the last three chapters are all trying to produce images that are indistinguishable from those in the training set.

You may be wondering: Can we translate images from one domain to another, such as transforming horses into zebras, converting black hair to blond hair or blond hair to black, adding or removing eyeglasses in images, turning photographs into paintings, or converting winter scenes to summer scenes? It turns out you can, and you'll acquire such skills in this chapter through CycleGAN!

CycleGAN was introduced in 2017.[1] The key innovation of CycleGAN is its ability to learn to translate between domains without paired examples. CycleGAN has a variety of interesting and useful applications, such as simulating the aging or rejuvenation process on faces to assist digital identity verification or visualizing clothing in different colors or patterns without physically creating each variant to streamline the design process.

CycleGAN uses a cycle consistency loss function to ensure the original image can be reconstructed from the transformed image, encouraging the preservation of key features. The idea behind cycle consistency loss is truly ingenious and deserves to be highlighted here. The CycleGAN in this chapter has two generators: let's call them the black hair generator and the blond hair generator, respectively. The black hair generator takes in an image with blond hair (instead of a random noise vector as you have seen before) and converts it to one with black hair, while the blond hair generator takes in an image with black hair and converts it to one with blond hair.

To train the model, we'll give a real image with black hair to the blond hair generator to produce a fake image with blond hair. We'll then give the fake blond hair image to the black hair generator to convert it back to an image with black hair. If both generators work well, there is little difference between the original image with black hair and the fake one after a round-trip conversion. To train the CycleGAN, we adjust the model parameters to minimize the sum of adversarial losses and cycle consistency losses. As in chapters 3 and 4, adversarial losses are used to quantify how well the generator can fool the discriminator and how well the discriminator can differentiate between real and fake samples. Cycle consistency loss, a unique concept in CycleGANs, measures the difference between the original image and the fake image after a round-trip conversion. The inclusion of the cycle consistency loss in the total loss function is the key innovation in CycleGANs.

We'll use black and blond hair images as examples of two domains when training CycleGAN. However, the model can be applied to any two domains of images. To drive home the message, I'll ask you to train the same CycleGAN model by using images with and without eyeglasses that you used in chapter 5. The solution is provided in the book's GitHub repository (https://github.com/markhliu/DGAI), and you'll see that the trained model can indeed add or remove eyeglasses from human face images.

6.1 CycleGAN and cycle consistency loss

CycleGAN extends the basic GAN architecture to include two generators and two discriminators. Each generator-discriminator pair is responsible for learning the mapping between two distinct domains. It aims to translate images from one domain to another (e.g., horses to zebras, summer to winter scenes, and so on) while retaining the key characteristics of the original images. It uses a cycle consistency loss that ensures the original image can be reconstructed from the transformed image, encouraging the preservation of key features.

---

[1] Jun-Yan Zhu, Taesung Park, Phillip Isola, and Alexie Efros, 2017, "Unpaired Image-to-Image Translation Using Cycle Consistent Adversarial Networks." https://arxiv.org/abs/1703.10593.

In this section, we'll first discuss the architecture of CycleGAN. We'll emphasize the key innovation of CycleGANs: cycle consistency loss.

6.1.1 What is CycleGAN?

CycleGAN consists of two generators and two discriminators. The generators translate images from one domain to another, while the discriminators determine the authenticity of the images in their respective domains. These networks are capable of transforming photographs into artworks mimicking the style of famous painters or specific art movements, thereby bridging the gap between art and technology. They can also be used in healthcare for tasks like converting MRI images to CT scans or vice versa, which can be helpful in situations where one type of imaging is unavailable or too costly.

For our project in this chapter, we'll convert between images with black hair and blond hair. We therefore use them as an example when explaining how CycleGAN works. Figure 6.1 is a diagram of the CycleGAN architecture.

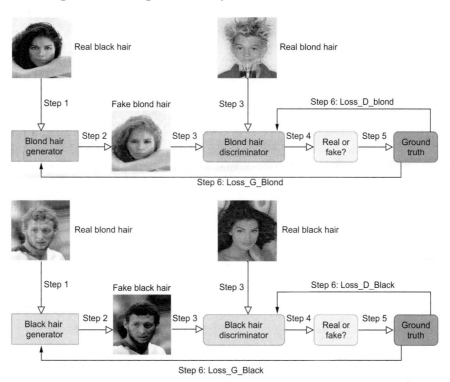

Figure 6.1 The architecture of a CycleGAN to convert images with black hair to ones with blond hair and to convert images with blond hair to ones with black hair. The diagram also outlines the training steps to minimize adversarial losses. How the model minimizes cycle consistency losses is explained in figure 6.2.

To train CycleGAN, we use unpaired datasets from the two domains we wish to translate between. We'll use 48,472 celebrity face images with black hair and 29,980 images with blond hair. We adjust the model parameters to minimize the sum of adversarial losses and cycle consistency losses. For ease of explanation, we'll explain only adversarial losses in figure 6.1. I'll explain how the model minimizes cycle consistency losses in the next subsection.

In each iteration of training, we feed real black hair images (top left in figure 6.1) to the blond hair generator to obtain fake blond hair images. We then feed the fake blond hair images, along with real blond hair images, to the blond hair discriminator (top middle). The blond hair discriminator produces a probability that each one is a real blond hair image. We then compare the predictions with the ground truth (whether an image is a true image with blond hair) and calculate the loss to the discriminator (`Loss_D_Blond`) as well as the loss to the generator (`Loss_G_Blond`).

At the same time, in each iteration of training, we feed real blond hair images (middle left) to the black hair generator (bottom left) to create fake black hair images. We present the fake black hair images, along with real ones, to the black hair discriminator (middle bottom) to obtain predictions that they are real. We compare the predictions from the black hair discriminator with the ground truth and calculate the loss to the discriminator (`Loss_D_Black`) and the loss to the generator (`Loss_G_Black`). We train the generators and discriminators simultaneously. To train the two discriminators, we adjust the model parameters to minimize the discriminator loss, which is the sum of `Loss_D_Black` and `Loss_D_Blond`.

6.1.2   *Cycle consistency loss*

To train the two generators, we adjust the model parameters to minimize the sum of the adversarial loss and cycle consistency loss. The adversarial loss is the sum of `Loss_G_Black` and `Loss_G_Blond` that we discussed in the previous subsection. To explain cycle consistency loss, let's look at figure 6.2.

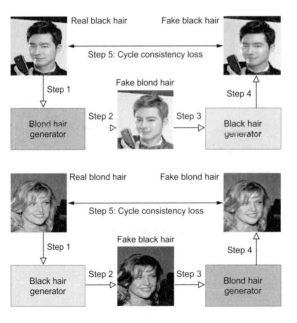

Figure 6.2   How CycleGAN minimizes cycle consistency losses between original black hair images and fake ones after round trips and cycle consistency losses between original blond hair images and fake ones after round trips

The loss function for the generators in CycleGAN consists of two parts. The first part, the adversarial loss, ensures that generated images are indistinguishable from real images in the target domain. For example, `Loss_G_Blond` (defined in the previous subsection) ensures that fake blond images produced by the blond hair generator resemble real images with blond hair in the training set. The second part, the cycle consistency loss, ensures that an image translated from one domain to another can be translated back to the original domain.

The cycle consistency loss is a crucial component of CycleGANs, ensuring that the original input image can be recovered after a round-trip translation. The idea is that if you translate a real black hair image (top left in figure 6.2) to a fake blond hair image and convert it back to a fake black hair image (top right), you should end up with an image close to the original black hair image. The cycle consistency loss for black hair images is the mean absolute error, at the pixel level, between the fake image and the original real one. Let's call this loss `Loss_Cycle_Black`. The same applies to translating blond hair to black hair and then back to blond hair, and we call this loss `Loss_Cycle_Blond`. The total cycle consistency loss is the sum of `Loss_Cycle_Black` and `Loss_Cycle_Blond`.

6.2 The celebrity faces dataset

We'll use celebrity face images with black hair and blond hair as the two domains. You'll first download the data in this section. You'll then process the images to get them ready for training later in this chapter.

You'll use two new Python libraries in this chapter: `pandas` and `albumentations`. To install these libraries, execute the following line of code in a new cell in your Jupyter Notebook application on your computer:

```
!pip install pandas albumentations
```

Follow the on-screen instructions to finish the installation.

6.2.1 Downloading the celebrity faces dataset

To download the celebrity faces dataset, log into Kaggle and go to the link https://mng.bz/Ompo. Unzip the dataset after downloading and place all image files inside the folder /files/img_align_celeba/img_align_celeba/ on your computer (note there is a subfolder with the same name in the folder itself). There are about 200,000 images in the folder. Also download the file `list_attr_celeba.csv` from Kaggle and place it in the /files/ folder on your computer. The CSV file specifies various attributes of each image.

The celebrity faces dataset contains images with many different hair colors: brown, gray, black, blond, and so on. We'll select images with black or blond hair as our training set because these two types are the most abundant in the celebrity faces dataset. Run the code in the following listing to select all images with black or blond hair.

Listing 6.1   Selecting images with black or blond hair

```
import pandas as pd
import os, shutil

df=pd.read_csv("files/list_attr_celeba.csv")
os.makedirs("files/black", exist_ok=True)
os.makedirs("files/blond", exist_ok=True)
folder="files/img_align_celeba/img_align_celeba"
for i in range(len(df)):
    dfi=df.iloc[i]
    if dfi['Black_Hair']==1:
        try:
            oldpath=f"{folder}/{dfi['image_id']}"
            newpath=f"files/black/{dfi['image_id']}"
            shutil.move(oldpath, newpath)
        except:
            pass
    elif dfi['Blond_Hair']==1:
        try:
            oldpath=f"{folder}/{dfi['image_id']}"
            newpath=f"files/blond/{dfi['image_id']}"
            shutil.move(oldpath, newpath)
        except:
            pass
```

Loads the CSV file that contains image attributes

Creates two folders to store images with black and blond hair

If the attribute Black_Hair is 1, moves the image to the black folder.

If the attribute Blond_Hair is 1, moves the image to the blond folder.

We first use the pandas library to load the file list_attr_celeba.csv so that we know whether each image has black or blond hair in it. We then create two folders locally, /files/black/ and /files/blond/, to store images with black and blond hair, respectively. Listing 6.1 then iterates through all images in the dataset. If an image's attribute Black_Hair is 1, we move it to the folder /files/black/; if an image's attribute Blond_Hair is 1, we move it to the folder /files/blond/. You'll see 48,472 images with black hair and 29,980 images with blond hair. Figure 6.3 shows some examples of the images.

Figure 6.3   Sample images of celebrity faces with black or blond hair

Images in the top row of figure 6.3 have black hair while images in the bottom row have blond hair. Further, the image quality is high: all faces are front and center, and hair colors are easy to identify. The quantity and quality of the training data will help the training of the CycleGAN model.

6.2.2 *Process the black and blond hair image data*

We'll generalize the CycleGAN model so that it can be trained on any dataset with two domains of images. We'll also define a `LoadData()` class to process the training dataset for the CycleGAN model. The function can be applied to any dataset with two domains, whether human face images with different hair colors, images with or without eyeglasses, or images with summer and winter scenes.

To that end, we have created a local module `ch06util`. Download the files `ch06util.py` and `__init__.py` from the book's GitHub repository (https://github .com/markhliu/DGAI) and place them in the folder /utils/ on your computer. In the local module, we have defined the following `LoadData()` class.

Listing 6.2 The `LoadData()` class to process the training data in CycleGAN

```
class LoadData(Dataset):
    def __init__(self, root_A, root_B, transform=None):       ◄──  The two folders
        super().__init__()                                          root_A and root_B
        self.root_A = root_A                                        are where the
        self.root_B = root_B                                        images in the two
        self.transform = transform                                  domains are stored
        self.A_images = []
        for r in root_A:
            files=os.listdir(r)
            self.A_images += [r+i for i in files]
        self.B_images = []                                     ◄──  Loads all images
        for r in root_B:                                            in each domain
            files=os.listdir(r)
            self.B_images += [r+i for i in files]
        self.len_data = max(len(self.A_images),
                            len(self.B_images))
        self.A_len = len(self.A_images)
        self.B_len = len(self.B_images)
    def __len__(self):                                         ◄──  Defines a method to
        return self.len_data                                        count the length of
                                                                    the dataset
    def __getitem__(self, index):                              ◄──  Defines a method to
        A_img = self.A_images[index % self.A_len]                   access individual
        B_img = self.B_images[index % self.B_len]                   elements in each
        A_img = np.array(Image.open(A_img).convert("RGB"))          domain
        B_img = np.array(Image.open(B_img).convert("RGB"))
        if self.transform:
            augmentations = self.transform(image=B_img,
                                           image0=A_img)
            B_img = augmentations["image"]
            A_img = augmentations["image0"]
        return A_img, B_img
```

The `LoadData()` class is inherited from the `Dataset` class in PyTorch. The two lists `root_A` and `root_B` contain folders of images in domains A and B, respectively. The class loads up images in the two domains and produces a pair of images, one from domain A and one from domain B so that we can use the pair to train the CycleGAN model later.

As we did in previous chapters, we create a data iterator with batches to improve computational efficiency, memory usage, and optimization dynamics in the training process.

Listing 6.3   Processing the black and blond hair images for training

```
transforms = albumentations.Compose(
    [albumentations.Resize(width=256, height=256),        ◄──  Resizes the images to
        albumentations.HorizontalFlip(p=0.5),                  256 by 256 pixels
        albumentations.Normalize(mean=[0.5, 0.5, 0.5],
        std=[0.5, 0.5, 0.5],max_pixel_value=255),         ◄──  Normalizes the images
        ToTensorV2()],                                          to the range of -1 to 1
    additional_targets={"image0": "image"})
dataset = LoadData(root_A=["files/black/"],
    root_B=["files/blond/"],                              ◄──  Applies the LoadData()
    transform=transforms)                                      class on the images
loader=DataLoader(dataset,batch_size=1,
    shuffle=True, pin_memory=True)                        ◄──  Creates a data iterator
                                                               for training
```

We first define an instance of the `Compose()` class in the `albumentations` library (which is famous for fast and flexible image augmentations) and call it `transforms`. The class transforms the images in several ways: it resizes images to 256 by 256 pixels and normalizes the values to the range –1 to 1. The `HorizontalFlip()` argument in listing 6.3 creates a mirror image of the original image in the training set. Horizontal flipping is a simple yet powerful augmentation technique that enhances the diversity of training data, helping models generalize better and become more robust. The augmentations and increase in size boost the performance of the CycleGAN model and make the generated images realistic.

We then apply the `LoadData()` class to the black and blond hair images. We set the batch size to 1 since the images have a large file size, and we use a pair of images to train the model in each iteration. Setting the batch size to more than 1 may result in your machine running out of memory.

6.3   *Building a CycleGAN model*

We'll build a CycleGAN model from scratch in this section. We'll take great care to make our CycleGAN model general so that it can be trained using any dataset with two domains of images. As a result, we'll use A and B to denote the two domains instead of, for example, black and blond hair images. As an exercise, you'll train the same Cycle-GAN model by using the eyeglasses dataset that you used in chapter 5. This helps you apply the skills you learned in this chapter to other real-world applications by using a different dataset.

6.3.1 Creating two discriminators

Even though CycleGAN has two discriminators, they are identical ex ante. Therefore, we'll create one single `Discriminator()` class and then instantiate the class twice: one instance is discriminator A and the other discriminator B. The two domains in Cycle-GAN are symmetric, and it doesn't matter which domain we call domain A: images with black hair or images with blond hair.

Open the file `ch06util.py` you just downloaded. In it, I have defined the `Discriminator()` class.

Listing 6.4 Defining the `Discriminator()` class in CycleGAN

```
class Discriminator(nn.Module):
    def __init__(self, in_channels=3, features=[64,128,256,512]):
        super().__init__()
        self.initial = nn.Sequential(
            nn.Conv2d(in_channels,features[0],
                kernel_size=4,stride=2,padding=1,
                padding_mode="reflect"),
            nn.LeakyReLU(0.2, inplace=True))
        layers = []
        in_channels = features[0]
        for feature in features[1:]:
            layers.append(Block(in_channels, feature,
                stride=1 if feature == features[-1] else 2))
            in_channels = feature
        layers.append(nn.Conv2d(in_channels,1,kernel_size=4,
                stride=1,padding=1,padding_mode="reflect"))
        self.model = nn.Sequential(*layers)
    def forward(self, x):
        out = self.model(self.initial(x))
        return torch.sigmoid(out)
```

The first Conv2d layer has 3 input channels and 64 output channels.

Three more Conv2d layers with 126, 256, and 512 output channels, respectively

The last Conv2d layer has 512 input channels and 1 output channel.

Applies the sigmoid activation function on the output so it can be interpreted as a probability

---

The previous code listing defines the discriminator network. The architecture is similar to the discriminator network in chapter 4 and the critic network in chapter 5. The main components are five `Conv2d` layers. We apply the sigmoid activation function on the last layer because the discriminator performs a binary classification problem. The discriminator takes a three-channel color image as input and produces a single number between 0 and 1, which can be interpreted as the probability that the input image is a real image in the domain.

The `padding_mode="reflect"` argument we used in listing 6.4 means the padding added to the input tensor is a reflection of the input tensor itself. Reflect padding helps in preserving the edge information by not introducing artificial zero values at the borders. It creates smoother transitions at the boundaries of the input tensor, which is beneficial for differentiating images in different domains in our setting.

We then create two instances of the class and call them `disc_A` and `disc_B`, respectively:

```
from utils.ch06util import Discriminator, weights_init
import torch

device = "cuda" if torch.cuda.is_available() else "cpu"
disc_A = Discriminator().to(device)
disc_B = Discriminator().to(device)
weights_init(disc_A)
weights_init(disc_B)
```

◄─── **Imports the Discriminator class from the local module**

◄─── **Creates two instances of the Discriminator class**

◄─── **Initializes weights**

In the local module `ch06util`, we also defined a `weights_init()` function to initialize model weights. The function is defined similarly to the one in chapter 5. We then initialize weights in the two newly created discriminators, `disc_A` and `disc_B`.

Now that we have two discriminators, we'll create two generators next.

6.3.2   Creating two generators

Similarly, we define a single `Generator()` class in the local module and instantiate the class twice: one instance is generator A, and the other is generator B. In the file `ch06util.py` you just downloaded, we have defined the `Generator()` class.

Listing 6.5   The `Generator()` class in CycleGAN

```
class Generator(nn.Module):
    def __init__(self, img_channels, num_features=64,
                 num_residuals=9):
        super().__init__()
        self.initial = nn.Sequential(
            nn.Conv2d(img_channels,num_features,kernel_size=7,
                stride=1,padding=3,padding_mode="reflect",),
            nn.InstanceNorm2d(num_features),
            nn.ReLU(inplace=True))
        self.down_blocks = nn.ModuleList(
            [ConvBlock(num_features,num_features*2,kernel_size=3,
                    stride=2, padding=1),
            ConvBlock(num_features*2,num_features*4,kernel_size=3,
                stride=2,padding=1)])
        self.res_blocks = nn.Sequential(
            *[ResidualBlock(num_features * 4)
            for _ in range(num_residuals)])
        self.up_blocks = nn.ModuleList(
            [ConvBlock(num_features * 4, num_features * 2,
                    down=False, kernel_size=3, stride=2,
                    padding=1, output_padding=1),
                ConvBlock(num_features * 2, num_features * 1,
                    down=False,kernel_size=3, stride=2,
                    padding=1, output_padding=1)])
        self.last = nn.Conv2d(num_features * 1, img_channels,
            kernel_size=7, stride=1,
            padding=3, padding_mode="reflect")
```

◄─── **Three Conv2d layers**

◄─── **Nine residual blocks**

◄─── **Two upsampling blocks**

```python
def forward(self, x):
    x = self.initial(x)
    for layer in self.down_blocks:
        x = layer(x)
    x = self.res_blocks(x)
    for layer in self.up_blocks:
        x = layer(x)
    return torch.tanh(self.last(x))
```

Applies tanh activation on the output

The generator network consists of several `Conv2d` layers, followed by nine residual blocks (which I'll explain in detail later). After that, the network has two upsampling blocks that consist of a `ConvTranspose2d` layer, an `InstanceNorm2d` layer, and a `ReLU` activation. As we have done in previous chapters, we use the tanh activation function at the output layer, so the output pixels are all in the range of –1 to 1, the same as the images in the training set.

The residual block in the generator is defined in the local module as follows:

```python
class ConvBlock(nn.Module):
    def __init__(self, in_channels, out_channels,
                 down=True, use_act=True, **kwargs):
        super().__init__()
        self.conv = nn.Sequential(
            nn.Conv2d(in_channels, out_channels,
                      padding_mode="reflect", **kwargs)
            if down
            else nn.ConvTranspose2d(in_channels,
                                    out_channels, **kwargs),
            nn.InstanceNorm2d(out_channels),
            nn.ReLU(inplace=True) if use_act else nn.Identity())
    def forward(self, x):
        return self.conv(x)

class ResidualBlock(nn.Module):
    def __init__(self, channels):
        super().__init__()
        self.block = nn.Sequential(
            ConvBlock(channels,channels,kernel_size=3,padding=1),
            ConvBlock(channels,channels,
                      use_act=False, kernel_size=3, padding=1))
    def forward(self, x):
        return x + self.block(x)
```

A residual connection is a concept in deep learning, particularly in the design of deep neural networks. You'll see it quite often later in this book. It's a technique used to address the problem of vanishing gradients, which often occurs in very deep networks. In a residual block, which is the basic unit of a network with residual connections, the input is passed through a series of transformations (like convolution, activation, and batch or instance normalization) and then added back to the output of these transformations. Figure 6.4 provides a diagram of the architecture of the residual block defined previously.

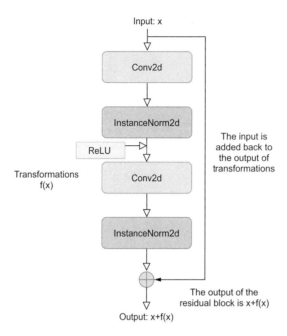

Figure 6.4   The architecture of a residual block. The input x is passed through a series of transformations (two sets of Conv2d layer and InstanceNorm2d layer and a ReLU activation). The input x is then added back to the output of these transformations, f(x). The output of the residual block is therefore x + f(x).

The transformations in each residual block are different. In this example, the input x is passed through two sets of `Conv2d` layer and `InstanceNorm2d` layer and a ReLU activation in between. The input x is then added back to the output of these transformations, f(x), to form the final output, x+f(x)—hence the name residual connection.

Next, we create two instances of the `Generator()` class and call one of them `gen_A` and the other `gen_B`:

```
from utils.ch06util import Generator

gen_A = Generator(img_channels=3, num_residuals=9).to(device)
gen_B = Generator(img_channels=3, num_residuals=9).to(device)
weights_init(gen_A)
weights_init(gen_B)
```

When training the model, we'll use the mean absolute error (i.e., L1 loss) to measure the cycle consistency loss. We'll use the mean squared error (i.e., L2 loss) to gauge the adversarial loss. L1 loss is often used if the data are noisy and have many outliers since it punishes extreme values less than the L2 loss. Therefore, we import the following loss functions:

```
import torch.nn as nn

l1 = nn.L1Loss()
mse = nn.MSELoss()
```

```
g_scaler = torch.cuda.amp.GradScaler()
d_scaler = torch.cuda.amp.GradScaler()
```

Both L1 and L2 losses are calculated at the pixel level. The original image has a shape of (3, 256, 256) and so is the fake image. To calculate the losses, we first calculate the difference (absolute value of this difference for L1 loss and the squared value of this difference for L2 loss) between the corresponding pixel values between two images at each of the $3 \times 256 \times 256 = 196608$ positions and average them over the positions.

We'll use PyTorch's automatic mixed precision package `torch.cuda.amp` to speed up training. The default data type in PyTorch tensors is `float32`, a 32-bit floating-point number, which takes up twice as much memory as a 16-bit floating number, `float16`. Operations on the former are slower than those on the latter. There is a trade-off between precision and computational costs. Which data type to use depends on the task at hand. `torch.cuda.amp` provides an automatic mixed precision, where some operations use `float32` and others `float16`. Mixed precision tries to match each operation to its appropriate data type to speed up training.

As we have done in chapter 4, we'll use the Adam optimizer for both the discriminators and the generators:

```
lr = 0.00001
opt_disc = torch.optim.Adam(list(disc_A.parameters()) +
  list(disc_B.parameters()),lr=lr,betas=(0.5, 0.999))
opt_gen = torch.optim.Adam(list(gen_A.parameters()) +
  list(gen_B.parameters()),lr=lr,betas=(0.5, 0.999))
```

Next, we'll train the CycleGAN model by using images with black or blond hair.

6.4   *Using CycleGAN to translate between black and blond hair*

Now that we have the training data and the CycleGAN model, we'll train the model by using images with black or blond hair. As with all GAN models, we'll discard the discriminators after training. We'll use the two trained generators to convert black hair images to blond hair ones and convert blond hair images to black hair ones.

6.4.1   *Training a CycleGAN to translate between black and blond hair*

As we explained in chapter 4, we'll use visual inspections to determine when to stop training. To that end, we create a function to test what the real images look like and what the corresponding generated images look like so that we can compare the two to visually inspect the effectiveness of the model. In the local module `ch06util`, we define a `test()` function:

```
def test(i,A,B,fake_A,fake_B):
    save_image(A*0.5+0.5,f"files/A{i}.png")
    save_image(B*0.5+0.5,f"files/B{i}.png")
    save_image(fake_A*0.5+0.5,f"files/fakeA{i}.png")
    save_image(fake_B*0.5+0.5,f"files/fakeB{i}.png")
```

Real images in domains A and B, saved in a local folder

The corresponding fake images in domains A and B, created by the generators in batch i

We save four images after every 100 batches of training. We save real images and the corresponding fake images in the two domains in the local folder so we can periodically check the generated images and compare them with the real ones to assess the progress of training. We made the function general so that it can be applied to images from any two domains.

Further, we define a `train_epoch()` function in the local module ch06util to train the discriminators and the generators for an epoch. The following listing highlights the code we use to train the two discriminators.

Listing 6.6   Training the two discriminators in CycleGAN

```
def train_epoch(disc_A, disc_B, gen_A, gen_B, loader, opt_disc,
        opt_gen, l1, mse, d_scaler, g_scaler,device):
    loop = tqdm(loader, leave=True)
    for i, (A,B) in enumerate(loop):                    ◄──┐ Iterates through all pairs of
        A=A.to(device)                                      │ images in the two domains
        B=B.to(device)
        with torch.cuda.amp.autocast():                 ◄──┐ Uses PyTorch automatic
            fake_A = gen_A(B)                               │ mixed precision package to
            D_A_real = disc_A(A)                            │ speed up training
            D_A_fake = disc_A(fake_A.detach())
            D_A_real_loss = mse(D_A_real,
                            torch.ones_like(D_A_real))
            D_A_fake_loss = mse(D_A_fake,
                            torch.zeros_like(D_A_fake))
            D_A_loss = D_A_real_loss + D_A_fake_loss
            fake_B = gen_B(A)
            D_B_real = disc_B(B)
            D_B_fake = disc_B(fake_B.detach())
            D_B_real_loss = mse(D_B_real,
                            torch.ones_like(D_B_real))
            D_B_fake_loss = mse(D_B_fake,
                            torch.zeros_like(D_B_fake))
            D_B_loss = D_B_real_loss + D_B_fake_loss
            D_loss = (D_A_loss + D_B_loss) / 2          ◄──┐ The total loss for the two
        opt_disc.zero_grad()                                │ discriminators is the simple
        d_scaler.scale(D_loss).backward()                   │ average of the adversarial
        d_scaler.step(opt_disc)                             │ losses to the two
        d_scaler.update()                                   │ discriminators.
        ...
```

We use the `detach()` method here to remove gradients in tensors `fake_A` and `fake_B` to reduce memory and speed up computations. The training for the two discriminators is similar to what we have done in chapter 4, with a couple of differences. First, instead of having just one discriminator, we have two discriminators here: one for images in domain A and one for images in domain B. The total loss for the two discriminators is the simple average of the adversarial losses of the two discriminators. Second, we use the PyTorch automatic mixed precision package to speed up training, reducing the training time by more than 50%.

We simultaneously train the two generators in the same iteration. The following listing highlights the code we use to train the two generators.

Listing 6.7 Training the two generators in CycleGAN

```
def train_epoch(disc_A, disc_B, gen_A, gen_B, loader, opt_disc,
        opt_gen, l1, mse, d_scaler, g_scaler,device):
        ...
        with torch.cuda.amp.autocast():
            D_A_fake = disc_A(fake_A)
            D_B_fake = disc_B(fake_B)
            loss_G_A = mse(D_A_fake, torch.ones_like(D_A_fake))
            loss_G_B = mse(D_B_fake, torch.ones_like(D_B_fake))
            cycle_B = gen_B(fake_A)
            cycle_A = gen_A(fake_B)
            cycle_B_loss = l1(B, cycle_B)
            cycle_A_loss = l1(A, cycle_A)
            G_loss=loss_G_A+loss_G_B+cycle_A_loss*10+cycle_B_loss*10
        opt_gen.zero_grad()
        g_scaler.scale(G_loss).backward()
        g_scaler.step(opt_gen)
        g_scaler.update()
        if i % 100 == 0:
            test(i,A,B,fake_A,fake_B)
        loop.set_postfix(D_loss=D_loss.item(),G_loss=G_loss.item())
```

Adversarial losses to the two generators → `loss_G_B = mse(D_B_fake, torch.ones_like(D_B_fake))`

Cycle consistency losses for the two generators

The total loss for the two generators is the weighted sum of adversarial losses and cycle consistency losses. → `G_loss=loss_G_A+loss_G_B+cycle_A_loss*10+cycle_B_loss*10`

Generates images for visual inspection after every 100 batches of training

The training for the two generators is different from what we have done in chapter 4 in two important ways. First, instead of having just one generator, we train two generators simultaneously here. Second, the total loss for the two generators is the weighted sum of adversarial losses and cycle consistency losses, and we weigh the latter 10 times more than the former loss. However, if you change the value 10 to other numbers such as 9 or 12, you'll get similar results.

The cycle consistency loss is the mean absolute error between the original image and the fake image that's translated back to the original domain.

Now that we have everything ready, we'll start the training loop:

```
from utils.ch06util import train_epoch

for epoch in range(1):
    train_epoch(disc_A, disc_B, gen_A, gen_B, loader, opt_disc,
        opt_gen, l1, mse, d_scaler, g_scaler, device)
torch.save(gen_A.state_dict(), "files/gen_black.pth")
torch.save(gen_B.state_dict(), "files/gen_blond.pth")
```

Trains the CycleGAN for one epoch using the black and blond hair images

Saves the trained model weights

The preceding training takes a couple of hours if you use GPU training. It may take a whole day otherwise. If you don't have the computing resources to train the model, download the pretrained generators from my website: https://gattonweb.uky.edu/faculty/lium/ml/hair.zip. Unzip the file and place the files `gen_black.pth` and `gen_blond.pth` in the folder /files/ on your computer. You'll be able to convert between black hair images and blond hair ones in the next subsection.

> **Exercise 6.1**
>
> When training the CycleGAN model, we assume that domain A contains images with black hair and domain B contains images with blond hair. Modify the code in listing 6.2 so that domain A contains images with blond hair and domain B contains images with black hair.

6.4.2   *Round-trip conversions of black hair images and blond hair images*

Due to the high quality and the abundant quantity of the training dataset, we have trained the CycleGAN with great success. We'll not only convert between images with black hair and images with blond hair, but we'll also conduct round-trip conversions. For example, we'll convert images with black hair to images with blond hair and then convert them back to images with black hair. That way, we can compare the original images with the generated images in the same domain after a round trip and see the difference.

The following listing performs conversions of images between the two domains as well as round-trip conversions of images in each domain.

Listing 6.8   Round-trip conversions of images with black or blond hair

```
gen_A.load_state_dict(torch.load("files/gen_black.pth",
    map_location=device))
gen_B.load_state_dict(torch.load("files/gen_blond.pth",
    map_location=device))
i=1
for black,blond in loader:
    fake_blond=gen_B(black.to(device))
    save_image(black*0.5+0.5,f"files/black{i}.png")          Original image with
                                                             black hair
    save_image(fake_blond*0.5+0.5,f"files/fakeblond{i}.png")
    fake2black=gen_A(fake_blond)
    save_image(fake2black*0.5+0.5,                            A fake image with black
        f"files/fake2black{i}.png")                          hair after a round trip
    fake_black=gen_A(blond.to(device))
    save_image(blond*0.5+0.5,f"files/blond{i}.png")          Original image with
    save_image(fake_black*0.5+0.5,f"files/fakeblack{i}.png") blond hair
    fake2blond=gen_B(fake_black)
    save_image(fake2blond*0.5+0.5,
```

```
    f"files/fake2blond{i}.png")
i=i+1
if i>10:
    break
```

A fake image with blond
hair after a round trip

We have saved six sets of images in your local folder /files/. The first set is the original images with black hair. The second set is the fake blond images produced by the trained blond hair generator: the images are saved as `fakeblond0.png`, `fakeblond1.png`, and so on. The third set is the fake images with black hair after a round trip: we feed the fake images we just created to the trained black hair generator to obtain fake images with black hair. They are saved as `fake2black0.png`, `fake2black1.png`, and so on. Figure 6.5 shows the three sets of images.

Original images with black hair:

Fake images with blond hair:

Fake images translated to black hair:

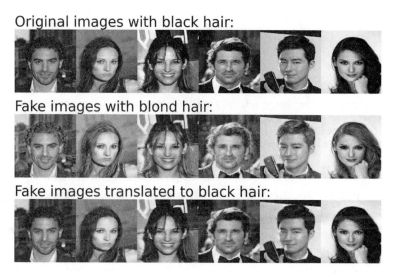

Figure 6.5   A round-trip conversion of images with black hair. Images in the top row are the original images with black hair from the training set. Images in the middle row are the corresponding fake images with blond hair, produced by the trained blond hair generator. Images in the bottom row are fake images with black hair after a round trip: we feed the images in the middle row to the trained black hair generator to create fake images with black hair.

There are three rows of images in figure 6.5. The top row displays original images with black hair from the training set. The middle row displays fake blond hair images produced by the trained blond hair. The bottom row contains fake black hair images after a round-trip conversion: the images look almost identical to the ones in the top row! Our trained CycleGAN model works extremely well.

The fourth set of images in the local folder /files/ are the original images with blond hair. The fifth set is the fake image produced by the trained black hair generator. Finally, the sixth set contains fake images with blond hair after a round trip. Figure 6.6 compares these three sets of images.

Original images with blond hair:

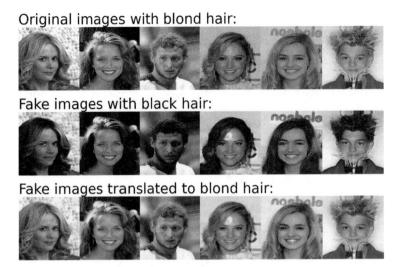

Fake images with black hair:

Fake images translated to blond hair:

Figure 6.6   A round-trip conversion of images with blond hair. Images in the top row are the original images with blond hair from the training set. Images in the middle row are the corresponding fake images with black hair, produced by the trained black hair generator. Images in the bottom row are fake images with blond hair after a round-trip conversion: we feed the images in the middle row to the trained blond hair generator to create fake images with blond hair.

In figure 6.6, fake black hair images produced by the trained black hair generator are shown in the middle row: they have black hair on the same human faces as the top row. Fake blond hair images after a round trip are shown in the bottom row: they look almost identical to the original blond hair images in the top row.

Exercise 6.2

The CycleGAN model is general and can be applied to any training dataset with two domains of images. Train the CycleGAN model using the eyeglasses images that you downloaded in chapter 5. Use images with glasses as domain A and images without glasses as domain B. Then use the trained CycleGAN to add and remove eyeglasses from images (i.e., translating images between the two domains). An example implementation and results are in the book's GitHub repository.

So far, we have focused on one type of generative model, GANs. In the next chapter, you'll learn to use another type of generative model, variational autoencoders (VAEs), to generate high-resolution images. You'll learn the advantages and disadvantages of VAEs compared to GANs. More importantly, you'll learn the encoder-decoder architecture in VAEs. The architecture is widely used in generative models, including Transformers, which we'll study later in the book.

Summary

- CycleGAN can translate images between two domains without paired examples. It consists of two discriminators and two generators. One generator converts images in domain A to domain B while the other generator converts images in domain B to domain A. The two discriminators classify if a given image is from a specific domain.

- CycleGAN uses a cycle consistency loss function to ensure the original image can be reconstructed from the transformed image, encouraging the preservation of key features.

- A properly constructed CycleGAN model can be applied to any dataset with images from two domains. The same model can be trained with different datasets and be used to translate images in different domains.

- When we have abundant high-quality training data, the trained CycleGAN can convert images in one domain to another and convert them back to the original domain. The images after a round-trip conversion can potentially look almost identical to the original images.

Image generation
with variational
autoencoders

This chapter covers

- Autoencoders vs. variational autoencoders
- Building and training an Autoencoder to reconstruct handwritten digits
- Building and training a variational autoencoder to generate human face images
- Performing encoding arithmetic and interpolation with a trained variational autoencoder

So far, you have learned how to generate shapes, numbers, and images, all by using generative adversarial networks (GANs). In this chapter, you'll learn to create images by using another generative model: variational autoencoders (VAEs). You'll also learn the practical uses of VAEs by performing encoding arithmetic and encoding interpolation.

To know how VAEs work, we first need to understand autoencoders (AEs). AEs have a dual-component structure: an encoder and a decoder. The encoder compresses the data into an abstract representation in a lower-dimensional space (the latent space), and the decoder decompresses the encoded information and reconstructs the data. The primary goal of an AE is to learn a compressed representation of the input data, focusing on minimizing the reconstruction error—the difference between the original input and its reconstruction (at the pixel level, as we have seen in chapter 6 when calculating cycle consistency loss). The encoder-decoder architecture is a cornerstone in various generative models, including Transformers, which you'll explore in detail in the latter half of this book. For example, in chapter 9, you'll build a Transformer for machine language translation: the encoder converts an English phrase into an abstract representation while the decoder constructs the French translation based on the compressed representation generated by the encoder. Text-to-image Transformers like DALL-E 2 and Imagen also utilize an AE architecture in their design. This involves first encoding an image into a compact, low-dimensional probability distribution. Then, they decode from this distribution. Of course, what constitutes an encoder and a decoder is different in different models.

Your first project in this chapter involves constructing and training an AE from scratch to generate handwritten digits. You'll use 60,000 grayscale images of handwritten digits (0 to 9), each with a size of $28 \times 28 = 784$ pixels, as the training data. The encoder in the AE compresses each image into a deterministic vector representation with only 20 values. The decoder in the AE reconstructs the image with the aim of minimizing the difference between the original image and the reconstructed image. This is achieved by minimizing the mean absolute error between the two images at the pixel level. The end result is an AE capable of generating handwritten digits almost identical to those in the training set.

While AEs are good at replicating the input data, they often falter in generating new samples that are not present in the training set. More importantly, AEs are not good at input interpolation: they often fail to generate intermediate representations between two input data points. This leads us to VAEs. VAEs differ from AEs in two critical ways. First, while an AE encodes each input into a specific point in the latent space, a VAE encodes it into a probability distribution within this space. Second, an AE focuses solely on minimizing the reconstruction error, whereas a VAE learns the parameters of the probability distribution for latent variables, minimizing a loss function that includes both reconstruction loss and a regularization term, the Kullback–Liebler (KL) divergence.

The KL-divergence encourages the latent space to approximate a certain distribution (a normal distribution in our example) and ensures that the latent variables don't just memorize the training data but rather capture the underlying distribution. It helps in achieving a well-structured latent space where similar data points are mapped closely together, making the space continuous and interpretable. As a result, we can manipulate the encodings to achieve new outcomes, which makes encoding arithmetic and input interpolation possible in VAEs.

In the second project in this chapter, you'll build and train a VAE from the ground up to generate human face images. Here, your training set comprises eyeglasses images that you downloaded in chapter 5. The VAE's encoder compresses an image of size $3 \times 256 \times 256 = 196,608$ pixels into a 100-value probabilistic vector, each following a normal distribution. The decoder then reconstructs the image based on this probabilistic vector. The trained VAE can not only replicate human faces from the training set but also generate novel ones.

You'll learn how to conduct encoding arithmetic and input interpolation in VAEs. You'll manipulate the encoded representations (latent vectors) of different inputs to achieve specific outcomes (i.e., with or without certain characteristics in images) when decoded. The latent vectors control different characteristics in the decoded images such as gender, whether there are eyeglasses in an image, and so on. For example, you can first obtain the latent vectors for men with glasses ($z1$), women with glasses ($z2$), and women without glasses ($z3$). You then calculate a new latent vector, $z4 = z1 - z2 + z3$. Since both $z1$ and $z2$ lead to eyeglasses in images when decoded, $z1 - z2$ cancels out the eyeglasses feature in the resulting image. Similarly, since both $z2$ and $z3$ lead to a female face, $z3 - z2$ cancels out the female feature in the resulting image. Therefore, if you decode $z4 = z1 - z2 + z3$ with the trained VAE, you'll get an image of a man without glasses.

You'll also create a series of images transitioning from a woman with glasses to a woman without glasses by varying the weight assigned to the latent vectors $z1$ and $z2$. These exercises exemplify the versatility and creative potential of VAEs in the field of generative models.

Compared to GANs, which we studied in the last few chapters, AEs and VAEs have a simple architecture and are easy to construct. Further, AEs and VAEs are generally easier and more stable to train relative to GANs. However, images generated by AEs and VAEs tend to be blurrier compared to those generated by GANs. GANs excel in generating high-quality, realistic images but suffer from training difficulties and resource intensiveness. The choice between GANs and VAEs largely depends on the specific requirements of the task at hand, including the desired quality of the output, computational resources available, and the importance of having a stable training process.

VAEs have a wide range of practical applications in the real world. Consider, for instance, that you run an eyewear store and have successfully marketed a new style of men's glasses online. Now, you wish to target the female market with the same style but lack images of women wearing these glasses, and you face high costs for a professional photo shoot. Here's where VAEs come into play: you can combine existing images of men wearing the glasses with pictures of both men and women without glasses. This way, you can create realistic images of women sporting the same eyewear style, as illustrated in figure 7.1, through encoding arithmetic, a technique you'll learn in this chapter.

woman without glasses - man without glasses + man with glasses = woman with glasses

Figure 7.1 Generating images of women with glasses by performing encoding arithmetic

In another scenario, suppose your store offers eyeglasses with dark and light frames, both of which are popular. You want to introduce a middle option with frames of an intermediate shade. With VAEs, through a method called encoding interpolation, you can effortlessly generate a smooth transition series of images, as shown in figure 7.2. These images would vary from dark to light-framed glasses, offering customers a visual spectrum of choices.

Figure 7.2   Generating a series of images that transition from glasses with dark frames to those with light frames

The use of VAEs is not limited to eyeglasses; it extends to virtually any product category, be it clothing, furniture, or food. The technology provides a creative and cost-effective solution for visualizing and marketing a wide range of products. Furthermore, although image generation is a prominent example, VAEs can be applied to many other types of data, including music and text. Their versatility opens up endless possibilities in terms of practical use!

7.1   An overview of AEs

This section discusses what an AE is and its basic structure. For you to have a deep understanding of the inner workings of AEs, you'll build and train an AE to generate handwritten digits as your first project in this chapter. This section provides an overview of an AE's architecture and a blueprint for completing the first project.

7.1.1   What is an AE?

AEs are a type of neural network used in unsupervised learning that are particularly effective for tasks like image generation, compression, and denoising. An AE consists of two main parts: an encoder and a decoder. The encoder compresses the input into a lower-dimensional representation (latent space), and the decoder reconstructs the input from this representation.

The compressed representation, or latent space, captures the most important features of the input data. In image generation, this space encodes crucial aspects of the images that the network has been trained on. AEs are useful for their efficiency in learning data representations and their ability to work with unlabeled data, making them suitable for tasks like dimensionality reduction and feature learning. One challenge with AEs is the risk of losing information in the encoding process, which can lead to less accurate reconstructions. Using deeper architectures with multiple hidden layers can help in learning more complex and abstract representations, potentially mitigating information loss in AEs. Also, training AEs to generate high-quality images can be computationally intensive and requires large datasets.

As we mentioned in chapter 1, the best way to learn something is to create it from scratch. To that end, you'll learn to create an AE to generate handwritten digits in the first project in this chapter. The next subsection provides a blueprint for how to do that.

7.1.2   *Steps in building and training an AE*

Imagine that you must build and train an AE from the ground up to generate grayscale images of handwritten digits so that you acquire the skills needed to use AEs for more complicated tasks such as color image generation or dimensionality reduction. How should you go about this task?

Figure 7.3 provides a diagram of the architecture of an AE and the steps involved in training an AE to generate handwritten digits.

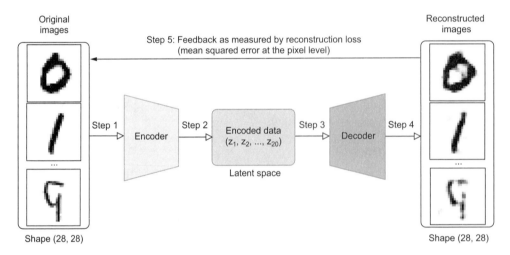

Figure 7.3   The architecture of an AE and the steps to train one to generate handwritten digits. An AE consists of an encoder (middle left) and a decoder (middle right). In each iteration of training, images of handwritten digits are fed to the encoder (step 1). The encoder compresses the images to deterministic points in the latent space (step 2). The decoder takes the encoded vectors (step 3) from the latent space and reconstructs the images (step 4). The AE adjusts its parameters to minimize the reconstruction loss, the difference between the originals and the reconstructions (step 5).

As you can see from the figure, the AE has two main parts: an encoder (middle left) that compresses images of handwritten digits into vectors in the latent space and a decoder (middle right) that reconstructs these images based on the encoded vectors. Both the encoder and decoder are deep neural networks that can potentially include different types of layers such as dense layers, convolutional layers, transposed convolutional layers, and so on. Since our example involves grayscale images of handwritten digits, we'll use only dense layers. However, AEs can also be used to generate higher-resolution color images; for those tasks, convolutional neural networks (CNNs) are usually included in encoders and decoders. Whether to use CNNs in AEs depends on the resolution of the images you want to generate.

When an AE is built, the parameters in it are randomly initialized. We need to obtain a training set to train the model: PyTorch provides 60,000 grayscale images of handwritten digits, evenly distributed among the 10 digits 0 to 9. The left side of figure 7.3 shows three examples, and they are images of digits 0, 1, and 9, respectively. In the first step in the training loop, we feed images in the training set to the encoder. The encoder compresses the images to 20-value vectors in the latent space (step 2). There is nothing magical about the number 20. If you use 25-value vectors in the latent space, you'll get similar results. We then feed the vector representations to the decoder (step 3) and ask it to reconstruct the images (step 4). We calculate the reconstruct loss, which is the mean squared error, over all the pixels, between the original image and the reconstructed image. We then propagate this loss back through the network to update the parameters in the encoder and decoder to minimize the reconstruction loss (step 5) so that in the next iteration, the AE can reconstruct images closer to the original ones. This process is repeated for many epochs over the dataset.

After the model is trained, you'll feed unseen images of handwritten digits to the encoder and obtain encodings. You then feed the encodings to the decoder to obtain reconstructed images. You'll notice that the reconstructed images look almost identical to the originals. The right side of figure 7.3 shows three examples of reconstructed images: they do look similar to the corresponding originals on the left side of the figure.

7.2   Building and training an AE to generate digits

Now that you have a blueprint to build and train an AE to generate handwritten digits, let's dive into the project and implement the steps outlined in the last section.

Specifically, in this section, you'll learn first how to obtain a training set and a test set of images of handwritten digits. You'll then build an encoder and decoder with dense layers. You'll train the AE with the training dataset and use the trained encoder to encode images in the test set. Finally, you'll learn to use the trained decoder to reconstruct images and compare them to the originals.

7.2.1   Gathering handwritten digits

You can download grayscale images of handwritten images using the *datasets* package in the Torchvision library, similar to how you downloaded images of clothing items in chapter 2.

First, let's download a training set and a test set:

```
import torchvision
import torchvision.transforms as T

transform=T.Compose([
    T.ToTensor()])
train_set=torchvision.datasets.MNIST(root=".",
```

Downloads handwritten digits by using the MNIST() class in torchvision.datasets

```
        train=True,download=True,transform=transform)
test_set=torchvision.datasets.MNIST(root=".",
        train=False,download=True,transform=transform)
```

The train=True argument means you download the training set.

The train=False argument means you download the test set.

Instead of using the `FashionMNIST()` class as we did in chapter 2, we use the `MNIST()` class here. The `train` argument in the class tells PyTorch whether to download the training set (when the argument is set to `True`) or the test set (when the argument is set to `False`). Before transformation, the image pixels are integers ranging from 0 to 255. The `ToTensor()` class in the preceding code block converts them to PyTorch float tensors with values between 0 to 1. There are 60,000 images in the training set and 10,000 in the test set, evenly distributed among 10 digits, 0 to 9, in each set.

We'll create batches of data for training and testing, with 32 images in each batch:

```
import torch

batch_size=32
train_loader=torch.utils.data.DataLoader(
    train_set,batch_size=batch_size,shuffle=True)
test_loader=torch.utils.data.DataLoader(
    test_set,batch_size=batch_size,shuffle=True)
```

Now that we have the data ready, we'll build and train an AE next.

7.2.2 Building and training an AE

An AE consists of two parts: the encoder and the decoder. We'll define an `AE()` class, as shown in the following listing, to represent the AE.

Listing 7.1 Creating an AE to generate handwritten digits

```
import torch.nn.functional as F
from torch import nn

device="cuda" if torch.cuda.is_available() else "cpu"
input_dim = 784
z_dim = 20
h_dim = 200
class AE(nn.Module):
    def __init__(self,input_dim,z_dim,h_dim):
        super().__init__()
        self.common = nn.Linear(input_dim, h_dim)
        self.encoded = nn.Linear(h_dim, z_dim)
        self.l1 = nn.Linear(z_dim, h_dim)
        self.decode = nn.Linear(h_dim, input_dim)
    def encoder(self, x):
        common = F.relu(self.common(x))
        mu = self.encoded(common)
        return mu
    def decoder(self, z):
```

The input to the AE has 28 × 28 = 784 values in it.

The latent variable (encoding) has 20 values in it.

The encoder compresses images to latent variables.

The decoder reconstructs the images based on encodings.

```
        out=F.relu(self.l1(z))
        out=torch.sigmoid(self.decode(out))
        return out
    def forward(self, x):                          ◄─────┐  The encoder and
        mu=self.encoder(x)                               │  decoder form the AE.
        out=self.decoder(mu)
        return out, mu
```

The input size is 784 because the grayscale images of handwritten digits have a size of 28 by 28 pixels. We flatten the images to 1D tensors and feed them to the AE. The images first go through the encoder: they are compressed into encodings in a lower dimensional space. Each image is now represented by a 20-value latent variable. The decoder reconstructs the images based on the latent variables. The output from the AE has two tensors: `out`, the reconstructed images, and `mu`, latent variables (i.e., encodings).

Next, we instantiate the `AE()` class we defined earlier to create an AE. We also use the Adam optimizer during training, as we did in previous chapters:

```
model = AE(input_dim,z_dim,h_dim).to(device)
lr=0.00025
optimizer = torch.optim.Adam(model.parameters(), lr=lr)
```

We define a function `plot_digits()` to visually inspect the reconstructed handwritten digits after each epoch of training, as shown in the following listing.

Listing 7.2 The `plot_digits()` function to inspect reconstructed images

```
import matplotlib.pyplot as plt

originals = []                                      ◄─────┐  Collects a sample image of
idx = 0                                                   │  each digit in the test set
for img,label in test_set:
    if label == idx:
        originals.append(img)
        idx += 1
    if idx == 10:
        break
def plot_digits():                                        Feeds the image to the AE
    reconstructed=[]                                      to obtain a reconstructed
    for idx in range(10):                                 image
        with torch.no_grad():
            img = originals[idx].reshape((1,input_dim))
            out,mu = model(img.to(device))        ◄──────┘
        reconstructed.append(out)                 ◄─────┐  Collects the reconstructed
    imgs=originals+reconstructed                        │  image of each original
    plt.figure(figsize=(10,2),dpi=50)                   │  image
    for i in range(20):
        ax = plt.subplot(2,10, i + 1)
        img=(imgs[i]).detach().cpu().numpy()
        plt.imshow(img.reshape(28,28),            ◄─────┐  Compares the originals
                cmap="binary")                          │  to the reconstructed
        plt.xticks([])                                  │  digits visually
        plt.yticks([])
    plt.show()
```

We first collect 10 sample images, one representing a different digit, and place them in a list, `originals`. We feed the images to the AE to obtain the reconstructed images. Finally, we plot both the originals and the reconstructed images so that we can compare them and assess the performance of the AE periodically.

Before training starts, we call the function `plot_digits()` to visualize the output:

```
plot_digits()
```

You'll see the output as shown in figure 7.4.

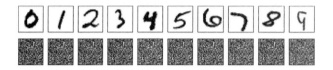

Figure 7.4   Comparing reconstructed images by the AE with the originals before training starts. The top row shows 10 original images of handwritten digits in the test set. The bottom row shows the reconstructed images by the AE before training. The reconstructions are nothing more than pure noise.

Though we could divide our data into training and validation sets and train the model until no further improvements are seen on the validation set (as we have done in chapter 2), our primary aim here is to grasp how AEs work, not necessarily to achieve the best parameter tuning. Therefore, we'll train the AE for 10 epochs.

Listing 7.3   Training the AE to generate handwritten digits

```
for epoch in range(10):
    tloss=0
    for imgs, labels in train_loader:          Iterates through batches
        imgs=imgs.to(device).view(-1, input_dim)   in the training set
        out, mu=model(imgs)                    Uses the AE to reconstruct images
        loss=((out-imgs)**2).sum()
        optimizer.zero_grad()                  Calculates reconstruct loss as
        loss.backward()                        measured by mean squared error
        optimizer.step()
        tloss+=loss.item()
    print(f"at epoch {epoch} toal loss = {tloss/len(train_loader)}")
    plot_digits()                              Visually inspects the
                                               performance of the AE
```

In each epoch of training, we iterate through all batches of data in the training set. We feed the original images to the AE to obtain the reconstructed images. We then calculate the reconstruction loss, which is the mean squared error between the original images and the reconstructed images. Specifically, the reconstruction loss is obtained by first calculating the difference between the two images, pixel by pixel, squaring the values and averaging the squared difference. We adjust the model parameters to minimize the reconstruction loss, utilizing the Adam optimizer, which is a variation of the gradient descent method.

The model takes about 2 minutes to train if you are using GPU training. Alternatively, you can download the trained model from my website: https://mng.bz/YV6K.

7.2.3 *Saving and using the trained AE*

We'll save the model in the local folder on your computer:

```
scripted = torch.jit.script(model)
scripted.save('files/AEdigits.pt')
```

To use it to reconstruct an image of handwritten digits, we load up the model:

```
model=torch.jit.load('files/AEdigits.pt',map_location=device)
model.eval()
```

We can use it to generate handwritten digits by calling the `plot_digits()` function we defined earlier:

```
plot_digits()
```

The output is shown in figure 7.5.

Figure 7.5 Comparing reconstructed images by the trained AE with the originals. The top row shows 10 original images of handwritten digits in the test set. The bottom row shows the reconstructed images by the trained AE. The reconstructed images look similar to the original ones.

The reconstructed handwritten digits do resemble the original ones, although the reconstruction is not perfect. Some information gets lost during the encoding–decoding process. However, compared to GANs, AEs are easy to construct and take less time to train. Further, the encoder–decoder architecture is employed by many generative models. This project will help your understanding of later chapters, especially when we explore Transformers.

7.3 *What are VAEs?*

While AEs are good at reconstructing original images, they fail at generating novel images that are unseen in the training set. Further, AEs tend not to map similar inputs to nearby points in the latent space. As a result, the latent space associated with an AE is neither continuous nor easily interpretable. For example, you cannot interpolate two input data points to generate meaningful intermediate representations. For these reasons, we'll study an improvement in AEs: VAEs.

In this section, you'll first learn the key differences between AEs and VAEs and why these differences lead to the ability of the latter to generate realistic images that are unseen in the training set. You'll then learn the steps involved in training VAEs in general and training one to generate high-resolution human face images in particular.

7.3.1   Differences between AEs and VAEs

VAEs were first proposed by Diederik Kingma and Max Welling in 2013.[1] They are a variant of AEs. Like an AE, a VAE also has two main parts: an encoder and a decoder.

However, there are two key differences between AEs and VAEs. First, the latent space in an AE is deterministic. Each input is mapped to a fixed point in the latent space. In contrast, the latent space in a VAE is probabilistic. Instead of encoding an input as a single vector in the latent space, a VAE encodes an input as a distribution over possible values. In our second project, for example, we'll encode a color image into a 100-value probabilistic vector. Additionally, we'll assume that each element in this vector adheres to an independent normal distribution. Since defining a normal distribution requires just the mean (μ) and standard deviation (σ), each element in our 100-element probabilistic vector will be characterized by these two parameters. To reconstruct the image, we sample a vector from this distribution and decode it. The uniqueness of VAEs is highlighted by the fact that each sampling from the distribution results in a slightly varied output.

In statistical terms, the encoder in a VAE is trying to learn the true distribution of the training data x, $p(x|\theta)$, where θ is the parameters defining the distribution. For tractability, we usually assume that the distribution of the latent variable is normal. Because we only need the mean, μ, and standard deviation, σ, to define a normal distribution, we can rewrite the true distribution as $p(x|\theta) = p(x|\mu,\sigma)$. The decoder in the VAE generates a sample based on the distribution learned by the encoder. That is, the decoder generates an instance probabilistically from the distribution $p(x|\mu,\sigma)$.

The second key difference between AEs and VAEs lies in the loss function. When training an AE, we minimize the reconstruction loss so that the reconstructed images are as close to the originals as possible. In contrast, in VAEs, the loss function consists of two parts: the reconstruction loss and the KL divergence. KL divergence is a measure of how one probability distribution diverges from a second, expected probability distribution. In VAEs, KL divergence is used to regularize the encoder by penalizing deviations of the learned distribution (the encoder's output) from a prior distribution (a standard normal distribution). This encourages the encoder to learn meaningful and generalizable latent representations. By penalizing distributions that are too far from the prior, KL divergence helps to avoid overfitting.

The KL divergence is calculated as follows in our setting since we assume a normal distribution (the formula is different if a nonnormal distribution is assumed):

$$\text{KL Divergence} = \sum_{n=1}^{100}\left(\frac{\sigma_n^2}{2} + \frac{\mu_n^2}{2} - \log(\sigma_n^2) - \frac{1}{2}\right) \tag{7.1}$$

The summation is taken over all 100 dimensions of the latent space. When the encoder compresses the images into standard normal distributions in the latent space, such that

[1]   Diederik P Kingma and Max Welling, 2013, "Auto-Encoding Variational Bayes." https://arxiv.org/abs/1312.6114.

μ=0 and σ=1, the KL divergence becomes 0. In any other scenario, the value exceeds 0. Thus, the KL divergence is minimized when the encoder successfully compresses the images into standard normal distributions within the latent space.

7.3.2 *The blueprint to train a VAE to generate human face images*

In the second project in this chapter, you'll build and train a VAE from scratch to generate color images of human faces. The trained model can generate images that are unseen in the training set. Further, you can interpolate inputs to generate novel images that are intermediate representations between two input data points. The following is a blueprint for this second project.

Figure 7.6 provides a diagram of the architecture of a VAE and the steps in training a VAE to generate human face images.

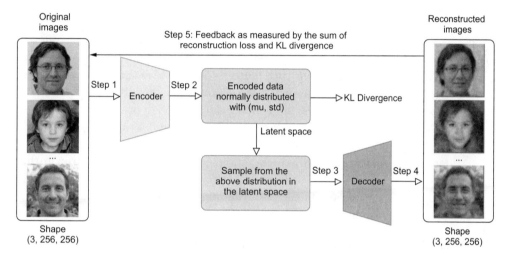

Figure 7.6   The architecture of a VAE and the steps to train one to generate human face images.
A VAE consists of an encoder (middle upper left) and a decoder (middle bottom right). In each iteration of training, human face images are fed to the encoder (step 1). The encoder compresses the images to probabilistic points in the latent space (step 2; since we assume normal distributions, each probability point is characterized by a vector of means and a vector of standard deviations). We then sample encodings from the distribution and present them to the decoder. The decoder takes sampled encodings (step 3) and reconstructs images (step 4). The VAE adjusts its parameters to minimize the sum of reconstruction loss and the KL divergence. The KL divergence measures the difference between the encoder's output and a standard normal distribution.

Figure 7.6 shows that a VAE also has two parts: an encoder (middle top left) and a decoder (middle bottom right). Since the second project involves high-resolution color images, we'll use CNNs to create the VAE. As we discussed in chapter 4, high-resolution color images contain many more pixels than low-resolution grayscale images. If we use fully connected (dense) layers only, the number of parameters in the model is too large, making learning slow and ineffective. CNNs require fewer parameters than fully connected networks of similar size, leading to faster and more effective learning.

Once the VAE is created, you'll use the eyeglasses dataset that you downloaded in chapter 5 to train the model. The left side of figure 7.6 shows three examples of the original human face images in the training set. In the first step in the training loop, we feed images in the training set, with a size of $3 \times 256 \times 256 = 196,608$ pixels, to the encoder. The encoder compresses the images to 100-value probabilistic vectors in the latent space (step 2; vectors of means and standard deviations due to the assumption of normal distribution). We then sample from the distribution and feed the sampled vector representations to the decoder (step 3) and ask it to reconstruct the images (step 4). We calculate the total loss as the sum of the reconstruction loss at the pixel level and the KL divergence as specified in equation 7.1. We propagate this loss back through the network to update the parameters in the encoder and decoder to minimize the total loss (step 5). The total loss encourages the VAE to encode the inputs into more meaningful and generalizable latent representations and to reconstruct images closer to the originals.

After the model is trained, you'll feed human face images to the encoder and obtain encodings. You then feed the encodings to the decoder to obtain reconstructed images. You'll notice that the reconstructed images look close to the originals. The right side of figure 7.6 shows three examples of reconstructed images: they look similar to the corresponding originals on the left side of the figure, though not perfectly.

More importantly, you can discard the encoder and randomly draw encodings from the latent space and feed them to the trained decoder in VAE to generate novel human face images that are unseen in the training set. Further, you can manipulate the encoded representations of different inputs to achieve specific outcomes when decoded. You can also create a series of images transitioning from one instance to another by varying the weight assigned to any two encodings.

7.4   A VAE to generate human face images

This section creates and trains a VAE from scratch to generate human face images by following the steps outlined in the last section.

Compared to what we have done to build and train AEs, our approach for the second project incorporates several modifications. Firstly, we plan to use CNNs in both the encoders and decoders of VAEs, particularly because high-resolution color images possess a greater number of pixels. Relying solely on fully connected (dense) layers would result in an excessively large number of parameters, leading to slow and inefficient learning. Second, as part of our process to compress images into vectors that follow a normal distribution in the latent space, we will generate both a mean vector and a standard deviation vector during the encoding of each image. This differs from the fixed value vector used in AEs. From the encoded normal distribution, we'll then sample to obtain encodings, which are subsequently decoded to produce images. Notably, each reconstructed image will vary slightly every time we sample from this distribution, which gives rise to VAEs' ability to generate novel images.

7.4.1   Building a VAE

If you recall, the eyeglasses dataset that you downloaded in chapter 5 is saved in the folder /files/glasses/ on your computer after some labels are manually corrected. We'll resize the images to 256 by 256 pixels with values between 0 and 1. We then create a batch iterator with 16 images in each batch:

```
transform = T.Compose([
          T.Resize(256),                      ◄──── Resizes images to
          T.ToTensor(),                              256 by 256 pixels
          ])                              ◄────
data = torchvision.datasets.ImageFolder(           Converts images to tensors
    root="files/glasses",                          with values between 0 and 1
    transform=transform)
batch_size=16                             ◄────   Loads images from the folder
loader = torch.utils.data.DataLoader(data,         and apply the transformations
    batch_size=batch_size,shuffle=True)   ◄────
                                                   Places the data in a
                                                   batch iterator
```

Next, we'll create a VAE that includes convolutional and transposed convolutional layers. We first define an Encoder() class as follows.

Listing 7.4   The encoder in the VAE

```
latent_dims=100                                    ◄────
class Encoder(nn.Module):                                The dimension of the latent
    def __init__(self, latent_dims=100):                 space is 100.
        super().__init__()
        self.conv1 = nn.Conv2d(3, 8, 3, stride=2, padding=1)
        self.conv2 = nn.Conv2d(8, 16, 3, stride=2, padding=1)
        self.batch2 = nn.BatchNorm2d(16)
        self.conv3 = nn.Conv2d(16, 32, 3, stride=2, padding=0)
        self.linear1 = nn.Linear(31*31*32, 1024)
        self.linear2 = nn.Linear(1024, latent_dims)
        self.linear3 = nn.Linear(1024, latent_dims)
        self.N = torch.distributions.Normal(0, 1)
        self.N.loc = self.N.loc.cuda()
        self.N.scale = self.N.scale.cuda()
    def forward(self, x):
        x = x.to(device)
        x = F.relu(self.conv1(x))
        x = F.relu(self.batch2(self.conv2(x)))
        x = F.relu(self.conv3(x))              The mean of the distribution
        x = torch.flatten(x, start_dim=1)      of the encodings
        x = F.relu(self.linear1(x))
        mu =  self.linear2(x)                          The standard deviation
        std = torch.exp(self.linear3(x))   ◄────       of the encodings
        z = mu + std*self.N.sample(mu.shape) ◄────
        return mu, std, z                   ◄────   The encoded vector
                                                    representation
```

The encoder network consists of several convolutional layers, which extract the spatial features of the input images. The encoder compresses the inputs into vector representations, z, which are normally distributed with means, mu, and standard deviations, `std`. The output from the encoder consists of three tensors: `mu`, `std`, and `z`. While the `mu` and `std` are the mean and standard deviation of the probabilistic vector, respectively, `z` is an instance sampled from this distribution.

Specifically, the input image, with a size of (3, 256, 256), first goes through a Conv2d layer with a stride value of 2. As we explained in chapter 4, this means the filter skips two pixels each time it moves on the input image, which leads to downsampling of the image. The output has a size of (8, 128, 128). It then goes through two more Conv2d layers, and the size becomes (32, 31, 31). It is flattened and passed through linear layers to obtain values of `mu` and `std`.

We define a `Decoder()` class to represent the decoder in the VAE.

Listing 7.5 The decoder in the VAE

```
class Decoder(nn.Module):
    def __init__(self, latent_dims=100):
        super().__init__()
        self.decoder_lin = nn.Sequential(          Encodings first go through
            nn.Linear(latent_dims, 1024),          two dense layers.
            nn.ReLU(True),
            nn.Linear(1024, 31*31*32),             Reshapes encodings into
            nn.ReLU(True))                         multidimensional objects
        self.unflatten = nn.Unflatten(dim=1,       so we can perform
                unflattened_size=(32,31,31))       transposed convolutional
        self.decoder_conv = nn.Sequential(         operations on them
            nn.ConvTranspose2d(32,16,3,stride=2,
                              output_padding=1),   Passes the encodings
            nn.BatchNorm2d(16),                    through three transposed
            nn.ReLU(True),                         convolutional layers
            nn.ConvTranspose2d(16, 8, 3, stride=2,
                              padding=1, output_padding=1),
            nn.BatchNorm2d(8),
            nn.ReLU(True),
            nn.ConvTranspose2d(8, 3, 3, stride=2,
                              padding=1, output_padding=1))

    def forward(self, x):
        x = self.decoder_lin(x)
        x = self.unflatten(x)                      Squeezes the output to values
        x = self.decoder_conv(x)                   between 0 and 1, the same as
        x = torch.sigmoid(x)                       the values in the input images
        return x
```

The decoder is a mirror image of the encoder: instead of performing convolutional operations, it performs transposed convolutional operations on the encodings to generate feature maps. It gradually converts encodings in the latent space back into high-resolution color images.

Specifically, the encoding first goes through two linear layers. It's then unflattened to a shape (32, 31, 31), mirroring the size of the image after the last Conv2d layer in the encoder. It then goes through three ConvTranspose2d layers, mirroring the Conv2d layers in the encoder. The output from the decoder has a shape of (3, 256, 256), the same as that of the training image.

We'll combine the encoder with the decoder to create a VAE:

```
class VAE(nn.Module):
    def __init__(self, latent_dims=100):          Creates an encoder by
        super().__init__()                         instantiating the Encoder() class
        self.encoder = Encoder(latent_dims)
        self.decoder = Decoder(latent_dims)        Creates a decoder by
    def forward(self, x):                          instantiating the Decoder() class
        x = x.to(device)
        mu, std, z = self.encoder(x)               Passes the input through
        return mu, std, self.decoder(z)            the encoder to obtain
                                                   the encoding
```

The output of the VAE is the mean and standard deviation of the encodings, as well as the reconstructed images.

The VAE consists of an encoder and a decoder, as defined by the `Encoder()` and `Decoder()` classes. When we pass images through the VAE, the output consists of three tensors: the mean and standard deviation of the encodings and the reconstructed images.

Next, we create a VAE by instantiating the `VAE()` class and define the optimizer for the model:

```
vae=VAE().to(device)
lr=1e-4
optimizer=torch.optim.Adam(vae.parameters(),
                           lr=lr,weight_decay=1e-5)
```

We'll manually calculate the reconstruction loss and the KL-divergence loss during training. Therefore, we don't define a loss function here.

7.4.2 Training the VAE

To train the model, we first define a `train_epoch()` function to train the model for one epoch.

Listing 7.6 Defining the `train_epoch()` function

```
def train_epoch(epoch):                               Obtains the
    vae.train()                                       reconstructed images
    epoch_loss = 0.0
    for imgs, _ in loader:                            Calculates the
        imgs = imgs.to(device)                        reconstruction loss
        mu, std, out = vae(imgs)
        reconstruction_loss = ((imgs-out)**2).sum()   Calculates the
        kl = ((std**2)/2 + (mu**2)/2 - torch.log(std) - 0.5).sum()   KL divergence
        loss = reconstruction_loss + kl
        optimizer.zero_grad()
                                                      Sum of the reconstruction loss
                                                      and the KL divergence.
```

```
        loss.backward()
        optimizer.step()
        epoch_loss+=loss.item()
    print(f'at epoch {epoch}, loss is {epoch_loss}')
```

We iterate through all batches in the training set. We pass images through the VAE to obtain reconstructed images. The total loss is the sum of the reconstruction loss and the KL divergence. The model parameters are adjusted in each iteration to minimize the total loss.

We also define a `plot_epoch()` function to visually inspect the generated images by the VAE:

```
import numpy as np
import matplotlib.pyplot as plt

def plot_epoch():
    with torch.no_grad():
        noise = torch.randn(18,latent_dims).to(device)
        imgs = vae.decoder(noise).cpu()
        imgs = torchvision.utils.make_grid(imgs,6,3).numpy()
        fig, ax = plt.subplots(figsize=(6,3),dpi=100)
        plt.imshow(np.transpose(imgs, (1, 2, 0)))
        plt.axis("off")
        plt.show()
```

A well-trained VAE can map similar inputs to nearby points in the latent space, leading to a more continuous and interpretable latent space. As a result, we can randomly draw vectors from the latent space, and the VAE can decode the vectors into meaningful outputs. Therefore, in the previous function `plot_epoch()`, we randomly draw 18 vectors from the latent space and use them to generate 18 images after each epoch of training. We plot them in a 3×6 grid and visually inspect them to see how the VAE is performing during the training process.

Next, we train the VAE for 10 epochs:

```
for epoch in range(1,11):
    train_epoch(epoch)
    plot_epoch()
torch.save(vae.state_dict(),"files/VAEglasses.pth")
```

This training takes about half an hour if you use GPU training or several hours otherwise. The trained model weights are saved on your computer. Alternatively, you can download the trained weights from my website: https://mng.bz/GNRR. Make sure you unzip the file after downloading.

7.4.3   *Generating images with the trained VAE*

Now that the VAE is trained, we can use it to generate images. We first load the weights of the trained model that we saved in the local folder:

```
vae.eval()
vae.load_state_dict(torch.load('files/VAEglasses.pth',
    map_location=device))
```

We then check the VAE's ability to reconstruct images and see how closely they resemble the originals:

```
imgs,_=next(iter(loader))
imgs = imgs.to(device)
mu, std, out = vae(imgs)
images=torch.cat([imgs[:8],out[:8],imgs[8:16],out[8:16]],
                 dim=0).detach().cpu()
images = torchvision.utils.make_grid(images,8,4)
fig, ax = plt.subplots(figsize=(8,4),dpi=100)
plt.imshow(np.transpose(images, (1, 2, 0)))
plt.axis("off")
plt.show()
```

If you run the previous code block, you'll see an output similar to figure 7.7.

Figure 7.7   Comparing the reconstructed images by a trained VAE with the originals. The first and the third rows are the original images. We feed them to the trained VAE to obtain the reconstructed images, which are shown below the original images.

The original images are shown in the first and third rows, while the reconstructed images are shown below the originals. The reconstructed images resemble the originals, as shown in figure 7.7. However, some information gets lost during the reconstruction process: they don't look as realistic as the originals.

Next, we test the VAE's ability to generate novel images that are unseen in the training set, by calling the plot_epoch() function we defined before:

```
plot_epoch()
```

The function randomly draws 18 vectors from the latent space and passes them to the trained VAE to generate 18 images. The output is shown in figure 7.8.

Figure 7.8 Novel images generated by the trained VAE. We randomly draw vector representations in the latent space and feed them to the decoder in the trained VAE. The decoded images are shown in this figure. Since the vector representations are randomly drawn, the images don't correspond to any originals in the training set.

These images are not present in the training set: the encodings are randomly drawn from the latent space, not the encoded vectors after passing images in the training set through the encoder. This is because the latent space in VAEs is continuous and interpretable. New and unseen encodings in the latent space can be meaningfully decoded into images that resemble but differ from those in the training set.

7.4.4   *Encoding arithmetic with the trained VAE*

VAEs include a regularization term (KL divergence) in their loss function, which encourages the latent space to approximate a normal distribution. This regularization ensures that the latent variables don't just memorize the training data but rather capture the underlying distribution. It helps to achieve a well-structured latent space where similar data points are mapped closely together, making the space continuous and interpretable. As a result, we can manipulate the encodings to achieve new outcomes.

To make results reproducible, I encourage you to download the trained weights from my website (https://mng.bz/GNRR) and use the same code blocks for the rest of the chapter. As we explained in the introduction, encoding arithmetic allows us to generate images with certain features. To illustrate how encoding arithmetic works in VAEs, let's first hand-collect three images in each of the following four groups: men with glasses, men without glasses, women with glasses, and women without glasses.

Listing 7.7 Collecting images with different characteristics

```
torch.manual_seed(0)
glasses=[]
for i in range(25):
```

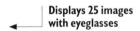
Displays 25 images with eyeglasses

```
        img,label=data[i]
        glasses.append(img)
        plt.subplot(5,5,i+1)
        plt.imshow(img.numpy().transpose((1,2,0)))
        plt.axis("off")
plt.show()
men_g=[glasses[0],glasses[3],glasses[14]]
women_g=[glasses[9],glasses[15],glasses[21]]

noglasses=[]
for i in range(25):
        img,label=data[-i-1]
        noglasses.append(img)
        plt.subplot(5,5,i+1)
        plt.imshow(img.numpy().transpose((1,2,0)))
        plt.axis("off")
plt.show()
men_ng=[noglasses[1],noglasses[7],noglasses[22]]
women_ng=[noglasses[4],noglasses[9],noglasses[19]])
```

Selects three images of
men with glasses

Selects three images of
women with glasses

Displays 25 images
without eyeglasses

Selects three images of
men without glasses

Selects three images of
women without glasses

We select three images in each group instead of just one so that we can calculate the average of multiple encodings in the same group when performing encoding arithmetic later. VAEs are designed to learn the distribution of the input data in the latent space. By averaging multiple encodings, we effectively smooth out the representation in this space. This helps us find an average representation that captures common features among different samples within a group.

Next we feed the three images of men with glasses to the trained VAE to obtain their encodings in the latent space. We then calculate the average encoding for the three images and use it to obtain a reconstructed image of a man with glasses. We then repeat this for the other three groups.

Listing 7.8 Encoding and decoding images in four different groups

```
# create a batch of images of men with glasses
men_g_batch = torch.cat((men_g[0].unsqueeze(0),
            men_g[1].unsqueeze(0),
            men_g[2].unsqueeze(0)), dim=0).to(device)
# Obtain the three encodings
_,_,men_g_encodings=vae.encoder(men_g_batch)
# Average over the three images to obtain the encoding for the group
men_g_encoding=men_g_encodings.mean(dim=0)
# Decode the average encoding to create an image of a man with glasses
men_g_recon=vae.decoder(men_g_encoding.unsqueeze(0))

# Do the same for the other three groups
# group 2, women with glasses
women_g_batch = torch.cat((women_g[0].unsqueeze(0),
            women_g[1].unsqueeze(0),
            women_g[2].unsqueeze(0)), dim=0).to(device)
# group 3, men without glasses
men_ng_batch = torch.cat((men_ng[0].unsqueeze(0),
            men_ng[1].unsqueeze(0),
```

Creates a batch of images
of men with glasses

Obtains the
average
encoding for
men with
glasses

Decodes the
average encoding
for men with glasses

```
            men_ng[2].unsqueeze(0)), dim=0).to(device)
# group 4, women without glasses
women_ng_batch = torch.cat((women_ng[0].unsqueeze(0),
            women_ng[1].unsqueeze(0),
            women_ng[2].unsqueeze(0)), dim=0).to(device)
# obtain average encoding for each group
_,_,women_g_encodings=vae.encoder(women_g_batch)
women_g_encoding=women_g_encodings.mean(dim=0)
_,_,men_ng_encodings=vae.encoder(men_ng_batch)
men_ng_encoding=men_ng_encodings.mean(dim=0)
_,_,women_ng_encodings=vae.encoder(women_ng_batch)
women_ng_encoding=women_ng_encodings.mean(dim=0)
# decode for each group
women_g_recon=vae.decoder(women_g_encoding.unsqueeze(0))
men_ng_recon=vae.decoder(men_ng_encoding.unsqueeze(0))
women_ng_recon=vae.decoder(women_ng_encoding.unsqueeze(0))
```

> Obtains the average encodings for the other three groups

> Decodes the average encodings for the other three groups

The average encodings for the four groups are men_g_encoding, women_g_encoding, men_ng_encoding, and women_ng_encoding, respectively, where g stands for glasses and ng for no glasses. The decoded images for the four groups are men_g_recon, women_g_recon, men_ng_recon, and women_ng_recon, respectively. We plot the four images:

```
imgs=torch.cat((men_g_recon,
            women_g_recon,
            men_ng_recon,
            women_ng_recon),dim=0)
imgs=torchvision.utils.make_grid(imgs,4,1).cpu().numpy()
imgs=np.transpose(imgs,(1,2,0))
fig, ax = plt.subplots(figsize=(8,2),dpi=100)
plt.imshow(imgs)
plt.axis("off")
plt.show()
```

You'll see the output as shown in figure 7.9.

Figure 7.9   Decoded images based on average encodings. We first obtain three images in each of the following four groups: men with glasses, women with glasses, men without glasses, and women without glasses. We feed the 12 images to the encoder in the trained VAE to obtain their encodings in the latent space. We then calculate the average encoding of the three images in each group. The four average encodings are fed to the decoder in the trained VAE to obtain four images and they are shown in this figure.

The four decoded images are shown in figure 7.9. They are the composite images representing the four groups. Notice that they are different from any of the original 12 images. At the same time, they preserve the defining characteristics of each group.

Next, let's manipulate the encodings to create a new encoding and then use the trained decoder in the VAE to decode the new encoding and see what happens. For example, we can subtract the average encoding of women with glasses from the average encoding of men with glasses and add the average encoding of women without glasses. We then feed the result to the decoder and see the output.

Listing 7.9 An example of encoding arithmetic

```
z=men_g_encoding-women_g_encoding+women_ng_encoding
out=vae.decoder(z.unsqueeze(0))
imgs=torch.cat((men_g_recon,
                women_g_recon,
                women_ng_recon,out),dim=0)
imgs=torchvision.utils.make_grid(imgs,4,1).cpu().numpy()
imgs=np.transpose(imgs,(1,2,0))
fig, ax = plt.subplots(figsize=(8,2),dpi=100)
plt.imshow(imgs)
plt.title("man with glasses - woman \
with glasses + woman without \
glasses = man without glasses ",fontsize=10,c="r")
plt.axis("off")
plt.show()
```

Defines z as the encoding of men with glasses – women with glasses + women without glasses

Decodes z to generate an image

Displays the four images

Displays a title on top of the images

If you run the code block in listing 7.9, you'll see an output as shown in figure 7.10.

man with glasses - woman with glasses + woman without glasses = man without glasses

Figure 7.10 An example of encoding arithmetic with the trained VAE. We first obtain the average encodings for the following three groups: men with glasses (z1), women with glasses (z2), and women without glasses (z3). We define a new encoding z = z1 – z2 + z3. We then feed z to the decoder in the trained VAE and obtain the decoded image, as shown at the far right of this figure.

The first three images in figure 7.10 are the composite images representing the three input groups. The output image, at the far right, is an image of a man without glasses.

Since both men_g_encoding and women_g_encoding lead to eyeglasses in images when decoded, men_g_encoding − women_g_encoding cancels out eyeglasses features in the resulting image. Similarly, since both women_ng_encoding and women_g_encoding lead to a female face, women_ng_encoding − women_g_encoding cancels out female features in the resulting image. Therefore, if you decode men_g_encoding

+ women_g_encoding —women_ng_encoding with the trained VAE, you'll get an image of a man without glasses. The encoding arithmetic in this example shows that an encoding for men without glasses can be obtained by manipulating the average encodings in the other three groups.

Exercise 7.1

Perform the following encoding arithmetics by modifying code listing 7.9:

1. Subtract the average encoding of men without glasses from the average encoding of men with glasses and add the average encoding of women without glasses. Feed the result to the decoder and see what happens.
2. Subtract the average encoding of women without glasses from the average encoding of men without glasses and add the average encoding of women with glasses. Feed the result to the decoder and see what happens.
3. Subtract the average encoding of men without glasses from the average encoding of women without glasses and add the average encoding of men with glasses. Feed the result to the decoder and see what happens. Make sure you modify the image titles to reflect the changes. The solutions are provided in the book's GitHub repository: https://github.com/markhliu/DGAI.

Further, we can interpolate any two encodings in the latent space by assigning different weights to them and creating a new encoding. We can then decode the new encoding and create a composite image as a result. By choosing different weights, we can create a series of intermediate images that transition from one image to another.

Let's use the encodings of women with and without glasses as an example. We'll define a new encoding z as w*women_ng_encoding+(1-w)*women_g_encoding, where w is the weight we put on women_ng_encoding. We'll change the value of w from 0 to 1 with an increment of 0.2 in each step. We then decode them and display the resulting six images.

Listing 7.10   Interpolating two encodings to create a series of images

```
results=[]
for w in [0, 0.2, 0.4, 0.6, 0.8, 1.0]:          ◄─── Iterates through six
    z=w*women_ng_encoding+(1-w)*women_g_encoding ◄───  different values of w
    out=vae.decoder(z.unsqueeze(0))              ◄───
    results.append(out)
imgs=torch.cat((results[0],results[1],results[2],    Interpolates between
            results[3],results[4],results[5]),dim=0)  two encodings
imgs=torchvision.utils.make_grid(imgs,6,1).cpu().numpy()  Decodes the
imgs=np.transpose(imgs,(1,2,0))                           interpolated encoding
fig, ax = plt.subplots(dpi=100)
plt.imshow(imgs)
plt.axis("off")                              ◄─── Displays the six
plt.show()                                        resulting images
```

After running the code in listing 7.10, you'll see an output as shown in figure 7.11.

Figure 7.11 Interpolating encodings to create a series of intermediate images. We first obtain the average encodings for women with glasses (`women_g_encoding`) and women without glasses (`women_ng_encoding`). The interpolated encoding z is defined as `w*women_ng_encoding+(1-w)*women_g_encoding`, where w is the weight on `women_ng_encoding`. We change the value of w from 0 to 1 with an increment of 0.2 to create six interpolated encodings. We then decode them and display the resulting six images in the figure.

As you can see in figure 7.11, as you move from left to right, the image gradually transitions from a woman with glasses to a woman without glasses. This shows that the encodings in the latent space are continuous, meaningful, and interpolatable.

> **Exercise 7.2**
>
> Modify listing 7.10 to create a series of intermediate images by using the following pairs of encodings: (i) `men_ng_encoding` and `men_g_encoding`; (ii) `men_ng_encoding` and `women_ng_encoding`; (iii) `men_g_encoding` and `women_g_encoding`. The solutions are provided in the book's GitHub repository: https://github.com/markhliu/DGAI.

Starting in the next chapter, you'll embark on a journey in natural language processing. This will enable you to generate another form of content: text. However, many tools you have used so far will be used again in later chapters, such as deep neural networks and the encoder-decoder architecture.

Summary

- AEs have a dual-component structure: an encoder and a decoder. The encoder compresses the data into an abstract representation in a lower-dimensional space (the latent space), and the decoder decompresses the encoded information and reconstructs the data.
- VAEs also consist of an encoder and a decoder. They differ from AEs in two critical ways. First, while an AE encodes each input into a specific point in the latent space, a VAE encodes it into a probability distribution within this space. Second, an AE focuses solely on minimizing the reconstruction error, whereas a VAE learns the parameters of the probability distribution for latent variables, minimizing a loss function that includes both reconstruction loss and a regularization term, the KL divergence.
- The KL divergence in the loss function when training VAEs ensures the distribution for latent variables resembles a normal distribution. This

encourages the encoder to learn continuous, meaningful, and generalizable latent representations.

- A well-trained VAE can map similar inputs to nearby points in the latent space, leading to a more continuous and interpretable latent space. As a result, VAEs can decode random vectors in the latent space into meaningful outputs, leading to images that are unseen in the training set.
- The latent space in a VAE is continuous and interpretable, different from that in an AE. As a result, we can manipulate the encodings to achieve new outcomes. We can also create a series of intermediate images transitioning from one instance to another by varying weights on two encodings in the latent space.

Part 3

Natural language processing and Transformers

Part III focuses on text generation.

In chapter 8, you'll learn to build and train a recurrent neural network to generate text. Along the way, you'll learn how tokenization and word embedding work. You'll also learn to generate text autoregressively and how to use temperature and top-K sampling to control the creativity of the generated text. In chapters 9 and 10, you'll build a Transformer from scratch, based on the paper "Attention Is All You Need," to translate English to French. In chapter 11, you'll learn to build GPT-2XL, the largest version of GPT-2, from scratch. After that, you'll learn how to extract the pretrained weights from Hugging Face and load them to your own GPT-2 model. You'll use your GPT-2 to generate text by feeding a prompt to the model. In chapter 12, you'll build and train a GPT model to generate text in Hemingway style.

Text generation with recurrent neural networks

So far in this book, we have discussed how to generate shapes, numbers, and images. Starting from this chapter, we'll focus mainly on text generation. Generating text is often considered the holy grail of generative AI for several compelling reasons. Human language is incredibly complex and nuanced. It involves understanding not only grammar and vocabulary but also context, tone, and cultural references. Successfully generating coherent and contextually appropriate text is a significant challenge that requires deep understanding and processing of language.

As humans, we primarily communicate through language. AI that can generate human-like text can interact more naturally with users, making technology more accessible and user-friendly. Text generation has many applications, from automating customer service responses to creating entire articles, scripting for games and movies, aiding in creative writing, and even building personal assistants. The potential effect across industries is enormous.

In this chapter, we'll make our first attempt at building and training models to generate text. You'll learn to tackle three main challenges in modeling text generation. First, text is sequential data, consisting of data points organized in a specific sequence, where each point is successively ordered to reflect the inherent order and interdependencies within the data. Predicting outcomes for sequences is challenging due to their sensitive ordering. Altering the sequence of elements changes their meaning. Second, text exhibits long-range dependencies: the meaning of a certain part of the text depends on elements that appeared much earlier in the text (e.g., 100 words ago). Understanding and modeling these long-range dependencies is essential for generating coherent text. Lastly, human language is ambiguous and context dependent. Training a model to understand nuances, sarcasm, idioms, and cultural references to generate contextually accurate text is challenging.

You'll explore a specific neural network designed for handling sequential data, such as text or time series: the recurrent neural network (RNN). Traditional neural networks, such as feedforward neural networks or fully connected networks, treat each input independently. This means that the network processes each input separately, without considering any relationship or order between different inputs. In contrast, RNNs are specifically designed to handle sequential data. In an RNN, the output at a given time step depends not only on the current input but also on previous inputs. This allows RNNs to maintain a form of memory, capturing information from previous time steps to influence the processing of the current input.

This sequential processing makes RNNs suitable for tasks where the order of the inputs matters, such as language modeling, where the goal is to predict the next word in a sentence based on previous words. We'll focus on one variant of RNN, long short-term memory (LSTM) networks, which can recognize both short-term and long-term data patterns in sequential data like text. LSTM models use a hidden state to capture information in previous time steps. Therefore, a trained LSTM model can produce coherent text based on the context.

The style of the generated text depends on the training data. Additionally, as we plan to train a model from scratch for text generation, the length of the training text is a crucial factor. It needs to be sufficiently extensive for the model to effectively learn and mimic a particular writing style yet concise enough to avoid excessive computational demands during training. As a result, we'll use the text from the novel *Anna Karenina*, which appears to be of the right length for our purposes, to train an LSTM model. Since neural networks like an LSTM cannot accept text as input directly, you'll learn to break down text into tokens (individual words in this chapter but can be parts of words, as you'll see in later chapters), a process known as *tokenization*. You'll then create a dictionary to map each unique token into an integer (i.e., an index). Based on this dictionary, you'll convert the text into a long sequence of integers, ready to be fed into a neural network.

You'll use sequences of indexes of a certain length as the input to train the LSTM model. You shift the sequence of inputs by one token to the right and use it as the output: you are effectively training the model to predict the next token in a sentence. This is the so-called *sequence-to-sequence* prediction problem in natural language processing (NLP), and you'll see it again in later chapters.

Once the LSTM is trained, you'll use it to generate text one token at a time based on previous tokens in the sequence as follows: you feed a prompt (part of a sentence such as "Anna and the") to the trained model. The model then predicts the most likely next token and appends the selected token to your prompt. The updated prompt serves again as the input, and the model is used once more to predict the next token. The iterative process continues until the prompt reaches a certain length. This approach is similar to the mechanism employed by more advanced generative models like ChatGPT (though ChatGPT is not an LSTM). You'll witness the trained LSTM model generating grammatically correct and coherent text, with a style matching that of the original novel.

Finally, you also learn how to control the creativeness of the generated text using temperature and top-K sampling. Temperature controls the randomness of the predictions of the trained model. A high temperature makes the generated text more creative while a low temperature makes the text more confident and predictable. Top-K sampling is a method where you select the next token from the top K most probable tokens, rather than selecting from the entire vocabulary. A small value of K leads to the selection of highly likely tokens in each step, and this, in turn, makes the generated text less creative and more coherent.

The primary goal of this chapter is not necessarily to generate the most coherent text possible, which, as mentioned earlier, presents substantial challenges. Instead, our objective is to demonstrate the limitations of RNNs, thereby setting the stage for the introduction of Transformers in subsequent chapters. More importantly, this chapter establishes the basic principles of text generation, including tokenization, word embedding, sequence prediction, temperature settings, and top-K sampling. Consequently, in later chapters, you will have a solid understanding of the fundamentals of NLP. This foundation will allow us to concentrate on other, more advanced aspects of NLP, such as how the attention mechanism functions and the architecture of Transformers.

8.1 Introduction to RNNs

At the beginning of this chapter, we touched upon the complexities involved in generating text, particularly when aiming for coherence and contextual relevance. This section dives deeper into these challenges and explores the architecture of RNNs. We'll explain why RNNs are suitable for the task and their limitations (which are the reasons they have been overtaken by Transformers).

RNNs are specifically designed to handle sequential data, making them capable of text generation, a task inherently sequential in nature. They utilize a form of memory, known as hidden states, to capture and retain information from earlier parts of the sequence. This capability is crucial for maintaining context and understanding dependencies as the sequence progresses.

In this chapter, we will specifically utilize LSTM networks, advanced versions of RNNs, for text generation, using their advanced capabilities to tackle the challenges in this task.

8.1.1   Challenges in generating text

Text represents a quintessential example of *sequential data*, which is defined as any dataset where the order of elements is critical. This structuring implies that the positioning of individual elements relative to each other holds significant meaning, often conveying essential information for understanding the data. Examples of sequential data include time series (like stock prices), textual content (such as sentences), and musical compositions (a succession of notes).

This book primarily zeroes in on text generation, although it also ventures into music generation in chapters 13 and 14. The process of generating text is fraught with complexities. A primary challenge lies in modeling the sequence of words within sentences, where altering the order can drastically change the meaning. For instance, in the sentence "Kentucky defeated Vanderbilt in last night's football game," swapping 'Kentucky' and 'Vanderbilt' entirely reverses the sentence's implication, despite using the same words. Furthermore, as mentioned in the introduction, text generation encounters challenges in handling long-range dependencies and dealing with the problem of ambiguity.

In this chapter, we will explore one approach to tackle these challenges—namely, by using RNNs. While this method isn't flawless, it lays the groundwork for more advanced techniques you'll encounter in later chapters. This approach will provide insight into managing word order, addressing long-range dependencies, and navigating the inherent ambiguity in text, equipping you with fundamental skills in text generation. The journey through this chapter serves as a stepping stone to more sophisticated methods and deeper understanding in the subsequent parts of the book. Along the way, you'll acquire many valuable skills in NLP, such as text tokenization, word embedding, and sequence-to-sequence predictions.

8.1.2   How do RNNs work?

RNNs are a specialized form of artificial neural network designed to recognize patterns in sequences of data, such as text, music, or stock prices. Unlike traditional neural networks, which process inputs independently, RNNs have loops in them, allowing information to persist.

One of the challenges in generating text is how to predict the next word based on all previous words so that the prediction captures both the long-range dependencies and contextual meaning. RNNs take input not just as a standalone item but as a sequence (like words in a sentence, for example). At each time step, the prediction is based on not only the current input but also all previous inputs in the form of a summary through a hidden state. Let's consider the phrase "a frog has four legs" as an example. In the first time step, we use the word "a" to predict the second word "frog." In the second time step, we predict the next word using both "a" and "frog." By the time we predict the last word, we need to use all four previous words "a frog has four."

A key feature of RNNs is the so-called hidden state, which captures information in all previous elements in a sequence. This feature is crucial for the network's ability to process and generate sequential data effectively. The functioning of RNNs and this sequential processing is depicted in figure 8.1, which illustrates how a layer of recurrent neurons unfolds over time.

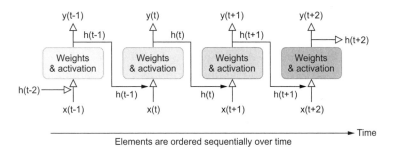

Figure 8.1   **How a layer of recurrent neurons unfolds through time. When a recurrent neural network makes a prediction on sequential data, it takes the hidden state from the previous time step, h(t − 1), along with the input at the current time step, x(t), and generates the output, y(t), and the updated hidden state, h(t). The hidden state at time step t captures the information in all previous time steps, x(0), x(1), …, x(t).**

The hidden state in RNNs plays a pivotal role in capturing information across all time steps. This allows RNNs to make predictions that are informed not just by the current input, x(t), but also by the accumulated knowledge from all previous inputs, x(0), x(1), …, x(t − 1). This attribute makes RNNs capable of understanding temporal dependencies. They can grasp the context from an input sequence, which is indispensable for tasks like language modeling, where the preceding words in a sentence set the stage for predicting the next word.

However, RNNs are not without their drawbacks. Though standard RNNs are capable of handling short-term dependencies, they struggle with longer-range dependencies within text. This difficulty stems from the vanishing gradient problem, which occurs in long sequences where the gradients (essential for training the network) diminish, hindering the model's ability to learn relationships over longer distances. To mitigate this, advanced versions of RNNs, such as LSTM networks, have been developed.

LSTM networks were introduced by Hochreiter and Schmidhuber in 1997.[1] An LSTM network is composed of LSTM units (or cells), each of which has a more complex structure than a standard RNN neuron. The cell state is the key innovation of LSTMs: it acts as a kind of conveyor belt, running straight down the entire chain of LSTM units. It

---

[1]   Sepp Hochreiter and Jurgen Schmidhuber, 1997, "Long Short-Term Memory," *Neural Computation* 9(8): 1735-1780.

has the ability to carry relevant information through the network. The ability to add or remove information to the cell state allows LSTMs to capture long-term dependencies and remember information for long periods. This makes them more effective for tasks like language modeling and text generation. In this chapter, we will harness the LSTM model to undertake a project on text generation, aiming to mimic the style of the novel *Anna Karenina*.

However, it's noteworthy that even advanced RNN variants like LSTMs encounter hurdles in capturing extremely long-range dependencies in sequence data. We will discuss these challenges and provide solutions in the next chapter, continuing our exploration of sophisticated models for effective sequence data processing and generation.

8.1.3   *Steps in training a LSTM model*

Next, we'll discuss the steps involved in training an LSTM model to generate text. This overview aims to provide a foundational understanding of the training process before embarking on the project.

The choice of text for training depends on the desired output. A lengthy novel serves as a good starting point. Its extensive content enables the model to learn and replicate a specific writing style effectively. An ample amount of text data enhances the model's proficiency in this style. At the same time, novels are generally not excessively long, which helps in managing the training time. For our LSTM model training, we'll utilize the text from *Anna Karenina*, aligning with our previously outlined training data criteria.

Similar to other deep neural networks, LSTM models cannot process raw text directly. Instead, we'll convert the text into numerical form. This begins by breaking down the text into smaller pieces, a process known as tokenization, where each piece is a token. Tokens can be entire words, punctuation marks (like an exclamation mark or a comma), or special characters (such as & or %). For this chapter, each of these elements will be treated as separate tokens. Although this method of tokenization may not be the most efficient, it is easy to implement since all we need is to map words to tokens. We will use subword tokenization in subsequent chapters where some infrequent words are broken into smaller pieces such as syllables. Following tokenization, we assign a unique integer to each token, creating a numerical representation of the text as a sequence of integers.

To prepare the training data, we divide this long sequence into shorter sequences of equal length. For our project, we'll use sequences comprising 100 integers each. These sequences form the features (the x variable) of our model. We then generate the output y by shifting the input sequence one token to the right. This setup enables the LSTM model to predict the next token in a sequence. The pairs of input and output serve as the training data. Our model includes LSTM layers to understand long-term patterns in the text and an embedding layer to grasp semantic meanings.

Let's revisit the example of predicting the sentence "a frog has four legs" that we mentioned earlier. Figure 8.2 is a diagram of how the training of the LSTM model works.

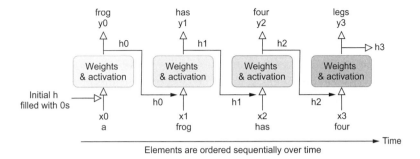

Figure 8.2 **An example of how an LSTM model is trained. We first break down the training text into tokens and assign a unique integer to each token, creating a numerical representation of the text as a sequence of indexes. We then divide this long sequence into shorter sequences of equal length. These sequences form the features (the x variable) of our model. We then generate the output y by shifting the input sequence one token to the right. This setup enables the LSTM model to predict the next token based on previous tokens in the sequence.**

In the first time step, the model uses the word "a" to predict the word "frog." Since there's no preceding word for "a," we initialize the hidden state with zeros. The LSTM model receives both the index for "a" and this initial hidden state as input and outputs the predicted next word along with an updated hidden state, h0. In the subsequent time step, the word "frog" and the updated state h0 are used to predict "has" and generate a new hidden state, h1. This sequence of predicting the next word and updating the hidden state continues until the model forecasts the final word in the sentence, "legs."

The predictions are then compared to the actual next word in the sentence. Since the model is effectively predicting the next token out of all possible tokens in the vocabulary, there is a multicategory classification problem. We tweak the model parameters in each iteration to minimize the cross-entropy loss so that in the next iteration, the model predictions move closer to actual outputs in the training data.

Once the model is trained, generating text begins with a seed sequence input into the model. The model predicts the next token, which is then appended to your sequence. This iterative process of prediction and sequence updating is repeated to generate text for as long as desired.

8.2 *Fundamentals of NLP*

Deep learning models, including the LSTM models we discussed earlier and Transformers, which you'll learn in later chapters, cannot process raw text directly because they are designed to work with numerical data, typically in the form of vectors or matrices. The processing and learning capabilities of neural networks are based on mathematical operations like addition, multiplication, and activation functions, which require numerical input. Consequently, it's essential first to break down text into smaller, more manageable elements known as tokens. These tokens can range from individual characters and words to subword units.

The next crucial step in NLP tasks is transforming these tokens into numerical representations. This conversion is necessary for feeding them into deep neural networks, which is a fundamental part of training our models.

In this section, we'll discuss different tokenization methods, along with their advantages and drawbacks. Additionally, you'll gain insights into the process of converting tokens into dense vector representations—a method known as word embedding. This technique is crucial for capturing the meaning of language in a format that deep learning models can effectively utilize.

8.2.1 Different tokenization methods

Tokenization involves dividing text into smaller parts, known as tokens, which can be in the form of words, characters, symbols, or other significant units. The primary goal of tokenization is to streamline the process of text data analysis and processing.

Broadly speaking, there are three approaches to tokenization. The first is character tokenization, where the text is divided into its constituent characters. This method is used in languages with complex morphological structures, such as Turkish or Finnish, in which the meaning of words can change significantly with slight variations in characters. Take the English phrase "It is unbelievably good!" as an example; it's broken down into individual characters as follows: ['I', 't', ' ', 'i', 's', ' ', 'u', 'n', 'b', 'e', 'l', 'i', 'e', 'v', 'a', 'b', 'l', 'y', ' ', 'g', 'o', 'o', 'd', '!']. A key advantage of character tokenization is the limited number of unique tokens. This limitation significantly reduces the parameters in deep learning models, leading to faster and more efficient training. However, the major drawback is that individual characters often lack significant meaning, making it challenging for machine learning models to derive meaningful insights from a sequence of characters.

> **Exercise 8.1**
> Use character tokenization to divide the phrase "Hi, there!" into individual tokens.

The second approach is word tokenization, where the text is split into individual words and punctuation marks. It is used often in situations where the number of unique words is not too large. For instance, the same phrase "It is unbelievably good!" becomes five tokens: ['It', 'is', 'unbelievably', 'good', '!']. The main advantage of this method is that each word inherently carries semantic meaning, making it more straightforward for models to interpret the text. The downside, however, lies in the substantial increase in unique tokens, which increases the number of parameters in deep learning models. This increase can lead to slower and less efficient training processes.

> **Exercise 8.2**
> Use word tokenization to break down the phrase "Hi, how are you?" into individual tokens.

The third approach is subword tokenization. This method, a key concept in NLP, breaks text into smaller, meaningful components called subwords. For instance, the phrase "It is unbelievably good!" would be divided into tokens like `['It', 'is', 'un', 'believ', 'ably', 'good', '!']`. Most advanced language models, including ChatGPT, use subword tokenization, and you'll use this method in the next few chapters. Subword tokenization strikes a balance between the more traditional tokenization techniques that typically split text into either individual words or characters. Word-based tokenization, while capturing more meaning, leads to a vast vocabulary. Conversely, character-based tokenization results in a smaller vocabulary, but each token carries less semantic value.

Subword tokenization effectively mitigates these problems by keeping frequently used words whole in the vocabulary while dividing less common or more complex words into subcomponents. This technique is particularly advantageous for languages with large vocabularies or those exhibiting a high degree of word form variation. By adopting subword tokenization, the overall vocabulary size is substantially reduced. This reduction enhances the efficiency and effectiveness of language processing tasks, especially when dealing with a wide range of linguistic structures.

In this chapter, we will focus on word tokenization, as it offers a straightforward foundation for beginners. As we progress to later chapters, our attention will shift to subword tokenization, utilizing models that have already been trained with this technique. This approach allows us to concentrate on more advanced topics, such as understanding the Transformer architecture and exploring the inner workings of the attention mechanism.

8.2.2   Word embedding

Word embedding is a method that transforms tokens into compact vector representations, capturing their semantic information and interrelationships. This technique is vital in NLP, especially since deep neural networks, including models like LSTM and Transformers, require numerical input.

Traditionally, tokens are converted into numbers using one-hot encoding before being fed into NLP models. In one-hot encoding, each token is represented by a vector where only one element is '1', and the rest are '0's. For example, in this chapter, there are 12,778 unique word-based tokens in the text for the novel *Anna Karenina*. Each token is represented by a vector of 12,778 dimensions. Consequently, a phrase like "happy families are all alike" is represented as a $5 \times 12{,}778$ matrix, where 5 represents the number of tokens. This representation, however, is highly inefficient due to its large dimensionality, leading to an increased number of parameters, which can hinder training speed and efficiency.

LSTMs, Transformers, and other advanced NLP models address this inefficiency through word embedding. Instead of bulky one-hot vectors, word embedding uses continuous, lower-dimensional vectors (e.g., 128-value vectors we use in this chapter). As a result, the phrase "happy families are all alike" is represented by a more compact $5 \times$

128 matrix after word embedding. This streamlined representation drastically reduces the model's complexity and enhances training efficiency.

Word embedding not only reduces word complexity by condensing it into a lower-dimensional space but also effectively captures the context and the nuanced semantic relationships between words, a feature that simpler representations like one-hot encoding lack, for the following reasons. In one-hot encoding, all tokens have the same distance from each other in vector space. However, in word embeddings, tokens with similar meanings are represented by vectors close to each other in the embedding space. Word embeddings are learned from the text in the training data; the resulting vectors capture contextual information. Tokens that appear in similar contexts will have similar embeddings, even if they are not explicitly related.

Word embedding in NLP

Word embeddings are a powerful method for representing tokens in NLP that offer significant advantages over traditional one-hot encoding in capturing context and semantic relationships between words.

One-hot encoding represents tokens as sparse vectors with a dimension equal to the size of the vocabulary, where each token is represented by a vector with all zeros except for a single one at the index corresponding to the token. In contrast, word embeddings represent tokens as dense vectors with much lower dimensions (e.g., 128 dimensions in this chapter and 256 dimensions in chapter 12). This dense representation is more efficient and can capture more information.

Specifically, in one-hot encoding, all tokens have the same distance from each other in the vector space, meaning there is no notion of similarity between tokens. However, in word embeddings, similar tokens are represented by vectors that are close to each other in the embedding space. For example, the words "king" and "queen" would have similar embeddings, reflecting their semantic relationship.

Word embeddings are learned from the text in the training data. The embedding process uses the context in which tokens appear to learn their embeddings, meaning that the resulting vectors capture contextual information. Tokens that appear in similar contexts will have similar embeddings, even if they are not explicitly related.

Overall, word embeddings provide a more nuanced and efficient representation of words that captures semantic relationships and contextual information, making them more suitable for NLP tasks compared to one-hot encoding.

In practical terms, particularly in frameworks like PyTorch, word embedding is implemented by passing indexes through a linear layer, which compresses them into a lower-dimensional space. That is, when you pass an index to the `nn.Embedding()` layer, it looks up the corresponding row in the embedding matrix and returns the embedding vector for that index, avoiding the need to create potentially very large one-hot vectors. The weights of this embedding layer are not predefined but are learned during the training process. This learning aspect enables the model to refine its understanding of word semantics based on the training data, leading to a more nuanced and context-aware representation of language in the neural network. This approach significantly enhances the model's ability to process and interpret language data efficiently and meaningfully.

8.3   *Preparing data to train the LSTM model*

In this section, we'll process text data and get it ready for training. We'll first break text down into individual tokens. Our next step involves creating a dictionary that assigns each token an index, essentially mapping them to integers. After this setup, we will organize these tokens into batches of training data, which will be crucial for training an LSTM model in the subsequent section.

We'll walk through the tokenization process in a detailed, step-by-step manner, ensuring you gain a thorough understanding of how tokenization functions. We'll use word tokenization, owing to its simplicity in dividing text into words, as opposed to the more complex subword tokenization that demands a nuanced grasp of linguistic structure. In later chapters, we'll employ pretrained tokenizers for subword tokenization using more sophisticated methods. This will allow us to focus on advanced topics, such as the attention mechanism and the Transformer architecture, without getting bogged down in the initial stages of text processing.

8.3.1   *Downloading and cleaning up the text*

We'll use the text from the novel *Anna Karenina* to train our model. Go to https://mng .bz/znmX to download the text file and save it as anna.txt in the folder /files/ on your computer. After that, open the file and delete everything after line 39888, which says, `"END OF THIS PROJECT GUTENBERG EBOOK ANNA KARENINA."` Or you can simply download the file anna.txt from the book's GitHub repository: https://github.com/ markhliu/DGAI.

First, we load up the data and print out some passages to get a feeling about the dataset:

```
with open("files/anna.txt","r") as f:
    text=f.read()
words=text.split(" ")
print(words[:20])
```

The output is

```
['Chapter', '1\n\n\nHappy', 'families', 'are', 'all', 'alike;', 'every',
 'unhappy', 'family', 'is', 'unhappy', 'in', 'its',
'own\nway.\n\nEverything', 'was', 'in', 'confusion', 'in', 'the',
"Oblonskys'"]
```

As you can see, line breaks (represented by \n) are considered part of the text. Therefore, we should replace these line breaks with spaces so they are not in the vocabulary. Additionally, converting all words to lowercase is helpful in our setting, as it ensures words like "The" and "the" are recognized as the same token. This step is vital for reducing the variety of unique tokens, thereby making the training process more efficient. Furthermore, punctuation marks should be spaced apart from the words they follow. Without this separation, combinations like "way." and "way" would be erroneously treated as different tokens. To address these problems, we'll clean up the text:

```
clean_text=text.lower().replace("\n", " ")
clean_text=clean_text.replace("-", " ")
for x in ",.:;?!$()/_&%*@'`":
    clean_text=clean_text.replace(f"{x}", f" {x} ")
clean_text=clean_text.replace('"', ' " ')
text=clean_text.split()
```

Replaces line break with a space

Replaces a hyphen with a space

Adds a space around punctuation marks and special characters

Next, we obtain unique tokens:

```
from collections import Counter
word_counts = Counter(text)
words=sorted(word_counts, key=word_counts.get,
                    reverse=True)
print(words[:10])
```

The list `words` contains all the unique tokens in the text, with the most frequent one appearing first, and the least frequent one last. The output from the preceding code block is

```
[',', '.', 'the', '"', 'and', 'to', 'of', 'he', "'", 'a']
```

The preceding output shows the most frequent 10 tokens. The comma (`,`) and the period (`.`) are the most and the second most frequent tokens, respectively. The word "the" is the third most frequent token, and so on.

We now create two dictionaries: one mapping tokens to indexes and the other mapping indexes to tokens.

Listing 8.1 Dictionaries to map tokens to indexes and indexes to tokens

The length of text (how many tokens in the text)

The length of unique tokens

Maps tokens to indexes

Maps indexes to tokens

```
text_length=len(text)
num_unique_words=len(words)
print(f"the text contains {text_length} words")
print(f"there are {num_unique_words} unique tokens")
word_to_int={v:k for k,v in enumerate(words)}
int_to_word={k:v for k,v in enumerate(words)}
print({k:v for k,v in word_to_int.items() if k in words[:10]})
print({k:v for k,v in int_to_word.items() if v in words[:10]})
```

The output from the preceding code block is

```
the text contains 437098 words
there are 12778 unique tokens
{',': 0, '.': 1, 'the': 2, '"': 3, 'and': 4, 'to': 5, 'of': 6, 'he': 7,
"'": 8, 'a': 9}
{0: ',', 1: '.', 2: 'the', 3: '"', 4: 'and', 5: 'to', 6: 'of', 7: 'he',
 8: "'", 9: 'a'}
```

The text for the novel *Anna Karenina* has a total of 437,098 tokens. There are 12,778 unique tokens. The dictionary `word_to_int` assigns an index to each unique token. For example, the comma (`,`) is assigned an index of 0, and the period (`.`) is assigned an index of 1. The dictionary `int_to_word` translates an index back to a token. For example, index 2 is translated back to the token "`the`". Index 4 is translated back to the token "`and`", and so on.

Finally, we convert the whole text to indexes:

```
print(text[0:20])
wordidx=[word_to_int[w] for w in text]
print([word_to_int[w] for w in text[0:20]])
```

The output is

```
['chapter', '1', 'happy', 'families', 'are', 'all', 'alike', ';', 'every',
 'unhappy', 'family', 'is', 'unhappy', 'in', 'its', 'own', 'way', '.',
 'everything', 'was']
[208, 670, 283, 3024, 82, 31, 2461, 35, 202, 690, 365, 38, 690, 10, 234,
 147, 166, 1, 149, 12]
```

We convert all tokens in the text into the corresponding indexes and save them in a list `wordidx`. The preceding output shows the first 20 tokens in the text, as well as the corresponding indexes. For example, the first token in the text is `chapter`, with an index value of 208.

Exercise 8.3

Find out the index value of the token `anna` in the dictionary `word_to_int`.

8.3.2   Creating batches of training data

Next, we create pairs of (x, y) for training purposes. Each x is a sequence with 100 indexes. There is nothing magical about the number 100, and you can easily change it to 90 or 110 and have similar results. Setting the number too large may slow down training, while setting the number too small may lead to the model's failure to capture long-range dependencies. We then slide the window right by one token and use it as the target y. Shifting the sequence by one token to the right and using it as the output during sequence generation is a common technique in training language models, including Transformers. The code block in the following listing creates the training data.

Listing 8.2   Creating training data

```
import torch
seq_len=100                                          Each input contains
xys=[]                                               100 indexes.
for n in range(0, len(wordidx)-seq_len-1):

                                                     Starting from the first token in text,
                                                     slides to the right one at a time
```

```
x = wordidx[n:n+seq_len]
y = wordidx[n+1:n+seq_len+1]
xys.append((torch.tensor(x),(torch.tensor(y))))
```

◄────── **Defines the input x**

Shifts the input x to the right by one token and uses it as the output y

By shifting the sequence one token to the right and using it as output, the model is trained to predict the next token given the previous tokens. For instance, if the input sequence is "how are you", then the shifted sequence would be "are you today". During training, the model learns to predict 'are' after seeing 'how', 'you' after seeing 'are', and so on. This helps the model learn the probability distribution of the next token in a sequence. You'll see this practice again and again later in this book.

We'll create batches of data for training, with 32 pairs of (x, y) in each batch:

```
from torch.utils.data import DataLoader

torch.manual_seed(42)
batch_size=32
loader = DataLoader(xys, batch_size=batch_size, shuffle=True)
```

We now have the training dataset. Next, we'll create an LSTM model and train it using the data we just processed.

8.4   Building and training the LSTM model

In this section, you'll begin by constructing an LSTM model using PyTorch's built-in LSTM layer. This model will start with a word embedding layer, which transforms each index into a dense vector of 128 dimensions. Your training data will pass through this embedding layer before being fed into the LSTM layer. This LSTM layer is designed to process elements of a sequence in a sequential manner. Following the LSTM layer, the data will proceed to a linear layer, which has an output size matching the size of your vocabulary. The outputs generated by the LSTM model are essentially logits, serving as inputs for the softmax function to compute probabilities.

Once you have built the LSTM model, the next step will involve using your training data to train this model. This training phase is crucial to refine the model's ability to understand and generate patterns consistent with the data it has been fed.

8.4.1   Building an LSTM model

In listing 8.3, we define a WordLSTM() class to serve as our LSTM model to be trained to generate text in the style of *Anna Karenina*. The class is defined as shown in the following listing.

Listing 8.3   Defining the WordLSTM() class

```
from torch import nn
device="cuda" if torch.cuda.is_available() else "cpu"
class WordLSTM(nn.Module):
    def __init__(self, input_size=128, n_embed=128,
            n_layers=3, drop_prob=0.2):
```

```
        super().__init__()
        self.input_size=input_size
        self.drop_prob = drop_prob
        self.n_layers = n_layers
        self.n_embed = n_embed
        vocab_size=len(word_to_int)
        self.embedding=nn.Embedding(vocab_size,n_embed)
        self.lstm = nn.LSTM(input_size=self.input_size,
            hidden_size=self.n_embed,
            num_layers=self.n_layers,
            dropout=self.drop_prob,batch_first=True)
        self.fc = nn.Linear(input_size, vocab_size)

    def forward(self, x, hc):
        embed=self.embedding(x)
        x, hc = self.lstm(embed, hc)
        x = self.fc(x)
        return x, hc

    def init_hidden(self, n_seqs):
        weight = next(self.parameters()).data
        return (weight.new(self.n_layers,
                        n_seqs, self.n_embed).zero_(),
            weight.new(self.n_layers,
                        n_seqs, self.n_embed).zero_())
```

Training data first goes through an embedding layer.

Creates an LSTM layer with the PyTorch LSTM() class

In each time step, the LSTM layer uses the previous token and the hidden state to predict the next token and the next hidden state.

Initiates the hidden state for the first token in the input sequence

The WordLSTM() class defined previously has three layers: the word embedding layer, the LSTM layer, and a final linear layer. We set the value of the argument n_layers to 3, which means the LSTM layer stacks three LSTMs together to form a stacked LSTM, with the last two LSTMs taking the output from the previous LSTM as input. The init_hidden() method fills the hidden state with zeros when the model uses the first element in the sequence to make predictions. In each time step, the input is the current token and the previous hidden state while the output is the next token and the next hidden state.

How the `torch.nn.Embedding()` class works

The `torch.nn.Embedding()` class in PyTorch is used to create an embedding layer in a neural network. An embedding layer is a trainable lookup table that maps integer indexes to dense, continuous vector representations (embeddings).

When you create an instance of `torch.nn.Embedding()`, you need to specify two main parameters: num_embeddings, the size of the vocabulary (total number of unique tokens), and embedding_dim, the size of each embedding vector (the dimensionality of the output embeddings).

Internally, the class creates a matrix (or lookup table) of shape (num_embeddings, embedding_dim) where each row corresponds to the embedding vector for a particular index. Initially, these embeddings are randomly initialized but are learned and updated during training through backpropagation.

(continued)

When you pass a tensor of indexes to the embedding layer (during the forward pass of the network), it looks up the corresponding embedding vectors in the lookup table and returns them. More information about the class is provided by PyTorch at https://mng .bz/n0Zd.

We create an instance of the `WordLSTM()` class and use it as our LSTM model, as follows:

```
model=WordLSTM().to(device)
```

When the LSTM model is created, the weights are randomly initialized. When we use pairs of (x, y) to train the model, LSTM learns to predict the next token based on all previous tokens in the sequence by adjusting the model parameters. As we have illustrated in figure 8.2, LSTM learns to predict the next token and the next hidden state based on the current token and the current hidden state, which is a summary of the information in all previous tokens.

We use the Adam optimizer with a learning rate of 0.0001. The loss function is the cross-entropy loss since this is essentially a multicategory classification problem: the model is trying to predict the next token from a dictionary with 12,778 choices:

```
lr=0.0001
optimizer = torch.optim.Adam(model.parameters(), lr=lr)
loss_func = nn.CrossEntropyLoss()
```

Now that the LSTM model is built, we'll train the model with the batches of training data we prepared before.

8.4.2   *Training the LSTM model*

During each training epoch, we go through all data batches of data (x, y) in the training set. The LSTM model receives the input sequence, x, and generates a predicted output sequence, $\hat{y}$. This prediction is compared with the actual output sequence, y, to compute the cross-entropy loss since we essentially conduct a multicategory classification here. We then tweak the model's parameters to reduce this loss, as we did in chapter 2 when classifying clothing items.

Though we could divide our data into training and validation sets, training the model until no further improvements are seen on the validation set (as we have done in chapter 2), our primary aim here is to grasp how LSTM models function, not necessarily to achieve the best parameter tuning. Therefore, we'll train the model for 50 epochs.

Listing 8.4   Training the LSTM model to generate text

```
model.train()

for epoch in range(50):
    tloss=0
```

```
sh,sc = model.init_hidden(batch_size)
for i, (x,y) in enumerate(loader):
    if x.shape[0]==batch_size:
        inputs, targets = x.to(device), y.to(device)
        optimizer.zero_grad()
        output, (sh,sc) = model(inputs, (sh,sc))
        loss = loss_func(output.transpose(1,2),targets)
        sh,sc=sh.detach(),sc.detach()
        loss.backward()
        nn.utils.clip_grad_norm_(model.parameters(), 5)
        optimizer.step()
        tloss+=loss.item()
    if (i+1)%1000==0:
        print(f"at epoch {epoch} iteration {i+1}\
        average loss = {tloss/(i+1)}")
```

Iterates through all batches of (x,y) in the training data

Uses the model to predict the output sequence

Compares the predictions with the actual output and calculates the loss

Tweaks model parameters to minimize loss

In the preceding code listing, sh and sc together form the hidden state. In particular, the cell state sc acts as a conveyor belt, carrying information over many time steps, with information added or removed in each time step. The component sh is the output of the LSTM cell at a given time step. It contains information about the current input and is used to pass information to the next LSTM cell in the sequence.

If you have a CUDA-enabled GPU, this training takes about 6 hours. If you use CPU only, it may take a day or two, depending on your hardware. Or you can download the pretrained weights from my website: https://mng.bz/vJZa.

Next, we save the trained model weights in the local folder:

```
import pickle

torch.save(model.state_dict(),"files/wordLSTM.pth")
with open("files/word_to_int.p","wb") as fb:
    pickle.dump(word_to_int, fb)
```

The dictionary word_to_int is also saved on your computer, which is a practical step ensuring that you can generate text using the trained model without needing to repeat the tokenization process.

8.5 Generating text with the trained LSTM model

Now that you have a trained LSTM model, you'll learn how to use it to generate text in this section. The goal is to see if the trained model can generate grammatically correct and coherent text by iteratively predicting the next token based on previous tokens. You'll also learn to use temperature and top-K sampling to control the creativeness of the generated text.

When generating text with the trained LSTM model, we start with a prompt as the initial input to the model. We use the trained model to predict the most likely next token. After appending the next token to the prompt, we feed the new sequence to the trained model to predict the next token again. We repeat this process until the sequence reaches a certain length.

8.5.1   *Generating text by predicting the next token*

First, we load the trained model weights and the dictionary `word_to_int` from the local folder:

```
model.load_state_dict(torch.load("files/wordLSTM.pth",
                                 map_location=device))
with open("files/word_to_int.p","rb") as fb:
    word_to_int = pickle.load(fb)
int_to_word={v:k for k,v in word_to_int.items()}
```

The file `word_to_int.p` is also available in the book's GitHub repository. We switch the positions of keys and values in the dictionary `word_to_int` to create the dictionary `int_to_word`.

To generate text with the trained LSTM model, we need a prompt as the starting point of the generated text. We'll set the default prompt to "Anna and the." An easy way to determine when to stop is to limit the generated text to a certain length, say 200 tokens: once the desired length is reached, we ask the model to stop generating.

The following listing defines a `sample()` function to generate text based on a prompt.

Listing 8.5   A `sample()` function to generate text

```
import numpy as np
def sample(model, prompt, length=200):
    model.eval()
    text = prompt.lower().split(' ')
    hc = model.init_hidden(1)
    length = length - len(text)
    for i in range(0, length):
        if len(text)<= seq_len:
            x = torch.tensor([[word_to_int[w] for w in text]])
        else:
            x = torch.tensor([[word_to_int[w] for w \
in text[-seq_len:]]])
        inputs = x.to(device)
        output, hc = model(inputs, hc)
        logits = output[0][-1]
        p = nn.functional.softmax(logits, dim=0).detach().cpu().numpy()
        idx = np.random.choice(len(logits), p=p)
        text.append(int_to_word[idx])
    text=" ".join(text)
    for m in ",.:;?!$()/_&%*@'`":
        text=text.replace(f" {m}", f"{m} ")
    text=text.replace('" ', '"')
    text=text.replace(" ' ", " ' ")
    text=text.replace(" ' ", "'")
    text=text.replace(" ' ", "'")
    return text
```

- Determines how many tokens need to be generated
- The input is the current sequence; trims it if it's longer than 100 tokens
- Makes a prediction using the trained model
- Selects the next token based on predicted probabilities
- Appends the predicted next token to the sequence and repeats

The function `sample()` takes three arguments. The first is the trained LSTM model you will be using. The second is the starting prompt for text generation, which can be a phrase of any length, in quotes. The third parameter specifies the length of the text to be generated, measured in tokens, with a default value of 200 tokens.

Within the function, we first deduct the number of tokens in the prompt from the total desired length to determine the number of tokens that need to be generated. When generating the next token, we consider the current sequence's length. If it's under 100 tokens, we input the entire sequence into the model; if it's over 100 tokens, only the last 100 tokens of the sequence are used as input. This input is then fed into the trained LSTM model to predict the subsequent token, which we then add to the current sequence. We continue this process until the sequence reaches the desired length.

When generating the next token, the model employs the random.choice(len(logits), p = p) method from NumPy. Here, the method's first parameter indicates the range of choices, which in this case is len(logits) = 12778. This signifies that the model will randomly select an integer from 0 to 12,777, with each integer corresponding to a different token in the vocabulary. The second parameter, p, is an array containing 12,778 elements where each element denotes the probability of selecting a corresponding token from the vocabulary. Tokens with a higher probability in this array are more likely to be chosen.

Let's generate a passage with the model using "Anna and the prince" as the prompt (make sure you put a space before punctuation marks when you use your own prompt):

```
torch.manual_seed(42)
np.random.seed(42)
print(sample(model, prompt='Anna and the prince'))
```

Here, I fixed the random seed number to 42 in both PyTorch and NumPy in case you want to reproduce results. The generated passage is

```
anna and the prince did not forget what he had not spoken. when the
softening barrier was not so long as he had talked to his brother, all the
hopelessness of the impression. "official tail, a man who had tried him,
though he had been able to get across his charge and locked close, and the
light round the snow was in the light of the altar villa. the article in law
levin was first more precious than it was to him so that if it was most easy
as it would be as the same. this was now perfectly interested. when he had
got up close out into the sledge, but it was locked in the light window with
their one grass, and in the band of the leaves of his projects, and all the
same stupid woman, and really, and i swung his arms round that thinking of
bed. a little box with the two boys were with the point of a gleam of filling
the boy, noiselessly signed the bottom of his mouth, and answering them
took the red
```

You may have noticed that the text generated is entirely in lowercase. This is because, during the text processing stage, we converted all uppercase letters to lowercase to minimize the number of unique tokens.

The text generated from 6 hours of training is quite impressive! Most of the sentences adhere to grammatical norms. While it may not match the level of sophistication seen in text generated by advanced systems like ChatGPT, it's a significant achievement.

With skills acquired in this exercise, you are ready to train more advanced text generation models in later chapters.

8.5.2   *Temperature and top-K sampling in text generation*

The creativity of the generated text can be controlled by using techniques like temperature and top-K sampling.

Temperature adjusts the distribution of probabilities assigned to each potential
token before selecting the next one. It effectively scales the logits, which are the inputs
to the softmax function calculating these probabilities, by the value of the temperature. Logits are the outputs of the LSTM model prior to the application of the softmax
function.

In the `sample()` function we just defined, we didn't adjust the logits, implying a
default temperature of 1. A lower temperature (below 1; e.g., 0.8) results in fewer variations, making the model more deterministic and conservative, favoring more likely
choices. Conversely, a higher temperature (above 1; e.g., 1.5) makes it more likely to
choose improbable words in text generation, leading to more varied and inventive outputs. However, this could also make the text less coherent or relevant, as the model
might opt for less probable words.

Top-K sampling is another method to influence the output. This approach involves
selecting the next word from the top K most probable options as predicted by the
model. The probability distribution is truncated to include only the top K words. With a
small K value, such as 5, the model's choices are limited to a few highly probable words,
resulting in more predictable and coherent but potentially less diverse and interesting
outputs. In the `sample()` function we defined earlier, we did not apply top-K sampling,
so the value of K was effectively the size of the vocabulary (12,778 in our case).

Next, we introduce a new function, `generate()`, for text generation. This function is
similar to the `sample()` function but includes two additional parameters: `temperature`
and `top_k`, allowing for more control over the creativity and randomness of the
generated text. The function `generate()` is defined in the following listing.

> **Listing 8.6   Generating text with temperature and top-K sampling**

```
def generate(model, prompt , top_k=None,
             length=200, temperature=1):
    model.eval()
    text = prompt.lower().split(' ')
    hc = model.init_hidden(1)
    length = length - len(text)
    for i in range(0, length):
        if len(text)<= seq_len:
            x = torch.tensor([[word_to_int[w] for w in text]])
        else:
            x = torch.tensor([[word_to_int[w] for w in text[-seq_len:]]])
        inputs = x.to(device)
```

```
output, hc = model(inputs, hc)                          Scales the logits with
logits = output[0][-1]                                  temperature
logits = logits/temperature
p = nn.functional.softmax(logits, dim=0).detach().cpu()
if top_k is None:
    idx = np.random.choice(len(logits), p=p.numpy())    Keeps only the K
else:                                                   most probable
    ps, tops = p.topk(top_k)                            candidates
    ps=ps/ps.sum()
    idx = np.random.choice(tops, p=ps.numpy())          Selects the next
text.append(int_to_word[idx])                           token from the top
                                                        K candidates
text=" ".join(text)
for m in ",.:;?!$()/_&%*@'`":
    text=text.replace(f" {m}", f"{m} ")
text=text.replace('" ', '"')
text=text.replace("' ", "'")
text=text.replace('" ', '"')
text=text.replace("' ", "'")
return text
```

Compared to the `sample()` function, the new function `generate()` has two more optional arguments: `top_k` and `temperature`. By default, `top_k` is set to `None`, and `temperature` is set to 1. Therefore, if you call the `generate()` function without specifying these two arguments, the output will be the same as what you would get from the function `sample()`.

Let's illustrate the variations in generated text by focusing on the creation of a single token. For this purpose, we'll use "I ' m not going to see" as the prompt (note the space before the apostrophe, as we previously have done in the chapter). We call the `generate()` function 10 times, setting its length argument to be one more than the prompt's length. This approach ensures that the function appends only one extra token to the prompt:

```
prompt="I ' m not going to see"
torch.manual_seed(42)
np.random.seed(42)
for _ in range(10):
    print(generate(model, prompt, top_k=None,
        length=len(prompt.split(" "))+1, temperature=1))
```

The output is

```
i'm not going to see you
i'm not going to see those
i'm not going to see me
i'm not going to see you
i'm not going to see her
i'm not going to see her
i'm not going to see the
i'm not going to see my
i'm not going to see you
i'm not going to see me
```

With the default setting of top_k = None and temperature = 1, there is some degree of repetition in the output. For example, the word "you" was repeated three times. There are a total of six unique tokens.

However, the functionality of generate() expands when you adjust these two arguments. For instance, setting a low temperature, like 0.5, and a small top_k value, such as 3, results in generated text that is more predictable and less creative.

Let's repeat the single token example. This time, we set the temperature to 0.5 and top_k value to 3:

```
prompt="I ' m not going to see"
torch.manual_seed(42)
np.random.seed(42)
for _ in range(10):
    print(generate(model, prompt, top_k=3,
        length=len(prompt.split(" "))+1, temperature=0.5))
```

The output is

```
i'm not going to see you
i'm not going to see the
i'm not going to see her
i'm not going to see you
i'm not going to see you
i'm not going to see you
i'm not going to see you
i'm not going to see her
i'm not going to see you
i'm not going to see her
```

The output has fewer variations: there are only 3 unique tokens from 10 attempts, "you," "the," and "her."

Let's see this in action by using "Anna and the prince" as our starting prompt when we set the temperature to 0.5 and top_k value to 3:

```
torch.manual_seed(42)
np.random.seed(42)
print(generate(model, prompt='Anna and the prince',
            top_k=3,
            temperature=0.5))
```

The output is

```
anna and the prince had no milk. but,  "answered levin,  and he stopped.
"i've been skating to look at you all the harrows,  and i'm glad. . .  ""no,
i'm going to the country. ""no,  it's not a nice fellow. ""yes,  sir.
""well,  what do you think about it? ""why,  what's the matter? ""yes,  yes,
"answered levin,  smiling,  and he went into the hall. "yes,  i'll come for
him and go away,  "he said,  looking at the crumpled front of his shirt. "i
have not come to see him,  "she said,  and she went out. "i'm very glad,
"she said,  with a slight bow to the ambassador's hand. "i'll go to the door.
"she looked at her watch,  and she did not know what to say
```

Exercise 8.4

Generate text by setting temperature to 0.6 and `top_k` to 10 and using "Anna and the nurse" as the starting prompt. Set the random seed number to 0 in both PyTorch and NumPy.

Conversely, opting for a higher `temperature` value, like 1.5, coupled with a higher `top_k` value, for instance, `None` (enabling selection from the entire pool of 12,778 tokens), leads to outputs that are more creative and less predictable. This is demonstrated next, in the single token example. This time, we set the temperature to 2 and `top_k` value to `None`:

```
prompt="I ' m not going to see"
torch.manual_seed(42)
np.random.seed(42)
for _ in range(10):
    print(generate(model, prompt, top_k=None,
        length=len(prompt.split(" "))+1, temperature=2))
```

The output is

```
i'm not going to see them
i'm not going to see scarlatina
i'm not going to see behind
i'm not going to see us
i'm not going to see it
i'm not going to see it
i'm not going to see a
i'm not going to see misery
i'm not going to see another
i'm not going to see seryozha
```

The output has almost no repetition: there are 9 unique tokens from 10 attempts; only the word "it" was repeated.

Let's again use "Anna and the prince" as the initial prompt but set the temperature to 2 and top_k value to None and see what happens:

```
torch.manual_seed(42)
np.random.seed(42)
print(generate(model, prompt='Anna and the prince',
            top_k=None,
            temperature=2))
```

The generated text is

```
anna and the prince took sheaves covered suddenly people. "pyotr marya
borissovna, propped mihail though her son will seen how much evening her
husband; if tomorrow she liked great time too. "adopted heavens details
for it women from this terrible, admitting this touching all everything
ill with flirtation shame consolation altogether: ivan only all the circle
with her honorable carriage in its house dress, beethoven ashamed had the
conversations raised mihailov stay of close i taste work? "on new farming
```

```
show ivan nothing. hat yesterday if interested understand every hundred of
two with six thousand roubles according to women living over a thousand:
snetkov possibly try disagreeable schools with stake old glory mysterious one
have people some moral conclusion,  got down and then their wreath. darya
alexandrovna thought inwardly peaceful with varenka out of the listen from
and understand presented she was impossible anguish. simply satisfied with
staying after presence came where he pushed up his hand as marya her pretty
hands into their quarters. waltz was about the rider gathered;  sviazhsky
further alone have an hand paused riding towards an exquisite
```

The output generated is not repetitive, although it lacks coherence in many places.

Exercise 8.5

Generate text by setting temperature to 2 and `top_k` to 10000 and using "Anna and the nurse" as the starting prompt. Set the random seed number to 0 in both PyTorch and NumPy.

In this chapter, you have acquired foundational skills in NLP, including word-level tokenization, word embedding, and sequence prediction. Through these exercises, you've learned to construct a language model based on word-level tokenization and have trained it using LSTM for text generation. Moving forward, the next few chapters will introduce you to training Transformers, the type of models used in systems like ChatGPT. This will provide you with a more in-depth understanding of advanced text generation techniques.

Summary

- RNNs are a specialized form of artificial neural network designed to recognize patterns in sequences of data, such as text, music, or stock prices. Unlike traditional neural networks, which process inputs independently, RNNs have loops in them, allowing information to persist. LSTM networks are improved versions of RNNs.

- There are three approaches to tokenization. The first is character tokenization, where the text is divided into its constituent characters. The second approach is word tokenization, where the text is split into individual words. The third approach is subword tokenization, which breaks words into smaller, meaningful components called subwords.

- Word embedding is a method that transforms words into compact vector representations, capturing their semantic information and interrelationships. This technique is vital in NLP, especially since deep neural networks, including models like LSTM and Transformers, require numerical input.

- Temperature is a parameter that influences the behavior of text generation models. It controls the randomness of the predictions by scaling the logits (the inputs to the softmax function for probability calculation) before applying softmax.

Low temperature makes the model more conservative in its predictions but also more repetitive. At higher temperatures, the model becomes less repetitive and more innovative, increasing the diversity of the generated text.

- Top-K sampling is another way to influence the behavior of text generation models. It involves selecting the next word from the K most likely candidates, as determined by the model. The probability distribution is truncated to keep only the top K words. Small values of K make the output more predictable and coherent but potentially less diverse and interesting.

9

A line-by-line implementation of attention and Transformer

This chapter covers

- The architecture and functionalities of encoders and decoders in Transformers
- How the attention mechanism uses query, key, and value to assign weights to elements in a sequence
- Different types of Transformers
- Building a Transformer from scratch for language translation

Transformers are advanced deep learning models that excel in handling sequence-to-sequence prediction challenges, outperforming older models like recurrent neural networks (RNNs) and convolutional neural networks (CNNs). Their strength lies in effectively understanding the relationships between elements in input and output sequences over long distances, such as two words far apart in the text. Unlike RNNs, Transformers are capable of parallel training, significantly cutting down training times and enabling the handling of vast datasets. This transformative architecture has been pivotal in the development of large language models (LLMs) like ChatGPT, BERT, and T5, marking a significant milestone in AI progress.

Prior to the introduction of Transformers in the groundbreaking 2017 paper "Attention Is All You Need" by a group of Google researchers,[1] natural language processing (NLP) and similar tasks primarily relied on RNNs, including long short-term memory (LSTM) models. RNNs, however, process information sequentially, limiting their speed due to the inability to train in parallel and struggling with maintaining information about earlier parts of a sequence, thus failing to capture long-term dependencies.

The revolutionary aspect of the Transformer architecture is its attention mechanism. This mechanism assesses the relationship between words in a sequence by assigning weights, determining the degree of relatedness in meaning among words based on the training data. This enables models like ChatGPT to comprehend relationships between words, thus understanding human language more effectively. The nonsequential processing of inputs allows for parallel training, reducing training time and facilitating the use of large datasets, thereby powering the rise of knowledgeable LLMs and the current surge in AI advancements.

In this chapter, we will implement, line by line, the creation of a Transformer from the ground up, based on the paper "Attention Is All You Need." The Transformer, once trained, can handle translations between any two languages (such as German to English or English to Chinese). In the next chapter, we'll focus on training the Transformer developed here to perform English to French translations.

To build the Transformer from scratch, we'll explore the inner workings of the self-attention mechanism, including the roles of query, key, and value vectors, and the computation of scaled dot product attention (SDPA). We'll construct an encoder layer by integrating layer normalization and residual connection into a multihead attention layer and combining it with a feed-forward layer. We'll then stack six of these encoder layers to form the encoder. Similarly, we'll develop a decoder in the Transformer that is capable of generating translation one token at a time, based on previous tokens in the translation and the encoder's output.

This groundwork will equip you to train the Transformer for translations between any two languages. In the next chapter, you'll learn to train the Transformer using a dataset containing more than 47,000 English-to-French translations. You'll witness the trained model translating common English phrases to French with an accuracy comparable to using Google Translate.

9.1   *Introduction to attention and Transformer*

To grasp the concept of Transformers in machine learning, it's essential to first understand the attention mechanism. This mechanism allows Transformers to recognize long-range dependencies between sequence elements, a feature that sets them apart from earlier sequence prediction models like RNNs. With this mechanism, Transformers can simultaneously focus on every element in a sequence, comprehending the context of each word.

---

[1]   Vaswani et al., 2017, "Attention Is All You Need." https://arxiv.org/abs/1706.03762.

Consider the word "bank" to illustrate how the attention mechanism interprets words based on context. In the sentence "I went fishing by the river yesterday, remaining near the bank the whole afternoon," the word "bank" is linked to "fishing" because it refers to the area beside a river. Here, a Transformer understands "bank" as part of the river's terrain.

By contrast, in "Kate went to the bank after work yesterday and deposited a check there," "bank" is connected to "check," leading the Transformer to identify "bank" as a financial institution. This example showcases how Transformers discern word meanings based on their surrounding context.

In this section, you'll dive deeper into the attention mechanism, exploring how it works. This process is crucial for determining the importance, or weights, of various words within a sentence. After that, we'll examine the structure of different Transformer models, including one that can translate between any two languages.

9.1.1 *The attention mechanism*

The attention mechanism is a method used to determine the interconnections between elements in a sequence. It calculates scores to indicate how one element relates to others in the sequence, with higher scores denoting a stronger relationship. In NLP, this mechanism is instrumental in linking words within a sentence meaningfully. This chapter will guide you through implementing the attention mechanism for language translation.

We'll construct a Transformer composed of an encoder and a decoder for that purpose. We'll then train the Transformer to translate English to French in the next chapter. The encoder transforms an English sentence, such as "How are you?", into vector representations that capture its meaning. The decoder then uses these vector representations to generate the French translation.

To transform the phrase "How are you?" into vector representations, the model first breaks it down into tokens [how, are, you, ?], a process similar to what you have done in chapter 8. These tokens are each represented by a 256-dimensional vector known as word embeddings, which capture the meaning of each token. The encoder also employs positional encoding, a method to determine the positions of tokens in the sequence. This positional encoding is added to the word embeddings to create input embeddings, which are then used to calculate self-attention. The input embedding for "How are you?" forms a tensor with dimensions (4, 256), where 4 represents the number of tokens and 256 is the dimensionality of each embedding.

While there are different ways to calculate attention, we'll use the most common method, SDPA. This mechanism is also called self-attention because the algorithm calculates how a word attends to all words in the sequence, including the word itself. Figure 9.1 provides a diagram of how to calculate SDPA.

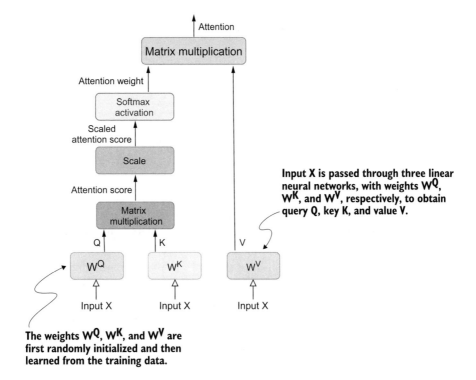

The weights W^Q, W^K, and W^V are first randomly initialized and then learned from the training data.

Figure 9.1 **A diagram of the self-attention mechanism. To calculate attention, the input embedding X is first passed through three neural layers with weights, W^Q, W^K, and W^V, respectively. The outputs are query Q, key K, and value V. The scaled attention score is the product of Q and K divided by the square root of the dimension of K, d_k. We apply the softmax function on the scaled attention score to obtain the attention weight. The attention is the product of the attention weight and value V.**

The utilization of query, key, and value in calculating attention is inspired by retrieval systems. Consider visiting a public library to find a book. If you search for "machine learning in finance" in the library's search engine, this phrase becomes your query. The book titles and descriptions in the library serve as the keys. Based on the similarity between your query and these keys, the library's retrieval system suggests a list of books (values). Books containing "machine learning," "finance," or both in their titles or descriptions are likely to rank higher. In contrast, books unrelated to these terms will have a lower matching score and thus are less likely to be recommended.

To calculate SDPA, the input embedding X is processed through three distinct neural network layers. The corresponding weights for these layers are W^Q, W^K, and W^V; each has a dimension of 256×256. These weights are learned from data during the training phase. Thus, we can calculate query Q, key K, and value V as $Q = X * W^Q$, $K = X * Q^K$, and $V = X * W^V$. The dimensions of Q, K, and V match those of the input embedding X, which are 4×256.

Similar to the retrieval system example we mentioned earlier, in the attention mechanism, we assess the similarities between the query and key vectors using the SDPA approach. SDPA involves calculating the dot product of the query (Q) and key (K) vectors. A high dot product indicates a strong similarity between the two vectors and vice versa. For instance, in the sentence "How are you?", the scaled attention score is computed as follows:

$$\text{AttentionScore}(Q, K) = \frac{Q * K^T}{\sqrt{d_k}} \tag{9.1}$$

where d_k represents the dimension of the key vector K, which in our case is 256. We scale the dot product of Q and K by the square root of d_k to stabilize training. This scaling is done to prevent the dot product from growing too large in magnitude. The dot product between the query and key vectors can become very large when the dimension of these vectors (i.e., the depth of the embedding) is high. This is because each element of the query vector is multiplied by each element of the key vector, and these products are then summed up.

The next step is to apply the softmax function to these attention scores, converting them into attention weights. This ensures that the total attention a word gives to all words in the sentence sums to 100%.

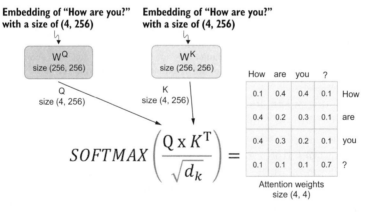

Figure 9.2 **Steps to calculate attention weights. The input embedding is passed through two neural networks to obtain query Q and key K. The scaled attention scores are calculated as the dot product of Q and K divided by the square root of the dimension of K. Finally, we apply the softmax function on the scaled attention scores to obtain attention weights, which demonstrate how each element is related to all other elements in the sequence.**

Figure 9.2 shows how this is done. For the sentence "How are you?", the attention weights form a 4×4 matrix, which shows how each token in ["How", "are," "you," "?"] is related to all other tokens (including itself). The numbers in figure 9.2 are made-up numbers to illustrate the point. For example, the first row in the attention weights shows that the token "How" gives 10% of its attention to itself and 40%, 40%, and 10% to the other three tokens, respectively.

The final attention is then calculated as the dot product of these attention weights and the value vector V (also illustrated in figure 9.3):

$$\text{Attention}(Q, K, V) = \text{softmax}\left(\frac{Q * K^T}{\sqrt{d_k}}\right) * V \qquad (9.2)$$

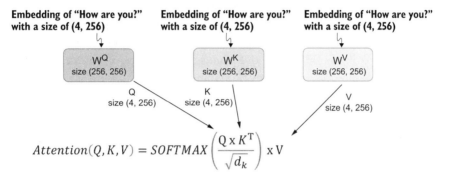

Figure 9.3 Use attention weights and the value vector to calculate the attention vector. The input embedding is passed through a neural network to obtain value V. The final attention is the dot product of the attention weights that we calculated earlier and the value vector V.

This output also maintains a dimension of 4 × 256, consistent with our input dimensions.

To summarize, the process begins with the input embedding X of the sentence "How are you?", which has a dimension of 4 × 256. This embedding captures the meanings of the four individual tokens but lacks contextualized understanding. The attention mechanism ends with the output attention(Q,K,V), which maintains the same dimension of 4 × 256. This output can be viewed as a contextually enriched combination of the original four tokens. The weighting of the original tokens varies based on the contextual relevance of each token, granting more significance to words that are more important within the sentence's context. Through this procedure, the attention mechanism transforms vectors representing isolated tokens into vectors imbued with contextualized meanings, thereby extracting a richer, more nuanced understanding from the sentence.

Further, instead of using one set of query, key, and value vectors, Transformer models use a concept called multihead attention. For example, the 256-dimensional query, key, and value vectors can be split into say, 8, heads, and each head has a set of query, key, and value vectors with dimensions of 32 (because 256/8 = 32). Each head pays attention to different parts or aspects of the input, enabling the model to capture a broader range of information and form a more detailed and contextual understanding of the input data. Multihead attention is especially useful when a word has multiple meanings in a sentence, such as in a pun. Let's continue the "bank" example we mentioned earlier. Consider the pun joke, "Why is the river so rich? Because it has two banks." In the project of translating English to French in the next chapter, you'll implement first-hand splitting Q, K, and V into multiple heads to calculate attention in each head before concatenating them back into one single attention vector.

9.1.2   *The Transformer architecture*

The concept of the attention mechanism was introduced by Bahdanau, Cho, and Bengio in 2014.[2] It became widely used after the groundbreaking paper "Attention Is All You Need," which focused on creating a model for machine language translation. The architecture of this model, known as the Transformer, is depicted in figure 9.4. It features an encoder-decoder structure that relies heavily on the attention mechanism. In this chapter, you'll build this model from scratch, coding it line by line, intending to train it for translation between any two languages.

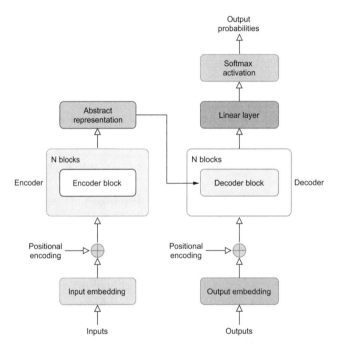

Figure 9.4   The Transformer architecture. The encoder in the Transformer (left side of the diagram), which consists of N identical encoder layers, learns the meaning of the input sequence and converts it into vectors that represent its meaning. It then passes these vectors to the decoder (right side of the diagram), which consists of N identical decoder layers. The decoder constructs the output (e.g., the French translation of an English phrase) by predicting one token at a time, based on previous tokens in the sequence and vector representations from the encoder. The generator on the top right is the head attached to the output from the decoder so that the output is the probability distribution over all tokens in the target language (e.g., the French vocabulary).

---

[2]   Dzmitry Bahdanau, Kyunghyun Cho, and Yoshua Bengio, 2014, "Neural Machine Translation by Jointly Learning to Align and Translate." https://arxiv.org/abs/1409.0473.

Let's use English-to-French translation as our example. The Transformer's encoder transforms an English sentence like "I don't speak French" into vector representations that store its meaning. The Transformer's decoder then processes them to produce the French translation "Je ne parle pas français." The encoder's role is to capture the essence of the original English sentence. For instance, if the encoder is effective, it should translate both "I don't speak French" and "I do not speak French" into similar vector representations. Consequently, the decoder will interpret these vectors and generate similar translations. Interestingly, when using ChatGPT, these two English phrases indeed result in the same French translation.

The encoder in the Transformer approaches the task by first tokenizing both the English and French sentences. This is similar to the process described in chapter 8 but with a key difference: it employs subword tokenization. Subword tokenization is a technique used in NLP to break words into smaller components, or subwords, allowing for more efficient and nuanced processing. For example, as you'll see in the next chapter, the English phrase "I do not speak French" is divided into six tokens: (i, do, not, speak, fr, ench). Similarly, its French counterpart "Je ne parle pas français" is tokenized into six parts: (je, ne, parle, pas, franc, ais). This method of tokenization enhances the Transformer's ability to handle language variations and complexities.

Deep learning models, including Transformers, can't directly process text, so tokens are indexed using integers before being fed to the model. These tokens are typically first represented using one-hot encoding, as we discussed in chapter 8. We then pass them through a word embedding layer to compress them into vectors with continuous values of a much smaller size, such as a length of 256. Thus, after applying word embedding, the sentence "I do not speak French" is represented by a 6×256 matrix.

Transformers process input data such as sentences in parallel, unlike RNNs, which handle data sequentially. This parallelism enhances their efficiency but doesn't inherently allow them to recognize the sequence order of the input. To address this, Transformers add positional encodings to the input embeddings. These positional encodings are unique vectors assigned to each position in the input sequence and align in dimension with the input embeddings. The vector values are determined by a specific positional function, particularly involving sine and cosine functions of varying frequencies, defined as

$$\text{PositionalEncoding}\,(\text{pos}, 2i) = \sin\left(\frac{\text{pos}}{n^{2i/d}}\right)$$

$$\text{PositionalEncoding}\,(\text{pos}, 2i + 1) = \cos\left(\frac{\text{pos}}{n^{2i/d}}\right) \tag{9.3}$$

In these equations, vectors are calculated using the sine function for even indexes and the cosine function for odd indexes. The two parameters *pos* and i represent the position of a token within the sequence and the index within the vector, respectively. As an illustration, consider the positional encoding for the phrase "I do not speak French." This is depicted as a 6×256 matrix, the same size as the word embedding for the sentence. Here, *pos* ranges from 0 to 5, and the indexes 2i and 2i + 1 collectively span 256 distinct values (from 0 to 255). A beneficial aspect of this positional encoding approach is that all values are constrained within the range of –1 to 1.

It's important to note that each token position is uniquely identified by a 256-dimensional vector, and these vector values remain constant throughout training. Before being input to the attention layers, these positional encodings are added to the word embeddings of the sequence. In the example of the sentence "I do not speak French," the encoder generates both word embedding and positional encoding, each having dimensions of 6×256, before combining them into a single 6×256-dimensional representation. Subsequently, the encoder applies the attention mechanism to refine this embedding into more sophisticated vector representations that capture the overall meaning of the phrase, before passing them to the decoder.

The Transformer's encoder, as depicted in figure 9.5, is made up of six identical layers (N = 6). Each of these layers comprises two distinct sublayers. The first sublayer is a multihead self-attention layer, similar to what was discussed earlier. The second sublayer is a basic, position-wise, fully connected feed-forward network. This network treats each position in the sequence independently rather than as sequential elements. In the model's architecture, each sublayer incorporates layer normalization and a residual connection. Layer normalization normalizes observations to have zero mean and unit standard deviation. Such normalization helps stabilize the training process. After the normalization layer, we perform the residual connection. This means the input to each sublayer is added to its output, enhancing the flow of information through the network.

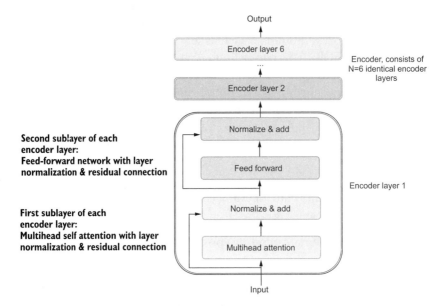

Figure 9.5 **The structure of the encoder in the Transformer. The encoder consists of N = 6 identical encoder layers. Each encoder layer contains two sublayers. The first sublayer is a multihead self-attention layer and the second is a feed-forward network. Each sublayer uses layer normalization and residual connection.**

The decoder of the Transformer model, as seen in figure 9.6, is comprised of six identical decoder layers (N = 6). Each of these decoder layers features three sublayers: a multihead self-attention sublayer, a sublayer that performs multihead cross attention between the output from the first sublayer and the encoder's output, and a feed-forward sublayer. Note that the input to each sublayer is the output from the previous sublayer. Further, the second sublayer in the decoder layer also takes the output from the encoder as input. This design is crucial for integrating information from the encoder: this is how the decode generates translations based on the output from the encoder.

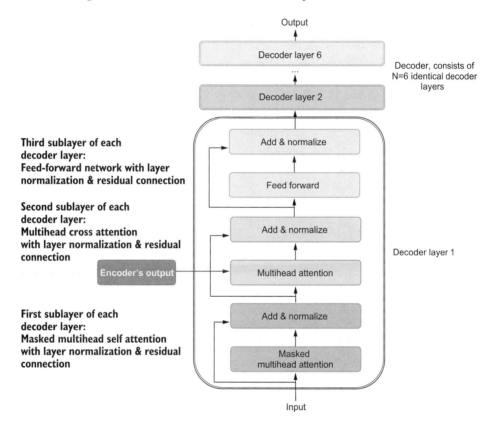

Figure 9.6   The structure of the decoder in the Transformer. The decoder consists of N = 6 identical decoder layers. Each decoder layer contains three sublayers. The first sublayer is a masked multihead self-attention layer. The second is a multihead cross-attention layer to calculate the cross attention between the output from the first sublayer and the output from the encoder. The third sublayer is a feed-forward network. Each sublayer uses layer normalization and residual connection.

A key aspect of the decoder's self-attention sublayer is the masking mechanism. This mask prevents the model from accessing future positions in the sequence, ensuring that predictions for a particular position can only depend on previously known elements. This sequential dependency is vital for tasks like language translation or text generation.

The decoding process begins with the decoder receiving an input phrase in French. The decoder transforms the French tokens into word embeddings and positional encodings before combining them into a single embedding. This step ensures that the model not only understands the semantic content of the phrase but also maintains the sequential context, which is crucial for accurate translation or generation tasks.

The decoder operates in an autoregressive manner, generating the output sequence one token at a time. At the first time step, it starts with the `"BOS"` token, which indicates the beginning of a sentence. Using this start token as its initial input, the decoder examines vector representations of the English phrase "I do not speak French" and attempts to predict the first token following `"BOS"`. Suppose the decoder's first prediction is `"Je"`. In the next time step, it then uses the sequence `"BOS Je"` as its new input to predict the following token. This process continues iteratively, with the decoder adding each newly predicted token to its input sequence for the subsequent prediction.

The translation process is designed to conclude when the decoder predicts the `"EOS"` token, signifying the end of the sentence. When preparing for the training data, we add EOS to the end of each phrase, so the model has learned that it means the end of a sentence. Upon reaching this token, the decoder recognizes the completion of the translation task and ceases its operation. This autoregressive approach ensures that each step in the decoding process is informed by all previously predicted tokens, allowing for coherent and contextually appropriate translations.

9.1.3   *Different types of Transformers*

There are three types of Transformers: encoder-only Transformers, decoder-only Transformers, and encoder-decoder Transformers. We are using an encoder-decoder Transformer in this chapter and the next, but you'll get a chance to explore firsthand decoder-only Transformers later in the book.

An encoder-only Transformer consists of N identical encoder layers as shown on the left side of figure 9.4 and is capable of converting a sequence into abstract continuous vector representations. For example, BERT is an encoder-only Transformer that contains 12 encoder layers. An encoder-only Transformer can be used for text classification, for example. If two sentences have similar vector representations, we can classify the two sentences into one category. On the other hand, if two sequences have very different vector representations, we can put them in different categories.

A decoder-only Transformer also consists of N identical layers, and each layer is a decoder layer as shown on the right side of figure 9.4. For example, ChatGPT is a decoder-only Transformer that contains many decoder layers. The decoder-only Transformer can generate text based on a prompt, for example. It extracts the semantic meaning of the words in the prompt and predicts the most likely next token. It then adds the token to the end of the prompt and repeats the process until the text reaches a certain length.

The machine language translation Transformer we discussed earlier is an example of an encoder-decoder Transformer. They are needed for handling complicated tasks, such as text-to-image generation or speech recognition. Encoder-decoder Transformers combine the strengths of both encoders and decoders. Encoders are efficient in processing and understanding input data, while decoders excel in generating output. This combination allows the model to effectively understand complex inputs (like text or speech) and generate intricate outputs (like images or transcribed text).

9.2 Building an encoder

We'll develop and train an encoder-decoder Transformer designed for machine language translation. The coding in this project is adapted from the work of Chris Cui in translating Chinese to English (https://mng.bz/9o1o) and Alexander Rush's German-to-English translation project (https://mng.bz/j0mp).

This section discusses how to construct an encoder in the Transformer. Specifically, we'll dive into the process of building various sublayers within each encoder layer and implementing the multihead self-attention mechanism.

9.2.1 The attention mechanism

While there are different attention mechanisms, we'll use the SDPA because it's widely used and effective. The SDPA attention mechanism uses query, key, and value to calculate the relationships among elements in a sequence. It assigns scores to show how an element is related to all elements in a sequence (including the element itself).

Instead of using one set of query, key, and value vectors, the Transformer model uses a concept called multihead attention. Our 256-dimensional query, key, and value vectors are split into 8 heads, and each head has a set of query, key, and value vectors with dimensions of 32 (because $256/8 = 32$). Each head pays attention to different parts or aspects of the input, enabling the model to capture a broader range of information and form a more detailed and contextual understanding of the input data. For example, multihead attention allows the model to capture the multiple meanings of the word "bank" in the pun joke, "Why is the river so rich? Because it has two banks."

To implement this, we define an `attention()` function in the local module ch09util. Download the file ch09util.py from the book's GitHub repository (https://github.com/markhliu/DGAI) and store it in the /utils/ directory on your computer. The attention() function is defined as shown in the following listing.

Listing 9.1 Calculating attention based on query, key, and value

Scaled attention score is the dot product of query and key, scaled by the square root of d_k.

```
def attention(query, key, value, mask=None, dropout=None):
    d_k = query.size(-1)
    scores = torch.matmul(query,
            key.transpose(-2, -1)) / math.sqrt(d_k)      ◀── If there is a
    if mask is not None:                                         mask, hides
        scores = scores.masked_fill(mask == 0, -1e9)      ◀──    future
    p_attn = nn.functional.softmax(scores, dim=-1)        ◀──    elements in
    if dropout is not None:                                      the sequence
        p_attn = dropout(p_attn)                          ◀── Calculates attention
    return torch.matmul(p_attn, value), p_attn                  weights
                                                          ◀── Returns both attention
                                                              and attention weights
```

The `attention()` function takes query, key, and value as inputs and calculates attention and attention weights as we discussed earlier in this chapter. The scaled attention score is the dot product of query and key, scaled by the square root of the dimension of the key, d_k. We apply the softmax function on the scaled attention score to obtain attention weights. Finally, attention is calculated as the dot product of attention weights and value.

Let's use our running example to show how multihead attention works (see figure 9.7). The embedding for "How are you?" is a tensor with a size of (1, 6, 256), as we explained in the last section (after we add positional encoding to word embedding). Note that 1 means there is one sentence in the batch, and there are six tokens in the sentence instead of four because we add BOS and EOS to the beginning and the end of the sequence. This embedding is passed through three linear layers to obtain query Q, key K, and value V, each of the same size (1, 6, 256). These are divided into eight heads, resulting in eight distinct sets of Q, K, and V, now sized (1, 6, 256/8 = 32) each. The attention function, as defined earlier, is applied to each of these sets, yielding eight attention outputs, each also sized (1, 6, 32). We then concatenate the eight attention outputs into one single attention, and the result is a tensor with a size of (1, 6, 32 × 8 = 256). Finally, this combined attention passes through another linear layer sized 256 × 256, leading to the output from the `MultiHeadAttention()` class. This output maintains the original input's dimensions, which are (1, 6, 256).

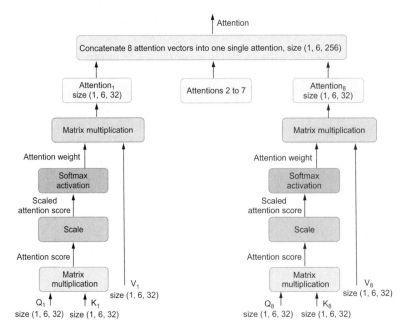

Figure 9.7 An example of multihead attention. This diagram uses the calculation of the multihead self attention for the phrase "How are you?" as an example. We first pass the embedding through three neural networks to obtain query Q, key K, and value V, each with a size of (1, 6, 256). We split them into eight heads, each with a set of Q, k, and V, with a size of (1, 6, 32). We calculate the attention in each head. The attention vectors from the eight heads are then joined back into one single attention vector, with a size of (1, 6, 256).

This is implemented in the following code listing in the local module.

Listing 9.2 Calculating multihead attention

```
from copy import deepcopy
class MultiHeadedAttention(nn.Module):
    def __init__(self, h, d_model, dropout=0.1):
        super().__init__()
        assert d_model % h == 0
        self.d_k = d_model // h
        self.h = h
        self.linears = nn.ModuleList([deepcopy(
            nn.Linear(d_model, d_model)) for i in range(4)])
        self.attn = None
        self.dropout = nn.Dropout(p=dropout)

    def forward(self, query, key, value, mask=None):
        if mask is not None:
            mask = mask.unsqueeze(1)
        nbatches = query.size(0)
        query, key, value = [l(x).view(nbatches, -1, self.h,
            self.d_k).transpose(1, 2)
          for l, x in zip(self.linears, (query, key, value))]
        x, self.attn = attention(
            query, key, value, mask=mask, dropout=self.dropout)
        x = x.transpose(1, 2).contiguous().view(
            nbatches, -1, self.h * self.d_k)
        output = self.linears[-1](x)
        return output
```

Passes input through three linear layers to obtain Q, K, V, and splits them into multiheads

Calculates attention and attention weights for each head

Concatenates attention vectors from multiheads into one single attention vector

Passes the output through a linear layer

Each encoder layer and decoder layer also contain a feed-forward sublayer, which is a two-layer fully connected neural network, with the purpose of enhancing the model's ability to capture and learn intricate features in the training dataset. Further, the neural network processes each embedding independently. It doesn't treat the sequence of embeddings as a single vector. Therefore, we often call it a position-wide feed-forward network (or a 1D convolutional network). For that purpose, we define a PositionwiseFeedForward() class in the local module as follows:

```
class PositionwiseFeedForward(nn.Module):
    def __init__(self, d_model, d_ff, dropout=0.1):
        super().__init__()
        self.w_1 = nn.Linear(d_model, d_ff)
        self.w_2 = nn.Linear(d_ff, d_model)
        self.dropout = nn.Dropout(dropout)
    def forward(self, x):
        h1 = self.w_1(x)
        h2 = self.dropout(h1)
        return self.w_2(h2)
```

The `PositionwiseFeedForward()` class is defined with two key parameters: `d_ff`, the dimensionality of the feed-forward layer, and `d_model`, representing the model's dimension size. Typically, `d_ff` is chosen to be four times the size of `d_model`. In our example, `d_model` is 256, and we therefore set `d_ff` to 256 * 4 = 1024. This practice of enlarging the hidden layer in comparison to the model size is a standard approach in Transformer architectures. It enhances the network's ability to capture and learn intricate features in the training dataset.

9.2.2 Creating an encoder

To create an encoder layer, we first define the following `EncoderLayer()` class and `SublayerConnection()` class.

Listing 9.3 A class to define an encoder layer

```
class EncoderLayer(nn.Module):
    def __init__(self, size, self_attn, feed_forward, dropout):
        super().__init__()
        self.self_attn = self_attn
        self.feed_forward = feed_forward
        self.sublayer = nn.ModuleList([deepcopy(
        SublayerConnection(size, dropout)) for i in range(2)])
        self.size = size
    def forward(self, x, mask):
        x = self.sublayer[0](
            x, lambda x: self.self_attn(x, x, x, mask))
        output = self.sublayer[1](x, self.feed_forward)
        return output
class SublayerConnection(nn.Module):
    def __init__(self, size, dropout):
        super().__init__()
        self.norm = LayerNorm(size)
        self.dropout = nn.Dropout(dropout)
    def forward(self, x, sublayer):
        output = x + self.dropout(sublayer(self.norm(x)))
        return output
```

The first sublayer in each encoder layer is a multihead self-attention network.

The second sublayer in each encoder layer is a feed-forward network.

Each sublayer goes through residual connection and layer normalization.

Each encoder layer is composed of two distinct sublayers: one is a multihead self-attention layer, as outlined in the `MultiHeadAttention()` class, and the other is a straightforward, position-wise, fully connected feed-forward network, as specified in the `PositionwiseFeedForward()` class. Additionally, both of these sublayers incorporate layer normalization and residual connections. As explained in chapter 6, a residual connection involves passing the input through a sequence of transformations (either the attention or the feed-forward layer in this context) and then adding the input back to these transformations' output. The method of residual connection is employed to combat the problem of vanishing gradients, which is a common challenge in very deep networks. Another benefit of residual connections in Transformers is to provide a passage to pass the positional encodings (which are calculated only before the first layer) to subsequent layers.

Layer normalization is somewhat similar to the batch normalization we implemented in chapter 4. It standardizes the observations in a layer to have a zero mean and a unit standard deviation. To achieve this within the local module, we define the `LayerNorm()` class, which executes layer normalization as follows:

```
class LayerNorm(nn.Module):
    def __init__(self, features, eps=1e-6):
        super().__init__()
        self.a_2 = nn.Parameter(torch.ones(features))
        self.b_2 = nn.Parameter(torch.zeros(features))
        self.eps = eps
    def forward(self, x):
        mean = x.mean(-1, keepdim=True)
        std = x.std(-1, keepdim=True)
        x_zscore = (x - mean) / torch.sqrt(std ** 2 + self.eps)
        output = self.a_2*x_zscore+self.b_2
        return output
```

The `mean` and `std` values in the preceding `LayerNorm()` class are the mean and standard deviation of the inputs in each layer. The a_2 and b_2 layers in the `LayerNorm()` class expand x_zscore back to the shape of the input x.

We can now create an encoder by stacking six encoder layers together. For that purpose, we define the `Encoder()` class in the local module:

```
from copy import deepcopy
class Encoder(nn.Module):
    def __init__(self, layer, N):
        super().__init__()
        self.layers = nn.ModuleList(
            [deepcopy(layer) for i in range(N)])
        self.norm = LayerNorm(layer.size)
    def forward(self, x, mask):
        for layer in self.layers:
            x = layer(x, mask)
            output = self.norm(x)
        return output
```

Here, the `Encoder()` class is defined with two arguments: `layer`, which is an encoder layer as defined in the `EncoderLayer()` class in listing 9.3, and `N`, the number of encoder layers in the encoder. The `Encoder()` class takes input x (for example, a batch of English phrases) and the mask (to mask out sequence padding, as I'll explain in chapter 10) to generate output (vector representations that capture the meanings of the English phrases).

With that, you have created an encoder. Next, you'll learn how to create a decoder.

9.3 *Building an encoder-decoder Transformer*

Now that you understand how to create an encoder in the Transformer, let's move on to the decoder. You'll first learn how to create a decoder layer in this section. You'll then stack N = 6 identical decoder layers to form a decoder.

We then create an encoder-decoder transformer with five components: `encoder`, `decoder`, `src_embed`, `tgt_embed`, and `generator`, which I'll explain in this section.

9.3.1 *Creating a decoder layer*

Each decoder layer consists of three sublayers: (1) a multihead self-attention layer, (2) the cross attention between the output from the first sublayer and the encoder's output, and (3) a feed-forward network. Each of these three sublayers incorporates a layer normalization and the residual connection, similar to what we have done in encoder layers. Furthermore, the decoder stack's multihead self-attention sublayer is masked to prevent positions from attending to subsequent positions. The mask forces the model to use previous elements in a sequence to predict later elements. I'll explain how masked multihead self-attention works in a moment. To implement this, we define the `DecoderLayer()` class in the local module.

Listing 9.4   Creating a decoder layer

```
class DecoderLayer(nn.Module):
    def __init__(self, size, self_attn, src_attn,
                 feed_forward, dropout):
        super().__init__()
        self.size = size
        self.self_attn = self_attn
        self.src_attn = src_attn
        self.feed_forward = feed_forward
        self.sublayer = nn.ModuleList([deepcopy(
        SublayerConnection(size, dropout)) for i in range(3)])
    def forward(self, x, memory, src_mask, tgt_mask):
        x = self.sublayer[0](x, lambda x:
                self.self_attn(x, x, x, tgt_mask))
        x = self.sublayer[1](x, lambda x:
                self.src_attn(x, memory, memory, src_mask))
        output = self.sublayer[2](x, self.feed_forward)
        return output
```

> The first sublayer is a masked multihead self-attention layer.

> The second sublayer is a cross-attention layer between the target language and the source language.

> The third sublayer is a feed-forward network.

To illustrate the operation of a decoder layer, let's consider our ongoing example. The decoder takes in tokens `['BOS', 'comment', 'et', 'es-vous', '?']`, along with the output from the encoder (referred to as `memory` in the preceding code block), to predict the sequence ['comment', 'et', 'es-vous', '?', 'EOS']. The embedding of ['BOS', 'comment', 'et', 'es-vous', '?'] is a tensor of size (1, 5, 256): 1 is the number of sequences in the batch, 5 is the number of tokens in the sequence, and 256 means each token is represented by a 256-value vector. We pass this embedding through the first sublayer, a masked multihead self-attention layer. This process is similar to the multihead self-attention calculation you saw earlier in the encoder layer. However, the process utilizes a mask, designated as tgt_mask in the preceding code block, which is a 5 × 5 tensor with the following values in the ongoing example:

```
tensor([[ True, False, False, False, False],
        [ True,  True, False, False, False],
        [ True,  True,  True, False, False],
        [ True,  True,  True,  True, False],
        [ True,  True,  True,  True,  True]], device='cuda:0')
```

As you may have noticed, the lower half of the mask (values below the main diagonal in the tensor) is turned on as True, and the upper half of the mask (values above the main diagonal) is turned off as False. When this mask is applied to the attention scores, it results in the first token attending only to itself during the first time step. In the second time step, attention scores are calculated exclusively between the first two tokens. As the process continues, for example, in the third time step, the decoder uses tokens ['BOS', 'comment', 'et'] to predict the token 'es-vous', and the attention scores are computed only among these three tokens, effectively hiding the future tokens ['es-vous', '?']

Following this process, the output generated from the first sublayer, which is a tensor of size (1, 5, 256), matches the input's size. This output, which we can refer to as x, is then fed into the second sublayer. Here, cross attention is computed between x and the output of the encoder stack, termed memory. You may remember that memory has a dimension of (1, 6, 256) since the English phrase "How are you?" is converted to six tokens ['BOS', 'how', 'are', 'you', '?', 'EOS'].

Figure 9.8 shows how cross-attention weights are calculated. To calculate the cross attention between x and memory, we first pass x through a neural network to obtain query, which has a dimension of (1, 5, 256). We then pass memory through two neural networks to obtain key and value, each having a dimension of (1, 6, 256). The scaled attention score is calculated using the formula as specified in equation 9.1. This scaled attention score has a dimension of (1, 5, 6): the query Q has a dimension of (1, 5, 256) and the transposed key K has a dimension of (1, 256, 6). Therefore, the scaled attention score, which is the dot product of the two, scaled by $\sqrt{d_k}$, has a size of (1, 5, 6). After applying the softmax function to the scaled attention score, we obtain attention weights, which is a 5 × 6 matrix. This matrix tells us how the five tokens in the French input ['BOS', 'comment', 'et', 'es-vous', '?'] attend to the six tokens in the English phrase ['BOS', 'how', 'are', 'you', '?', 'EOS']. This is how the decoder captures the meaning of the English phrase when translating.

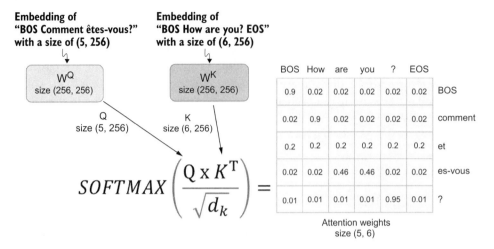

Figure 9.8 An example of how cross-attention weights are calculated between the input to the decoder and the output from the encoder. The input to the decoder is passed through a neural network to obtain query Q. The output from the encoder is passed through a different neural network to obtain key K. The scaled cross-attention scores are calculated as the dot product of Q and K divided by the square root of the dimension of K. Finally, we apply the softmax function on the scaled cross-attention scores to obtain the cross-attention weights, which demonstrate how each element in Q is related to all elements in K.

The final cross attention in the second sublayer is then calculated as the dot product of attention weights and the value vector V. The attention weights have a dimension of $(1, 5, 6)$ and the value vector has a dimension of $(1, 6, 256)$, so the final cross attention, which is the dot product of the two, has a size of $(1, 5, 256)$. Therefore, the input and output of the second sublayer have the same dimension of $(1, 5, 256)$. After processing through this second sublayer, the output is then directed through the third sublayer, which is a feed-forward network.

9.3.2 Creating an encoder-decoder Transformer

The decoder consists of N = 6 identical decoder layers.

The `Decoder()` class is defined in the local module as follows:

```
class Decoder(nn.Module):
    def __init__(self, layer, N):
        super().__init__()
        self.layers = nn.ModuleList(
            [deepcopy(layer) for i in range(N)])
        self.norm = LayerNorm(layer.size)
    def forward(self, x, memory, src_mask, tgt_mask):
        for layer in self.layers:
            x = layer(x, memory, src_mask, tgt_mask)
        output = self.norm(x)
        return output
```

To create an encoder-decoder transformer, we first define a `Transformer()` class in the local module. Open the file ch09util.py, and you'll see the definition of the class as shown in the following listing.

Listing 9.5   A class to represent an encoder-decoder Transformer

```
class Transformer(nn.Module):
    def __init__(self, encoder, decoder,
                 src_embed, tgt_embed, generator):
        super().__init__()
        self.encoder = encoder
        self.decoder = decoder
        self.src_embed = src_embed
        self.tgt_embed = tgt_embed
        self.generator = generator
    def encode(self, src, src_mask):
        return self.encoder(self.src_embed(src), src_mask)
    def decode(self, memory, src_mask, tgt, tgt_mask):
        return self.decoder(self.tgt_embed(tgt),
                            memory, src_mask, tgt_mask)
    def forward(self, src, tgt, src_mask, tgt_mask):
        memory = self.encode(src, src_mask)
        output = self.decode(memory, src_mask, tgt, tgt_mask)
        return output
```

Defines the encoder in the Transformer

Defines the decoder in the Transformer

Source language is encoded into abstract vector representations.

The decoder uses these vector representations to generate translation in the target language.

The `Transformer()` class is constructed with five key components: `encoder`, `decoder`, `src_embed`, `tgt_embed`, and `generator`. The encoder and decoder are represented by the `Encoder()` and `Decoder()` classes defined previously. In the next chapter, you'll learn to generate the source language embedding: we'll process numerical representations of English phrases using word embedding and positional encoding, combining the results to form the `src_embed` component. Similarly, for the target language, we process numerical representations of French phrases in the same manner, using the combined output as the `tgt_embed` component. The generator produces predicted probabilities for each index that corresponds to the tokens in the target language. We'll define a `Generator()` class in the next section for this purpose.

9.4   *Putting all the pieces together*

In this section, we'll put all the pieces together to create a model that can translate between any two languages.

9.4.1   *Defining a generator*

First, we define a `Generator()` class in the local module to generate the probability distribution of the next token (see figure 9.9). The idea is to attach a head to the decoder for downstream tasks. In our example in the next chapter, the downstream task is to predict the next token in the French translation.

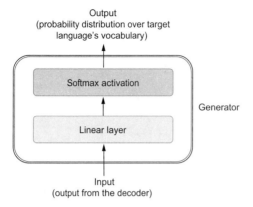

Figure 9.9   The structure of the generator in the Transformer. The generator converts the output from the decoder stack to a probability distribution over the target language's vocabulary, so that the Transformer can use the distribution to predict the next token in the French translation of an English phrase. The generator contains a linear layer so that the number of outputs is the same as the number of tokens in the French vocabulary. The generator also applies a softmax activation to the output so that the output is a probability distribution.

The class is defined as follows:

```
class Generator(nn.Module):
    def __init__(self, d_model, vocab):
        super().__init__()
        self.proj = nn.Linear(d_model, vocab)

    def forward(self, x):
        out = self.proj(x)
        probs = nn.functional.log_softmax(out, dim=-1)
        return probs
```

The Generator() class produces predicted probabilities for each index that corresponds to the tokens in the target language. This enables the model to sequentially predict tokens in an autoregressive manner, utilizing previously generated tokens and the encoder's output.

9.4.2   *Creating a model to translate between two languages*

Now we are ready to create a Transformer model to translate between any two languages (e.g., English to French or Chinese to English). The create_model() function defined in the local module accomplishes that.

> **Listing 9.6   Creating a Transformer to translate between two languages**

```
def create_model(src_vocab, tgt_vocab, N, d_model,
                 d_ff, h, dropout=0.1):
    attn=MultiHeadedAttention(h, d_model).to(DEVICE)
    ff=PositionwiseFeedForward(d_model, d_ff, dropout).to(DEVICE)
    pos=PositionalEncoding(d_model, dropout).to(DEVICE)
```

Creates an encoder by
instantiating the Encoder() class

```
model = Transformer(
    Encoder(EncoderLayer(d_model,deepcopy(attn),deepcopy(ff),
                      dropout).to(DEVICE),N).to(DEVICE),
    Decoder(DecoderLayer(d_model,deepcopy(attn),
        deepcopy(attn),deepcopy(ff), dropout).to(DEVICE),
            N).to(DEVICE),
    nn.Sequential(Embeddings(d_model, src_vocab).to(DEVICE),
                deepcopy(pos)),
    nn.Sequential(Embeddings(d_model, tgt_vocab).to(DEVICE),
                deepcopy(pos)),
    Generator(d_model, tgt_vocab)).to(DEVICE)
for p in model.parameters():
    if p.dim() > 1:
        nn.init.xavier_uniform_(p)
return model.to(DEVICE)
```

Creates a
decoder by
instantiating
the Decoder()
class

Creates src_embed
by passing source
language through
word embedding
and positional
encoding

Creates tgt_embed
by passing target
language through
word embedding
and positional
encoding

Creates a generator by instantiating
the Generator() class

The primary element of the `create_model()` function is the `Transformer()` class, which was previously defined. Recall that the `Transformer()` class is built with five essential elements: `encoder`, `decoder`, `src_embed`, `tgt_embed`, and `generator`. Within the create_model() function, we sequentially construct these five components, using the recently defined `Encoder()`, `Decoder()`, and `Generator()` classes. In the next chapter, we'll discuss in detail how to generate the source and target language embeddings, `src_embed` and `tgt_embed`.

In the next chapter, you'll apply the Transformer you created here to English-to-French translation. You'll train the model using more than 47,000 pairs of English-to-French translations. You'll then use the trained model to translate common English phrases into French.

Summary

- Transformers are advanced deep-learning models that excel in handling sequence-to-sequence prediction challenges. Their strength lies in effectively understanding the relationships between elements in input and output sequences over long distances.

- The revolutionary aspect of the Transformer architecture is its attention mechanism. This mechanism assesses the relationship between words in a sequence by assigning weights, determining how closely words are related based on the training data. This enables Transformer models like ChatGPT to comprehend relationships between words, thus understanding human language more effectively.

- To calculate SDPA, the input embedding X is processed through three distinct neural network layers, query (Q), key (K), and value (V). The corresponding weights for these layers are W^Q, W^K, and W^V. We can calculate Q, K, and V as Q = X * W^Q, K = X * Q^K, and V = X * W^V. SDPA is calculated as follows:

$$\text{Attention}\ (Q, K, V) = \text{softmax}\left(\frac{Q * K^T}{\sqrt{d_k}}\right) * V$$

where d_k represents the dimension of the key vector K. The softmax function is applied to the attention scores, converting them into attention weights. This ensures that the total attention a word gives to all words in the sentence sums to 100%. The final attention is the dot product of these attention weights and the value vector V.

- Instead of using one set of query, key, and value vectors, Transformer models use a concept called multihead attention. The query, key, and value vectors are split into multiple heads. Each head pays attention to different parts or aspects of the input, enabling the model to capture a broader range of information and form a more detailed and contextual understanding of the input data. Multihead attention is especially useful when a word has multiple meanings in a sentence.

Training a Transformer to translate English to French

10

This chapter covers

- Tokenizing English and French phrases to subwords
- Understanding word embedding and positional encoding
- Training a Transformer from scratch to translate English to French
- Using the trained Transformer to translate an English phrase into French

In the last chapter, we built a Transformer from scratch that can translate between any two languages, based on the paper "Attention Is All You Need."[1] Specifically, we implemented the self-attention mechanism, using query, key, and value vectors to calculate scaled dot product attention (SDPA).

To have a deeper understanding of self-attention and Transformers, we'll use English-to-French translation as our case study in this chapter. By exploring the

---

[1] Vaswani et al, 2017, "Attention Is All You Need." https://arxiv.org/abs/1706.03762.

process of training a model for converting English sentences into French, you will gain a deep understanding of the Transformer's architecture and the functioning of the attention mechanism.

Picture yourself having amassed a collection of more than 47,000 English-to-French translation pairs. Your objective is to train the encoder-decoder Transformer from the last chapter using this dataset. This chapter will walk you through all phases of the project. You'll first use subword tokenization to break English and French phrases into tokens. You'll then build your English and French vocabularies, which contain all unique tokens in each language. The vocabularies allow you to represent English and French phrases as sequences of indexes. After that, you'll use word embedding to transform these indexes (essentially one-hot vectors) into compact vector representations. We'll add positional encodings to the word embeddings to form input embeddings. Positional encodings allow the Transformer to know the ordering of tokens in the sequence.

Finally, you'll train the encoder-decoder Transformer from chapter 9 to translate English to French by using the collection of English-to-French translations as the training dataset. After training, you'll learn to translate common English phrases to French with the trained Transformer. Specifically, you'll use the encoder to capture the meaning of the English phrase. You'll then use the decoder in the trained Transformer to generate the French translation in an autoregressive manner, starting with the beginning token "BOS". In each time step, the decoder generates the most likely next token based on previously generated tokens and the encoder's output, until the predicted token is "EOS", which signals the end of the sentence. The trained model can translate common English phrases accurately as if you were using Google Translate for the task.

10.1   Subword tokenization

As we discussed in chapter 8, there are three tokenization methods: character-level tokenization, word-level tokenization, and subword tokenization. In this chapter, we'll use subword tokenization, which strikes a balance between the other two methods. It keeps frequently used words whole in the vocabulary and splits less common or more complex words into subcomponents.

In this section, you'll learn to tokenize both English and French phrases into subwords. You'll then create dictionaries to map tokens to indexes. The training data are then converted to sequences of indexes and placed in batches for training purposes.

10.1.1   Tokenizing English and French phrases

Go to https://mng.bz/WVAw to download the zip file that contains the English-to-French translations I collected from various sources. Unzip the file and place en2fr.csv in the folder /files/ on your computer.

We'll load the data and print out an English phrase, along with its French translation, as follows:

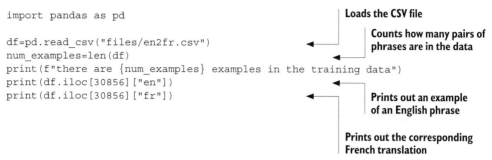

```
import pandas as pd

df=pd.read_csv("files/en2fr.csv")
num_examples=len(df)
print(f"there are {num_examples} examples in the training data")
print(df.iloc[30856]["en"])
print(df.iloc[30856]["fr"])
```

Loads the CSV file

Counts how many pairs of phrases are in the data

Prints out an example of an English phrase

Prints out the corresponding French translation

The output from the preceding code snippet is

```
there are 47173 examples in the training data
How are you?
Comment êtes-vous?
```

There are 47,173 pairs of English-to-French translations in the training data. We have printed out the English phrase "How are you?" and the corresponding French translation "Comment êtes-vous?" as an example.

Run the following line of code in a new cell in this Jupyter Notebook to install the transformers library on your computer:

```
!pip install transformers
```

Next, we'll tokenize both the English and the French phrases in the dataset. We'll use the pretrained XLM model from Hugging Face as the tokenizer because it excels at handling multiple languages, including English and French phrases.

Listing 10.1 A pretrained tokenizer

Imports the pretrained tokenizer

```
from transformers import XLMTokenizer

tokenizer = XLMTokenizer.from_pretrained("xlm-clm-enfr-1024")

tokenized_en=tokenizer.tokenize("I don't speak French.")
print(tokenized_en)
tokenized_fr=tokenizer.tokenize("Je ne parle pas français.")
print(tokenized_fr)
print(tokenizer.tokenize("How are you?"))
print(tokenizer.tokenize("Comment êtes-vous?"))
```

Uses the tokenizer to tokenize an English sentence

Tokenizes a French sentence

The output from code listing 10.1 is

```
['i</w>', 'don</w>', "'t</w>", 'speak</w>', 'fr', 'ench</w>', '.</w>']
['je</w>', 'ne</w>', 'parle</w>', 'pas</w>', 'franc', 'ais</w>', '.</w>']
['how</w>', 'are</w>', 'you</w>', '?</w>']
['comment</w>', 'et', 'es-vous</w>', '?</w>']
```

In the preceding code block, we use a pretrained tokenizer from the XLM model to divide the English sentence "I don't speak French." into a group of tokens. In chapter 8, you developed a custom word-level tokenizer. However, this chapter introduces the use of a more efficient pretrained subword tokenizer, surpassing the word-level tokenizer in effectiveness. The sentence "I don't speak French." is thus tokenized into ['i', 'don', "'t", 'speak', 'fr', 'ench', '.']. Similarly, the French sentence "Je ne parle pas français." is split into six tokens: ['je', 'ne', 'parle', 'pas', 'franc', 'ais', '.']. We have also tokenized the English phrase "How are you?" and its French translation. The results are shown in the last two lines of the preceding output.

> **NOTE** You may have noticed that the XLM model uses '</w>' as a token separator, except in cases where two tokens are part of the same word. Subword tokenization typically results in each token being either a complete word or a punctuation mark, but there are occasions when a word is divided into syllables. For example, the word "French" is divided into "fr" and "ench." It's noteworthy that the model doesn't insert </w> between "fr" and "ench," as these syllables jointly constitute the word "French."

Deep-learning models such as Transformers cannot process raw text directly; hence we need to convert text into numerical representations before feeding them to the models. For that purpose, we create a dictionary to map all English tokens to integers.

Listing 10.2   Mapping English tokens to indexes

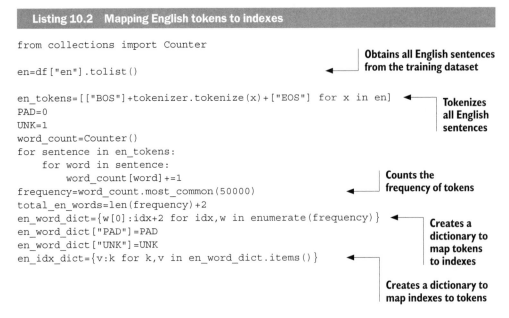

```
from collections import Counter

en=df["en"].tolist()                                    Obtains all English sentences
                                                        from the training dataset

en_tokens=[["BOS"]+tokenizer.tokenize(x)+["EOS"] for x in en]    Tokenizes
PAD=0                                                            all English
UNK=1                                                            sentences
word_count=Counter()
for sentence in en_tokens:
    for word in sentence:
        word_count[word]+=1
frequency=word_count.most_common(50000)                 Counts the
total_en_words=len(frequency)+2                          frequency of tokens
en_word_dict={w[0]:idx+2 for idx,w in enumerate(frequency)}
en_word_dict["PAD"]=PAD                                  Creates a
en_word_dict["UNK"]=UNK                                  dictionary to
en_idx_dict={v:k for k,v in en_word_dict.items()}        map tokens
                                                         to indexes

                                      Creates a dictionary to
                                      map indexes to tokens
```

We insert the tokens "BOS" (beginning of the sentence) and "EOS" (end of the sentence) at the start and end of each phrase, respectively. The dictionary en_word_dict assigns each token a unique integer value. Further, the `"PAD"` token, used for padding, is allocated the integer 0, while the `"UNK"` token, representing unknown tokens, is given the integer 1. A reverse dictionary, `en_idx_dict`, maps integers (indexes) back to their corresponding tokens. This reverse mapping is essential for converting a sequence of integers back into a sequence of tokens, enabling us to reconstruct the original English phrase.

Using the dictionary `en_word_dict`, we can transform the English sentence "I don't speak French." into its numerical representation. This process involves looking up each token in the dictionary to find its corresponding integer value. For instance:

```
enidx=[en_word_dict.get(i,UNK) for i in tokenized_en]
print(enidx)
```

The preceding lines of code produce the following output:

```
[15, 100, 38, 377, 476, 574, 5]
```

This means that the English sentence "I don't speak French." is now represented by a sequence of integers [15, 100, 38, 377, 476, 574, 5].

We can also revert the numerical representations into tokens using the dictionary `en_idx_dict`. This process involves mapping each integer in the numerical sequence back to its corresponding token as defined in the dictionary. Here's how it is done:

```
entokens=[en_idx_dict.get(i,"UNK") for i in enidx]    ◀── Converts indexes to tokens
print(entokens)
en_phrase="".join(entokens)                           ◀── Joins tokens into a string
en_phrase=en_phrase.replace("</w>"," ")               ◀──
for x in '''?:;.,'("-!&)%''':
    en_phrase=en_phrase.replace(f" {x}",f"{x}")       ◀── Replaces the separator with a space
print(en_phrase)
                                                         Removes the space before punctuations
```

The output of the preceding code snippet is

```
['i</w>', 'don</w>', "'t</w>", 'speak</w>', 'fr', 'ench</w>', '.</w>']
i don't speak french.
```

The dictionary `en_idx_dict` is used to translate numbers back into their original tokens. Following this, these tokens are transformed into the complete English phrase. This is done by first joining the tokens into a single string and then substituting the separator `'</w>'` with a space. We also remove the space before punctuation marks. Notice that the restored English phrase has all lowercase letters because the pretrained tokenizer automatically converts uppercase letters into lowercase to reduce the number of unique tokens. As you'll see in the next chapter, some models, such as GPT2 and ChatGPT, don't do this; hence, they have a larger vocabulary.

Exercise 10.1

In listing 10.1, we have split the sentence "How are you?" into tokens `['how</w>'`, `'are</w>'`, `'you</w>'`, `'?</w>']`. Follow the steps in this subsection to (i) convert the tokens into indexes using the dictionary `en_word_dict`; (ii) convert the indexes back to tokens using the dictionary `en_idx_dict`; (iii) restore the English sentence by joining the tokens into a string, changing the separator `'</w>'` to a space, and removing the space before punctuation marks.

We can apply the same steps to French phrases to map tokens to indexes and vice versa.

Listing 10.3 Mapping French tokens to indexes

```
fr=df["fr"].tolist()
fr_tokens=[["BOS"]+tokenizer.tokenize(x)+["EOS"] for x in fr]    ◀── Tokenizes all French sentences
word_count=Counter()
for sentence in fr_tokens:
    for word in sentence:
        word_count[word]+=1
frequency=word_count.most_common(50000)    ◀── Counts the frequency of French tokens
total_fr_words=len(frequency)+2
fr_word_dict={w[0]:idx+2 for idx,w in enumerate(frequency)}    ◀── Creates a dictionary to map French tokens to indexes
fr_word_dict["PAD"]=PAD
fr_word_dict["UNK"]=UNK
fr_idx_dict={v:k for k,v in fr_word_dict.items()}    ◀── Creates a dictionary to map indexes to French tokens
```

The dictionary `fr_word_dict` assigns an integer to each French token, while `fr_idx_dict` maps these integers back to their corresponding French tokens. Next, I'll demonstrate how to transform the French phrase "Je ne parle pas français." into its numerical representation:

```
fridx=[fr_word_dict.get(i,UNK) for i in tokenized_fr]
print(fridx)
```

The output from the preceding code snippet is

```
[28, 40, 231, 32, 726, 370, 4]
```

The tokens for the French phrase "Je ne parle pas français." are converted into a sequence of integers, as shown.

We can transform the numerical representations back into French tokens using the dictionary `fr_idx_dict`. This involves translating each number in the sequence back to its respective French token in the dictionary. Once the tokens are retrieved, they can be joined to reconstruct the original French phrase. Here's how it's done:

```
frtokens=[fr_idx_dict.get(i,"UNK") for i in fridx]
print(frtokens)
```

```
fr_phrase="".join(frtokens)
fr_phrase=fr_phrase.replace("</w>"," ")
for x in '''?:;.,'("-!&)%''':
    fr_phrase=fr_phrase.replace(f" {x}",f"{x}")
print(fr_phrase)
```

The output from the preceding code block is

```
['je</w>', 'ne</w>', 'parle</w>', 'pas</w>', 'franc', 'ais</w>', '.</w>']
je ne parle pas francais.
```

It's important to recognize that the restored French phrase doesn't exactly match its original form. This discrepancy is due to the tokenization process, which transforms all uppercase letters into lowercase and eliminates accent marks in French.

Exercise 10.2

In listing 10.1, we have split the sentence "Comment êtes-vous?" into tokens `['comment</w>', 'et', 'es-vous</w>', '?</w>']`. Follow the steps in this subsection to (i) convert the tokens into indexes using the dictionary `fr_word_dict`; (ii) convert the indexes back to tokens using the dictionary `fr_idx_dict`; (iii) restore the French phrase by joining the tokens into a string, changing the separator `'</w>'` to a space, and removing the space before punctuation marks.

Save the four dictionaries in the folder /files/ on your computer so that you can load them up and start translating later without worrying about first mapping tokens to indexes and vice versa:

```
import pickle

with open("files/dict.p","wb") as fb:
    pickle.dump((en_word_dict,en_idx_dict,
                 fr_word_dict,fr_idx_dict),fb)
```

The four dictionaries are now saved in a single pickle file `dict.p`. Alternatively, you can download the file from the book's GitHub repository.

10.1.2 *Sequence padding and batch creation*

We'll divide the training data into batches during training for computational efficiency and accelerated convergence, as we have done in previous chapters.

Creating batches for other data formats such as images is straightforward: simply group a specific number of inputs to form a batch since they all have the same size. However, in natural language processing, batching can be more complex due to the varying lengths of sentences. To standardize the length within a batch, we pad the shorter sequences. This uniformity is crucial since the numerical representations fed into the Transformer need to have the same length. For instance, English phrases in a batch may vary in length (this can also happen to French phrases in a batch). To address this, we append zeros to the end of the numerical representations of shorter phrases in a batch, ensuring that all inputs to the Transformer model are of equal length.

NOTE Incorporating BOS and EOS tokens at the beginning and end of each sentence, as well as padding shorter sequences within a batch, is a distinctive feature in machine language translation. This distinction arises from the fact that the input consists of entire sentences or phrases. In contrast, as you will see in the next two chapters, training a text generation model does not entail these processes; the model's input contains a predetermined number of tokens.

We start by converting all English phrases into their numerical representations and then apply the same process to the French phrases:

```
out_en_ids=[[en_word_dict.get(w,UNK) for w in s] for s in en_tokens]
out_fr_ids=[[fr_word_dict.get(w,UNK) for w in s] for s in fr_tokens]
sorted_ids=sorted(range(len(out_en_ids)),
                  key=lambda x:len(out_en_ids[x]))
out_en_ids=[out_en_ids[x] for x in sorted_ids]
out_fr_ids=[out_fr_ids[x] for x in sorted_ids]
```

Next, we put the numerical representations into batches for training:

```
import numpy as np

batch_size=128
idx_list=np.arange(0,len(en_tokens),batch_size)
np.random.shuffle(idx_list)

batch_indexs=[]
for idx in idx_list:
    batch_indexs.append(np.arange(idx,min(len(en_tokens),
                                       idx+batch_size)))
```

Note that we have sorted observations in the training dataset by the length of the English phrases before placing them into batches. This method ensures that the observations within each batch are of a comparable length, consequently decreasing the need for padding. As a result, this approach not only reduces the overall size of the training data but also accelerates the training process.

To pad sequences in a batch to the same length, we define the following function:

```
def seq_padding(X, padding=0):
    L = [len(x) for x in X]
    ML = max(L)
    padded_seq = np.array([np.concatenate([x, [padding] * (ML - len(x))])
        if len(x) < ML else x for x in X])
    return padded_seq
```

Find out the length of the longest sequence in the batch.

If a batch is shorter than the longest sequence, add 0s to the sequence at the end.

The function seq_padding() first identifies the longest sequence within the batch. Then it appends zeros to the end of shorter sequences to ensure that every sequence in the batch matches this maximum length.

To conserve space, we have created a Batch() class within the local module ch09util.py that you downloaded in the last chapter (see figure 10.1).

Listing 10.4 Creating a `Batch()` class in the local module

```
import torch
DEVICE = "cuda" if torch.cuda.is_available() else "cpu"

class Batch:
    def __init__(self, src, trg=None, pad=0):
        src = torch.from_numpy(src).to(DEVICE).long()
        self.src = src
        self.src_mask = (src != pad).unsqueeze(-2)
        if trg is not None:
            trg = torch.from_numpy(trg).to(DEVICE).long()
            self.trg = trg[:, :-1]
            self.trg_y = trg[:, 1:]
            self.trg_mask = make_std_mask(self.trg, pad)
            self.ntokens = (self.trg_y != pad).data.sum()
```

Creates a source mask to hide padding at the end of the sentence

Creates input to the decoder

Shifts the input one token to the right and uses it as output

Creates a target mask

src: sequence of indexes for the source language; e.g., those for the English phrase "How are you?"

trg: sequence of indexes for the target language; e.g., those for the French phrase "Comment êtes-vous?"

The Batch() Class

src_mask: source mask to conceal padding at the end of the source

trg: input to the decoder; e.g., indexes for ['BOS', 'comment', 'et', 'es-vous', '?']

trg_y: output of the decoder; e.g., indexes for ['comment', 'et', 'es-vous', '?', 'EOS']

trg_mask: target mask to conceal padding and to hide future tokens

Figure 10.1 What does the `Batch()` class do? The `Batch()` class takes two inputs: `src` and `trg`, sequences of indexes for the source language and the target language, respectively. It adds several attributes to the training data: `src_mask`, the source mask to conceal padding; modified `trg`, the input to the decoder; `trg_y`, the output to the decoder; `trg_mask`, the target mask to hide padding and future tokens.

The `Batch()` class processes a batch of English and French phrases, converting them into a format suitable for training. To make this explanation more tangible, consider the English phrase "How are you?" and its French equivalent "Comment êtes-vous?" as our example. The `Batch()` class receives two inputs: `src`, which is the sequence of indexes representing the tokens in "How are you?", and `trg`, the sequence of indexes for the tokens in "Comment êtes-vous?". This class generates a tensor, `src_mask`, to conceal the padding at the sentence's end. For instance, the sentence "How are you?" is broken down into six tokens: `['BOS', 'how', 'are', 'you', '?', 'EOS']`. If this sequence is part of a batch with a maximum length of eight tokens, two zeros are added to the end. The `src_mask` tensor instructs the model to disregard the final two tokens in such scenarios.

The Batch() class additionally prepares the input and output for the Transformer's decoder. Consider the French phrase "Comment êtes-vous?", which is transformed into six tokens: ['BOS', 'comment', 'et', 'es-vous', '?', 'EOS']. The indexes of these first five tokens serve as the input to the decoder, named trg. Next, we shift this input one token to the right to form the decoder's output, trg_y. Hence, the input comprises indexes for ['BOS', 'comment', 'et', 'es-vous', '?'], while the output consists of indexes for ['comment', 'et', 'es-vous', '?', 'EOS']. This approach mirrors what we discussed in chapter 8 and is designed to force the model to predict the next token based on the previous ones.

The Batch() class also generates a mask, trg_mask, for the decoder's input. The aim of this mask is to conceal the subsequent tokens in the input, ensuring that the model relies solely on previous tokens for making predictions. This mask is produced by the make_std_mask() function, which is defined within the local module ch09util:

```
import numpy as np
def subsequent_mask(size):
    attn_shape = (1, size, size)
    subsequent_mask = np.triu(np.ones(attn_shape),k=1).astype('uint8')
    output = torch.from_numpy(subsequent_mask) == 0
    return output
def make_std_mask(tgt, pad):
    tgt_mask=(tgt != pad).unsqueeze(-2)
    output=tgt_mask & subsequent_mask(tgt.size(-1)).type_as(tgt_mask.data)
    return output
```

The subsequent_mask() function generates a mask specifically for a sequence, instructing the model to focus solely on the actual sequence and disregard the padded zeros at the end, which are used only to standardize sequence lengths. The make_std_mask() function, on the other hand, constructs a standard mask for the target sequence. This standard mask has the dual role of concealing both the padded zeros and the future tokens in the target sequence.

Next, we import the Batch() class from the local module and use it to create batches of training data:

```
from utils.ch09util import Batch

class BatchLoader():
    def __init__(self):
        self.idx=0
    def __iter__(self):
        return self
    def __next__(self):
        self.idx += 1
        if self.idx<=len(batch_indexs):
            b=batch_indexs[self.idx-1]
            batch_en=[out_en_ids[x] for x in b]
            batch_fr=[out_fr_ids[x] for x in b]
            batch_en=seq_padding(batch_en)
            batch_fr=seq_padding(batch_fr)
            return Batch(batch_en,batch_fr)
        raise StopIteration
```

The `BatchLoader()` class creates data batches intended for training. Each batch in this list contains 128 pairs, where each pair contains numerical representations of an English phrase and its corresponding French translation.

10.2 *Word embedding and positional encoding*

After tokenization in the last section, English and French phrases are represented by sequences of indexes. In this section, you'll use word embedding to transform these indexes (essentially one-hot vectors) into compact vector representations. Doing so captures the semantic information and interrelationship of tokens in a phrase. Word embedding also improves training efficiency: instead of bulky one-hot vectors, word embedding uses continuous, lower-dimensional vectors to reduce the model's complexity and dimensionality.

The attention mechanism processes all tokens in a phrase at the same time instead of sequentially. This enhances its efficiency but doesn't inherently allow it to recognize the sequence order of the tokens. Therefore, we'll add positional encodings to the input embeddings by using sine and cosine functions of varying frequencies.

10.2.1 *Word embedding*

The numerical representations of the English and French phrases involve a large number of indexes. To determine the exact number of distinct indexes required for each language, we can count the number of unique elements in the `en_word_dict` and `fr_word_dict` dictionaries. Doing so generates the total number of unique tokens in each language's vocabulary (we'll use them as inputs to the Transformer later):

```
src_vocab = len(en_word_dict)
tgt_vocab = len(fr_word_dict)
print(f"there are {src_vocab} distinct English tokens")
print(f"there are {tgt_vocab} distinct French tokens")
```

The output is

```
there are 11055 distinct English tokens
there are 11239 distinct French tokens
```

In our dataset, there are 11,055 unique English tokens and 11,239 unique French tokens. Utilizing one-hot encoding for these would result in an excessively high number of parameters to train. To address this, we will employ word embeddings, which compress the numerical representations into continuous vectors, each with a length of `d_model = 256`.

This is achieved through the use of the `Embeddings()` class, which is defined in the local module ch09util:

```
import math

class Embeddings(nn.Module):
    def __init__(self, d_model, vocab):
        super().__init__()
        self.lut = nn.Embedding(vocab, d_model)
```

```
        self.d_model = d_model

    def forward(self, x):
        out = self.lut(x) * math.sqrt(self.d_model)
        return out
```

The `Embeddings()` class defined previously utilizes PyTorch's `Embedding()` class. It also multiplies the output by the square root of d_model, which is 256. This multiplication is intended to counterbalance the division by the square root of d_model that occurs later during the computation of attention scores. The `Embeddings()` class decreases the dimensionality of the numerical representations of English and French phrases. We discussed in detail how PyTorch's `Embedding()` class works in chapter 8.

10.2.2 *Positional encoding*

To accurately represent the sequence order of elements in both input and output, we introduce the `PositionalEncoding()` class in the local module.

> **Listing 10.5   A class to calculate positional encoding**

```
class PositionalEncoding(nn.Module):
    def __init__(self, d_model, dropout, max_len=5000):     ◄───  Initiates the
        super().__init__()                                        class, allowing a
        self.dropout = nn.Dropout(p=dropout)                      maximum of
        pe = torch.zeros(max_len, d_model, device=DEVICE)         5,000 positions
        position = torch.arange(0., max_len,
                         device=DEVICE).unsqueeze(1)
        div_term = torch.exp(torch.arange(
            0., d_model, 2, device=DEVICE)                   Applies sine function
            * -(math.log(10000.0) / d_model))               to even indexes in
        pe_pos = torch.mul(position, div_term)              the vector
        pe[:, 0::2] = torch.sin(pe_pos)           ◄───
        pe[:, 1::2] = torch.cos(pe_pos)           ◄───      Applies cosine
        pe = pe.unsqueeze(0)                                function to odd
        self.register_buffer('pe', pe)                      indexes in the vector

    def forward(self, x):
        x=x+self.pe[:,:x.size(1)].requires_grad_(False)     ◄───  Adds positional
        out=self.dropout(x)                                       encoding to word
        return out                                                embedding
```

The `PositionalEncoding()` class generates vectors for sequence positions using sine functions for even indexes and cosine functions for odd indexes. It's important to note that in the `PositionalEncoding()` class, the `requires_grad_(False)` argument is included because there is no need to train these values. They remain constant across all inputs, and they don't change during the training process.

For example, the indexes for the six tokens ['BOS', 'how', 'are', 'you', '?', 'EOS'] from the English phrase are first processed through a word embedding layer. This step transforms these indexes into a tensor with the dimensions of (1, 6, 256): 1 means there is only 1 sequence in the batch; 6 means there are 6 tokens in the sequence; 256 means each token is represented by a 256-value vector. After this word embedding process, the `PositionalEncoding()` class is employed to calculate the positional encodings for the indexes corresponding to the tokens [`'BOS'`, `'how'`, `'are'`, `'you'`, `'?'`, `'EOS'`]. This is done to provide the model with information about the position of each token in the sequence. Better yet, we can tell you the exact values of the positional encodings for the previous six tokens by using the following code block:

```
from utils.ch09util import PositionalEncoding
import torch
DEVICE = "cuda" if torch.cuda.is_available() else "cpu"

pe = PositionalEncoding(256, 0.1)
x = torch.zeros(1, 8, 256).to(DEVICE)
y = pe.forward(x)
print(f"the shape of positional encoding is {y.shape}")
print(y)
```

Instantiates the PositionalEncoding() class and set the model dimension to 256

Creates a word embedding and fills it with zeros

Calculates the input embedding by adding positional encoding to the word embedding

Prints out the input embedding, which is the same as positional encoding since word embedding is set to zero

We first create an instance, `pe`, of the `PositionalEncoding()` class by setting the model dimension to 256 and the dropout rate to 0.1. Since the output from this class is the sum of word embedding and positional encoding, we create a word embedding filled with zeros and feed it to `pe`: this way, the output is the same as the positional encoding.

After running the preceding code block, you'll see the following output:

```
the shape of positional encoding is torch.Size([1, 8, 256])
tensor([[[ 0.0000e+00,  1.1111e+00,  0.0000e+00,  ...,  0.0000e+00,
           0.0000e+00,  1.1111e+00],
         [ 9.3497e-01,  6.0034e-01,  8.9107e-01,  ...,  1.1111e+00,
           1.1940e-04,  1.1111e+00],
         [ 0.0000e+00, -4.6239e-01,  1.0646e+00,  ...,  1.1111e+00,
           2.3880e-04,  1.1111e+00],
         ...,
         [-1.0655e+00,  3.1518e-01, -1.1091e+00,  ...,  1.1111e+00,
           5.9700e-04,  1.1111e+00],
         [-3.1046e-01,  1.0669e+00, -0.0000e+00,  ...,  0.0000e+00,
           7.1640e-04,  1.1111e+00],
         [ 7.2999e-01,  8.3767e-01,  2.5419e-01,  ...,  1.1111e+00,
           8.3581e-04,  1.1111e+00]]], device='cuda:0')
```

The preceding tensor represents the positional encoding for the English phrase "How are you?" It's important to note that this positional encoding also has the dimensions of (1, 6, 256), which matches the size of the word embedding for "How are you?". The next step involves combining the word embedding and positional encoding into a single tensor.

An essential characteristic of positional encodings is that their values are the same no matter what the input sequences are. This means that regardless of the specific input sequence, the positional encoding for the first token will always be the same 256-value vector, [0.0000e+00, 1.1111e+00, ..., 1.1111e+00], as shown in the above output. Similarly, the positional encoding for the second token will always be [9.3497e-01, 6.0034e-01, ..., 1.1111e+00], and so on. Their values don't change during the training process either.

10.3 *Training the Transformer for English-to-French translation*

Our constructed English-to-French translation model can be viewed as a multicategory classifier. The core objective is to predict the next token in the French vocabulary when translating an English sentence. This is somewhat similar to the image classification project we discussed in chapter 2, though this model is significantly more complex. This complexity necessitates careful selection of the loss function, optimizer, and training loop parameters.

In this section, we will detail the process of selecting an appropriate loss function and optimizer. We will train the Transformer using batches of English-to-French translations as our training dataset. After the model is trained, you'll learn how to translate common English phrases into French.

10.3.1 *Loss function and the optimizer*

First, we import the `create_model()` function from the local module ch09util.py and construct a Transformer so that we can train it to translate English to French:

```
from utils.ch09util import create_model

model = create_model(src_vocab, tgt_vocab, N=6,
    d_model=256, d_ff=1024, h=8, dropout=0.1)
```

The paper "Attention Is All You Need" uses various combinations of hyperparameters when constructing the model. Here we choose a model dimension of 256 with 8 heads because we find this combination does a good job translating English to French in our setting. Interested readers could potentially use a validation set to tune hyperparameters to select the best model in their own projects.

We'll follow the original paper "Attention Is All You Need" and use label smoothing during training. Label smoothing is commonly used in training deep neural networks to improve the generalization of the model. It is used to address overconfidence problems (the predicted probability is greater than the true probability) and overfitting in classifications. Specifically, it modifies the way the model learns by adjusting the target labels, aiming to reduce the model's confidence in the training data, which can lead to better performance on unseen data.

In a typical classification task, target labels are represented in a one-hot encoding format. This representation implies absolute certainty about the correctness of the label for each training sample. Training with absolute certainty can lead to two main problems. The first is overfitting: the model becomes overly confident in its predictions, fitting too closely to the training data, which can harm its performance on new, unseen data. The second problem is poor calibration: models trained this way often output overconfident probabilities. For instance, they might output a probability of 99% for a correct class when, realistically, the confidence should be lower.

Label smoothing adjusts the target labels to be less confident. Instead of having a target label of [1, 0, 0] for a three-class problem, you might have something like [0.9, 0.05, 0.05]. This approach encourages the model not to be too confident about its predictions by penalizing overconfident outputs. The smoothed labels are a mixture of the original label and some distribution over the other labels (usually the uniform distribution).

We define the following LabelSmoothing() class in the local module ch09util.

Listing 10.6 A class to conduct label smoothing

```
class LabelSmoothing(nn.Module):
    def __init__(self, size, padding_idx, smoothing=0.1):
        super().__init__()
        self.criterion = nn.KLDivLoss(reduction='sum')
        self.padding_idx = padding_idx
        self.confidence = 1.0 - smoothing
        self.smoothing = smoothing
        self.size = size
        self.true_dist = None
    def forward(self, x, target):
        assert x.size(1) == self.size
        true_dist = x.data.clone()
        true_dist.fill_(self.smoothing / (self.size - 2))
        true_dist.scatter_(1,
                target.data.unsqueeze(1), self.confidence)
        true_dist[:, self.padding_idx] = 0
        mask = torch.nonzero(target.data == self.padding_idx)
        if mask.dim() > 0:
            true_dist.index_fill_(0, mask.squeeze(), 0.0)
        self.true_dist = true_dist
        output = self.criterion(x, true_dist.clone().detach())
        return output
```

Extracts predictions from the model

Extracts actual labels from the training data and adds noise to them

Uses the smoothed labels as targets when calculating loss

The LabelSmoothing() class first extracts the predictions from the model. It then smoothes the actual labels in the training dataset by adding noise to it. The parameter smoothing controls how much noise we inject into the actual label. The label [1, 0, 0] is smoothed to [0.9, 0.05, 0.05] if you set smoothing=0.1, and it is smoothed to [0.95, 0.025, 0.025] if you set smoothing=0.05, for example. The class then calculates the loss by comparing the predictions with the smoothed labels.

As in previous chapters, the optimizer we use is the Adam optimizer. However, instead of using a constant learning rate throughout training, we define the `NoamOpt()` class in the local module to change the learning rate during the training process:

```
class NoamOpt:
    def __init__(self, model_size, factor, warmup, optimizer):
        self.optimizer = optimizer
        self._step = 0
        self.warmup = warmup                            ◄──── Defines warm-up steps
        self.factor = factor
        self.model_size = model_size
        self._rate = 0
    def step(self):                                     ◄──── A step() method to apply
        self._step += 1                                        the optimizer to adjust
        rate = self.rate()                                     model parameters
        for p in self.optimizer.param_groups:
            p['lr'] = rate
        self._rate = rate
        self.optimizer.step()
    def rate(self, step=None):
        if step is None:                                      Calculates
            step = self._step                                 the learning
        output = self.factor * (self.model_size ** (-0.5) *   rate based
        min(step ** (-0.5), step * self.warmup ** (-1.5)))  ◄─ on steps
        return output
```

The `NoamOpt()` class, as defined previously, implements a warm-up learning rate strategy. First, it increases the learning rate linearly during the initial warmup steps of training. Following this warm-up period, the class then decreases the learning rate, adjusting it in proportion to the inverse square root of the training step number.

Next, we create the optimizer for training:

```
from utils.ch09util import NoamOpt

optimizer = NoamOpt(256, 1, 2000, torch.optim.Adam(
    model.parameters(), lr=0, betas=(0.9, 0.98), eps=1e-9))
```

To define the loss function for training, we first create the following `SimpleLoss-Compute()` class in the local module.

Listing 10.7   A class to compute loss

```
class SimpleLossCompute:
    def __init__(self, generator, criterion, opt=None):
        self.generator = generator
        self.criterion = criterion
        self.opt = opt                              Uses the model to
    def __call__(self, x, y, norm):                 make predictions
        x = self.generator(x)
        loss = self.criterion(x.contiguous().view(-1, x.size(-1)),
                              y.contiguous().view(-1)) / norm  ◄──

                                           Compares the predictions
                                       with labels to calculate loss,
                                       utilizing label smoothing
```

```
        loss.backward()
        if self.opt is not None:
            self.opt.step()
            self.opt.optimizer.zero_grad()
        return loss.data.item() * norm.float()
```

Calculates gradients with respect to model parameters

Adjusts model parameters (backpropagate)

The `SimpleLossCompute()` class is designed with three key elements: `generator`, serving as the prediction model; `criterion`, which is a function to calculate loss; and `opt`, the optimizer. This class processes a batch of training data, denoted as (x, y), by utilizing the generator for predictions. It subsequently evaluates the loss by comparing these predictions with the actual labels y (which is handled by the `LabelSmoothing()` class defined earlier; the actual labels y will be smoothed in the process). The class computes gradients relative to the model parameters and utilizes the optimizer to update these parameters accordingly.

We are now ready to define the loss function:

```
from utils.ch09util import (LabelSmoothing,
        SimpleLossCompute)

criterion = LabelSmoothing(tgt_vocab,
                            padding_idx=0, smoothing=0.1)
loss_func = SimpleLossCompute(
        model.generator, criterion, optimizer)
```

Next, we'll train the Transformer by using the data we prepared earlier in the chapter.

10.3.2 *The training loop*

We could potentially divide the training data into a train set and a validation set and train the model until the performance of the model doesn't improve on the validation set, similar to what we have done in chapter 2. However, to save space, we'll train the model for 100 epochs. We'll calculate the loss and the number of tokens from each batch. After each epoch, we calculate the average loss in the epoch as the ratio between the total loss and the total number of tokens.

Listing 10.8   Training a Transformer to translate English to French

```
for epoch in range(100):
    model.train()
    tloss=0
    tokens=0
    for batch in BatchLoader():
        out = model(batch.src, batch.trg,
                    batch.src_mask, batch.trg_mask)
        loss = loss_func(out, batch.trg_y, batch.ntokens)
        tloss += loss
        tokens += batch.ntokens
    print(f"Epoch {epoch}, average loss: {tloss/tokens}")
torch.save(model.state_dict(),"files/en2fr.pth")
```

Makes predictions using the Transformer

Calculates loss and adjusts model parameters

Counts the number of tokens in the batch

Saves the weights in the trained model after training

This training process takes a couple of hours if you are using a CUDA-enabled GPU. It may take a full day if you are using CPU training. Once the training is done, the model weights are saved as en2fr.pth on your computer. Alternatively, you can download the trained weights from my website (https://gattonweb.uky.edu/faculty/lium/gai/ch9 .zip).

10.4 *Translating English to French with the trained model*

Now that you have trained the Transformer, you can use it to translate any English sentence to French. We define a function `translate()` as shown in the following listing.

Listing 10.9   Defining a `translate()` function to translate English to French

```
def translate(eng):
    tokenized_en=tokenizer.tokenize(eng)
    tokenized_en=["BOS"]+tokenized_en+["EOS"]
    enidx=[en_word_dict.get(i,UNK) for i in tokenized_en]
    src=torch.tensor(enidx).long().to(DEVICE).unsqueeze(0)
    src_mask=(src!=0).unsqueeze(-2)
    memory=model.encode(src,src_mask)                      ◀── Uses encoder
    start_symbol=fr_word_dict["BOS"]                            to convert the
    ys = torch.ones(1, 1).fill_(start_symbol).type_as(src.data)   English phrase
    translation=[]                                              to a vector
    for i in range(100):                                        representation
        out = model.decode(memory,src_mask,ys,
        subsequent_mask(ys.size(1)).type_as(src.data))     ◀── Predicts the next
        prob = model.generator(out[:, -1])                      token using the
        _, next_word = torch.max(prob, dim=1)                   decoder
        next_word = next_word.data[0]
        ys = torch.cat([ys, torch.ones(1, 1).type_as(
            src.data).fill_(next_word)], dim=1)
        sym = fr_idx_dict[ys[0, -1].item()]
        if sym != 'EOS':
            translation.append(sym)
        else:                                              ◀── Stops translating when the
            break                                              next token is "EOS"
    trans="".join(translation)
    trans=trans.replace("</w>"," ")
    for x in '''?:;.,'("-!&)%''':                          ◀── Joins the predicted tokens
        trans=trans.replace(f" {x}",f"{x}")                    to form a French sentence
    print(trans)
    return trans
```

To translate an English phrase to French, we first use the tokenizer to convert the English sentence to tokens. We then add `"BOS"` and `"EOS"` at the beginning and the end of the phrase. We use the dictionary `en_word_dict` we created earlier in the chapter to convert tokens to indexes. We feed the sequence of indexes to the encoder in the trained model. The encoder produces an abstract vector representation and passes it on to the decoder.

Based on the abstract vector representation of the English sentence produced by the encoder, the decoder in the trained model starts translating in an autoregressive manner, starting with the beginning token `"BOS"`. In each time step, the decoder generates the most likely next token based on previously generated tokens, until the predicted token is `"EOS"`, which signals the end of the sentence. Note this is slightly different from the text generation approach discussed in chapter 8, where the next token is chosen randomly in accordance with its predicted probabilities. Here, the method for selecting the next token is deterministic, meaning the token with the highest probability is chosen with certainty because we mainly care about accuracy. However, you can switch to stochastic prediction as we did in chapter 8 and use `top-K` sampling and temperature if you want your translation to be creative.

Finally, we change the token separator to a space and remove the space before the punctuation marks. The output is the French translation in a clean format.

Let's try the `translate()` function with the English phrase "Today is a beautiful day!":

```
from utils.ch09util import subsequent_mask

with open("files/dict.p","rb") as fb:
    en_word_dict,en_idx_dict,\
    fr_word_dict,fr_idx_dict=pickle.load(fb)
trained_weights=torch.load("files/en2fr.pth",
                            map_location=DEVICE)
model.load_state_dict(trained_weights)
model.eval()
eng = "Today is a beautiful day!"
translated_fr = translate(eng)
```

The output is

```
aujourd'hui est une belle journee!
```

You can verify that the French translation indeed means "Today is a beautiful day!" by using, say, Google Translate.

Let's try a longer sentence and see if the trained model can successfully translate:

```
eng = "A little boy in jeans climbs a small tree while another child looks on."
translated_fr = translate(eng)
```

The output is

```
un petit garcon en jeans grimpe un petit arbre tandis qu'un autre enfant regarde.
```

When I translate the preceding output back to English using Google Translate, it says, "a little boy in jeans climbs a small tree while another child watches"—not exactly the same as the original English sentence, but the meaning is the same.

Next, we'll test if the trained model generates the same translation for the two English sentences "I don't speak French." and "I do not speak French." First, let's try the sentence "I don't speak French.":

```
eng = "I don't speak French."
translated_fr = translate(eng)
```

The output is

```
je ne parle pas francais.
```

Now let's try the sentence "I do not speak French.":

```
eng = "I do not speak French."
translated_fr = translate(eng)
```

The output this time is

```
je ne parle pas francais.
```

The results indicate that French translations of the two sentences are exactly the same. This suggests that the encoder component of the Transformer successfully grasps the semantic essence of the two phrases. It then represents them as similar abstract continuous vector forms, which are subsequently passed on to the decoder. The decoder then generates translations based on these vectors and produces identical results.

Exercise 10.3

Use the `translate()` function to translate the following two English sentences to French. Compare the results with those from Google Translate and see if they are the same: (i) I love skiing in the winter! (ii) How are you?

In this chapter, you trained an encoder-decoder Transformer to translate English to French by using more than 47,000 pairs of English-to-French translations. The trained model works well, translating common English phrases correctly!

In the following chapters, you'll explore decoder-only Transformers. You'll learn to build them from scratch and use them to generate coherent text, better than the text you generated in chapter 8 using long short-term memory.

Summary

- Transformers process input data such as sentences in parallel, unlike recurrent neural networks, which handle data sequentially. This parallelism enhances their efficiency but doesn't inherently allow them to recognize the sequence order of the input. To address this, Transformers add positional encodings to the input embeddings. These positional encodings are unique vectors assigned to each position in the input sequence and align in dimension with the input embeddings.

- Label smoothing is commonly used in training deep neural networks to improve the generalization of the model. It is used to address overconfidence problems (the predicted probability is greater than the true probability) and overfitting in classifications. Specifically, it modifies the way the model learns by adjusting the target labels, aiming to reduce the model's confidence in the training data, which can lead to better performance on unseen data.

- Based on the encoder's output that captures the meaning of the English phrase, the decoder in the trained Transformer starts translating in an autoregressive manner, starting with the beginning token `"BOS"`. In each time step, the decoder generates the most likely next token based on previously generated tokens, until the predicted token is `"EOS"`, which signals the end of the sentence.

Building a generative pretrained Transformer from scratch

This chapter covers

- Building a generative pretrained Transformer from scratch
- Causal self-attention
- Extracting and loading weights from a pretrained model
- Generating coherent text with GPT-2, the predecessor of ChatGPT and GPT-4

Generative Pretrained Transformer 2 (GPT-2) is an advanced large language model (LLM) developed by OpenAI and announced in February 2019. It represents a significant milestone in the field of natural language processing (NLP) and has paved the way for the development of even more sophisticated models, including its successors, ChatGPT and GPT-4.

GPT-2, an improvement over its predecessor, GPT-1, was designed to generate coherent and contextually relevant text based on a given prompt, demonstrating a remarkable ability to mimic human-like text generation across various styles and topics. Upon its announcement, OpenAI initially decided not to release to the public the most powerful version of GPT-2 (also the one you'll build from scratch in this chapter, with 1.5 billion parameters). The main concern was potential misuse, such as generating misleading news articles, impersonating individuals online, or automating the production of abusive or fake content. This decision sparked a significant debate within the AI and tech communities about the ethics of AI development and the balance between innovation and safety.

OpenAI later adopted a staggered release strategy, gradually making smaller versions of the model available while monitoring the effect and exploring safe deployment strategies. Eventually, in November 2019, OpenAI released the full model, along with several datasets and a tool to detect model-generated text, contributing to discussions on responsible AI usage. Because of this release, you'll learn to extract the pretrained weights from GPT-2 and load them to the GPT-2 model that you create.

GPT-2 is based on the Transformer architecture that we discussed in chapters 9 and 10. However, unlike the English-to-French translator you created before, GPT-2 is a decoder-only Transformer, meaning there is no encoder stack in the model. When translating an English phrase into French, the encoder captures the meaning of the English phrase and passes it to the decoder to generate the translation. However, in text generation tasks, the model does not need an encoder to understand a different language. Instead, it generates text based on the previous tokens in the sentence, using only a decoder-only architecture. Like other Transformer models, GPT-2 uses self-attention mechanisms to process input data in parallel, significantly improving the efficiency and effectiveness of training LLMs.

GPT-2 is pretrained on a large corpus of text data, essentially predicting the next word in a sentence given the words that precede it. This training enables the model to learn a wide range of language patterns, grammar, and knowledge.

In this chapter, you'll learn to build GPT-2XL, the largest version of GPT-2, from scratch. After that, you'll learn how to extract the pretrained weights from Hugging Face (an AI community that hosts and collaborates on machine learning models, datasets, and applications) and load them to your own GPT-2 model. You'll use your GPT-2 to generate text by feeding a prompt to the model. GPT-2 calculates the probabilities of possible next tokens and samples from these probabilities. It can produce coherent and contextually relevant paragraphs of text based on the input prompt it receives. Additionally, as you did in chapter 8, you can control the creativeness of the generated text by using `temperature` and `top-K` sampling.

While GPT-2 marks a notable advance in NLP, it's essential to moderate your expectations and recognize its inherent limitations. It's crucial not to compare GPT-2 with ChatGPT or GPT-4 directly, as GPT-2XL has only 1.5 billion parameters compared to ChatGPT's 175 billion and GPT-4's estimated 1.76 trillion parameters. One of the main limitations of GPT-2 is its lack of genuine comprehension of the content it generates.

The model predicts the next word in a sequence based on the probability distribution of words in its training data, which can produce syntactically correct and seemingly logical text. However, the model lacks a true understanding of the meaning behind the words, leading to potential inaccuracies, nonsensical statements, or superficial content.

Another key factor is GPT-2's limited contextual awareness. While it can maintain coherence over short spans of text, it struggles with longer passages, potentially resulting in a loss of coherence, contradictions, or irrelevant content. We should be cautious not to overestimate the model's ability to generate long-form content that requires sustained attention to context and detail. Therefore, while GPT-2 represents a significant step forward in NLP, it's important to approach its generated text with a healthy dose of skepticism and set realistic expectations.

11.1 *GPT-2 architecture and causal self-attention*

GPT-2 operates as a solely decoder-based Transformer (it generates text based on previous tokens in the sentence without the need for an encoder to understand a different language), mirroring the decoder component of the English-to-French translator discussed in chapters 9 and 10. Unlike its bilingual counterpart, GPT-2 lacks an encoder and thus does not incorporate encoder-derived inputs in its output generation process. The model relies entirely on preceding tokens within the sequence to produce its output.

In this section, we'll discuss the architecture of GPT-2. We will also dive into the causal self-attention mechanism, which is the core of the GPT-2 model.

11.1.1 *The architecture of GPT-2*

GPT-2 comes in four different sizes: small (S), medium (M), large (L), and extra-large (XL), each varying in capability. Our primary focus will be on the most powerful version, GPT-2XL. The smallest GPT-2 model has around 124 million parameters, while the extra-large version has about 1.5 billion parameters. It is the most powerful among the GPT-2 models, with the highest number of parameters. GPT-2XL can understand complex contexts, generating coherent and nuanced text.

GPT-2 consists of many identical decoder blocks. The extra-large version has 48 decoder blocks, while the other three versions have 12, 24, and 36 decoder blocks, respectively. Each of these decoder blocks comprises two distinct sublayers. The first sublayer is a causal self-attention layer, which I'll explain in detail soon. The second sublayer is a basic, position-wise, fully connected feed-forward network, as we have seen in the encoder and decoder blocks in the English-to-French translator. Each sublayer incorporates layer normalization and a residual connection to stabilize the training process.

Figure 11.1 is a diagram of the architecture of GPT-2.

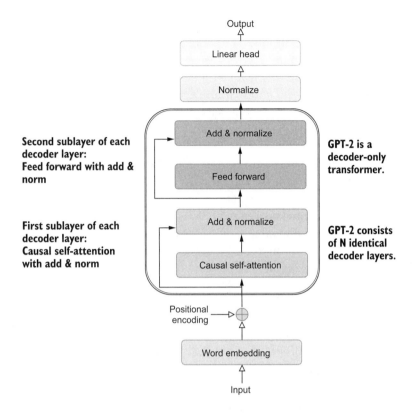

Figure 11.1 The architecture of the GPT-2 model. GPT-2 is a decoder-only Transformer, consisting of N identical decoder layers. Each decoder block contains two sublayers. The first sublayer is a causal self-attention layer. The second is a feed-forward network. Each sublayer uses layer normalization and a residual connection. The input is first passed through word embedding and positional encoding, and the sum is then passed through the decoder. The output from the decoder goes through layer normalization and a linear layer.

GPT-2 first passes indexes for a sequence of tokens through word embedding and positional encoding to obtain input embedding (I'll explain soon how this process works). The input embedding is passed through N decoder blocks sequentially. After that, the output is passed through layer normalization and a linear layer. The number of outputs in GPT-2 is the number of unique tokens in the vocabulary (50,257 tokens for all GPT-2 versions). The model is designed to predict the next token based on all previous tokens in the sequence.

To train GPT-2, OpenAI used a dataset called WebText, which was collected automatically from the internet. The dataset contained a wide variety of text, including websites like Reddit links that were highly upvoted, aiming to cover a broad spectrum of human languages and topics. This dataset is estimated to contain about 40GB of text.

The training data was broken into sequences of a fixed length (1,024 tokens for all GPT-2 versions) and used as inputs. The sequences were shifted to the right by one token and used as outputs to the model during training. Since the model uses causal self-attention, in which future tokens in a sequence are masked (i.e., hidden) during the training process, this is effectively training the model to predict the next token based on all previous tokens in the sequence.

11.1.2 *Word embedding and positional encoding in GPT-2*

GPT-2 uses a subword tokenization method called the Byte Pair Encoder (BPE) to break text into individual tokens (whole words or punctuation marks in most cases but syllables for uncommon words). These tokens are then mapped into an index between 0 and 50,256 since the vocabulary size is 50,257. GPT-2 transforms text in the training data into vector representations that capture its meaning through word embedding, similar to what you've done in the previous two chapters.

To give you a concrete example, the phrase "this is a prompt" is first converted into four tokens through BPE tokenization, [`'this'`, `' is'`, `' a'`, `' prompt'`]. Each token is then represented by a one-hot variable of size 50,257. The GPT-2 model passes them through a word embedding layer to compress them into condensed vectors with floating point values of a much smaller size, such as a length of 1,600 in GPT-2XL (the lengths are 768, 1,024, and 1,280, for the other three versions of GPT-2, respectively). With word embedding, the phrase "this is a prompt" is represented by a matrix with size $4 \times 1,600$ instead of the original $4 \times 50,257$. Word embedding significantly reduces the number of the model's parameters and makes training more efficient. The left side of figure 11.2 depicts how word embedding works.

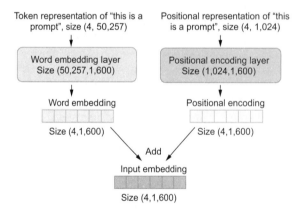

Figure 11.2   GPT-2 first represents each token in a sequence with a 50,276-value one-hot vector. The token representation of the sequence goes through a word embedding layer to compress it into an embedding with a dimension of 1,600. GPT-2 also represents each position in a sequence with a 1,024-value one-hot vector. The positional representation of the sequence goes through a positional encoding layer to compress it into an embedding also with a dimension of 1,600. The word embedding and positional encoding are added together to form the input embedding.

GPT-2, like other Transformers, processes input data in parallel, and this inherently doesn't allow it to recognize the sequence order of the input. To address this, we need to add positional encodings to the input embeddings. GPT-2 adopts a unique approach to positional encoding, diverging from the methodology outlined in the seminal 2017 "Attention Is All You Need" paper. Instead, GPT-2's technique for positional encoding parallels that of word embeddings. Given the model's capacity to handle up to 1,024 tokens in an input sequence, each position within the sequence is initially denoted by a one-hot vector of the same size. For instance, in the sequence "this is a prompt," the first token is represented by a one-hot vector where all elements are zero except for the first, which is set to one. The second token follows suit, represented by a vector where all but the second element are zero. Consequently, the positional representation for the phrase "this is a prompt" manifests as a 4 × 1,024 matrix, as illustrated in the upper right section of figure 11.2.

To generate positional encoding, the sequence's positional representation undergoes processing through a linear neural network, which is dimensioned at 1,024 × 1,600. The weights within this network are randomly initialized and subsequently refined through the training process. As a result, the positional encoding for each token in the sequence is a 1,600-value vector, matching the dimension of the word embedding vector. A sequence's input embedding is the sum of its word embedding and positional encoding, as depicted at the bottom of figure 11.2. In the context of the phrase "this is a prompt," both the word embedding and positional encoding are structured as 4 × 1,600 matrices. Therefore, the input embedding for "this is a prompt," which is the sum of these two matrices, maintains a dimensionality of 4 × 1,600.

11.1.3 Causal self-attention in GPT-2

Causal self-attention is a crucial mechanism within the GPT-2 model (and broadly in the GPT series of models), enabling the model to generate text by conditioning on the sequence of previously generated tokens. It's similar to the masked self-attention in the first sublayer of each decoder layer in the English-to-French translator we discussed in chapters 9 and 10, though the implementation differs slightly.

> **NOTE** The concept of "causal" in this context refers to the model's ability to ensure that predictions for a given token can only be influenced by the tokens that precede it in the sequence, respecting the causal (time-forward) direction of text generation. This is essential for generating coherent and contextually relevant text outputs.

Self-attention is a mechanism that allows each token in the input sequence to attend to all other tokens in the same sequence. In the context of Transformer models like GPT-2, self-attention enables the model to weigh the importance of other tokens when processing a specific token, thereby capturing the context and relationships between words in a sentence.

To ensure causality, GPT-2's self-attention mechanism is modified so that any given token can only attend to itself and the tokens that have come before it in the sequence. This is achieved by masking future tokens (i.e., tokens that come after the current token in the sequence) in the attention calculation, ensuring that the model cannot "see" or be influenced by future tokens when predicting the next token in a sequence. For example, in the phrase "this is a prompt," the mask hides the last three words in the first time step when the model uses the word "this" to predict the word "is." To implement this, positions corresponding to future tokens are set to minus infinity when we compute the attention scores. After softmax activation, future tokens are allocated zero weights, effectively removing them from the attention calculation.

Let's use a concrete example to illustrate exactly how causal self-attention works in code. The input embedding for the phrase "this is a prompt" is a $4 \times 1,600$ matrix after word embedding and positional encoding. We then pass this input embedding through N decoder layers in GPT-2. In each decoder layer, it first goes through the causal self-attention sublayer as follows. The input embedding is passed through three neural networks to create query Q, key K, and value V, as shown in the following listing.

> **Listing 11.1   Creating `query`, `key`, and `value` vectors**

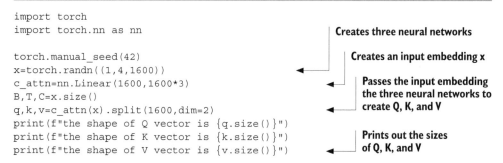

```
import torch
import torch.nn as nn                                    Creates three neural networks

torch.manual_seed(42)                                    Creates an input embedding x
x=torch.randn((1,4,1600))
c_attn=nn.Linear(1600,1600*3)                            Passes the input embedding
B,T,C=x.size()                                           the three neural networks to
q,k,v=c_attn(x).split(1600,dim=2)                        create Q, K, and V
print(f"the shape of Q vector is {q.size()}")
print(f"the shape of K vector is {k.size()}")            Prints out the sizes
print(f"the shape of V vector is {v.size()}")            of Q, K, and V
```

We first create a matrix with size $4 \times 1,600$, the same size as the input embedding for "this is a prompt". We then pass the input embedding through three neural networks, each with a size of $1,600 \times 1,600$, to obtain query Q, key K, and value V. If you run the preceding code block, you'll see the following output:

```
the shape of Q vector is torch.Size([1, 4, 1600])
the shape of K vector is torch.Size([1, 4, 1600])
the shape of V vector is torch.Size([1, 4, 1600])
```

The shapes of Q, K, and V are all $4 \times 1,600$. Next, instead of using one head, we split them into 25 parallel heads. Each head pays attention to different parts or aspects of the input, enabling the model to capture a broader range of information and form a more detailed and contextual understanding of the input data. As a result, we have 25 sets of Q, K, and V:

```
hs=C//25
k = k.view(B, T, 25, hs).transpose(1, 2)
q = q.view(B, T, 25, hs).transpose(1, 2)
v = v.view(B, T, 25, hs).transpose(1, 2)
print(f"the shape of Q vector is {q.size()}")
print(f"the shape of K vector is {k.size()}")
print(f"the shape of V vector is {v.size()}")
```

← Splits Q, K, and V into 25 heads

← Prints out the size of the multihead Q, K, and V

If you run the preceding code block, you'll see the following output:

```
the shape of Q vector is torch.Size([1, 25, 4, 64])
the shape of K vector is torch.Size([1, 25, 4, 64])
the shape of V vector is torch.Size([1, 25, 4, 64])
```

The shapes of Q, K, and V are now $25 \times 4 \times 64$: this means we have 25 heads; each head has a set of query, key, and value, all having a size of 4×64.

Next, we calculate the scaled attention scores in each head:

```
import math
scaled_att = (q @ k.transpose(-2, -1)) *\
             (1.0 / math.sqrt(k.size(-1)))
print(scaled_att[0,0])
```

The scaled attention scores are the dot product of Q and K in each head, scaled by the square root of the dimension of K, which is $1,600/25 = 64$. The scaled attention scores form a 4×4 matrix in each head, and we print out those in the first head:

```
tensor([[ 0.2334,  0.1385, -0.1305,  0.2664],
        [ 0.2916,  0.1044,  0.0095,  0.0993],
        [ 0.8250,  0.2454,  0.0214,  0.8667],
        [-0.1557,  0.2034,  0.2172, -0.2740]], grad_fn=<SelectBackward0>)
```

The scaled attention scores in the first head are also shown in the bottom left table in figure 11.3.

Exercise 11.1

The tensor `scaled_att` contains the scaled attention scores in the 25 heads. We have printed out those in the first head previously. How do you print out the scaled attention scores in the second head?

Next, we apply a mask to the scaled attention scores to hide future tokens in the sequence:

```
mask=torch.tril(torch.ones(4,4))
print(mask)
masked_scaled_att=scaled_att.masked_fill(\
    mask == 0, float('-inf'))
print(masked_scaled_att[0,0])
```

← Creates a mask

← Applies the mask on the scaled attention scores by changing the values to $-\infty$ for future tokens

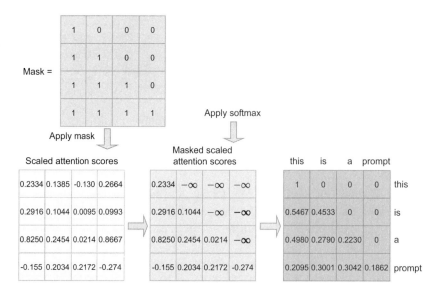

Figure 11.3 How to calculate masked attention weights in causal self-attention. A mask is applied to the scaled attention scores so that values corresponding to future tokens (those above the main diagonal in the matrix) become $-\infty$. We then apply the softmax function on the masked scaled attention scores and obtain the masked attention weights. The masking ensures that predictions for a given token can only be influenced by the tokens that precede it in the sequence, not by future tokens. This is essential for generating coherent and contextually relevant text outputs.

If you run the preceding code, you'll see the following output:

```
tensor([[1., 0., 0., 0.],
        [1., 1., 0., 0.],
        [1., 1., 1., 0.],
        [1., 1., 1., 1.]])
tensor([[ 0.2334,    -inf,    -inf,    -inf],
        [ 0.2916,  0.1044,    -inf,    -inf],
        [ 0.8250,  0.2454,  0.0214,    -inf],
        [-0.1557,  0.2034,  0.2172, -0.2740]], grad_fn=<SelectBackward0>)
```

The mask is a 4 × 4 matrix as shown at the top of figure 11.3. The lower half of the mask (values below the main diagonal) are 1s while the upper half of the mask (values above the main diagonal) are 0s. When this mask is applied to the scaled attention scores, the values in the upper half of the matrix become $-\infty$ (the middle bottom of figure 11.3). This way, when we apply the softmax function on the scaled attention scores, the upper half of the attention weights matrix is filled with 0s (bottom right of figure 11.3):

```
import torch.nn.functional as F
att = F.softmax(masked_scaled_att, dim=-1)
print(att[0,0])
```

We print out the attention weights in the first head with the following values:

```
tensor([[1.0000, 0.0000, 0.0000, 0.0000],
        [0.5467, 0.4533, 0.0000, 0.0000],
```

```
           [0.4980, 0.2790, 0.2230, 0.0000],
           [0.2095, 0.3001, 0.3042, 0.1862]]], grad_fn=<SelectBackward0>)
```

The first row means in the first time step, the token "this" attends only to itself and not to any future tokens. Similarly, if you look at the second row, the tokens "this is" attend to each other but not to future tokens "a prompt".

> **NOTE** The weights in this numerical example are not trained, so don't take these values in attention weights literally. We use them as an example to illustrate how causal self-attention works.

Exercise 11.2

We have printed out the attention weights in the first head. How do you print out the attention weights in the last (i.e., the 25th) head?

Finally, we calculate the attention vector in each head as the dot product of attention weights and the value vector. The attention vectors in the 25 heads are then joined together as one single attention vector:

```
y=att@v
y = y.transpose(1, 2).contiguous().view(B, T, C)
print(y.shape)
```

The output is

```
torch.Size([1, 4, 1600])
```

The final output after causal self-attention is a $4 \times 1,600$ matrix, the same size as the input to the causal self-attention sublayer. The decoder layers are designed in such a way that the input and output have the same dimensions, and this allows us to stack many decoder layers together to increase the representation capacity of the model and to enable hierarchical feature extraction during training.

11.2 Building GPT-2XL from scratch

Now that you understand the architecture of GPT-2 and how its core ingredient, causal self-attention, functions, let's create the largest version of GPT-2 from scratch.

In this section, you'll first learn to use the subword tokenization method in GPT-2, the byte pair encoder (BPE) tokenizer, to break text into individual tokens. You'll also learn the GELU activation function used in the feed-forward network in GPT-2. After that, you'll code in the causal self-attention mechanism and combine it with a feed-forward network to form a decoder block. Finally, you'll stack 48 decoder blocks to create the GPT-2XL model. The code in this chapter is adapted from the excellent GitHub repository by Andrej Kaparthy (https://github.com/karpathy/minGPT). I encourage you to read through the repository if you want to dive deeper into how GPT-2 works.

11.2.1 *BPE tokenization*

GPT-2 uses a subword tokenization method called byte pair encoder (BPE), which is a data compression technique that has been adapted for use in tokenizing text in NLP tasks. It's particularly well-known for its application in training LLMs, such as the GPT series and BERT (Bidirectional Encoder Representations from Transformers). The primary goal of BPE is to encode a piece of text into a sequence of tokens in a way that balances the vocabulary size and the length of the tokenized text.

BPE operates by iteratively merging the most frequent pair of consecutive characters in a dataset into a single new token, subject to certain conditions. This process is repeated until a desired vocabulary size is reached or no more merges are beneficial. BPE allows for an efficient representation of text, balancing between character-level and word-level tokenization. It helps to reduce the vocabulary size without significantly increasing the sequence length, which is crucial for the performance of NLP models.

We discussed the pros and cons of the three types of tokenization methods (character-level, word-level, and subword tokenizations) in chapter 8. Further, you implemented a word-level tokenizer from scratch in chapter 8 (and will do so again in chapter 12). Therefore, in this chapter, we'll borrow the tokenization method from OpenAI directly. The detailed workings of BPE are beyond the scope of this book. All you need to know is that it first converts text into subword tokens and then the corresponding indexes.

Download the file `bpe.py` from Andrej Karpathy's GitHub repository, https://mng .bz/861B, and place the file in the folder /utils/ on your computer. We'll use the file as a local module in this chapter. As Andrej Karpathy explained in his GitHub repository, the module is based on OpenAI's implementation at https://mng.bz/EOlj but was mildly modified to make it easier to understand.

To see how the module `bpe.py` converts text into tokens and then indexes, let's try an example:

```
from utils.bpe import get_encoder

example="This is the original text."
bpe_encoder=get_encoder()
response=bpe_encoder.encode_and_show_work(example)
print(response["tokens"])
```

- ◄ **The text for an example sentence**
- ◄ **Instantiates the get_encoder() class from the bpe.py module**
- ◄ **Tokenizes the example text and print out the tokens**

The output is

```
['This', ' is', ' the', ' original', ' text', '.']
```

The BPE tokenizer splits the example text "This is the original text." into six tokens as shown in the preceding output. Note that the BPE tokenizer doesn't convert uppercase letters to lowercase ones. This leads to more meaningful tokenization but also a much larger number of unique tokens. In fact, all versions of GPT-2 models have a vocabulary size of 50,276, several times larger than the vocabulary size in the previous chapters.

We can also use the module bpe.py to map tokens to indexes:

```
print(response['bpe_idx'])
```

The output is

```
[1212, 318, 262, 2656, 2420, 13]
```

The preceding list contains the six indexes corresponding to the six tokens in the example text "This is the original text."

We can also restore the text based on the indexes:

```
from utils.bpe import BPETokenizer

tokenizer = BPETokenizer()
out=tokenizer.decode(torch.LongTensor(response['bpe_idx']))
print(out)
```

Instantiates the BPETokenizer() class from the bpe.py module

Uses the tokenizer to restore text based on indexes

The output from the preceding code block is

```
This is the original text.
```

As you can see, the BPE tokenizer has restored the example text to its original form.

> **Exercise 11.3**
>
> Use the BPE tokenizer to split the phrase "this is a prompt" into tokens. After that, map the tokens to indexes. Finally, restore the phrase based on the indexes.

11.2.2 *The Gaussian error linear unit activation function*

The Gaussian error linear unit (GELU) activation function is used in the feed-forward sublayers of each decoder block in GPT-2. GELU provides a blend of linear and non-linear activation properties that have been found to enhance model performance in deep learning tasks, particularly NLP.

GELU offers a nonlinear, smooth curve that allows for more nuanced adjustments during training compared to other functions like the rectified linear unit (ReLU). This smoothness helps in optimizing the neural network more effectively, as it provides a more continuous gradient for backpropagation. To compare GELU with ReLU, our go-to activation function, let's first define a GELU() class:

```
class GELU(nn.Module):
    def forward(self, x):
        return 0.5*x*(1.0+torch.tanh(math.sqrt(2.0/math.pi)*\
                     (x + 0.044715 * torch.pow(x, 3.0))))
```

The ReLU function is not differentiable everywhere since it has a kink in it. The GELU activation function, in contrast, is differentiable everywhere and provides a better learning process. Next we draw a picture of the GELU activation function and compare it to ReLU.

Listing 11.2   Comparing two activation functions: GELU and ReLU

```
import matplotlib.pyplot as plt
import numpy as np

genu=GELU()
def relu(x):
    y=torch.zeros(len(x))
    for i in range(len(x)):
        if x[i]>0:
            y[i]=x[i]
    return y
xs = torch.linspace(-6,6,300)
ys=relu(xs)
gs=genu(xs)
fig, ax = plt.subplots(figsize=(6,4),dpi=300)
plt.xlim(-3,3)
plt.ylim(-0.5,3.5)
plt.plot(xs, ys, color='blue', label="ReLU")
plt.plot(xs, gs, "--", color='red', label="GELU")
plt.legend(fontsize=15)
plt.xlabel("values of x")
plt.ylabel("values of $ReLU(x)$ and $GELU(x)$")
plt.title("The ReLU and GELU Activation Functions")
plt.show()
```

◄─── **Defines a function to represent ReLU**

◄─── **Plots the ReLU activation function in solid lines**

◄─── **Plots the GELU activation function in dashed lines**

If you run the preceding code block, you'll see a graph as shown in figure 11.4.

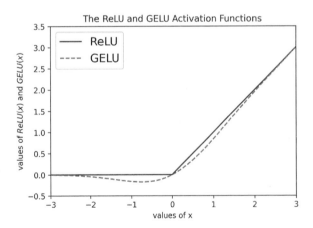

Figure 11.4   Comparing the GELU activation function with ReLU. The solid line is the ReLU activation function, while the dashed line is the GELU activation function. ReLU is not differentiable everywhere since there is a kink in it. GELU, in contrast, is differentiable everywhere. This smoothness in GELU helps to optimize the neural network more effectively, as it provides a more continuous gradient for backpropagation during the training process.

Furthermore, the formulation of GELU allows it to model input data distributions more effectively. It combines the properties of linear and Gaussian distribution modeling, which can be particularly beneficial for the complex, varied data encountered in NLP tasks. This capability helps in capturing subtle patterns in language data, improving the model's understanding and generation of text.

11.2.3 *Causal self-attention*

As we explained earlier, causal self-attention is the core element in GPT-2 models. Next, we'll implement this mechanism from scratch in PyTorch.

We first specify the hyperparameters in the GPT-2XL model that we'll build in this chapter. To that end, we define a `Config()` class with the values shown in the following listing.

Listing 11.3 Specifying hyperparameters in GPT-2XL

```
class Config():
    def __init__(self):                              ◄──  Defines a Config() class
        self.n_layer = 48
        self.n_head = 25
        self.n_embd = 1600
        self.vocab_size = 50257
        self.block_size = 1024                        ◄──  Places model
        self.embd_pdrop = 0.1                              hyperparameters as
        self.resid_pdrop = 0.1                             attributes in the class
        self.attn_pdrop = 0.1                         ◄──
                                                           Instantiates the
config=Config()                                       ◄──  Config() class
```

We define a `Config()` class and create several attributes in it to be used as the hyperparameters in the GPT-2XL model. The `n_layer` attribute means the GPT-2XL model we construct will have 48 decoder layers (we use the terms "decoder block" and "decoder layer" interchangeably). The `n_head` attribute means we'll split Q, K, and V into 25 parallel heads when calculating causal self-attention. The `n_embd` attribute means the embedding dimension is 1,600: each token will be represented by a 1,600-value vector. The `vocab_size` attribute means there are 50,257 unique tokens in the vocabulary. The `block_size` attribute means the input sequence to the GPT-2XL model contains at most 1,024 tokens. The dropout rates are all set to 0.1.

In the last section, I explained in detail how causal self-attention works. Next, we define a `CausalSelfAttention()` class to implement it.

Listing 11.4 Implementing causal self-attention

```
class CausalSelfAttention(nn.Module):
    def __init__(self, config):
        super().__init__()
        self.c_attn = nn.Linear(config.n_embd, 3 * config.n_embd)
        self.c_proj = nn.Linear(config.n_embd, config.n_embd)
        self.attn_dropout = nn.Dropout(config.attn_pdrop)
```

```
        self.resid_dropout = nn.Dropout(config.resid_pdrop)
        self.register_buffer("bias", torch.tril(torch.ones(\
            config.block_size, config.block_size))
          .view(1, 1, config.block_size, config.block_size))
        self.n_head = config.n_head
        self.n_embd = config.n_embd
    def forward(self, x):
        B, T, C = x.size()
        q, k ,v = self.c_attn(x).split(self.n_embd, dim=2)
        hs = C // self.n_head
        k = k.view(B, T, self.n_head, hs).transpose(1, 2)
        q = q.view(B, T, self.n_head, hs).transpose(1, 2)
        v = v.view(B, T, self.n_head, hs).transpose(1, 2)
        att - (q @ k.transpose(-2, -1)) *\
            (1.0 / math.sqrt(k.size(-1)))
        att = att.masked_fill(self.bias[:,:,:T,:T] == 0, \
                        float(,-inf'))
        att = F.softmax(att, dim=-1)
        att = self.attn_dropout(att)
        y = att @ v
        y = y.transpose(1, 2).contiguous().view(B, T, C)
        y = self.resid_dropout(self.c_proj(y))
        return y
```

Creates a mask and registers it as a buffer since it doesn't need to be updated

Passes input embedding through three neural networks to obtain Q, K, and V

Splits Q, K, and V into multiple heads

Calculates masked attention weights in each head

Concatenates attention vectors in all heads into one single attention vector

In PyTorch, register_buffer is a method used to register a tensor as a buffer. Variables in a buffer are not considered learnable parameters of the model; hence they are not updated during backpropagation. In the preceding code block, we have created a mask and registered it as a buffer. This has implications for how we extract and load model weights later: we'll omit the masks when retrieving weights from GPT-2XL.

As we explained in the first section, the input embedding is passed through three neural networks to obtain query Q, key K, and value V. We then split them into 25 heads and calculate masked self-attention in each head. After that, we join the 25 attention vectors back into one single attention vector, which is the output of the previous CausalSelfAttention() class.

11.2.4 Constructing the GPT-2XL model

Next, we add a feed-forward network to the causal self-attention sublayer to form a decoder block, as follows.

Listing 11.5 Constructing a decoder block

```
class Block(nn.Module):
    def __init__(self, config):
        super().__init__()
        self.ln_1 = nn.LayerNorm(config.n_embd)
        self.attn = CausalSelfAttention(config)
```

Initiates the Block() class

```
        self.ln_2 = nn.LayerNorm(config.n_embd)
        self.mlp = nn.ModuleDict(dict(
            c_fc   = nn.Linear(config.n_embd, 4 * config.n_embd),
            c_proj = nn.Linear(4 * config.n_embd, config.n_embd),
            act    = GELU(),
            dropout = nn.Dropout(config.resid_pdrop),
        ))
        m = self.mlp
        self.mlpf=lambda x:m.dropout(m.c_proj(m.act(m.c_fc(x))))
    def forward(self, x):
        x = x + self.attn(self.ln_1(x))
        x = x + self.mlpf(self.ln_2(x))
        return x
```

The first sublayer in the block is the causal self-attention sublayer, with layer normalization and residual connection.

The second sublayer in the block is a feed-forward network, with GELU activation, layer normalization, and residual connection.

Every decoder block is composed of two sublayers. The first sublayer is the causal self-attention mechanism, with the integration of layer normalization and residual connection. The second sublayer within the decoder block is the feed-forward network, which incorporates the GELU activation function, alongside layer normalization and residual connection.

We stack 48 decoder layers to form the main body of the GPT-2XL model, as shown in the following listing.

Listing 11.6 Building the GPT-2XL model

```
class GPT2XL(nn.Module):
    def __init__(self, config):
        super().__init__()
        self.block_size = config.block_size
        self.transformer = nn.ModuleDict(dict(
            wte = nn.Embedding(config.vocab_size, config.n_embd),
            wpe = nn.Embedding(config.block_size, config.n_embd),
            drop = nn.Dropout(config.embd_pdrop),
            h = nn.ModuleList([Block(config)
                            for _ in range(config.n_layer)]),
            ln_f = nn.LayerNorm(config.n_embd),))
        self.lm_head = nn.Linear(config.n_embd,
                            config.vocab_size, bias=False)
    def forward(self, idx, targets=None):
        b, t = idx.size()
        pos = torch.arange(0,t,dtype=torch.long).unsqueeze(0)
        tok_emb = self.transformer.wte(idx)
        pos_emb = self.transformer.wpe(pos)
        x = self.transformer.drop(tok_emb + pos_emb)
        for block in self.transformer.h:
            x = block(x)
```

Calculates input embedding as the sum of word embedding and positional encoding

Passes the input embedding through 48 decoder blocks

Applies layer normalization one more time

Attaches a linear head to the output so the number of outputs equals the number of unique tokens

```
x = self.transformer.ln_f(x)
logits = self.lm_head(x)
loss = None
if targets is not None:
    loss=F.cross_entropy(logits.view(-1,logits.size(-1)),
                targets.view(-1), ignore_index=-1)
return logits, loss
```

We construct the model in the GPT2XL() class as we explained in the first section of this chapter. The input to the model consists of sequences of indexes corresponding to tokens in the vocabulary. We first pass the input through word embedding and positional encoding; we then add the two to form the input embedding. The input embedding goes through 48 decoder blocks. After that, we apply layer normalization to the output and then attach a linear head to it so that the number of outputs is 50,257, the size of the vocabulary. The outputs are the logits corresponding to the 50,257 tokens in the vocabulary. Later, we'll apply the softmax activation on the logits to obtain the probability distribution over the unique tokens in the vocabulary when generating text.

NOTE Since the model size is too large, we didn't move the model to a GPU. This leads to a lower speed in text generation later in the chapter. However, if you have access to a CUDA-enabled GPU with large memory (say, above 32GB), you can move the model to a GPU for faster text generation.

Next, we'll create the GPT-2XL model by instantiating the GPT2XL() class we defined earlier:

```
model=GPT2XL(config)
num=sum(p.numel() for p in model.transformer.parameters())
print("number of parameters: %.2fM" % (num/1e6,))
```

We also count the number of parameters in the main body of the model. The output is

```
number of parameters: 1557.61M
```

The preceding output shows that GPT-2XL has more than 1.5 billion parameters. Note that the number doesn't include the parameters in the linear head at the end of the model. Depending on what the downstream task is, we can attach different heads to the model. Since our focus is on text generation, we have attached a linear head to ensure the number of outputs is equal to the number of unique tokens in the vocabulary.

NOTE In LLMs like GPT-2, ChatGPT, or BERT, an output head refers to the final layer of the model that is responsible for producing the actual output based on the processed input. This output can vary depending on the downstream task the model is performing. In text generation, the output head is often a linear layer that transforms the final hidden states into logits for each token in the vocabulary. These logits are then passed through a softmax function to generate a probability distribution over the vocabulary, which is used to predict the next token in a sequence. For classification tasks, the output head typically consists of a linear layer followed by a softmax function. The linear layer transforms the final hidden states of the model into logits for each class, and the softmax function converts these logits into probabilities for each class. The specific architecture of the output head can vary depending on the model and the task, but its primary function is to map the processed input to the desired output format (e.g., class probabilities, token probabilities, etc.).

Finally, you can print out the GPT-2XL model structure:

```
print(model)
```

The output is

```
GPT2XL(
  (transformer): ModuleDict(
    (wte): Embedding(50257, 1600)
    (wpe): Embedding(1024, 1600)
    (drop): Dropout(p=0.1, inplace=False)
    (h): ModuleList(
      (0-47): 48 x Block(
        (ln_1): LayerNorm((1600,), eps=1e-05, elementwise_affine=True)
        (attn): CausalSelfAttention(
          (c_attn): Linear(in_features=1600, out_features=4800, bias=True)
          (c_proj): Linear(in_features=1600, out_features=1600, bias=True)
          (attn_dropout): Dropout(p=0.1, inplace=False)
          (resid_dropout): Dropout(p=0.1, inplace=False)
        )
        (ln_2): LayerNorm((1600,), eps=1e-05, elementwise_affine=True)
        (mlp): ModuleDict(
          (c_fc): Linear(in_features=1600, out_features=6400, bias=True)
          (c_proj): Linear(in_features=6400, out_features=1600, bias=True)
          (act): GELU()
          (dropout): Dropout(p=0.1, inplace=False)
        )
      )
    )
    (ln_f): LayerNorm((1600,), eps=1e-05, elementwise_affine=True)
  )
  (lm_head): Linear(in_features=1600, out_features=50257, bias=False)
)
```

It shows the detailed blocks and layers in the GPT-2XL model.

And just like that, you have created the GPT-2XL model from scratch!

11.3 Loading up pretrained weights and generating text

Even though you have just created the GPT-2XL model, it is not trained. Therefore, you cannot use it to generate any meaningful text.

Given the sheer number of the model's parameters, it's impossible to train the model without supercomputing facilities, let alone the amount of data needed to train the model. Luckily, the pretrained weights of GPT-2 models, including the largest one, GPT-2XL, were released by OpenAI to the public on November 5, 2019 (see the statement on the OpenAI website, https://openai.com/research/gpt-2-1-5b-release, as well as a report by an American technology news website, The Verge, https://mng .bz/NBm7). We, therefore, will load up the pretrained weights to generate text in this section.

11.3.1 Loading up pretrained parameters in GPT-2XL

We'll use the `transformers` library developed by the Hugging Face team to extract pretrained weights in GPT-2XL.

First, run the following line of code in a new cell in this Jupyter Notebook to install the `transformers` library on your computer:

```
!pip install transformers
```

Next, we import the GPT2 model from the `transformers` library and extract the pretrained weights in GPT-2XL:

```
from transformers import GPT2LMHeadModel

model_hf = GPT2LMHeadModel.from_pretrained('gpt2-xl')
sd_hf = model_hf.state_dict()
print(model_hf)
```

◄—— **Loads the pretrained GPT-2XL model**

◄—— **Extracts model weights**

◄—— **Prints out the model structure of the original OpenAI GTP-2XL model**

The output from the preceding code block is

```
GPT2LMHeadModel(
  (transformer): GPT2Model(
    (wte): Embedding(50257, 1600)
    (wpe): Embedding(1024, 1600)
    (drop): Dropout(p=0.1, inplace=False)
    (h): ModuleList(
      (0-47): 48 x GPT2Block(
        (ln_1): LayerNorm((1600,), eps=1e-05, elementwise_affine=True)
        (attn): GPT2Attention(
          (c_attn): Conv1D()
          (c_proj): Conv1D()
          (attn_dropout): Dropout(p=0.1, inplace=False)
          (resid_dropout): Dropout(p=0.1, inplace=False)
        )
        (ln_2): LayerNorm((1600,), eps=1e-05, elementwise_affine=True)
        (mlp): GPT2MLP(
          (c_fc): Conv1D()
          (c_proj): Conv1D()
          (act): NewGELUActivation()
```

OpenAI used a Conv1d layer instead of a linear layer as we did.

OpenAI used a Conv1d layer instead of a linear layer as we did.

```
            (dropout): Dropout(p=0.1, inplace=False)
          )
       )
     )
     (ln_f): LayerNorm((1600,), eps=1e-05, elementwise_affine=True)
   )
   (lm_head): Linear(in_features=1600, out_features=50257, bias=False)
 )
```

If you compare this model structure with the one from the previous section, you'll notice that they are the same except that the linear layers are replaced with Conv1d layers. As we explained in chapters 9 and 10, in feed-forward networks, we treat values in an input as independent elements rather than a sequence. Therefore, we often call it a 1D convolutional network. OpenAI checkpoints use a Conv1d module in places of the model where we use a linear layer. As a result, we need to transpose certain weight matrices when we extract model weights from Hugging Face and place them in our model.

To understand how this works, let's look at the weights in the first layer of the feed-forward network in the first decoder block of the OpenAI GPT-2XL model. We can print out its shape as follows:

```
print(model_hf.transformer.h[0].mlp.c_fc.weight.shape)
```

The output is

```
torch.Size([1600, 6400])
```

The weight matrix in the Conv1d layer is a tensor with size (1,600, 6,400).

Now, if we look at the same weight matrix in the model we just constructed, its shape is

```
print(model.transformer.h[0].mlp.c_fc.weight.shape)
```

The output this time is

```
torch.Size([6400, 1600])
```

The weight matrix in the linear layer in our model is a tensor with size (6,400, 1,600), which is a transposed matrix of the weight matrix in OpenAI GPT-2XL. Therefore, we need to transpose the weight matrix in all Conv1d layers in the OpenAI GPT-2XL model before we place them in our model.

Next, we name the parameters in the original OpenAI GPT-2XL model as keys:

```
keys = [k for k in sd_hf if not k.endswith('attn.masked_bias')]
```

Note that we have excluded parameters ending with attn.masked_bias in the preceding line of code. OpenAI GPT-2 uses them to implement future token masking. Since we have created our own masking in the CausalSelfAttention() class and registered it as a buffer in PyTorch, we don't need to load parameters ending with attn.masked_bias from OpenAI.

We name the parameters in the GPT-2XL model we created from scratch as sd:

```
sd=model.state_dict()
```

Next, we'll extract the pretrained weights in OpenAI GPT-2XL and place them in our own model:

```
transposed = ['attn.c_attn.weight', 'attn.c_proj.weight',
              'mlp.c_fc.weight', 'mlp.c_proj.weight']
for k in keys:
    if any(k.endswith(w) for w in transposed):
        with torch.no_grad():
            sd[k].copy_(sd_hf[k].t())
    else:
        with torch.no_grad():
            sd[k].copy_(sd_hf[k])
```

Finds out layers that OpenAI uses a ConvId module instead of a linear module

For those layers, we transpose the weight matrix before placing weights in our model.

Otherwise, simply copies the weights from OpenAI and places them in our model

We extract the OpenAI pretrained weights from Hugging Face and place them in our own model. In the process, we make sure that we transpose the weight matrix whenever OpenAI checkpoints use a Conv1d module instead of a plain linear module.

Now our model is equipped with pre-trained weights from OpenAI. We can use the model to generate coherent text.

11.3.2 *Defining a generate() function to produce text*

Armed with pretrained weights from the OpenAI GPT-2XL model, we'll use the GPT2 model we created from scratch to generate text.

When generating text, we'll feed a sequence of indexes that correspond to tokens in a prompt to the model. The model predicts the index corresponding to the next token and attaches the prediction to the end of the sequence to form a new sequence. It then uses the new sequence to make predictions again. It keeps doing this until the model has generated a fixed number of new tokens or the conversation is over (signified by the special token `<|endoftext|>`).

> **The special token <|endoftext|> in GPTs**
>
> GPT models undergo training using text from a diverse range of sources. A unique token, `<|endoftext|>`, is employed during this phase to delineate text from different origins. In the text generation phase, it's crucial to halt the conversation upon encountering this special token. Failing to do so may trigger the initiation of an unrelated new topic, resulting in subsequent generated text that bears no relevance to the ongoing discussion.

To that end, we define a `sample()` function to add a certain number of new indexes to the current sequence. It takes a sequence of indexes as input to feed to the GPT-2XL model. It predicts one index at a time and adds the new index to the end of the running sequence. It stops until the specified number of time steps, `max_new_tokens`, is reached or when the predicted next token is `<|endoftext|>`, which signals the end of the conversation. If we don't stop, the model will randomly start an unrelated topic. The `sample()` function is defined as shown in the following listing.

Listing 11.7   Iteratively predicting the next index

```
model.eval()
def sample(idx, max_new_tokens, temperature=1.0, top_k=None):
    for _ in range(max_new_tokens):                          ◄──── Generates a fixed
        if idx.size(1) <= config.block_size:                       number of new indexes
            idx_cond = idx
        else:
            idx_cond = idx[:, -config.block_size:]
        logits, _ = model(idx_cond)                          ◄──── Predicts the next index
        logits = logits[:, -1, :] / temperature                    using GPT-2XL
        if top_k is not None:
            v, _ = torch.topk(logits, top_k)                       If using top-K
            logits[logits < v[:, [-1]]] = -float('Inf')      ◄──── sampling, sets the
        probs = F.softmax(logits, dim=-1)                          logits below the top
        idx_next = torch.multinomial(probs, num_samples=1)         K choices to −∞
        if idx_next.item()==tokenizer.encoder.encoder['<|endoftext|>']:
            break                                            ◄────
        idx = torch.cat((idx, idx_next), dim=1)  ◄───────┐        Stops predicting if
    return idx                                           │        the next token is
                                                         │        < | endoftext | >
                                                         │
                                                     Attaches the new prediction to
                                                     the end of the sequence
```

The `sample()` function uses GPT-2XL to add new indexes to a running sequence. It incorporates two arguments, `temperature` and `top_k`, to modulate the generated output's novelty, operating in the same manner as described in chapter 8. The function returns a new sequence of indexes.

Next, we define a `generate()` function to generate text based on a prompt. It first converts the text in the prompt to a sequence of indexes. It then feeds the sequence to the `sample()` function we just defined to generate a new sequence of indexes. Finally, the function `generate()` converts the new sequence of indexes back to text.

Listing 11.8   A function to generate text with GPT-2XL

```
def generate(prompt, max_new_tokens, temperature=1.0,
             top_k=None):
    if prompt == '':
        x=torch.tensor([[tokenizer.encoder.encoder['<|endoftext|>']]],
                        dtype=torch.long)
    else:                                                        If the prompt is
        x = tokenizer(prompt)                            ◄────   empty, uses
    y = sample(x, max_new_tokens, temperature, top_k)    ◄────   < | endoftext | >
    out = tokenizer.decode(y.squeeze())                  ◄──┐    as the prompt
    print(out)
                                                            │    Converts prompt
                        Converts the new sequence           │    into a sequence of
                        of indexes back to text             │    indexes

                                                     Uses the sample()
                                                     function to generate
                                                     new indexes
```

The `generate()` function bears resemblance to the version we introduced in chapter 8 but with a notable distinction: it employs GPT-2XL for prediction purposes, moving away from the LSTM model previously utilized. The function accepts a prompt as its initial input, transforming this prompt into a series of indexes that are then fed into the model to forecast the subsequent index. Upon producing a predetermined number of new indexes, the function reverts the entire index sequence back into textual form.

11.3.3   *Text generation with GPT-2XL*

Now that we have defined the `generate()` function, we can use it to generate text.

In particular, the `generate()` function allows for unconditional text generation, which means the prompt is empty. The model will generate text randomly. This can be beneficial in creative writing: the generated text can be used as inspiration or a starting point for one's own creative work. Let's try that:

```
prompt=""
torch.manual_seed(42)
generate(prompt, max_new_tokens=100, temperature=1.0,
         top_k=None)
```

The output is

```
<|endoftext|>Feedback from Ham Radio Recalls

I discovered a tune sticking in my head -- I'd heard it mentioned on several
occasions, but hadn't investigated further.

The tune sounded familiar to a tune I'd previously heard on the 550 micro.
During that same time period I've heard other people's receipients drone on
the idea of the DSH-94013, notably Kim Weaver's instructions in her
Interview on Radio Ham; and both Scott Mcystem and Steve Simmons' concepts.
```

As you can see, the preceding output is coherent and grammatically correct but may not be factually accurate. I did a quick Google search, and the text doesn't seem to be copied from any online source.

> ### Exercise 11.4
> Generate text unconditionally by setting the prompt as an empty string, temperature to 0.9, maximum number of new tokens to 100, and `top_k` to 40. Set the random seed number to 42 in PyTorch. See what the output is.

To evaluate whether GPT-2XL can produce coherent text based on preceding tokens, we will use the prompt "I went to the kitchen and" and generate 10 additional tokens after the prompt. We will repeat this process five times to determine if the generated text aligns with typical kitchen activities:

```
prompt="I went to the kitchen and"
for i in range(5):
    torch.manual_seed(i)
    generate(prompt, max_new_tokens=10, temperature=1.0,
                top_k=None)
```

The output is

```
I went to the kitchen and said, you're not going to believe this.
I went to the kitchen and noticed a female producer open a drawer in which was
I went to the kitchen and asked who was going to be right there and A
I went to the kitchen and took a small vial of bourbon and a little
I went to the kitchen and found the bottle of wine, and poured it into
```

These results indicate that the generated text includes activities such as conversing with someone, noticing something, and taking beverages, all of which are typical kitchen activities. This demonstrates that GPT-2XL can generate text relevant to the given context.

Next, we use "Lexington is the second largest city in the state of Kentucky" as the prompt and ask the generate() function to add up to 100 new tokens:

```
prompt="Lexington is the second largest city in the state of Kentucky"
torch.manual_seed(42)
generate(prompt, max_new_tokens=100, temperature=1.0,
            top_k=None)
```

The output is

```
Lexington is the second largest city in the state of Kentucky. It caters to
those who want to make everything in tune with being with friends and
enjoying a jaunt through the down to Earth lifestyle. To do so, they are
blessed with several venues large and small to fill their every need while
residing micro- cozy with nature within the landmarks of the city.

In a moment we look at ten up and coming suchache music acts from the
Lexington area to draw upon your attention.

Lyrikhop


This Lexington-based group
```

Again, this text is coherent. Even though the generated content may not be factually accurate. The GPT-2XL model is, fundamentally, trained to predict the next token based on preceding tokens in the sentence. The preceding output shows that the model has achieved that goal: the generated text is grammatically correct and seemingly logical. It shows the ability to remember the text in the early parts of the sequence and generate subsequent words that are relevant to the context. For example, while the first sentence discusses the city of Lexington, about 90 tokens later, the model mentions the music acts from the Lexington area.

Additionally, as noted in the introduction, GPT-2 has its limitations. It should not be held to the same standard as ChatGPT or GPT-4, given that its size is less than 1% of ChatGPT and less than 0.1% of GPT-4. GPT-3 has 175 billion parameters and produces more coherent text than GPT-2, but the pretrained weights are not released to the public.

Next, we'll explore how `temperature` and `top-K` sampling affect the generated text from GPT-2XL. We'll set the `temperature` to 0.9 and `top_k` to 50 and keep other arguments the same. Let's see what the generated text looks like:

```
torch.manual_seed(42)
generate(prompt, max_new_tokens=100, temperature=0.9,
         top_k=50)
```

The output is

```
Lexington is the second largest city in the state of Kentucky. It is also
the state capital. The population of Lexington was 1,731,947 in the 2011
Census. The city is well-known for its many parks, including Arboretum,
Zoo, Aquarium and the Kentucky Science Center, as well as its restaurants,
such as the famous Kentucky Derby Festival.

In the United States, there are at least 28 counties in this state with a
population of more than 100,000, according to the 2010 census.
```

The generated text seems more coherent than before. However, the content is not factually accurate. It made up many facts about the city of Lexington, Kentucky, such as "The population of Lexington was 1,731,947 in the 2011 Census."

Exercise 11.5

Generate text by setting the `temperature` to 1.2 and `top_k` to None and using "Lexington is the second largest city in the state of Kentucky" as the starting prompt. Set the random seed number to 42 in PyTorch and the maximum number of new tokens to 100.

In this chapter, you have learned how to build GPT-2, the predecessor of ChatGPT and GPT-4, from scratch. After that, you extracted the pretrained weights from the GPT-2XL model released by OpenAI and loaded them into your model. You witnessed the coherent text generated by the model.

Due to the large size of the GPT-2XL model (1.5 billion parameters), it's impossible to train the model without supercomputing facilities. In the next chapter, you'll create a smaller version of a GPT model, with a similar structure as GPT-2 but only about 5.12 million parameters. You'll train the model with the text from Ernest Hemingway's novels. The trained model will generate coherent text with a style matching that of Hemingway!

Summary

- GPT-2 is an advanced LLM developed by OpenAI and announced in February 2019. It represents a significant milestone in the field of NLP and has paved the way for the development of even more sophisticated models, including its successors, ChatGPT and GPT-4.

- GPT-2 is a decoder-only Transformer, meaning there is no encoder stack in the model. Like other Transformer models, GPT-2 uses self-attention mechanisms to process input data in parallel, significantly improving the efficiency and effectiveness of training LLMs.

- GPT-2 adopts a different approach to positional encoding than the one used in the seminal 2017 paper "Attention Is All You Need." Instead, GPT-2's technique for positional encoding parallels that of word embeddings.

- The GELU activation function is used in the feed-forward sublayers of GPT-2. GELU provides a blend of linear and nonlinear activation properties that have been found to enhance model performance in deep learning tasks, particularly in NLPs and in training LLMs.

- We can build a GPT-2 model from scratch and load up the pretrained weights released by OpenAI. The GPT-2 model you created can generate coherent text just as the original OpenAI GPT-2 model does.

Training a Transformer to generate text

This chapter covers

- Building a scaled-down version of the GPT-2XL model tailored to your needs
- Preparing data for training a GPT-style Transformer
- Training a GPT-style Transformer from scratch
- Generating text using the trained GPT model

In chapter 11, we developed the GPT-2XL model from scratch but were unable to train it due to its vast number of parameters. Training a model with 1.5 billion parameters requires supercomputing facilities and an enormous amount of data. Consequently, we loaded pretrained weights from OpenAI into our model and then used the GPT-2XL model to generate text.

However, learning how to train a Transformer model from scratch is crucial for several reasons. First, while this book doesn't directly cover fine-tuning a pretrained model, understanding how to train a Transformer equips you with the skills needed for fine-tuning. Training a model involves initializing parameters randomly, whereas fine-tuning involves loading pretrained weights and further training the model. Second, training or fine-tuning a Transformer enables you to customize the model to meet your specific needs and domain, which can significantly enhance its performance and relevance for your use case. Finally, training your own Transformer or fine-tuning an existing one provides greater control over data and privacy, which is particularly important for sensitive applications or handling proprietary data. In summary, mastering the training and fine-tuning of Transformers is essential for anyone looking to harness the power of language models for specific applications while maintaining privacy and control.

Therefore, in this chapter, we'll construct a scaled-down version of the GPT model with approximately 5 million parameters. This smaller model follows the architecture of the GPT-2XL model; the significant differences are its composition of only 3 decoder blocks and an embedding dimension of 256, compared to the original GPT-2XL's 48 decoder blocks and an embedding dimension of 1,600. By scaling down the GPT model to about 5 million parameters, we can train it on a regular computer.

The generated text's style will depend on the training data. When training a model from scratch for text generation, both text length and variation are crucial. The training material must be extensive enough for the model to learn and mimic a particular writing style effectively. At the same time, if the training material lacks variation, the model may simply replicate passages from the training text. On the other hand, if the material is too long, training may require excessive computational resources. Therefore, we will use three novels by Ernest Hemingway as our training material: *The Old Man and the Sea*, *A Farewell to Arms*, and *For Whom the Bell Tolls*. This selection ensures that our training data has sufficient length and variation for effective learning without being so long that training becomes impractical.

Since GPT models cannot process raw text directly, we will first tokenize the text into words. We will then create a dictionary to map each unique token to a different index. Using this dictionary, we will convert the text into a long sequence of integers, ready for input into a neural network.

We will use sequences of 128 indexes as input to train the GPT model. As in chapters 8 and 10, we will shift the input sequence by one token to the right and use it as the output. This approach forces the model to predict the next word in a sentence based on the current token and all previous tokens in the sequence.

A key challenge is determining the optimal number of epochs for training the model. Our goal is not merely to minimize the cross-entropy loss in the training set, as doing so could lead to overfitting, where the model simply replicates passages from the training text. To tackle this problem, we plan to train the model for 40 epochs. We will save the model at 10-epoch intervals and evaluate which version can generate coherent text without merely copying passages from the training material. Alternatively, one could potentially use a validation set to assess the performance of the model and decide when to stop training, as we did in chapter 2.

Once our GPT model is trained, we will use it to generate text autoregressively, as we did in chapter 11. We'll test different versions of the trained model. The model trained for 40 epochs produces very coherent text, capturing Hemingway's distinctive style. However, it may also generate text partly copied from the training material, especially if the prompt is similar to passages in the training text. The model trained for 20 epochs also generates coherent text, albeit with occasional grammatical errors, but is less likely to directly copy from the training text.

The primary goal of this chapter is not necessarily to generate the most coherent text possible, which presents significant challenges. Instead, our objective is to teach you how to build a GPT-style model from scratch, tailored to real-world applications and your specific needs. More importantly, this chapter outlines the steps involved in training a GPT model from scratch. You will learn how to select training text based on your objectives, tokenize the text and convert it to indexes, and prepare batches of training data. You will also learn how to determine the number of epochs for training. Once the model is trained, you will learn how to generate text using the model and how to avoid generating text directly copied from the training material.

12.1 Building and training a GPT from scratch

Our objective is to master building and training a GPT model from scratch, tailored to specific tasks. This skill is crucial for applying the concepts in this book to real-world problems.

Imagine you are an avid fan of Ernest Hemingway's work and wish to train a GPT model to generate text in Hemingway's style. How would you approach this? This section discusses the steps involved in this task.

The first step is to configure a GPT model suitable for training. You'll create a GPT model with a structure similar to the GPT-2 model you built in chapter 11 but with significantly fewer parameters to make training feasible in just a few hours. As a result, you'll need to determine key hyperparameters of the model, such as sequence length, embedding dimension, number of decoder blocks, and dropout rates. These hyperparameters are crucial as they influence both the quality of the output from the trained model and the speed of training.

Following that, you will gather the raw text of several Hemingway novels and clean it up to ensure it is suitable for training. You will tokenize the text and assign a different integer to each unique token so that you can feed it to the model. To prepare the training data, you will break down the text into sequences of integers of a certain length and use them as inputs. You will then shift the inputs one token to the right and use them as outputs. This approach forces the model to predict the next token based on the current token and all previous tokens in the sequence.

Once the model is trained, you will use it to generate text based on a prompt. You will first convert the text in the prompt to a sequence of indexes and feed it to the trained model. The model uses the sequence to predict the most likely next token iteratively. After that, you will convert the sequence of tokens generated by the model back to text.

In this section, we will first discuss the architecture of the GPT model for the task. After that, we will discuss the steps involved in training the model.

12.1.1 The architecture of a GPT to generate text

Although GPT-2 is available in various sizes, they all share a similar architecture. The GPT model we construct in this chapter follows the same structural design as GPT-2 but is significantly smaller, making it feasible to train without the need for supercomputing facilities. Table 12.1 presents a comparison between our GPT model and the four versions of the GPT-2 models.

Table 12.1 A comparison of our GPT with different versions of GPT-2 models

	GPT-2S	GPT-2M	GPT-2L	GPT-2XL	Our GPT
Embedding dimension	768	1,024	1,280	1,600	256
Number of decoder layers	12	24	36	48	3
Number of heads	12	16	20	25	4
Sequence length	1,024	1,024	1,024	1,024	128
Vocabulary size	50,257	50,257	50,257	50,257	10,600
Number of parameters	124 million	350 million	774 million	1,558 million	5.12 million

In this chapter, we'll construct a GPT model with three decoder layers and an embedding dimension of 256 (meaning each token is represented by a 256-value vector after word embedding). As we mentioned in chapter 11, GPT models use a different positional encoding method than the one used in the 2017 paper "Attention Is All You Need." Instead, we use embedding layers to learn the positional encodings for different positions in a sequence. As a result, each position in a sequence is also represented by a 256-value vector. For calculating causal self-attention, we use four parallel attention heads to capture different aspects of the meanings of a token in the sequence. Thus, each attention head has a dimension of $256/4 = 64$, similar to that in GPT-2 models. For example, in GPT-2XL, each attention head has a dimension of $1,600/25 = 64$.

The maximum sequence length in our GPT model is 128, which is much shorter than the maximum sequence length of 1,024 in GPT-2 models. This reduction is necessary to keep the number of parameters in the model manageable. However, even with 128 elements in a sequence, the model can learn the relationship between tokens in a sequence and generate coherent text.

While GPT-2 models have a vocabulary size of 50,257, our model has a much smaller vocabulary size of 10,600. It's important to note that the vocabulary size is mainly determined by the training data, rather than being a predefined choice. If you choose to use more text for training, you may end up with a larger vocabulary.

Figure 12.1 illustrates the architecture of the decoder-only Transformer we will create in this chapter. It is similar to the architecture of GPT-2 that you have seen in chapter 11, except that it is smaller in size. As a result, the total number of parameters in our model is 5.12 million, compared to the 1.558 billion in the GPT-2XL model that we built in chapter 11. Figure 12.1 shows the size of the training data at each step of training.

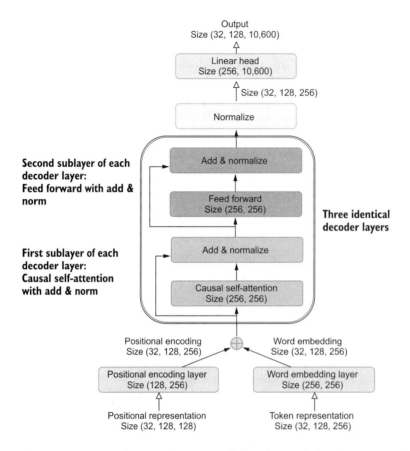

Figure 12.1 The architecture of a decoder-only Transformer, designed to generate text. The text from three Hemingway novels is tokenized and then converted into indexes. We arrange 128 indexes into a sequence, and each batch contains 32 such sequences. The input first undergoes word embedding and positional encoding, with the input embedding being the sum of these two components. This input embedding is then processed through three decoder layers. Following this, the output undergoes layer normalization and passes through a linear layer, resulting in an output size of 10,600, which corresponds to the number of unique tokens in the vocabulary.

The input to the GPT model we create consists of input embeddings, which are illustrated at the bottom of figure 12.1. We will discuss how to calculate these embeddings in detail in the next subsection. Briefly, they are the sum of word embeddings and positional encodings from the input sequence.

The input embedding is then passed sequentially through three decoder layers. Similar to the GPT-2XL model we built in chapter 11, each decoder layer consists of two sublayers: a causal self-attention layer and a feed-forward network. Additionally, we apply layer normalization and residual connections to each sublayer. After this, the output goes through a layer normalization and a linear layer. The number of outputs in our GPT model corresponds to the number of unique tokens in the vocabulary, which is 10,600. The output of the model is the logits for the next token. Later, we will apply the softmax function to these logits to obtain the probability distribution over the vocabulary. The model is designed to predict the next token based on the current token and all previous tokens in the sequence.

12.1.2 The training process of the GPT model to generate text

Now that we know how to construct the GPT model for text generation, let's explore the steps involved in training the model. We aim to provide an overview of the training process before diving into the coding aspect of the project.

The style of the generated text is influenced by the training text. Since our objective is to train the model to generate text in the style of Ernest Hemingway, we'll use the text from three of his novels: *The Old Man and the Sea, A Farewell to Arms,* and *For Whom the Bell Tolls.* If we were to choose just one novel, the training data would lack variety, leading the model to memorize passages from the novel and generate text identical to the training data. Conversely, using too many novels would increase the number of unique tokens, making it challenging to train the model effectively in a short amount of time. Therefore, we strike a balance by selecting three novels and combining them as our training data.

Figure 12.2 illustrates the steps involved in training the GPT model to generate text.

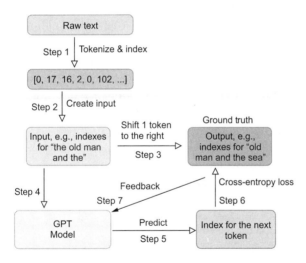

Figure 12.2 The training process for a decoder-only Transformer to generate text, Hemingway-style.

As in the previous three chapters, the first step in the training process is to convert text into a numerical form so that we can feed the training data to the model. Specifically, we first break down the text of the three novels into tokens using word-level tokenization, as we did in chapter 8. In this case, each token is a whole word or a punctuation mark (such as a colon, a parenthesis, or a comma). Word-level tokenization is easy to implement, and we can control the number of unique tokens. After tokenization, we assign a unique index (i.e., an integer) to each token, converting the training text into a sequence of integers (see step 1 in figure 12.2).

Next, we transform the sequence of integers into training data by first dividing this sequence into sequences of equal length (step 2 in figure 12.2). We allow a maximum length of 128 indexes in each sequence. The choice of 128 allows us to capture long-range dependencies among tokens in a sentence while keeping the model size manageable. However, the number 128 is not magical: changing the number to, say, 100 or 150 will lead to similar results. These sequences form the features (the x variable) of our model. As we did in previous chapters, we shift the input sequence one token to the right and use it as the output in the training data (the y variable; step 3 in figure 12.2).

The pairs of input and output serve as the training data (x, y). In the example of the sentence "the old man and the sea," we use indexes corresponding to "the old man and the" as the input x. We shift the input one token to the right and use the indexes for "old man and the sea" as the output y. In the first time step, the model uses "the" to predict "old." In the second time step, the model uses "the old" to predict "man," and so on.

During training, you will iterate through the training data. In the forward passes, you feed the input sequence x through the GPT model (step 4). The GPT then makes a prediction based on the current parameters in the model (step 5). You compute the cross-entropy loss by comparing the predicted next tokens with the output obtained from step 3. In other words, you compare the model's prediction with the ground truth (step 6). Finally, you will adjust the parameters in the GPT model so that in the next iteration, the model's predictions move closer to the actual output, minimizing the cross-entropy loss (step 7). Note that the model is essentially performing a multicategory classification problem: it's predicting the next token from all unique tokens in the vocabulary.

You will repeat steps 3 to 7 through many iterations. After each iteration, the model parameters are adjusted to improve the prediction of the next token. We will repeat this process for 40 epochs and save the trained model after every 10 epochs. As you will see later, if we train the model for too long, it becomes overfit, memorizing passages from the training data. The generated text then becomes identical to those in the original novels. We will test ex post which version of the model generates coherent text and, at the same time, does not simply copy from the training data.

12.2 *Tokenizing text of Hemingway novels*

Now that you understand the architecture of the GPT model and the training process, let's begin with the first step: tokenizing and indexing the text of Hemingway's novels.

First, we'll process the text data to prepare it for training. We'll break down the text into individual tokens, as we did in chapter 8. Since deep neural networks cannot directly process raw text, we'll create a dictionary that assigns an index to each token, effectively mapping them to integers. After that, we'll organize these indexes into batches of training data, which will be crucial for training the GPT model in the subsequent steps.

We'll use word-level tokenization for its simplicity in dividing text into words, as opposed to the more complex subword tokenization that requires a nuanced understanding of linguistic structure. Additionally, word-level tokenization results in a smaller number of unique tokens than subword tokenization, reducing the number of parameters in the GPT model.

12.2.1 Tokenizing the text

To train the GPT model, we'll use the raw text files of three novels by Ernest Hemingway: *The Old Man and the Sea*, *A Farewell to Arms*, and *For Whom the Bell Tolls*. The text files are downloaded from the Faded Page website: https://www.fadedpage.com. I have cleaned up the text by removing the top and bottom paragraphs that are not part of the original book. When preparing your own training text, it's crucial to eliminate all irrelevant information, such as vendor details, formatting, and license information. This ensures that the model focuses solely on learning the writing style present in the text. I have also removed the text between chapters that are not relevant to the main text. You can download the three files OldManAndSea.txt, FarewellToArms.txt, and ToWhomTheBellTolls.txt from the book's GitHub repository: https://github.com/markhliu/DGAI. Place them in the /files/ folder on your computer.

In the text file for *The Old Man and the Sea*, both the opening double quote (") and the closing double quote (") are represented by straight double quotes ("). This is not the case in the text files for the other two novels. Therefore, we load up the text for *The Old Man and the Sea* and change straight quotes to either an opening quote or a closing quote. Doing so allows us to differentiate between the opening and closing quotes. This will also aid in formatting the generated text later on: we'll remove the space after the opening quote and the space before the closing quote. This step is implemented as shown in the following listing.

Listing 12.1 Changing straight quotes to opening and closing quotes

```
with open("files/OldManAndSea.txt","r", encoding='utf-8-sig') as f:
    text=f.read()
text=list(text)
for i in range(len(text)):
    if text[i]=='"':
        if text[i+1]==' ' or text[i+1]=='\n':
            text[i]='"'
        if text[i+1]!=' ' and text[i+1]!='\n':
            text[i]='"'
    if text[i]=='"':
        if text[i-1]!=' ' and text[i-1]!='\n':
            text[i]='''
text="".join(text)
```

Loads up the raw text and breaks it into individual characters

If a straight double quote is followed by a space or a line break, changes it to a closing quote

Otherwise, changes it to an opening quote

Converts a straight single quote to an apostrophe

Joins individual characters back to text

If a double quote is followed by a space or a line break, we'll change it to a closing quote; otherwise, we'll change it to an opening quote. The apostrophe was entered as a single straight quote, and we have changed it to an apostrophe in the form of a closing single quote in listing 12.1.

Next, we load the text for the other two novels and combine the three novels into one single file.

Listing 12.2   Combining the text from three novels

```
with open("files/ToWhomTheBellTolls.txt","r", encoding='utf-8-sig') as f:
    text1=f.read()

with open("files/FarewellToArms.txt","r", encoding='utf-8-sig') as f:
    text2=f.read()

text=text+" "+text1+" "+text2

with open("files/ThreeNovels.txt","w",
        encoding='utf-8-sig') as f:
    f.write(text)
print(text[:250])
```

Reads the text from the second novel

Reads the text from the third novel

Combines the text from the three novels

Saves the combined text in the local folder

We load the text from the other two novels, *A Farewell to Arms* and *For Whom the Bell Tolls*. We then combine the text from all three novels to use as our training data. Additionally, we save the combined text in a local file named ThreeNovels.txt so that we can later verify if the generated text is directly copied from the original text.

The output from the preceding code listing is

```
He was an old man who fished alone in a skiff in the Gulf Stream and he
had gone eighty-four days now without taking a fish. In the first
forty days a boy had been with him. But after forty days without a
fish the boy's parents had told him that th
```

The output is the first 250 characters in the combined text.

We'll tokenize the text by using a space as the delimiter. As seen in the preceding output, punctuation marks such as periods (.), hyphens (-), and apostrophes (') are attached to the preceding words without a space. Therefore, we need to insert a space around all punctuation marks.

Additionally, we'll convert line breaks (\n) into spaces so that they are not included in the vocabulary. Converting all words to lowercase is also beneficial in our setting, as it ensures that words like "The" and "the" are recognized as the same token. This step helps reduce the number of unique tokens, thereby making the training process more efficient. To address these problems, we'll clean up the text as shown in the following listing.

Listing 12.3 Adding spaces around punctuation marks

```
text=text.lower().replace("\n", " ")

chars=set(text.lower())
punctuations=[i for i in chars if i.isalpha()==False
              and i.isdigit()==False]
print(punctuations)

for x in punctuations:
    text=text.replace(f"{x}", f" {x} ")
text_tokenized=text.split()

unique_tokens=set(text_tokenized)
print(len(unique_tokens))
```

- Replaces line breaks with spaces
- Identifies all punctuation marks
- Inserts spaces around punctuation marks
- Counts the number of unique tokens

We use the set() method to obtain all unique characters in the text. We then use the isalpha() and isdigit() methods to identify and remove letters and numbers from the set of unique characters, leaving us with only punctuation marks.

If you execute the preceding code block, the output will be as follows:

```
[')', '.', '&', ':', '(', ';', '-', '!', '"', ' ', '', '"', '?', ',', '']
10599
```

This list includes all punctuation marks in the text. We add spaces around them and break the text into individual tokens using the split() method. The output indicates that there are 10,599 unique tokens in the text from the three novels by Hemingway, a size that's much smaller than the 50,257 tokens in GPT-2. This will significantly reduce the model size and training time.

Additionally, we'll add one more token "UNK" to represent unknown tokens. This is useful in case we encounter a prompt with unknown tokens, allowing us to convert them to an index to feed to the model. Otherwise, we can only use a prompt with the preceding 10,599 tokens. Suppose you include the word "technology" in the prompt. Since "technology" is not one of the tokens in the dictionary word_to_int, the program will crash. By including the "UNK" token, you can prevent the program from crashing in such scenarios. When you train your own GPT, you should always include the "UNK" token since it's impossible to include all tokens in your vocabulary. To that end, we add "UNK" to the list of unique tokens and map them to indexes.

Listing 12.4 Mapping tokens to indexes

```
from collections import Counter

word_counts=Counter(text_tokenized)
words=sorted(word_counts, key=word_counts.get,
                    reverse=True)
words.append("UNK")
text_length=len(text_tokenized)
```

- Adds "UNK" to the list of unique tokens

Counts the size of the vocabulary,
ntokens, which will be a
hyperparamter in our model

```
ntokens=len(words)
print(f"the text contains {text_length} words")
print(f"there are {ntokens} unique tokens")
word_to_int={v:k for k,v in enumerate(words)}
int_to_word={v:k for k,v in word_to_int.items()}
print({k:v for k,v in word_to_int.items() if k in words[:10]})
print({k:v for k,v in int_to_word.items() if v in words[:10]})
```

Maps tokens to indexes

Maps indexes
to tokens

The output from the preceding code block is

```
the text contains 698207 words
there are 10600 unique tokens
{'.': 0, 'the': 1, ',': 2, '"': 3, '"': 4, 'and': 5, 'i': 6, 'to': 7, 'he':
8, 'it': 9}
{0: '.', 1: 'the', 2: ',', 3: '"', 4: '"', 5: 'and', 6: 'i', 7: 'to', 8:
'he', 9: 'it'}
```

The text from the three novels contains 698,207 tokens. After including "UNK" in the vocabulary, the total number of *unique* tokens is now 10,600. The dictionary word_to_ int assigns a different index to each unique token. For example, the most frequent token, the period (.), is assigned an index of 0, and the word "the" is assigned an index of 1. The dictionary int_to_word translates an index back to a token. For example, index 3 is translated back to the opening quote ("), and index 4 is translated back to the closing quote (").

We print out the first 20 tokens in the text and their corresponding indexes:

```
print(text_tokenized[0:20])
wordidx=[word_to_int[w] for w in text_tokenized]
print([word_to_int[w] for w in text_tokenized[0:20]])
```

The output is

```
['he', 'was', 'an', 'old', 'man', 'who', 'fished', 'alone', 'in', 'a',
'skiff', 'in', 'the', 'gulf', 'stream', 'and', 'he', 'had', 'gone',
 'eighty']
[8, 16, 98, 110, 67, 85, 6052, 314, 14, 11, 1039, 14, 1, 3193, 507, 5, 8,
25, 223, 3125]
```

Next, we'll break the indexes into sequences of equal length to use as training data.

12.2.2 *Creating batches for training*

We'll use a sequence of 128 tokens as the input to the model. We then shift the sequence one token to the right and use it as the output.

Specifically, we create pairs of (x, y) for training purposes. Each x is a sequence with 128 indexes. We choose 128 to strike a balance between training speed and the model's ability to capture long-range dependencies. Setting the number too high may slow down training, while setting it too low may prevent the model from capturing long-range dependencies effectively.

Once we have the sequence x, we slide the sequence window to the right by one token and use it as the target y. Shifting the sequence by one token to the right and using it as the output during sequence generation is a common technique in training language models, including GPTs. We have done this in chapters 8 to 10. The following code block creates the training data:

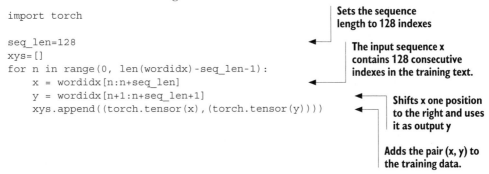

```
import torch

seq_len=128
xys=[]
for n in range(0, len(wordidx)-seq_len-1):
    x = wordidx[n:n+seq_len]
    y = wordidx[n+1:n+seq_len+1]
    xys.append((torch.tensor(x),(torch.tensor(y))))
```

Sets the sequence length to 128 indexes

The input sequence x contains 128 consecutive indexes in the training text.

Shifts x one position to the right and uses it as output y

Adds the pair (x, y) to the training data.

We have created a list xys to contain pairs of (x, y) as our training data. As we did in previous chapters, we organize the training data into batches to stabilize training. We choose a batch size of 32:

```
from torch.utils.data import DataLoader

torch.manual_seed(42)
batch_size=32
loader = DataLoader(xys, batch_size=batch_size, shuffle=True)

x,y=next(iter(loader))
print(x)
print(y)
print(x.shape,y.shape)
```

We print out a pair of x and y as an example. The output is

```
tensor([[   3,  129,    9,  ...,   11,  251,   10],
        [   5,   41,   32,  ...,  995,   52,   23],
        [   6,   25,   11,  ...,   15,    0,   24],
        ...,
        [1254,    0,    4,  ...,   15,    0,    3],
        [  17,    8, 1388,  ...,    0,    8,   16],
        [  55,   20,  156,  ...,   74,   76,   12]])
tensor([[ 129,    9,   23,  ...,  251,   10,    1],
        [  41,   32,   34,  ...,   52,   23,    1],
        [  25,   11,   59,  ...,    0,   24,   25],
        ...,
        [   0,    4,    3,  ...,    0,    3,   93],
        [   8, 1388,    1,  ...,    8,   16, 1437],
        [  20,  156,  970,  ...,   76,   12,   29]])
torch.Size([32, 128]) torch.Size([32, 128])
```

Each x and y have a shape of (32, 128). This means that in each batch of training data, there are 32 pairs of sequences, with each sequence containing 128 indexes. When an index is passed through the nn.Embedding() layer, PyTorch looks up the corresponding row in the embedding matrix and returns the embedding vector for that index, avoiding the need to create potentially very large one-hot vectors. Therefore, when x is passed through the word embedding layer, it's as if x is first converted to a one-hot tensor with a dimension of (32, 128, 256). Similarly, when x is passed through the positional encoding layer (which is implemented by the nn.Embedding() layer), it's as if x is first converted to a one-hot tensor with a dimension of (32, 128, 128).

12.3   *Building a GPT to generate text*

Now that we have the training data ready, we'll create a GPT model from scratch to generate text. The model we'll build has a similar architecture as the GPT-2XL model we built in chapter 11. However, instead of having 48 decoder layers, we'll use only 3 decoder layers. The embedding dimensions and the vocabulary size are both much smaller, as I have explained earlier in this chapter. As a result, our GPT model will have far fewer parameters than GPT-2XL.

We'll follow the same steps as those in chapter 11. Along the way, we'll highlight the differences between our GPT model and GPT-2XL and explain the reasons for these modifications.

12.3.1   *Model hyperparameters*

The feed-forward network in the decoder block uses the Gaussian error linear unit (GELU) activation function. GELU has been shown to enhance model performance in deep learning tasks, particularly in natural language processing. This has become a standard practice in GPT models. Therefore, we define a GELU class as follows, as we did in Chapter 11:

```
import torch
from torch import nn
import math

device="cuda" if torch.cuda.is_available() else "cpu"
class GELU(nn.Module):
    def forward(self, x):
        return 0.5*x*(1.0+torch.tanh(math.sqrt(2.0/math.pi)*\
                     (x + 0.044715 * torch.pow(x, 3.0))))
```

In chapter 11, we didn't use a GPU even during the text generation stage, as the model was simply too large and a regular GPU would run out of memory if we loaded the model onto it.

In this chapter, however, our model is significantly smaller. We'll move the model to the GPU for faster training. We'll also generate text using the model on the GPU.

We use a Config() class to include all the hyperparameters used in the model:

```
class Config():
    def __init__(self):
        self.n_layer = 3
        self.n_head = 4
        self.n_embd = 256
        self.vocab_size = ntokens
```

```
        self.block_size = 128
        self.embd_pdrop = 0.1
        self.resid_pdrop = 0.1
        self.attn_pdrop = 0.1
config=Config()
```

The attributes in the `Config()` class are used as hyperparameters in our GPT model. We set the n_layer attribute to 3, indicating our GPT model has three decoder layers. The n_head attribute is set to 4, meaning we'll split the query Q, key K, and value V vectors into 4 parallel heads when calculating causal self-attention. The n_embd attribute is set to 256, meaning the embedding dimension is 256: each token will be represented by a 256-value vector. The `vocab_size` attribute is determined by the number of unique tokens in the vocabulary. As explained in the last section, there are 10,600 unique tokens in our training text. The `block_size` attribute is set to 128, meaning the input sequence contains a maximum of 128 tokens. We set the dropout rates to 0.1, as we did in chapter 11.

12.3.2 *Modeling the causal self-attention mechanism*

The causal self-attention is defined in the same way as in chapter 11:

```
import torch.nn.functional as F
class CausalSelfAttention(nn.Module):
    def __init__(self, config):
        super().__init__()
        self.c_attn = nn.Linear(config.n_embd, 3 * config.n_embd)
        self.c_proj = nn.Linear(config.n_embd, config.n_embd)
        self.attn_dropout = nn.Dropout(config.attn_pdrop)
        self.resid_dropout = nn.Dropout(config.resid_pdrop)
        self.register_buffer("bias", torch.tril(torch.ones(\
                config.block_size, config.block_size))
            .view(1, 1, config.block_size, config.block_size))
        self.n_head = config.n_head
        self.n_embd = config.n_embd

    def forward(self, x):
        B, T, C = x.size()
        q, k ,v  = self.c_attn(x).split(self.n_embd, dim=2)
        hs = C // self.n_head
        k = k.view(B, T, self.n_head, hs).transpose(1, 2)
        q = q.view(B, T, self.n_head, hs).transpose(1, 2)
        v = v.view(B, T, self.n_head, hs).transpose(1, 2)

        att = (q @ k.transpose(-2, -1)) *\
            (1.0 / math.sqrt(k.size(-1)))
        att = att.masked_fill(self.bias[:,:,:T,:T] == 0, \
                            float(,-inf'))
        att = F.softmax(att, dim=-1)
        att = self.attn_dropout(att)
        y = att @ v
        y = y.transpose(1, 2).contiguous().view(B, T, C)
        y = self.resid_dropout(self.c_proj(y))
        return y
```

When calculating causal self-attention, the input embedding is passed through three neural networks to obtain the query Q, key K, and value V. We then split each of them into four parallel heads and calculate masked self-attention within each head. After that, we concatenate the four attention vectors back into a single attention vector, which is then used as the output of the `CausalSelfAttention()` class.

12.3.3 *Building the GPT model*

We combine a feed-forward network with the causal self-attention sublayer to form a decoder block. The feed-forward network injects nonlinearity into the model. Without it, the Transformer would simply be a series of linear operations, constraining its capacity to capture complex data relationships. Moreover, the feed-forward network processes each position independently and uniformly, enabling the transformation of features identified by the self-attention mechanism. This facilitates the capture of diverse aspects of the input data, thereby augmenting the model's ability to represent information. A decoder block is defined as follows:

```
class Block(nn.Module):
    def __init__(self, config):
        super().__init__()
        self.ln_1 = nn.LayerNorm(config.n_embd)
        self.attn = CausalSelfAttention(config)
        self.ln_2 = nn.LayerNorm(config.n_embd)
        self.mlp = nn.ModuleDict(dict(
            c_fc   = nn.Linear(config.n_embd, 4 * config.n_embd),
            c_proj = nn.Linear(4 * config.n_embd, config.n_embd),
            act    = GELU(),
            dropout = nn.Dropout(config.resid_pdrop),
        ))
        m = self.mlp
        self.mlpf=lambda x:m.dropout(m.c_proj(m.act(m.c_fc(x))))

    def forward(self, x):
        x = x + self.attn(self.ln_1(x))
        x = x + self.mlpf(self.ln_2(x))
        return x
```

Each decoder block in our GPT model consists of two sublayers: a causal self-attention sublayer and a feed-forward network. We apply layer normalization and a residual connection to each sublayer for improved stability and performance. We then stack three decoder layers on top of each other to form the main body of our GPT model.

Listing 12.5   Building a GPT model

```
class Model(nn.Module):
    def __init__(self, config):
        super().__init__()
        self.block_size = config.block_size
        self.transformer = nn.ModuleDict(dict(
            wte = nn.Embedding(config.vocab_size, config.n_embd),
            wpe = nn.Embedding(config.block_size, config.n_embd),
```

```
        drop = nn.Dropout(config.embd_pdrop),
        h = nn.ModuleList([Block(config)
                        for _ in range(config.n_layer)]),
        ln_f = nn.LayerNorm(config.n_embd),))
    self.lm_head = nn.Linear(config.n_embd,
                        config.vocab_size, bias=False)
    for pn, p in self.named_parameters():
        if pn.endswith('c_proj.weight'):
            torch.nn.init.normal_(p, mean=0.0,
                std=0.02/math.sqrt(2 * config.n_layer))
def forward(self, idx, targets=None):
    b, t = idx.size()
    pos=torch.arange(0,t,dtype=\
        torch.long).unsqueeze(0).to(device)       ◀── Moves the positional
    tok_emb = self.transformer.wte(idx)                encoding to CUDA-enabled
    pos_emb = self.transformer.wpe(pos)                GPU, if available
    x = self.transformer.drop(tok_emb + pos_emb)
    for block in self.transformer.h:
        x = block(x)
    x = self.transformer.ln_f(x)
    logits = self.lm_head(x)
    return logits
```

The positional encoding is created within the Model() class. Therefore, we need to move it to a compute unified device architecture (CUDA)-enabled GPU (if available) to ensure that all inputs to the model are on the same device. Failing to do this will result in an error message.

The input to the model consists of sequences of indexes corresponding to tokens in the vocabulary. We pass the input through word embedding and positional encoding and add the two to form the input embedding. The input embedding then goes through the three decoder blocks. After that, we apply layer normalization to the output and attach a linear head to it so that the number of outputs is 10,600, the size of the vocabulary. The outputs are the logits corresponding to the 10,600 tokens in the vocabulary. Later, we'll apply the softmax activation function to the logits to obtain the probability distribution over the unique tokens in the vocabulary when generating text.

Next, we'll create our GPT model by instantiating the Model() class we defined earlier:

```
model=Model(config)
model.to(device)
num=sum(p.numel() for p in model.transformer.parameters())
print("number of parameters: %.2fM" % (num/1e6,))
print(model)
```

The output is

```
number of parameters: 5.12M
Model(
  (transformer): ModuleDict(
    (wte): Embedding(10600, 256)
    (wpe): Embedding(128, 256)
    (drop): Dropout(p=0.1, inplace=False)
```

```
    (h): ModuleList(
      (0-2): 3 x Block(
        (ln_1): LayerNorm((256,), eps=1e-05, elementwise_affine=True)
        (attn): CausalSelfAttention(
          (c_attn): Linear(in_features=256, out_features=768, bias=True)
          (c_proj): Linear(in_features=256, out_features=256, bias=True)
          (attn_dropout): Dropout(p=0.1, inplace=False)
          (resid_dropout): Dropout(p=0.1, inplace=False)
        )
        (ln_2): LayerNorm((256,), eps=1e-05, elementwise_affine=True)
        (mlp): ModuleDict(
          (c_fc): Linear(in_features=256, out_features=1024, bias=True)
          (c_proj): Linear(in_features=1024, out_features=256, bias=True)
          (act): GELU()
          (dropout): Dropout(p=0.1, inplace=False)
        )
      )
    )
    (ln_f): LayerNorm((256,), eps=1e-05, elementwise_affine=True)
  )
  (lm_head): Linear(in_features=256, out_features=10600, bias=False)
)
```

Our GPT model has 5.12 million parameters. The structure of our model is similar to that of GPT-2XL. If you compare the output above with that from chapter 11, you'll see that the only differences are in the hyperparameters, such as the embedding dimension, number of decoder layers, vocabulary size, and so on.

12.4   *Training the GPT model to generate text*

In this section, you'll train the GPT model you just built using the batches of training data we prepared earlier in this chapter. A related question is how many epochs we should train the model. While training too few epochs may lead to incoherent text, training too many epochs may lead to an overfitted model, which may generate text identical to passages in the training text.

Therefore, we will train the model for 40 epochs. We'll save the model after every 10 epochs and assess which version of the trained model can generate coherent text without simply copying passages from the training text. Another potential approach is to create a validation set and stop training when the model's performance converges in the validation set, as we did in chapter 2.

12.4.1   *Training the GPT model*

As always, we'll use the Adam optimizer. Since our GPT model is essentially performing a multicategory classification, we'll use cross-entropy loss as our loss function:

```
lr=0.0001
optimizer = torch.optim.Adam(model.parameters(), lr=lr)
loss_func = nn.CrossEntropyLoss()
```

We will train the model for 40 epochs, as shown in the following listing.

Listing 12.6   Training the GPT model to generate text

```
model.train()
for i in range(1,41):
    tloss = 0.
    for idx, (x,y) in enumerate(loader):          Iterates through all
        x,y=x.to(device),y.to(device)             batches of training data
        output = model(x)
        loss=loss_func(output.view(-1,output.size(-1)),   Compares model
                        y.view(-1))                        predictions with
        optimizer.zero_grad()                              actual outputs
        loss.backward()
        nn.utils.clip_grad_norm_(model.parameters(),1)    Clips gradient
        optimizer.step()                                   norm to 1
        tloss += loss.item()
    print(f'epoch {i} loss {tloss/(idx+1)}')       Tweaks model parameters
    if i%10==0:                                     to minimize loss
        torch.save(model.state_dict(),f'files/GPTe{i}.pth')   Saves model
                                                              after every
                                                              ten epochs
```

During training, we pass all the input sequences x in a batch through the model to obtain predictions. We compare these predictions with the output sequences y in the batch and calculate the cross-entropy loss. We then adjust the model parameters to minimize this loss. Note that we have clipped the gradient norm to 1 to avoid the potential problem of exploding gradients.

Gradient norm clipping

Gradient norm clipping is a technique used in training neural networks to prevent the exploding gradient problem. This problem occurs when the gradients of the loss function with respect to the model's parameters become excessively large, leading to unstable training and poor model performance. In gradient norm clipping, the gradients are scaled down if their norm (magnitude) exceeds a certain threshold. This ensures that the gradients do not become too large, maintaining stable training and improving convergence.

This training process takes a couple of hours if you have a CUDA-enabled GPU. After training, four files, GPTe10.pth, GPTe20.pth, …, GPTe40.pth, will be saved on your computer. Alternatively, you can download the trained models from my website: https://gattonweb.uky.edu/faculty/lium/gai/GPT.zip.

12.4.2 A function to generate text

Now that we have multiple versions of the trained model, we can proceed to text generation and compare the performance of different versions. We can assess which version performs the best and use that version to generate text.

Similar to the process in GPT-2XL, text generation begins with feeding a sequence of indexes (representing tokens) to the model as a prompt. The model predicts the index of the next token, which is then appended to the prompt to form a new sequence. This new sequence is fed back into the model for further predictions, and this process is repeated until a desired number of new tokens is generated.

To facilitate this process, we define a `sample()` function. This function takes a sequence of indexes as input, representing the current state of the text. It then iteratively predicts and appends new indexes to the sequence until the specified number of new tokens, `max_new_tokens`, is reached. The following listing shows the implementation.

Listing 12.7   A `sample()` function to predict subsequent indexes

```
def sample(idx, weights, max_new_tokens, temperature=1.0, top_k=None):
    model.eval()
    model.load_state_dict(torch.load(weights,
        map_location=device))                        Loads up a version of
    original_length=len(idx[0])                      the trained model
    for _ in range(max_new_tokens):                  Generates a fixed
        if idx.size(1) <= config.block_size:         number of new indexes
            idx_cond = idx
        else:
            idx_cond = idx[:, -config.block_size:]
        logits = model(idx_cond.to(device))          Uses the model to
        logits = logits[:, -1, :] / temperature      make predictions
        if top_k is not None:
            v, _ = torch.topk(logits, top_k)
            logits[logits < v[:, [-1]]] = -float('Inf')   Attaches the new
        probs = F.softmax(logits, dim=-1)                 index to the end of
        idx_next=torch.multinomial(probs,num_samples=1)   the sequence
        idx = torch.cat((idx, idx_next.cpu()), dim=1)
    return idx[:, original_length:]                  Outputs only the
                                                     new indexes
```

One of the arguments of the `sample()` function is `weights`, which represents the trained weights of one of the models saved on your computer. Unlike the `sample()` function we defined in chapter 11, our function here returns only the newly generated indexes, not including the original indexes that were fed to the `sample()` function. We made this change to accommodate cases where the prompt contains unknown tokens. In such cases, our `sample()` function ensures that the final output retains the original prompt. Otherwise, all unknown tokens would be replaced with "UNK" in the final output.

Next, we define a `generate()` function to generate text based on a prompt. The function first converts the prompt to a sequence of indexes. It then uses the `sample()` function to generate a new sequence of indexes. After that, the `generate()` function concatenates all indexes together and converts them back to text. The implementation is shown in the following listing.

Listing 12.8   A function to generate text with the trained GPT model

```
UNK=word_to_int["UNK"]
def generate(prompt, weights, max_new_tokens, temperature=1.0,
            top_k=None):
```

Makes sure the
prompt is not empty

```
assert len(prompt)>0, "prompt must contain at least one token"
text=prompt.lower().replace("\n", " ")
for x in punctuations:
    text=text.replace(f"{x}", f" {x} ")
text_tokenized=text.split()
idx=[word_to_int.get(w,UNK) for w in text_tokenized]
idx=torch.LongTensor(idx).unsqueeze(0)
idx=sample(idx, weights, max_new_tokens,
           temperature=1.0, top_k=None)
tokens=[int_to_word[i] for i in idx.squeeze().numpy()]
text=" ".join(tokens)
for x in '''") .:;!?,-''''':
    text=text.replace(f" {x}", f"{x}")
for x in '''"(-''''':
    text=text.replace(f"{x} ", f"{x}")
return prompt+" "+text
```

Converts prompt
into a sequence of
indexes

Uses the sample()
function to generate
new indexes

Converts the
new sequence
of indexes back
to text

We ensure that the prompt is not empty. If it is, you'll receive an error message saying "prompt must contain at least one token." The `generate()` function allows you to select which version of the model to use by specifying the weights saved on your computer. For example, you can choose 'files/GPTe10.pth' as the value of the weights argument for the function. The function converts the prompt into a series of indexes, which are then fed into the model to predict the next index. After generating a fixed number of new indexes, the function converts the entire index sequence back into textual form.

12.4.3 *Text generation with different versions of the trained model*

Next, we'll experiment with different versions of the trained model to generate text.

We can use the unknown token `"UNK"` as the prompt for unconditional text generation. This is especially beneficial in our context because we want to check if the generated text is directly copied from the training text. While a unique prompt that's very different from the training text unlikely leads to passages directly from the training text, unconditionally generated text is more likely to be from the training text.

We first use the model after 20 epochs of training to generate text unconditionally:

```
prompt="UNK"
for i in range(10):
    torch.manual_seed(i)
    print(generate(prompt,'files/GPTe20.pth',max_new_tokens=20)[4:]))
```

The output is

```
way." "kümmel," i said. "it's the way to talk about it
--------------------------------------------------
," robert jordan said. "but do not realize how far he is ruined." "pero
--------------------------------------------------
in the fog, robert jordan thought. and then, without looking at last, so
good, he
--------------------------------------------------
```

```
pot of yellow rice and fish and the boy loved him. "no," the boy said.
------------------------------------------------
the line now. it's wonderful." "he's crazy about the brave."
------------------------------------------------
candle to us. "and if the maria kisses thee again i will commence kissing
thee myself. it
------------------------------------------------
?" "do you have to for the moment." robert jordan got up and walked away in
------------------------------------------------
. a uniform for my father, he thought. i'll say them later. just then he
------------------------------------------------
and more practical to read and relax in the evening; of all the things he
had enjoyed the next
------------------------------------------------
in bed and rolled himself a cigarette. when he gave them a log to a second
grenade. "
------------------------------------------------
```

We set the prompt to "UNK" and ask the generate() function to unconditionally generate 20 new tokens 10 times. We use the manual_seed() method to fix the random seeds so results are reproducible. As you can see, the 10 short passages generated here are all grammatically correct, and they sound like passages from Hemingway's novels. For example, the word "kummel" in the first passage was a type of liqueur that was mentioned in *A Farewell to Arms* quite often. At the same time, none of the above 10 passages are directly copied from the training text.

Next, we use the model after 40 epochs of training instead to generate text unconditionally and see what happens:

```
prompt="UNK"
for i in range(10):
    torch.manual_seed(i)
    print(generate(prompt,'files/GPTe40.pth',max_new_tokens=20)[4:]))
```

The output is

```
way." "kümmel, and i will enjoy the killing. they must have brought me a spit
------------------------------------------------
," robert jordan said. "but do not tell me that he saw anything." "not
------------------------------------------------
in the first time he had bit the ear like that and held onto it, his neck
and jaws
------------------------------------------------
pot of yellow rice with fish. it was cold now in the head and he could not
see the
------------------------------------------------
the line of his mouth. he thought." "the laughing hurt him." "i can
------------------------------------------------
candle made? that was the worst day of my life until one other day." "don'
------------------------------------------------
?" "do you have to for the moment." robert jordan took the glasses and
opened the
------------------------------------------------
. that's what they don't marry." i reached for her hand. "don
------------------------------------------------
```

```
and more grenades. that was the last for next year. it crossed the river
away from the front
-------------------------------------------------
in a revolutionary army," robert jordan said. "that's really nonsense. it's
-------------------------------------------------
```

The 10 short passages generated here are again all grammatically correct, and they sound like passages from Hemingway's novels. However, if you examine them closely, a large part of the eighth passage is directly copied from the novel *A Farewell to Arms*. The part `they don't marry." i reached for her hand. "don` appeared in the novel as well. You can verify by searching in the file ThreeNovels.txt that was saved on your computer earlier.

> ## Exercise 12.1
>
> Generate a passage of text with 50 new tokens unconditionally using the model trained for 10 epochs. Set the random seed to 42 and keep the `temperature` and `top-K` sampling at the default setting. Examine whether the generated passage is grammatically correct and if any parts are directly copied from the training text.

Alternatively, you can use a unique prompt that's not in the training text to generate new text. For example, you might use "the old man saw the shark near the" as the prompt and ask the `generate()` function to add 20 new tokens to the prompt, repeating this process 10 times:

```
prompt="the old man saw the shark near the"
for i in range(10):
    torch.manual_seed(i)
    print(generate(prompt,'files/GPTe40.pth',max_new_tokens=20))
    print("-"*50)
```

The output is

```
the old man saw the shark near the old man's head with his tail out and the
old man hit him squarely in the center of
-------------------------------------------------
the old man saw the shark near the boat with one hand. he had no feeling of
the morning but he started to pull on it gently
-------------------------------------------------
the old man saw the shark near the old man's head. then he went back to
another man in and leaned over and dipped the
-------------------------------------------------
the old man saw the shark near the fish now, and the old man was asleep in
the water as he rowed he was out of the
-------------------------------------------------
the old man saw the shark near the boat. it was a nice-boat. he saw the old
 man's head and he started
-------------------------------------------------
the old man saw the shark near the boat to see him clearly and he was
afraid that he was higher out of the water and the old
-------------------------------------------------
```

```
the old man saw the shark near the old man's head and then, with his tail
lashing and his jaws clicking, the shark plowed
---------------------------------------------------
the old man saw the shark near the line with his tail which was not sweet
smelling it. the old man knew that the fish was coming
---------------------------------------------------
the old man saw the shark near the fish with his jaws hooked and the old
man stabbed him in his left eye. the shark still hung
---------------------------------------------------
the old man saw the shark near the fish and he started to shake his head
again. the old man was asleep in the stern and he
---------------------------------------------------
```

The generated text is grammatically correct and coherent, closely resembling passages from Hemingway's novel *The Old Man and the Sea*. Since we used the model trained for 40 epochs, there's a higher likelihood of generating text that directly mirrors the training data. However, using a unique prompt can reduce this probability.

By setting the `temperature` and using `top-K` sampling, we can further control the diversity of the generated text. In this case, with a prompt like "the old man saw the shark near the," and a temperature of 0.9 with top-50 sampling, the output remains mostly grammatically correct:

```
prompt="the old man saw the shark near the"
for i in range(10):
    torch.manual_seed(i)
    print(generate(prompt,'files/GPTe20.pth',max_new_tokens=20,
                temperature=0.9,top_k=50))
    print("-"*50)
```

The output is

```
 The old man saw the shark near the boat. then he swung the great fish that
was more comfortable in the sun. the old man could
---------------------------------------------------
the old man saw the shark near the boat with one hand. he wore his overcoat
 and carried the submachine gun muzzle down, carrying it in
---------------------------------------------------
the old man saw the shark near the boat with its long dip sharply and the
old man stabbed him in the morning. he could not see
---------------------------------------------------
the old man saw the shark near the fish that was now heavy and long and
grave he had taken no part in. he was still under
---------------------------------------------------
the old man saw the shark near the boat. it was a nice little light. then
he rowed out and the old man was asleep over
---------------------------------------------------
the old man saw the shark near the boat to come. "old man's shack and i'll
fill the water with him in
---------------------------------------------------
the old man saw the shark near the boat and then rose with his lines close
him over the stern. "no," the old man
---------------------------------------------------
the old man saw the shark near the line with his tail go under. he was
cutting away onto the bow and his face was just a
---------------------------------------------------
```

```
the old man saw the shark near the fish with his tail that he swung him in.
 the shark's head was out of water and
--------------------------------------------------
the old man saw the shark near the boat and he started to cry. he could
almost have them come down and whipped him in again.
--------------------------------------------------
```

Since we used the model trained for 20 epochs instead of 40 epochs, the output is less coherent, with occasional grammar errors. For example, "with its long dip sharply" in the third passage is not grammatically correct. However, the risk of generating text directly copied from the training data is also lower.

> **Exercise 12.2**
>
> Generate a passage of text with 50 new tokens using the model trained for 40 epochs. Use "the old man saw the shark near the" as the prompt; set the `random seed` to 42, the `temperature` to 0.95, and the `top_k` to 100. Check if the generated passage is grammatically correct and if any part of the text is directly copied from the training text.

In this chapter, you've learned how to construct and train a GPT-style Transformer model from the ground up. Specifically, you've created a simplified version of the GPT-2 model with only 5.12 million parameters. Using three novels by Ernest Hemingway as training data, you have successfully trained the model. You have also generated text that is coherent and stylistically consistent with Hemingway's writing.

Summary

- The style of the generated text from a GPT model will be heavily influenced by the training data. For effective text generation, it's important to have a balance of text length and variation in the training material. The training dataset should be sufficiently large for the model to learn and emulate a specific writing style accurately. However, if the dataset lacks diversity, the model might end up reproducing passages directly from the training text. Conversely, overly long training datasets can require excessive computational resources for training.
- Choosing the right hyperparameters in the GPT model is crucial for successful model training and text generation. Setting the hyperparameters too large may lead to too many parameters. This results in longer training time and an overfitted model. Setting the hyperparameters too small may hinder the model's ability to learn effectively and capture the writing style in the training data. This may lead to incoherent generated text.
- The appropriate number of training epochs is important for text generation. While training too few epochs may lead to incoherent text, training for too many epochs may lead to an overfitted model that generates text identical to passages in the training text.

Part 4

Applications and new developments

This part covers some applications of the generative models from earlier chapters as well as some new developments in the field of generative AI.

In chapters 13 and 14, you'll learn two ways of generating music: MuseGAN, which treats a piece of music as a multidimensional object akin to an image, and Music Transformer, which treats a piece of music as a sequence of musical events. Chapter 15 introduces you to diffusion models, which form the foundation of all leading text-to-image Transformers (such as DALL-E 2 or Imagen). Chapter 16 uses the LangChain library to combine pretrained large language models with Wolfram Alpha and Wikipedia APIs to create a zero-shot know-it-all personal assistant.

Music generation with MuseGAN

Up to now, we have successfully generated shapes, numbers, images, and text. In this chapter and the next, we will explore two different ways of generating lifelike music. This chapter will apply the techniques from image GANs, treating a piece of music as a multidimensional object akin to an image. The generator will produce a complete piece of music and submit it to the critic (serving as the discriminator because we use the Wasserstein distance with gradient penalty, as discussed in chapter 5) for evaluation. The generator will then modify the music based on the critic's feedback until it closely resembles real music from the training dataset. In the next chapter, we will treat music as a sequence of musical events, employing natural language processing (NLP) techniques. We will use a GPT-style Transformer to predict the most probable musical event in a sequence based on previous events. This Transformer will generate a long sequence of musical events that can be converted into realistic-sounding music.

The field of music generation using AI has gained significant attention; MuseGAN is a prominent model, which was introduced by Dong, Hsiao, Yang, and Yang in 2017.[1] MuseGAN is a deep neural network that utilizes generative adversarial networks (GANs) to create multitrack music, with the word Muse signifying the creative inspiration behind music. The model is adept at understanding the complex interactions between different tracks that represent different musical instruments or different voices (which is the case in our training data). As a result, MuseGAN can generate compositions that are harmonious and cohesive.

MuseGAN, similar to other GAN models, consists of two primary components: the generator and the critic (who provides a continuous measure of how real the sample is rather than classifying a sample into real or fake). The generator's task is to generate music, whereas the critic assesses the music's quality and offers feedback to the generator. This adversarial interaction enables the generator to gradually improve, leading to the creation of more realistic and appealing music.

Suppose you're an avid fan of Johann Sebastian Bach and have listened to all his compositions. You might wonder if it's possible to use MuseGAN to create synthetic music that mimics his style. The answer is yes, and you'll learn how to do that in this chapter.

Specifically, you'll first explore how to represent a piece of multitrack music as a multidimensional object. A track is essentially an individual line of music or sound, which can be a different instrument such as piano, bass, or drums or a different voice such as soprano, alto, tenor, or bass. When composing a track in electronic music, you typically organize it into bars (segments of time), subdivide each bar into steps for finer control over rhythm, and then assign a specific note to each step to craft your melodies and rhythms. As a result, each piece of music in our training set is structured with a (4, 2, 16, 84) shape: this means there are four music tracks, with each track consisting of 2 bars, each bar containing 16 steps, and each step capable of playing one of the 84 different notes.

The style of the music generated by our MuseGAN will be influenced by the training data. Since you are interested in Bach's work, you'll be training MuseGAN with The JSB Chorales dataset, which is a collection of chorales composed by Bach, arranged for four tracks. These chorales have been converted into a piano roll representation, a method

[1]   Hao-Wen Dong, Wen-Yi Hsiao, Li-Chia Yang, Yi-Hsuan Yang, 2017, "MuseGAN: Multi-track Sequential Generative Adversarial Networks for Symbolic Music Generation and Accompaniment." https://arxiv.org/abs/1709.06298.

used for visualizing and encoding music, especially for digital processing purposes. You'll learn how to transform a piece of music represented in the shape of (4, 2, 16, 84) into a musical instrument digital interface (MIDI) file, which can then be played on your computer.

While the generator uses just one single noise vector from the latent space to generate different formats of content such as shapes, numbers, and images in earlier chapters, the generator in MuseGAN will use four noise vectors when producing a piece of music. The use of four separate noise vectors (chords, style, melody, and groove, which I'll explain in detail later in this chapter) is a design choice that allows for greater control and diversity in the music generation process. Each of these noise vectors represents a different aspect of music, and by manipulating them individually, the model can generate more complex and nuanced compositions.

Once the model is trained, we'll discard the critic network, a common practice in GAN models. We'll then utilize the trained generator to produce music pieces by inputting four noise vectors from the latent space. The music generated in this way closely mirrors the style of Bach.

13.1 Digital music representation

Our goal is to master the art of building and training a GAN model from scratch for music generation. To achieve this, we need to start with the fundamentals of music theory, including understanding musical notes, octaves, and pitch numbers. Following that, we'll dive into the inner workings of digital music, specifically focusing on MIDI files.

Depending on the type of machine learning model we use for music generation, the representation of a piece of music in digital form will vary. For instance, in this chapter, we'll represent music as a multidimensional object, while in the next chapter, we'll use a different format: a sequence of indexes.

In this section, we'll cover basic music theory and then move on to represent music digitally using piano rolls. You'll learn to load and play an example MIDI file on your computer. We'll also introduce the music21 Python library, which you'll install and use to visualize the staff notes associated with the music piece. Finally, you'll learn to represent a piece of music as a multidimensional object with the shape of (4, 2, 16, 84).

13.1.1 Musical notes, octave, and pitch

In this chapter, we'll be working with a training dataset that represents music pieces as 4D objects. To grasp the meaning of the music pieces in the training data, it's essential to first familiarize ourselves with some fundamental concepts in music theory, such as musical notes, octaves, and pitch. These concepts are interrelated and crucial for understanding the dataset.

Figure 13.1 illustrates the relationships among these concepts.

Octave	Note Numbers											
	C	C#	D	D#	E	F	F#	G	G#	A	A#	B
-1	0	1	2	3	4	5	6	7	8	9	10	11
0	12	13	14	15	16	17	18	19	20	21	22	23
1	24	25	26	27	28	29	30	31	32	33	34	35
2	36	37	38	39	40	41	42	43	44	45	46	47
3	48	49	50	51	52	53	54	55	56	57	58	59
4	60	61	62	63	64	65	66	67	68	69	70	71
5	72	73	74	75	76	77	78	79	80	81	82	83
6	84	85	86	87	88	89	90	91	92	93	94	95
7	96	97	98	99	100	101	102	103	104	105	106	107
8	108	109	110	111	112	113	114	115	116	117	118	119
9	120	121	122	123	124	125	126	127				

Figure 13.1   The relationship between musical notes, octaves, and pitches (also known as note numbers). The first column displays the 11 octaves (ranging from –1 to 9), representing different levels of musical sound. Each octave is subdivided into 12 semitones, which are listed in the top row: C, C#, D, D#, …, B. Within each octave, each note is assigned a specific pitch number, ranging from 0 to 127, as indicated in the figure.

A musical note is a symbol representing a specific sound in music. These notes are the foundational elements of music, used to craft melodies, chords, and rhythms. Each note is assigned a name (such as A, B, C, D, E, F, G) and corresponds to a specific frequency, which determines its pitch: whether the note sounds high or low. For instance, a middle C (C4) typically has a frequency of about 262 hertz, meaning its sound waves vibrate 262 times per second.

You might be wondering about the meaning of the term "middle C (C4)." The number 4 in C4 refers to the octave, which is the distance between one level of musical pitch and the next. In figure 13.1, the far-left column displays 11 octave levels, ranging from –1 to 9. The frequency of a sound doubles as you move from one octave level to the next. For example, note A4 is usually tuned to 440 hertz, while A5, one octave above A4, is tuned to 880 hertz..

In Western music, an octave is divided into 12 semitones, each corresponding to a specific note. The top row of figure 13.1 lists these 12 semitones: C, C#, D, D#, …, B. Moving up or down by 12 semitones takes you to the same note name but in a higher or lower octave. As mentioned earlier, A5 is one octave above A4.

Each note within a specific octave is assigned a pitch number, ranging from 0 to 127, as depicted in figure 13.1. For example, the note C4 has a pitch number of 60, while F3 has a pitch number of 53. The pitch number is a more efficient way to represent musical notes since it specifies both the octave level and the semitone. The training data you'll be using in this chapter is encoded using pitch numbers for this very reason.

13.1.2   *An introduction to multitrack music*

Let's first talk about how multitrack music works and how it is represented digitally. In electronic music production, a "track" typically refers to an individual layer or component of the music, such as a drum track, a bass track, or a melody track. In classical music, tracks might represent different vocal parts, like soprano, alto, tenor, and bass. For instance, the training dataset we're using in this chapter, the JSB Chorales dataset, consists of four tracks corresponding to four vocal parts. In music production, each track can be individually edited and processed within a digital audio workstation (DAW). These tracks are composed of various musical elements, including bars, steps, and notes.

A bar (or measure) is a segment of time defined by a specified number of beats, with each beat having a certain note duration. In many popular music genres, a bar typically contains four beats, although this can vary based on the time signature of the piece. The total number of bars in a track is determined by the track's length and structure. For example, in our training dataset, each track comprises two bars.

In the context of step sequencing, a technique commonly used for programming rhythms and melodies in electronic music, a "step" represents a subdivision of a bar. In a standard 4/4 time signature (four beats in a bar and four steps in a beat), you might find 16 steps per bar, with each step corresponding to a sixteenth of a bar.

Lastly, each step contains a musical note. In our dataset, we limit the range to the 84 most frequently used notes (with pitch numbers from 0 to 83). Therefore, the musical note in a step is encoded as a one-hot vector with 84 values.

To illustrate these concepts with a practical example, download the file example. midi from the book's GitHub repository at https://github.com/markhliu/DGAI and save it in the /files/ directory on your computer. A file with the .midi extension is a MIDI file. MIDI is a technical standard that outlines a protocol, digital interface, and connectors for enabling electronic musical instruments, computers, and other related devices to connect and communicate with each other.

MIDI files can be played on most music players on your computer. To get a sense of the type of music in our training data, open the file example.midi you just downloaded with a music player on your computer. It should sound like this music file I placed on my website: https://mng.bz/lrJB. The file example.midi is converted from one of the music pieces in the training dataset in this chapter. Later you'll learn how to convert a piece of music in the training dataset with a shape of (4, 2, 16, 84) into a MIDI file that can be played on your computer.

We'll use the music21 Python library, a powerful and comprehensive toolkit designed for music analysis, composition, and manipulation, to visualize how various music concepts work. Therefore, run the following line of code in a new cell in the Jupyter Notebook app on your computer:

```
!pip install music21
```

The music21 library enables you to visualize music as staff notation to have a better understanding of tracks, bars, steps, and notes. To achieve this, you must first install the MuseScore application on your computer. Visit https://musescore.org/en/download and download the most recent version of the MuseScore app for your operating system. As of this writing, the latest version is MuseScore 4, which we'll use as our example. Ensure you know the file path of the MuseScore app on your computer. For instance, in Windows, the path is C:\Program Files\MuseScore 4\bin\MuseScore4.exe. Run the code cell in the following listing to visualize the staff notation for the file example.midi.

Listing 13.1   Visualizing the staff notation using the music21 library

```
%matplotlib inline
from music21 import midi, environment

mf = midi.MidiFile()
mf.open("files/example.midi")
mf.read()
mf.close()
stream = midi.translate.midiFileToStream(mf)
us = environment.Environment()
path = r'C:\Program Files\MuseScore 4\bin\MuseScore4.exe'
us['musescoreDirectPNGPath'] = path
stream.show()
```

Shows the image in Jupyter notebook instead of in the original app

Opens the MIDI file

Defines the path of the MuseScore app

Shows the staff notation

For users of the macOS operating system, change the path in the preceding code cell to /Applications/MuseScore 4.app/Contents/MacOS/mscore. For Linux users, modify the path to /home/[user name]/.local/bin/mscore4portable, substituting [user name] with your actual username. For instance, my username is mark, so the path is /home/mark/.local/bin/mscore4portable.

Executing the previous code cell will display a staff notation similar to what is illustrated in figure 13.2. Please note that the annotations in the figure are added by me, so you will only see the staff notation without any annotations.

Figure 13.2   Staff notation for a piece of music in JSB Chorales dataset. The music has four tracks, representing the four voices in a chorale: soprano, alto, tenor, and bass. The notation is structured into two bars for each track, with the left and right halves representing the first and second bars, respectively. Each bar consists of 16 steps, aligning with the 4/4 time signature where a bar contains four beats, each subdivided into four sixteenth notes. A total of 84 different pitches are possible, and each note is represented as a one-hot vector with 84 values.

The JSB Chorales dataset, which consists of chorale music pieces by Johann Sebastian Bach, is often used for training machine learning models in music generation tasks. The shape (4, 2, 16, 84) of each music piece in the dataset can be explained as follows. Four represents the four voices in a chorale: soprano, alto, tenor, and bass. Each voice is treated as a separate track in the dataset. Each piece is divided into two bars (also called measures). The dataset is formatted this way to standardize the length of the music pieces for training purposes. The number 16 represents the number of steps (or subdivisions) in each bar. Finally, the note is one-hot encoded with 84 values, denoting the number of possible pitches (or notes) that can be played in each step.

13.1.3 *Digitally represent music: Piano rolls*

A piano roll is a visual representation of music often used in MIDI sequencing software and DAWs. It is named after the traditional piano rolls used in player pianos, which contained a physical roll of paper with holes punched in it to represent musical notes. In a digital context, the piano roll serves a similar function but in a virtual format.

The piano roll is displayed as a grid, with time represented horizontally (from left to right) and pitch represented vertically (from bottom to top). Each row corresponds to a specific musical note, with higher notes at the top and lower notes at the bottom, similar to the layout of a piano keyboard.

Notes are represented as bars or blocks on the grid. The position of a note block along the vertical axis indicates its pitch, while its position along the horizontal axis indicates its timing in the music. The length of the note block represents the duration of the note.

Let's use the music21 library to illustrate what a piano roll looks like. Run this line of code in a new cell in your Jupyter Notebook app:

```
stream.plot()
```

The output is shown in figure 13.3.

The music21 library also allows you to see the quantized notes corresponding to the preceding piano roll:

```
for n in stream.recurse().notes:
    print(n.offset, n.pitches)
```

The output is

```
0.0 (<music21.pitch.Pitch E4>,)
0.25 (<music21.pitch.Pitch A4>,)
0.5 (<music21.pitch.Pitch G4>,)
0.75 (<music21.pitch.Pitch F4>,)
1.0 (<music21.pitch.Pitch E4>,)
1.25 (<music21.pitch.Pitch D4>,)
1.75 (<music21.pitch.Pitch E4>,)
2.0 (<music21.pitch.Pitch E4>,)
2.5 (<music21.pitch.Pitch D4>,)
3.0 (<music21.pitch.Pitch C4>,)
3.25 (<music21.pitch.Pitch A3>,)
3.75 (<music21.pitch.Pitch B3>,)
```

```
0.0 (<music21.pitch.Pitch G3>,)
0.25 (<music21.pitch.Pitch A3>,)
0.5 (<music21.pitch.Pitch B3>,)
...
3.25 (<music21.pitch.Pitch F2>,)
3.75 (<music21.pitch.Pitch E2>,)
```

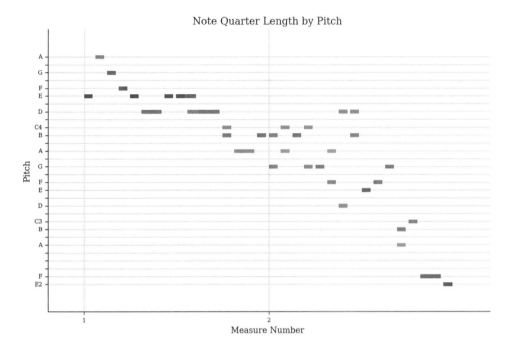

Figure 13.3   The piano roll for a piece of music. The piano roll is a graphical representation of a musical piece, depicted as a grid with time progressing horizontally from left to right and pitch represented vertically from bottom to top. Each row on the grid corresponds to a distinct musical note, arranged in a manner akin to the keyboard of a piano, with higher notes positioned at the top and lower notes at the bottom. This specific piece of music comprises two bars, resulting in two distinct sections visible in the graph. The vertical placement of a note block signifies its pitch, while its horizontal location indicates when the note is played in the piece. Additionally, the length of the note block reflects the duration for which the note is sustained.

I omitted most of the output. The first value in each line in the previous output represents time. It increases by 0.25 seconds after each line in most cases. If the time increase in the next line is more than 0.25 seconds, it means a note lasts more than 0.25 seconds. As you can see, the starting note is E4. After 0.25 seconds, the note changes to A4, and then G4, and so on. This explains the first three blocks (far left) in figure 13.3, which have values E, A, and G, respectively.

You might be curious about how to convert the sequence of musical notes into an object with the shape (4, 2, 16, 84). To understand this, let's examine the pitch number at each time step in the musical notes:

```
for n in stream.recurse().notes:
    print(n.offset,n.pitches[0].midi)
```

The output is

```
0.0 64
0.25 69
0.5 67
0.75 65
1.0 64
1.25 62
1.75 64
2.0 64
2.5 62
3.0 60
3.25 57
3.75 59
0.0 55
0.25 57
0.5 59
...
3.25 41
3.75 40
```

The preceding code block has converted the musical note in each time step into a pitch number, in the range of 0 to 83 based on the mapping used in figure 13.1. Each of the pitch numbers is then converted to a one-hot variable with 84 values, with value –1 everywhere, except 1 in one position. We use –1 and 1 in one-hot encoding instead of 0 and 1 because placing values between –1 and 1 centers the data around 0, which can make training more stable and faster. Many activation functions and weight initialization methods assume input data is centered around 0. Figure 13.4 illustrates how a piece of MIDI music is encoded into an object in the shape of (4, 2, 16, 84).

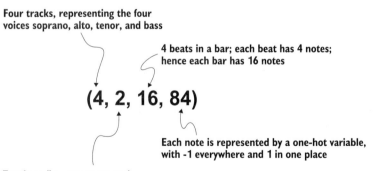

Four tracks, representing the four voices soprano, alto, tenor, and bass

4 beats in a bar; each beat has 4 notes; hence each bar has 16 notes

(4, 2, 16, 84)

Each note is represented by a one-hot variable, with -1 everywhere and 1 in one place

Two bars (i.e., two measures) in each music track

Figure 13.4 How to represent a piece of music using a 4D object. In our training data, each piece of music is represented by a 4D object in the shape of (4, 2, 16, 84). The first dimension represents the four music tracks, which are the four voices in the music (soprano, alto, tenor, and bass). Each music track is divided into two bars. There are four beats in each bar, and each beat has four notes; we therefore have 16 notes in a bar. Finally, each note is represented by a one-hot variable with 84 values, with –1 everywhere and 1 in one place.

Figure 13.4 explains the dimensions of the music object shaped (4, 2, 16, 84). In essence, each musical piece comprises four tracks, with each track containing two bars. Each bar is subdivided into 16 notes. Given that the pitch numbers range from 0 to 83 in our training set, each note is represented by a one-hot vector with 84 values.

In subsequent discussions on preparing training data, we will explore how to transform an object with the shape (4, 2, 16, 84) back into a music piece in MIDI format, enabling playback on a computer.

13.2   A blueprint for music generation

When creating music, we need to incorporate more detailed inputs for enhanced control and variety. Unlike the approach of utilizing a single noise vector from the latent space for generating shapes, numbers, and images, we will employ four distinct noise vectors in the music generation process. Since each music piece comprises four tracks and two bars, we'll utilize four vectors to manage this structure. We'll use one vector to govern all tracks and bars collectively, another vector to control each bar across all tracks, a third vector to oversee all tracks across bars, and a fourth one to manage each individual bar in each track. This section will introduce you to the concepts of chords, style, melody, and groove and explain how they influence various aspects of the music generation. After that, we'll discuss the steps involved in building and training the MuseGAN model.

13.2.1   Constructing music with chords, style, melody, and groove

Later, in the music generation stage, we obtain four noise vectors (chords, style, melody, and groove) from the latent space and feed them to the generator to create a piece of music. You may be wondering the meaning of these four pieces of information. In music, chords, style, melody, and groove are key elements that contribute to a piece's overall sound and feel. Next I provide a brief explanation of each element.

Style refers to the characteristic way in which music is composed, performed, and experienced. It includes the genre (such as jazz, classical, rock, and so on), the era in which the music was created, and the unique approach of the composer or performer. Style is influenced by cultural, historical, and personal factors, and it helps to define the music's identity.

Groove is the rhythmic feel or swing in music, especially in styles like funk, jazz, and soul. It's what makes you want to tap your foot or dance. A groove is created by the pattern of accents, the interplay between the rhythm section (drums, bass, etc.), and the tempo. It's the element that gives music its sense of motion and flow.

Chords are combinations of two or more notes played simultaneously. They provide the harmonic foundation for music. Chords are built on scales and are used to create progressions that give music its structure and emotional depth. Different chord types (major, minor, diminished, augmented, etc.) and their arrangements can evoke various moods and feelings in the listener.

Finally, melody is the sequence of notes that is most easily recognizable in a piece of music. It's the part that you might hum or sing along to. Melodies are often built from scales and are characterized by their pitch, rhythm, and contour (the pattern of rises and falls in pitch). A good melody is memorable and expressive, conveying the main musical and emotional themes of the piece.

Together, these elements work in harmony to create the overall sound and experience of a musical piece. Each element has its role, but they all interact and influence each other to produce the final music piece. Specifically, a music piece consists of four tracks, each with two bars, resulting in eight bar/track combinations. We'll use one noise vector for style, applied to all eight bars. We'll use eight different noise vectors for melody, each used in a unique bar. There are four noise vectors for groove, each applied to a different track, remaining the same across both bars. Two noise vectors will be used for chords, one for each bar. Figure 13.5 provides a diagram of how these four elements contribute to the creation of a complete piece of music.

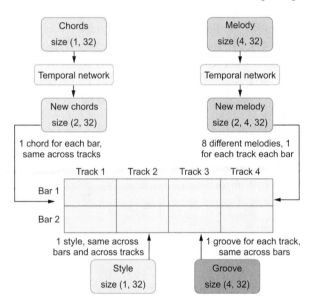

Figure 13.5 **Music generation using chords, style, melody, and groove. Each music composition consists of four tracks and spans two bars. We will extract four noise vectors from the latent space for this purpose. The first vector, representing chords, has a dimension of (1, 32). This vector will be processed through a temporal network to expand the chords into two (1, 32) vectors, corresponding to the two bars, with identical values across all tracks. The second vector, denoting style, also has a dimension of (1, 32) and remains constant across all tracks and bars. The third vector, melody, is shaped as (4, 32). It will be stretched through a temporal network into two (4, 32) vectors, resulting in eight (1, 32) vectors, each representing a unique track and bar combination. Lastly, the fourth vector, groove, with a dimension of (4, 32), will be applied to the four tracks, maintaining the same values for both bars.**

The generator creates a piece of music by generating one bar in one track at a time. For this, it requires four noise vectors, each with a shape of (1, 32), as input. These vectors represent chords, style, melody, and groove, and each controls a distinct aspect of the music, as previously explained. Since the music piece consists of four tracks, each with two bars, there are a total of eight bar/track combinations. Consequently, we need eight sets of chords, style, melody, and groove to generate all parts of the music piece.

We'll obtain four noise vectors from the latent space corresponding to chords, style, melody, and groove. We'll also introduce a temporal network later, whose role is to expand the input along the bar dimension. With two bars, this means doubling the size of the input. Music is inherently temporal, with patterns and structures that unfold over time. The temporal network in MuseGAN is designed to capture these temporal dependencies, ensuring that the generated music has a coherent and logical progression.

The noise vector for chords has a shape of $(1, 32)$. After processing it through the temporal network, we obtain two $(1, 32)$ sized vectors. The first vector is used across all four tracks in the first bar, while the second vector is used across all four tracks in the second bar.

The noise vector for style, also with a shape of $(1, 32)$, is applied uniformly across all eight track/bar combinations. Note that we'll not pass the style vector through the temporal network since the style vector is designed to be the same across bars.

The noise vector for melody has a shape of $(4, 32)$. When passed through the temporal network, it yields two $(4, 32)$ sized vectors, which further break down into eight $(1, 32)$ sized vectors. Each of these is used in a unique track/bar combination.

Lastly, the noise vector for groove, shaped as $(4, 32)$, is used such that each $(1, 32)$ sized vector is applied to a different track, remaining the same across both bars. We won't pass the groove vector through the temporal network since the groove vector is designed to be the same across bars.

After generating a bar of music for each of the eight bar/track combinations, we'll merge them to create a full piece of music, consisting of four distinct tracks, each comprising two unique bars.

13.2.2 A blueprint to train a MuseGAN

Chapter 1 provided an overview of the foundational concepts behind GANs. In chapters 3 to 5, you explored the creation and training of GANs for generating shapes, numbers, and images. This subsection will summarize the steps for building and training MuseGAN, highlighting the differences from the previous chapters.

The style of music generated by MuseGAN is influenced by the training data's style. Therefore, you should first collect a dataset of Bach's compositions in a format suitable for training. Next, you'll create a MuseGAN model, which consists of a generator and a critic. The generator network takes four random noise vectors as input (chords, style, melody, and groove) and outputs a piece of music. The critic network evaluates a piece of music and assigns a rating, with higher scores for real music (from the training set) and lower scores for fake music (produced by the generator). Both the generator and critic networks utilize deep convolutional layers to capture the spatial features of the inputs.

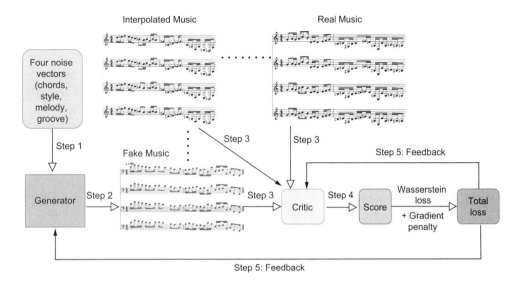

Figure 13.6   A diagram of the steps involved in training MuseGAN to generate music. The generator produces a fake music piece by drawing four random noise vectors from the latent space (top left) and presents it to the critic (middle). The critic evaluates the piece and assigns a rating. A high rating suggests that the piece is likely from the training dataset, while a lower rating indicates that the piece is likely fake (generated by the generator). Additionally, an interpolated music piece created from a mix of real and fake samples (top left) is presented to the critic. The training process incorporates a gradient penalty based on the critic's rating of this interpolated piece, which is added to the total loss. The ratings are then compared to the ground truth, allowing both the critic and the generator to learn from these evaluations. After numerous training iterations, the generator becomes proficient at producing music pieces that are virtually indistinguishable from real samples.

Figure 13.6 illustrates the training process of MuseGAN. The generator (the bottom left of the figure) receives four random noise vectors (chords, style, melody, and groove) as input and produces fake music pieces (step 1 in figure 13.6). These noise vectors are drawn from the latent space, which represents the range of potential outputs the GAN can generate, enabling the creation of diverse data samples. These fake music pieces, along with real ones from the training set (top right), are then evaluated by the critic (step 3). The critic (bottom center) assigns scores to all music pieces, aiming to give high scores to real music and low scores to fake music (step 4).

To guide the adjustment of model parameters, appropriate loss functions must be chosen for both the generator and the critic. The generator's loss function is designed to encourage the production of data points that closely resemble those from the training dataset. Specifically, the loss function for the generator is the negative of the critic's rating. By minimizing this loss function, the generator strives to create music pieces that receive high ratings from the critic. On the other hand, the critic's loss function is formulated to encourage accurate assessment of real and generated data points. Thus, the loss function for the critic is the rating itself if the music piece is from the training set and the negative of the rating if it is generated by the generator. In essence, the critic aims to assign high ratings to real music pieces and low ratings to fake ones.

Additionally, we incorporate the Wasserstein distance with gradient penalty into the loss function, as we did in chapter 5, to enhance the training stability and performance of GAN models. To achieve this, an interpolated music piece, blending real and fake music (top left in figure 13.6), is evaluated by the critic. The gradient penalty, based on the critic's rating of this interpolated piece, is then added to the total loss during the training process.

Throughout the training loop, we alternate between training the critic and the generator. In each training iteration, we sample a batch of real music pieces from the training set and a batch of fake music pieces generated by the generator. We calculate the total loss by comparing the critic's ratings (i.e., scores) with the ground truth (whether a music piece is real or fake). We then slightly adjust the weights in both the generator and critic networks so that, in subsequent iterations, the generator produces more realistic music pieces, and the critic assigns higher scores to real music and lower scores to fake music.

Once MuseGAN is fully trained, music can be created by inputting four random noise vectors into the trained generator.

13.3 Preparing the training data for MuseGAN

We'll use chorale compositions by Johann Sebastian Bach as our training dataset, expecting the generated music to resemble Bach's style. If you prefer the style of a different musician, you can use their work as the training data instead. In this section, we'll start by downloading the training data and organizing it into batches for later training.

Additionally, we've learned that the music pieces in the training set will be represented as 4D objects. In this section, you'll also learn how to convert these multidimensional objects into playable music pieces on a computer. This conversion is essential because MuseGAN generates multidimensional objects similar to those in the training set. Later in the chapter, we'll transform the multidimensional objects produced by MuseGAN into MIDI files, enabling you to listen to the generated music on your computer.

13.3.1 Downloading the training data

We'll use the JSB Chorales piano rolls dataset as our training set. Go to Cheng-Zhi Anna Huang's GitHub repository (https://github.com/czhuang/JSB-Chorales-dataset) and download the music file Jsb16thSeparated.npz. Save the file in the /files/ directory on your computer.

Then, download the two utility modules midi_util.py and MuseGAN_util.py from the book's GitHub repository (https://github.com/markhliu/DGAI) and save them in the /utils/ directory on your computer. The code in this chapter is adapted from the excellent GitHub repository by Azamat Kanametov (https://github.com/akanametov/musegan). With these files in place, we can now load the music files and organize them into batches for processing:

```
from torch.utils.data import DataLoader
from utils.midi_util import MidiDataset

dataset = MidiDataset('files/Jsb16thSeparated.npz')
first_song=dataset[0]
print(first_song.shape)
loader = DataLoader(dataset, batch_size=64,
                         shuffle=True, drop_last=True)
```

We load the dataset you just downloaded into Python, then extract the first song and name it `first_song`. Since songs are represented as multidimensional objects, we print out the shape of the first song. Finally, we place the training data in batches of 64, to be used later in the chapter.

The output from the preceding code block is

```
torch.Size([4, 2, 16, 84])
```

Each song in the dataset has a shape of (4, 2, 16, 84), as shown in the previous output. This indicates that each song consists of four tracks, each with two bars. Each bar contains 16 time steps, and at each time step, the musical note is represented by a one-hot vector with 84 values. In each one-hot vector, all values are set to –1, except for one position where the value is set to 1, indicating the presence of a note. You can verify the range of values in the dataset as follows:

```
flat=first_song.reshape(-1,)
print(set(flat.tolist()))
```

The output is

```
{1.0, -1.0}
```

The previous output shows that the values in each music piece are either –1 or 1.

13.3.2 Converting multidimensional objects to music pieces

Currently, the songs are formatted as PyTorch tensors and are ready to be inputted into the MuseGAN model. However, before we proceed, it's important to gain a better understanding of how to convert these multidimensional objects into playable music pieces on your computer. This will help us later to convert generated music pieces into playable files.

To begin, we'll convert all the 84-value one-hot variables into pitch numbers ranging from 0 to 83:

```
import numpy as np
from music21 import note, stream, duration, tempo

parts = stream.Score()
parts.append(tempo.MetronomeMark(number=66))
max_pitches = np.argmax(first_song, axis=-1)          ◀─── Converts 84-value one-hot
midi_note_score = max_pitches.reshape([2 * 16, 4])    ◀───     vectors to numbers
print(midi_note_score)                                          between 0 and 83

                                                            ◀─── Reshapes the
                                                                 result to (32, 4)
```

The output is

```
tensor([[74, 74, 74, 74],
…
        [70, 70, 69, 69],
        [67, 67, 69, 69],
        [70, 70, 70, 70],
        [69, 69, 69, 69],
        [69, 69, 69, 69],
        [65, 65, 65, 65],
        [58, 58, 60, 60],
…
        [53, 53, 53, 53]])
```

In the output displayed here, each column represents a music track, with numbers ranging from 0 to 83. These numbers correspond to pitch numbers, as you have seen earlier in figure 13.1.

Now, we'll proceed to convert the tensor `midi_note_score` in the previous code block into an actual MIDI file, allowing you to play it on your computer.

Listing 13.2   Converting pitch numbers to a MIDI file

```
for i in range(4):                                          ◀──   Iterates through
    last_x = int(midi_note_score[:, i][0])                         four music tracks
    s = stream.Part()
    dur = 0
    for idx, x in enumerate(midi_note_score[:, i]):         ◀──   Iterates through all
        x = int(x)                                                 notes in each track
        if (x != last_x or idx % 4 == 0) and idx > 0:
            n = note.Note(last_x)
            n.duration = duration.Duration(dur)
            s.append(n)
            dur = 0
        last_x = x                                          ───   Adds 0.25 seconds
        dur = dur + 0.25                                    ◀──   to each time step
    n = note.Note(last_x)
    n.duration = duration.Duration(dur)                     ───   Adds the note to
    s.append(n)                                             ◀──   the music stream
    parts.append(s)
parts.write("midi","files/first_song.midi")
```

After running the preceding code cell, you'll see a MIDI file, `first_song.midi`, on your computer. Play it with a music player on your computer to get a sense of what type of music we are using to train the MuseGAN.

Exercise 13.1

Convert the second song in the training dataset into a MIDI file. Save it as `second_song.midi` and play it using a music player on your computer.

13.4 Building a MuseGAN

In essence, we will treat a music piece as an object with multiple dimensions. Using techniques from chapters 4 to 6, we will tackle this task using deep convolutional neural networks for their ability to effectively extract spatial features from multidimensional objects. In MuseGAN, we'll construct a generator and a critic, similar to how a generator in image creation refines an image based on a critic's feedback. The generator will produce a music piece as a 4D object.

Both real music from our training set and fake music from the generator will be presented to the critic. The critic will score each piece from negative infinity to positive infinity, with higher scores indicating a higher likelihood of the music being real. The critic aims to give high scores to real music and low scores to fake music. Conversely, the generator aims to produce music that is indistinguishable from real music, thereby receiving high scores from the critic.

In this section, we will build a MuseGAN model, comprising a generator network and a critic network. The critic network employs deep convolutional layers to extract distinct features from multidimensional objects, enhancing its ability to evaluate music pieces. On the other hand, the generator network utilizes deep transposed convolutional layers to produce feature maps aimed at generating realistic music pieces. Later, we will train the MuseGAN model using music pieces from the training set.

13.4.1 A critic in MuseGAN

As explained in chapter 5, incorporating the Wasserstein distance into the loss function can help stabilize training. Therefore, in MuseGAN, we adopt a similar approach and use a critic instead of a discriminator. The critic is not a binary classifier; rather, it evaluates the output of the generator (in this case, a music piece) and assigns a score ranging from $-\infty$ to ∞. A higher score indicates a greater likelihood that the music is real (i.e., from the training set).

We construct a music critic neural network as shown in the following listing, and its definition can be found in the file MuseGAN_util.py that you downloaded earlier.

Listing 13.3   The critic network in MuseGAN

```
class MuseCritic(nn.Module):
    def __init__(self,hid_channels=128,hid_features=1024,
        out_features=1,n_tracks=4,n_bars=2,n_steps_per_bar=16,
        n_pitches=84):
        super().__init__()
        self.n_tracks = n_tracks
        self.n_bars = n_bars
        self.n_steps_per_bar = n_steps_per_bar
        self.n_pitches = n_pitches
        in_features = 4 * hid_channels if n_bars == 2\
            else 12 * hid_channels
        self.seq = nn.Sequential(
            nn.Conv3d(self.n_tracks, hid_channels,
                    (2, 1, 1), (1, 1, 1), padding=0),     ◄── Passes the input
                                                               through several
                                                               Conv3d layers
```

```
      nn.LeakyReLU(0.3, inplace=True),
      nn.Conv3d(hid_channels, hid_channels,
        (self.n_bars - 1, 1, 1), (1, 1, 1), padding=0),
      nn.LeakyReLU(0.3, inplace=True),
      nn.Conv3d(hid_channels, hid_channels,
              (1, 1, 12), (1, 1, 12), padding=0),
      nn.LeakyReLU(0.3, inplace=True),
      nn.Conv3d(hid_channels, hid_channels,
              (1, 1, 7), (1, 1, 7), padding=0),
      nn.LeakyReLU(0.3, inplace=True),
      nn.Conv3d(hid_channels, hid_channels,
              (1, 2, 1), (1, 2, 1), padding=0),
      nn.LeakyReLU(0.3, inplace=True),
      nn.Conv3d(hid_channels, hid_channels,
              (1, 2, 1), (1, 2, 1), padding=0),
      nn.LeakyReLU(0.3, inplace=True),
      nn.Conv3d(hid_channels, 2 * hid_channels,
              (1, 4, 1), (1, 2, 1), padding=(0, 1, 0)),
      nn.LeakyReLU(0.3, inplace=True),
      nn.Conv3d(2 * hid_channels, 4 * hid_channels,
              (1, 3, 1), (1, 2, 1), padding=(0, 1, 0)),
      nn.LeakyReLU(0.3, inplace=True),
      nn.Flatten(),                              ◀──── Flattens the output
      nn.Linear(in_features, hid_features),
      nn.LeakyReLU(0.3, inplace=True),
      nn.Linear(hid_features, out_features))     ◀──┐ Passes the output
def forward(self, x):                               │ through two linear layers
    return self.seq(x)
```

The input to the critic network is a music piece with dimensions (4, 2, 16, 84). The network primarily consists of several Conv3d layers. These layers treat each track of the music piece as a 3D object and apply filters to extract spatial features. The operation of the Conv3d layers is similar to the Conv2d layers used in image generation, as discussed in earlier chapters.

It's important to note that the final layer of the critic model is linear, and we do not apply any activation function to its output. As a result, the output from the critic model is a value ranging from $-\infty$ to ∞, which can be interpreted as the critic's rating of a music piece.

13.4.2 A generator in MuseGAN

As discussed earlier in this chapter, the generator will produce one bar of music at a time, and we will then combine these eight bars to form a complete piece of music.

Instead of using just a single noise vector, the generator in MuseGAN takes four independent noise vectors as input to control various aspects of the music being generated. Two of these vectors will be processed through a temporal network to extend them along the bar dimension. While the style and groove vectors are designed to remain constant across both bars, the chords and melody vectors are designed to vary between bars. Therefore, we will first establish a temporal network to stretch the chords and melody vectors across the two bars, ensuring that the generated music has a coherent and logical progression over time.

In the local module `MuseGAN_util` you downloaded earlier, we define the `TemporalNetwork()` class as follows:

```
class TemporalNetwork(nn.Module):
    def __init__(self,z_dimension=32,hid_channels=1024,n_bars=2):
        super().__init__()
        self.n_bars = n_bars
        self.net = nn.Sequential(
            Reshape(shape=[z_dimension, 1, 1]),          ◄── The input dimension to
            nn.ConvTranspose2d(z_dimension,hid_channels,     the TemporalNetwork()
                kernel_size=(2, 1),stride=(1, 1),padding=0,), class is (1, 32).
            nn.BatchNorm2d(hid_channels),
            nn.ReLU(inplace=True),
            nn.ConvTranspose2d(hid_channels,z_dimension,
                kernel_size=(self.n_bars - 1, 1),stride=(1, 1),
                padding=0,),
            nn.BatchNorm2d(z_dimension),
            nn.ReLU(inplace=True),                       ┐ The output
            Reshape(shape=[z_dimension, self.n_bars]),)  ◄── dimension is (2, 32).
    def forward(self, x):
        return self.net(x)
```

The `TemporalNetwork()` class described here employs two ConvTranspose2d layers to expand a single noise vector into two distinct noise vectors, each corresponding to one of the two bars. As we covered in chapter 4, transposed convolutional layers serve the purpose of upsampling and generating feature maps. In this context, they are utilized to extend noise vectors across different bars.

Instead of generating all bars in all tracks at once, we'll generate the music one bar at a time. Doing so allows MuseGAN to balance computational efficiency, flexibility, and musical coherence, resulting in more structured and appealing musical compositions. Therefore, we proceed to construct a bar generator that is responsible for generating a segment of the music piece: one bar within a track. We introduce the `BarGenerator()` class within the local `MuseGAN_util` module:

```
class BarGenerator(nn.Module):
    def __init__(self,z_dimension=32,hid_features=1024,hid_channels=512,
        out_channels=1,n_steps_per_bar=16,n_pitches=84):
        super().__init__()                               We concatenate
        self.n_steps_per_bar = n_steps_per_bar           chords, style,
        self.n_pitches = n_pitches                       melody, and groove
        self.net = nn.Sequential(                         into one vector, with
            nn.Linear(4 * z_dimension, hid_features),  ◄── a size of 4 * 32.
            nn.BatchNorm1d(hid_features),
            nn.ReLU(inplace=True),
            Reshape(shape=[hid_channels,hid_features//hid_channels,1]),
            nn.ConvTranspose2d(hid_channels,hid_channels,
                kernel_size=(2, 1),stride=(2, 1),padding=0),  ◄──
            nn.BatchNorm2d(hid_channels),                    The input is then
            nn.ReLU(inplace=True),                           reshaped into 2D,
            nn.ConvTranspose2d(hid_channels,hid_channels // 2, and we use several
                kernel_size=(2, 1),stride=(2, 1),padding=0),  ConvTranspose2d
            nn.BatchNorm2d(hid_channels // 2),               layers for
            nn.ReLU(inplace=True),                           upsampling and
                                                             music feature
                                                             generation.
```

```
        nn.ConvTranspose2d(hid_channels // 2,hid_channels // 2,
            kernel_size=(2, 1),stride=(2, 1),padding=0),
        nn.BatchNorm2d(hid_channels // 2),
        nn.ReLU(inplace=True),
        nn.ConvTranspose2d(hid_channels // 2,hid_channels // 2,
            kernel_size=(1, 7),stride=(1, 7),padding=0),
        nn.BatchNorm2d(hid_channels // 2),
        nn.ReLU(inplace=True),
        nn.ConvTranspose2d(hid_channels // 2,out_channels,
            kernel_size=(1, 12),stride=(1, 12),padding=0),
        Reshape([1, 1, self.n_steps_per_bar, self.n_pitches]))
    def forward(self, x):
        return self.net(x)
```

> **The output has a shape of (1, 1, 16, 84): 1 track, 1 bar, and 16 notes, and each note is represented by a 84-value vector.**

The `BarGenerator()` class accepts four noise vectors as input, each representing chords, style, melody, and groove for a specific bar in a different track, all with a shape of (1, 32). These vectors are concatenated into a single 128-value vector before being fed into the `BarGenerator()` class. The output from the `BarGenerator()` class is a bar of music, with dimensions (1, 1, 16, 84), indicating 1 track, 1 bar, and 16 notes, with each note represented by an 84-value vector.

Finally, we will employ the `MuseGenerator()` class to generate a complete piece of music, consisting of four tracks with two bars per track. Each bar is constructed using the `BarGenerator()` class defined earlier. To achieve this, we define the `MuseGenerator()` class in the local MuseGAN_util module.

Listing 13.4   The music generator in MuseGAN

```
class MuseGenerator(nn.Module):
    def __init__(self,z_dimension=32,hid_channels=1024,
        hid_features=1024,out_channels=1,n_tracks=4,
        n_bars=2,n_steps_per_bar=16,n_pitches=84):
        super().__init__()
        self.n_tracks = n_tracks
        self.n_bars = n_bars
        self.n_steps_per_bar = n_steps_per_bar
        self.n_pitches = n_pitches
        self.chords_network=TemporalNetwork(z_dimension,
                        hid_channels, n_bars=n_bars)
        self.melody_networks = nn.ModuleDict({})
        for n in range(self.n_tracks):
            self.melody_networks.add_module(
                "melodygen_" + str(n),
                TemporalNetwork(z_dimension,
                 hid_channels, n_bars=n_bars))
        self.bar_generators = nn.ModuleDict({})
        for n in range(self.n_tracks):
            self.bar_generators.add_module(
                „bargen_" + str(n),BarGenerator(z_dimension,
                hid_features,hid_channels // 2,out_channels,
                n_steps_per_bar=n_steps_per_bar,n_pitches=n_pitches))
```

```
def forward(self,chords,style,melody,groove):
    chord_outs = self.chords_network(chords)
    bar_outs = []
    for bar in range(self.n_bars):
        track_outs = []
        chord_out = chord_outs[:, :, bar]
        style_out = style
        for track in range(self.n_tracks):
            melody_in = melody[:, track, :]
            melody_out = self.melody_networks["melodygen_"\
                    + str(track)](melody_in)[:, :, bar]
            groove_out = groove[:, track, :]
            z = torch.cat([chord_out, style_out, melody_out,\
                    groove_out], dim=1)
            track_outs.append(self.bar_generators["bargen_"\
                    + str(track)](z))
        track_out = torch.cat(track_outs, dim=1)
        bar_outs.append(track_out)
    out = torch.cat(bar_outs, dim=2)
    return out
```

- Iterates through two bars
- Iterates through four tracks
- Concatenates chords, style, melody, and groove into one input
- Generates one bar using the bar generator
- Concatenates eight bars into one complete piece of music

The generator takes four noise vectors as inputs. It iterates through four tracks and two bars. In each iteration, it utilizes the bar generator to create a single bar of music. Upon completing all iterations, the MuseGenerator() class merges the eight bars into one cohesive music piece, which has dimensions of (4, 2, 16, 84).

13.4.3 *Optimizers and the loss function*

We create a generator and a critic based on the MuseGenerator() and MuseCritic() classes in the local module:

```
import torch
from utils.MuseGAN_util import (init_weights, MuseGenerator, MuseCritic)

device = "cuda" if torch.cuda.is_available() else "cpu"
generator = MuseGenerator(z_dimension=32, hid_channels=1024,
            hid_features=1024, out_channels=1).to(device)
critic = MuseCritic(hid_channels=128,
                hid_features=1024,
                out_features=1).to(device)
generator = generator.apply(init_weights)
critic = critic.apply(init_weights)
```

As we discussed in chapter 5, the critic generates a rating instead of a classification, so the loss function is defined as the negative average of the product between the prediction and the target. As a result, we define the following loss_fn() function in the local module MuseGAN_util:

```
def loss_fn(pred, target):
    return -torch.mean(pred*target)
```

During training, for the generator, we'll assign a value of 1 to the target argument in the loss_fn() function. This setting aims to guide the generator in producing music that can achieve the highest possible rating (i.e., the variable pred in the loss_fn() function). For the critic, we'll set the target to 1 for real music and –1 for fake music in the loss function. This setting guides the critic to assign a high rating to real music and a low rating to fake music.

Similar to the approach in chapter 5, we incorporate the Wasserstein distance with a gradient penalty into the critic's loss function to ensure training stability. The gradient penalty is defined in the MuseGAN_util.py file as follows:

```
class GradientPenalty(nn.Module):
    def __init__(self):
        super().__init__()
    def forward(self, inputs, outputs):
        grad = torch.autograd.grad(
            inputs=inputs,
            outputs=outputs,
            grad_outputs=torch.ones_like(outputs),
            create_graph=True,
            retain_graph=True,
        )[0]
        grad_=torch.norm(grad.view(grad.size(0),-1),p=2,dim=1)
        penalty = torch.mean((1. - grad_) ** 2)
        return penalty
```

The GradientPenalty() class requires two inputs: interpolated music, which is a blend of real and fake music, and the ratings assigned by the critic network to this interpolated music. The class computes the gradient of the critic's ratings concerning the interpolated music. The gradient penalty is then calculated as the squared difference between the norms of these gradients and the target value of 1, following a similar approach to what we did in chapter 5.

As usual, we'll use the Adam optimizer for both the critic and the generator:

```
lr = 0.001
g_optimizer = torch.optim.Adam(generator.parameters(),
                               lr=lr, betas=(0.5, 0.9))
c_optimizer = torch.optim.Adam(critic.parameters(),
                               lr=lr, betas=(0.5, 0.9))
```

With that, we have successfully constructed a MuseGAN, which is now ready to be trained using the data we prepared earlier in the chapter.

13.5   *Training the MuseGAN to generate music*

Now that we have both the MuseGAN model and the training data, we'll proceed to train the model in this section.

Similar to our approach in chapters 3 and 4, when training GANs, we'll alternate between training the critic and the generator. In each training iteration, we'll sample a batch of real music from the training dataset and a batch of generated music from the generator and present them to the critic for evaluation. During critic training, we compare the critic's ratings with the ground truth and adjust the critic network's weights slightly so that, in the next iteration, the ratings will be as high as possible for real music and as low as possible for generated music. During generator training, we feed generated music to the critic model to obtain a rating and then slightly adjust the generator network's weights so that, in the next iteration, the rating will be higher (as the generator aims to create music pieces that fool the critic into thinking they are real). We repeat this process for many iterations, gradually enabling the generator network to create more realistic music pieces.

Once the model is trained, we'll discard the critic network and use the trained generator to create music pieces by feeding it four noise vectors (chords, style, melody, and groove).

13.5.1 *Training the MuseGAN*

Before we embark on the training loops for the MuseGAN model, we first define a few hyperparameters and helper functions. The hyperparameter `repeat` controls how many times we train the critic in each iteration, `display_step` specifies how often we display output, and `epochs` is the number of epochs we train the model.

Listing 13.5   Hyperparameters and helper functions

```
from utils.MuseGAN_util import loss_fn, GradientPenalty

batch_size=64
repeat=5
display_step=10
epochs=500
alpha=torch.rand((batch_size,1,1,1,1)).requires_grad_().to(device)
gp=GradientPenalty()

def noise():
    chords = torch.randn(batch_size, 32).to(device)
    style = torch.randn(batch_size, 32).to(device)
    melody = torch.randn(batch_size, 4, 32).to(device)
    groove = torch.randn(batch_size, 4, 32).to(device)
    return chords,style,melody,groove
```

Defines a few hyperparameters

Defines alpha to create interpolated music

Defines a gp() function to calculate gradient penalty

Defines a noise() function to retrieve four random noise vectors

---

The batch size is set at 64, and this helps us determine how many sets of random noise vectors to retrieve to create a batch of fake music. We'll train the critic for five iterations and the generator just once in each training loop because an effective critic is essential for training the generator. We'll display training losses after every 10 epochs. We'll train the model for 500 epochs.

We instantiate the `GradientPenalty()` class in the local module to create a `gp()` function to calculate the gradient penalty. We also define a `noise()` function to generate four random noise vectors to feed to the generator.

Next, we define the following function, `train_epoch()`, to train the model for one epoch.

Listing 13.6   Training the MuseGAN model for one epoch

```
def train_epoch():
    e_gloss = 0
    e_closs = 0
    for real in loader:                              ← Iterates through
        real = real.to(device)                         all batches
        for _ in range(repeat):                      ← Trains the critic five
            chords,style,melody,groove=noise()          times in each iteration
            c_optimizer.zero_grad()
            with torch.no_grad():
                fake = generator(chords, style, melody,groove).detach()
            realfake = alpha * real + (1 - alpha) * fake
            fake_pred = critic(fake)
            real_pred = critic(real)
            realfake_pred = critic(realfake)
            fake_loss =  loss_fn(fake_pred,-torch.ones_like(fake_pred))
            real_loss = loss_fn(real_pred,torch.ones_like(real_pred))
            penalty = gp(realfake, realfake_pred)
            closs = fake_loss + real_loss + 10 * penalty    ← The total loss
            closs.backward(retain_graph=True)                 for the critic
            c_optimizer.step()                                has three
            e_closs += closs.item() / (repeat*len(loader))    components:
        g_optimizer.zero_grad()                               loss from
        chords,style,melody,groove=noise()                    evaluating real
        fake = generator(chords, style, melody, groove)       music, loss
        fake_pred = critic(fake)                              from
        gloss = loss_fn(fake_pred, torch.ones_like(fake_pred)) ← evaluating fake
        gloss.backward()                                       music, and the
        g_optimizer.step()                                     gradient
        e_gloss += gloss.item() / len(loader)                  penalty loss.
    return e_gloss, e_closs
                                                         Trains the
                                                         generator
```

The training process is very much like that we used in chapter 5 when we train the conditional GAN with gradient penalty.

We now train the model for 500 epochs:

```
for epoch in range(1,epochs+1):
    e_gloss, e_closs = train_epoch()
    if epoch % display_step == 0:
        print(f"Epoch {epoch}, G loss {e_gloss} C loss {e_closs}")
```

If you use GPU training, it takes about an hour. Otherwise, it may take several hours. Once done, you can save the trained generator to the local folder as follows:

```
torch.save(generator.state_dict(),'files/MuseGAN_G.pth')
```

Alternatively, you can download the trained generator from my website: https://mng .bz/Bglr.

Next, we'll discard the critic network and use the trained generator to create music that mimics the style of Bach.

13.5.2 *Generating music with the trained MuseGAN*

To generate music with the trained generator, we'll feed four noise vectors from the latent space to the generator. Note that we can generate multiple music objects at the same time and decode them together to form one continuous piece of music. You'll learn how to do that in this subsection.

We first load the trained weights in the generator:

```
generator.load_state_dict(torch.load('files/MuseGAN_G.pth',
    map_location=device))
```

Rather than producing a single 4D music object, we can simultaneously generate multiple 4D music objects and convert them into one continuous piece of music later. For instance, if we aim to create five music objects, we begin by sampling five sets of noise vectors from the latent spaces. Each set consists of four vectors: chords, style, melody, and groove, like so:

```
num_pieces = 5
chords = torch.rand(num_pieces, 32).to(device)
style = torch.rand(num_pieces, 32).to(device)
melody = torch.rand(num_pieces, 4, 32).to(device)
groove = torch.rand(num_pieces, 4, 32).to(device)
```

Each generated music object can be transformed into a music piece that lasts approximately 8 seconds. In this case, we choose to generate five music objects and decode them into a single music piece later, resulting in a duration of about 40 seconds. You can adjust the value of the variable `num_pieces` according to your preference, depending on the desired length of the music piece.

Next, we supply the generator with the five sets of latent variables to produce a set of music objects:

```
preds = generator(chords, style, melody, groove).detach()
```

The output, `preds`, consists of five music objects. Next, we decode these objects into a single piece of music, represented as a MIDI file:

```
from utils.midi_util import convert_to_midi

music_data = convert_to_midi(preds.cpu().numpy())
music_data.write('midi', 'files/MuseGAN_song.midi')
```

We import the `convert_to_midi()` function from the local module `midi_util`. Open the file `midi_util.py` that you downloaded earlier and review the definition of the `convert_to_midi()` function. This process is similar to what we have done earlier in this chapter when we converted the first music object in the training set into the file `first_song.midi`. Since MIDI files represent sequences of notes over time, we simply concatenate the five music pieces corresponding to the five music objects into one extended sequence of notes. This combined sequence is then saved as `MuseGAN_song.midi` on your computer.

Find the generated music piece, `MuseGAN_song.midi`, on your computer. Open it with a music player of your choice and listen to see if it resembles the music pieces from the training set. For comparison, you can listen to a piece of music generated by the trained model on my website at https://mng.bz/dZJv. Note that since the input to the generator, the noise vectors, are randomly drawn from the latent space, the music pieces you generate will sound different.

Exercise 13.2

Obtain three sets of random noise vectors (each set should contain chords, style, melody, and groove) from the latent space. Feed them to the trained generator to obtain three music objects. Decode them into one single piece of music in the form of a MIDI file. Save it as `generated_song.midi` on your computer, and play it using a music player.

In this chapter, you've learned how to build and train a MuseGAN to generate music in the style of Bach. Specifically, you've approached a piece of music as a 4D object and applied the techniques from chapter 4 on deep convolutional layers to develop a GAN model. In the next chapter, you'll explore a different way of generating music: treating a piece of music as a sequence of indexes and utilizing techniques from NLP to generate music pieces by predicting one index at a time.

Summary

- MuseGAN treats a piece of music as a multidimensional object akin to an image. The generator produces a piece of music and submits it, along with real music pieces from the training set, to the critic for evaluation. The generator then modifies the music based on the critic's feedback until it closely resembles real music from the training dataset.

- Musical notes, octaves, and pitch are fundamental concepts in music theory. Octaves represent different levels of musical sound. Each octave is subdivided into 12 semitones: C, C#, D, D#, E, F, F#, G, G#, A, A#, B. Within an octave, a note is assigned a specific pitch number.

- In electronic music production, a track typically refers to an individual layer or component of the music. Each track contains multiple bars (or measures). A bar is further divided into multiple steps.

- To represent a piece of music as a multidimensional object, we structure it with a (4, 2, 16, 84) shape: 4 music tracks, with each track consisting of 2 bars, each bar containing 16 steps, and each step capable of playing 1 of the 84 different notes.

- In music creation, incorporating more detailed inputs is essential for achieving greater control and variety. Instead of using a single noise vector from the latent space for generating shapes, numbers, and images as in previous chapters, we employ four distinct noise vectors in the music generation process. Given that each music piece consists of four tracks and two bars, we use these four vectors to effectively manage this structure. One vector controls all tracks and bars collectively, another controls each bar across all tracks, a third oversees all tracks across bars, and the fourth manages each individual bar in each track.

Building and training a music Transformer

This chapter covers

- Representing music with control messages and velocity values
- Tokenizing music into a sequence of indexes
- Building and training a music Transformer
- Generating musical events using the trained Transformer
- Converting musical events back to a playable MIDI file

Sad that your favorite musician is no longer with us? Sad no more: generative AI can bring them back to the stage!

Take, for example, Layered Reality, a London-based company that's working on a project called Elvis Evolution.[1] The goal? To resurrect the legendary Elvis Presley using AI. By feeding a vast array of Elvis' official archival material, including video clips, photographs, and music, into a sophisticated computer model, this AI Elvis

---

[1] Chloe Veltman, March 15, 2024. "Just because your favorite singer is dead doesn't mean you can't see them 'live.'" https://mng.bz/r1de.

learns to mimic his singing, speaking, dancing, and walking with remarkable resemblance. The result? A digital performance that captures the essence of the late King himself.

The Elvis Evolution project is a shining example of the transformative effect of generative AI across various industries. In the previous chapter, you explored the use of MuseGAN to create music that could pass as authentic multitrack compositions. Muse-GAN views a piece of music as a multidimensional object, similar to an image, and generates complete music pieces that resemble those in the training dataset. Both real and AI-generated music are then evaluated by a critic, which helps refine the AI-generated music until it's indistinguishable from the real thing.

In this chapter, you'll take a different approach to AI music creation, treating it as a sequence of musical events. We'll apply techniques from text generation, as discussed in chapters 11 and 12, to predict the next element in a sequence. Specifically, you'll develop a GPT-style model to predict the next musical event based on all previous events in the sequence. GPT-style Transformers are ideal for this task because of their scalability and the self-attention mechanism, which helps them capture long-range dependencies and understand context. This makes them highly effective for sequence prediction and generation across a wide range of content, including music. The music Transformer you will create has 20.16 million parameters, large enough to capture the long-term relations of different notes in music pieces but small enough to be trained in a reasonable amount of time.

We'll use the Maestro piano music from Google's Magenta group as our training data. You'll learn how to first convert a musical instrument digital interface (MIDI) file into a sequence of music notes, analogous to raw text data in natural language processing (NLP). You'll then break the musical notes down into small pieces called musical events, analogous to tokens in NLP. Since neural networks can only accept numerical inputs, you'll map each unique event token to an index. With this, the music pieces in the training data are converted into sequences of indexes, ready to be fed into neural networks.

To train the music Transformer to predict the next token based on the current token and all previous tokens in the sequence, we'll create sequences of 2,048 indexes as inputs (features x). We then shift the sequences one index to the right and use them as the outputs (targets y). We feed pairs of (x, y) to the music Transformer to train the model. Once trained, we'll use a short sequence of indexes as the prompt and feed it to the music Transformer to predict the next token, which is then appended to the prompt to form a new sequence. This new sequence is fed back into the model for further predictions, and this process is repeated until the sequence reaches a desired length.

You'll see that the trained music Transformer can generate lifelike music that mimics the style in the training dataset. Further, unlike the music generated in chapter 13, you'll learn to control the creativity of the music piece. You'll achieve this by scaling the predicted logits with the temperature parameter, just as you did in earlier chapters when controlling the creativity of the generated text.

14.1   Introduction to the music Transformer

The concept of the music Transformer was introduced in 2018.[2] This innovative approach extends the Transformer architecture, initially devised for NLP tasks, to the field of music generation. As discussed in previous chapters, Transformers employ self-attention mechanisms to effectively grasp the context and capture long-range dependencies among elements in a sequence.

In a similar vein, the music Transformer is engineered to generate a sequence of musical notes by learning from a vast dataset of existing music. The model is trained to predict the next musical event in a sequence based on preceding events by understanding the patterns, structures, and relationships between different musical elements in the training data.

A crucial step in training a music Transformer lies in figuring out how to represent music as a sequence of unique musical events, akin to tokens in NLP. In the previous chapter, you learned to represent a piece of music as a 4D object. In this chapter, you will explore an alternative approach to music representation, specifically performance-based music representation through control messages and velocity values.[3] Based on this, you will convert a piece of music into four types of musical events: note-on, note-off, time-shift, and velocity.

Note-on signals the start of a musical note being played, specifying the note's pitch. Note-off indicates the end of a note, telling the instrument to stop playing that note. Time-shift represents the amount of time that passes between two musical events. Velocity measures the force or speed with which a note is played, with higher values corresponding to a stronger, louder sound. Each type of musical event has many different values. Each unique event will be mapped to a different index, effectively transforming a piece of music into a sequence of indexes. You will then apply the GPT models, as discussed in chapters 11 and 12, to create a decoder-only music Transformer that predicts the next musical event in the sequence.

In this section, you will begin by learning about performance-based music representation through control messages and velocity values. You will then explore how to represent music pieces as sequences of musical events. Finally, you will learn the steps involved in building and training a Transformer to generate music.

14.1.1   Performance-based music representation

Performance-based music representation is often achieved using the MIDI format, which captures the nuances of a musical performance through control messages and velocity values. In MIDI, musical notes are represented by note-on and note-off messages, which include information about the pitch and velocity of each note.

---

[2]   Cheng-Zhi Anna Huang, Ashish Vaswani, Jakob Uszkoreit, Noam Shazeer, Ian Simon, Curtis Hawthorne, Andrew M. Dai, Matthew D. Hoffman, Monica Dinculescu, and Douglas Eck, 2018, "Music Transformer." https://arxiv.org/abs/1809.04281.

[3]   See, for example, Hawthorne et al., 2018, "Enabling Factorized Piano Music Modeling and Generation with the MAESTRO Dataset." https://arxiv.org/abs/1810.12247.

As we discussed in chapter 13, the pitch value ranges from 0 to 127, with each value corresponding to a semitone in an octave level. For instance, the pitch value 60 corresponds to a C4 note, while the pitch value 74 corresponds to a D5 note. The velocity value, also ranging from 0 to 127, represents the dynamics of the note, with higher values indicating louder or more forceful playing. By combining these control messages and velocity values, a MIDI sequence can capture the expressive details of a live performance, allowing for expressive playback through MIDI-compatible instruments and software.

To give you a concrete example of how a piece of music can be represented by control messages and velocity values, consider the five notes shown in the following listing.

Listing 14.1   Example notes in a performance-based music representation

```
<[SNote] time: 1.0325520833333333 type: note_on, value: 74, velocity: 86>
<[SNote] time: 1.0442708333333333 type: note_on, value: 38, velocity: 77>
<[SNote] time: 1.2265625 type: note_off, value: 74, velocity: None>
<[SNote] time: 1.2395833333333333 type: note_on, value: 73, velocity: 69>
<[SNote] time: 1.2408854166666665 type: note_on, value: 37, velocity: 64>
```

These are the first five notes from a piece of music in the training dataset you'll use in this chapter. The first note has a timestamp of approximately 1.03 seconds, with a note of pitch value 74 (D5) starting to play at a velocity of 86. Looking at the second note, you can infer that after about 0.01 seconds (since the timestamp is now 1.04 seconds), a note with a pitch value of 38 starts to play at a velocity of 77, and so on.

These musical notes are similar to raw text in NLP; we cannot directly feed them to a music Transformer to train the model. We first need to "tokenize" the notes and then convert the tokens to indexes before feeding them to the model.

To tokenize the musical notes, we'll represent the music using increments of 0.01 seconds to reduce the number of time steps in the music piece. Additionally, we'll separate control messages from velocity values and treat them as different elements of the music piece. Specifically, we'll represent music using a combination of note-on, note-off, time-shift, and velocity events. Once we do that, the preceding five musical notes can be represented by the following events (some events are omitted for brevity).

Listing 14.2   Tokenized representation of a piece of music

```
<Event type: time_shift, value: 99>,
 <Event type: time_shift, value: 2>,
 <Event type: velocity, value: 21>,
 <Event type: note_on, value: 74>,
 <Event type: time_shift, value: 0>,
 <Event type: velocity, value: 19>,
 <Event type: note_on, value: 38>,
 <Event type: time_shift, value: 17>,
 <Event type: note_off, value: 74>,
 <Event type: time_shift, value: 0>,
 <Event type: velocity, value: 17>,
 <Event type: note_on, value: 73>,
```

```
<Event type: velocity, value: 16>,
<Event type: note_on, value: 37>,
<Event type: time_shift, value: 0>
...
```

We'll count time shifts in increments of 0.01 seconds and tokenize time shifts from 0.01 seconds to 1 second with 100 different values. Thus, time-shift events are tokenized into 1 of 100 unique event tokens: a value of 0 indicates a time lapse of 0.01 seconds, 1 indicates a time lapse of 0.02 seconds, and so on, up to 99, which indicates a time lapse of 1 second. If a time-shift lasts more than 1 second, you can use multiple time-shift tokens to indicate it. For example, the first two tokens in listing 14.2 are both time-shift tokens, with values 99 and 2, respectively, indicating time lapses of 1 second and 0.03 seconds. This matches the timestamp of the first musical note in listing 14.1: 1.0326 seconds.

Listing 14.2 also shows that velocity is a separate type of musical event. We place the value of velocity into 32 equally spaced bins, converting the original velocity values, which range from 0 to 127, into 1 of 32 values, ranging from 0 to 31. This is why the original velocity value of 86 in the first note in listing 14.1 is now represented as a velocity event with a value of 21 in listing 14.2 (the number 86 falls into the 22nd bin, and Python uses zero-based indexing).

Table 14.1 shows the meaning of four types of different tokenized events, their value ranges, and the meaning of each event token.

Table 14.1   Meanings of different event tokens

Event token type	Event token value range	Meaning of the event tokens
note_on	0–127	Starting to play at a certain pitch value. For example, note_on with value 74 means starting to play note D5.
note_off	0–127	Releasing a certain note. For example, note_off with value 60 means to stop playing note C4.
time_shift	0–99	The time_shift values are increments of 0.01 seconds. For example, 0 indicates 0.01 seconds, 2 indicates 0.03 seconds, and 99 indicates 1 second.
velocity	0–31	The original velocity values are placed into 32 bins. The bin value is used. For example, an original velocity value of 86 now has a tokenized value of 21.

Similar to the approach taken in NLP, we'll convert each unique token into an index so that we can input the data into neural networks. According to table 14.1, there are 128 unique note-on event tokens, 128 note-off event tokens, 32 velocity event tokens, and 100 time-shift event tokens. This results in a total of 128 + 128 + 32 + 100 = 388 unique tokens. Consequently, we convert these 388 unique tokens into indexes ranging from 0 to 387, based on the mappings provided in table 14.2.

Table 14.2 Mapping event tokens to indexes and indexes to event tokens

Token type	Index range	Event token to index	Index to event token
note_on	0–127	The value of the note_on token. For example, the note_on token with a value of 74 is assigned an index value of 74.	If the index range is 0 to 127, set token type to note_on and value to the index value. For example, the index value 63 is mapped to a note_on token with a value of 63.
note_off	128–255	128 plus the value of the note_off token. For example, the note_off token with a value of 60 is assigned an index value of 188 (since 128 + 60 = 188).	If the index range is 128 to 255, set token type to note_off and value to index minus 128. For example, index 180 is mapped to the note_off token with value 52.
time_shift	256–355	256 plus the value of the time_shift token. For example, the time_shift token with a value of 16 is assigned an index value of 272 (since 256 + 16 = 272).	If the index range is 256 to 355, set token type to time_shift and value to index minus 256. For example, index 288 is mapped to the time_shift token with value 32.
velocity	356–387	356 plus the value of the velocity token. For example, the velocity token with a value of 21 is assigned an index value of 377 (since 356+21=377).	If the index range is 356 to 387, set token type to velocity and value to index minus 356. For example, index 380 is mapped to the velocity token with value 24.

The third column in table 14.2 outlines the conversion of event tokens to indexes. Note-on tokens are assigned index values ranging from 0 to 127, where the index value corresponds to the pitch number in the token. Note-off tokens are assigned index values from 128 to 255, with the index value being 128 plus the pitch number. Time-shift tokens are assigned index values from 256 to 355, with the index value being 256 plus the time-shift value. Lastly, velocity tokens are assigned index values from 356 to 387, with the index value being 356 plus the velocity bin number.

Using this token-to-index mapping, we'll convert each piece of music into a sequence of indexes. We'll apply this conversion to all music pieces in the training dataset and use the resulting sequences to train our music Transformer (the details of which will be explained later). Once trained, we'll use the Transformer to generate music in the form of a sequence of indexes. The final step is to convert this sequence back into MIDI format so that we can play and enjoy the music on a computer.

The last column in table 14.2 provides guidance on converting indexes back to event tokens. We first determine the token type based on the range in which the index falls. The four ranges in the second column of table 14.2 correspond to the four token types in the first column of the table. To obtain the value for each token type, we subtract the index value by 0, 128, 256, and 356 for the four types of tokens, respectively. These tokenized events are then converted into musical notes in MIDI format, ready to be played on a computer.

14.1.2   *The music Transformer architecture*

In chapter 9, we built an encoder-decoder Transformer, and in chapters 11 and 12, we focused on decoder-only Transformers. Unlike language translation tasks where the encoder captures the meaning of the source language and passes it to the decoder for generating the translation, music generation does not require an encoder to understand a different language. Instead, the model generates subsequent event tokens based on previous event tokens in the music sequence. Therefore, we'll construct a decoder-only Transformer for our music generation task.

Our music Transformer, like other Transformer models, utilizes self-attention mechanisms to capture the long-range dependencies among different musical events in a piece of music, thereby generating coherent and lifelike music. Although our music Transformer differs in size from the GPT models we built in chapters 11 and 12, it shares the same core architecture. It follows the same structural design as GPT-2 models but is significantly smaller, making it feasible to train without the need for supercomputing facilities.

Specifically, our music Transformer consists of 6 decoder layers with an embedding dimension of 512, meaning each token is represented by a 512-value vector after word embedding. Instead of using sine and cosine functions for positional encoding as in the original 2017 paper "Attention Is All You Need," we use embedding layers to learn the positional encodings for different positions in a sequence. As a result, each position in a sequence is also represented by a 512-value vector. For calculating causal self-attention, we use 8 parallel attention heads to capture different aspects of the meanings of a token in the sequence, giving each attention head a dimension of 64 (512/8).

Compared to the vocabulary size of 50,257 in GPT-2 models, our model has a much smaller vocabulary size of 390 (388 different event tokens, plus a token to signify the end of a sequence and a token to pad shorter sequences; I'll explain later why padding is needed). This allows us to set the maximum sequence length in our music Transformer to 2,048, which is much longer than the maximum sequence length of 1,024 in GPT-2 models. This choice is necessary to capture the long-term relations of music notes in a sequence. With these hyperparameter values, our music Transformer has a size of 20.16 million parameters.

Figure 14.1 illustrates the architecture of the music Transformer we will create in this chapter. It is similar to the architecture of the GPT models you built in chapters 11 and 12. Figure 14.1 also shows the size of the training data as it passes through the model during training.

The input to the music Transformer we constructed comprises input embeddings, as depicted at the bottom of figure 14.1. The input embedding is the sum of the word embedding and positional encoding of the input sequence. This input embedding is then passed sequentially through six decoder blocks.

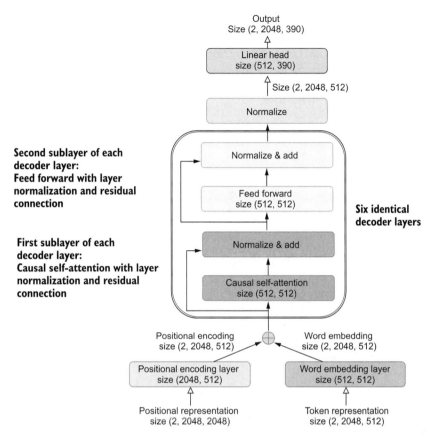

Figure 14.1 The architecture of a music Transformer. Music files in MIDI formats are first converted into sequences of musical events. These events are then tokenized and converted into indexes. We organize these indexes into sequences of 2,048 elements, and each batch contains 2 such sequences. The input sequence first undergoes word embedding and positional encoding; the input embedding is the sum of these two components. This input embedding is then processed through six decoder layers, each utilizing self-attention mechanisms to capture the relationships among different musical events in the sequence. After passing through the decoder layers, the output undergoes layer normalization to ensure stability in the training process. It then passes through a linear layer, resulting in an output size of 390, which corresponds to the number of unique tokens in the vocabulary. This final output represents the predicted logits for the next musical event in the sequence.

As discussed in chapters 11 and 12, each decoder layer consists of two sublayers: a causal self-attention layer and a feed-forward network. In addition, we apply layer normalization and residual connections to each sublayer to enhance the model's stability and learning capability.

After passing through the decoder layers, the output undergoes layer normalization and is then fed into a linear layer. The number of outputs in our model corresponds to the number of unique musical event tokens in the vocabulary, which is 390. The output of the model is the logits for the next musical event token.

Later, we will apply the softmax function to these logits to obtain the probability distribution over all possible event tokens. The model is designed to predict the next event token based on the current token and all previous tokens in the music sequence, enabling it to generate coherent and musically sensible sequences.

14.1.3 *Training the music Transformer*

Now that we understand how to construct a music Transformer for music generation, let's outline the training process for the music Transformer.

The style of the music generated by the model is influenced by the music pieces used for training. We'll use piano performances from Google's Magenta group to train our model. Figure 14.2 illustrates the steps involved in training the Transformer for music generation.

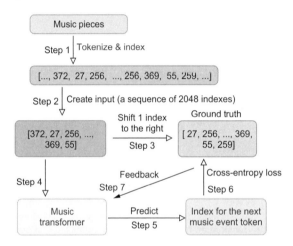

Figure 14.2   **The training process for a music Transformer to generate music**

Similar to the approach we've taken in NLP tasks, the first step in the training process for our music Transformer is to convert the raw training data into a numerical form so that it can be fed into the model. Specifically, we start by converting MIDI files in the training set into sequences of musical notes. We then further tokenize these notes by converting them into 1 of 388 unique events/tokens. After tokenization, we assign a unique index (i.e., an integer) to each token, converting the music pieces in the training set into sequences of integers (see step 1 in figure 14.2).

Next, we transform the sequence of integers into training data by dividing this sequence into sequences of equal length (step 2 in figure 14.2). We allow a maximum length of 2,048 indexes in each sequence. The choice of 2,048 enables us to capture long-range dependencies among musical events in a music sequence to create lifelike music. These sequences form the features (the x variable) of our model. As we did in previous chapters when training GPT models to generate text, we slide the input sequence window one index to the right and use it as the output in the training data (the y variable; step 3 in figure 14.2). Doing so forces our model to predict the next music token in a sequence based on the current token and all previous tokens in the music sequence.

The input and output pairs serve as the training data (x, y) for the music Transformer. During training, you will iterate through the training data. In the forward passes, you feed the input sequence x through the music Transformer (step 4). The music Transformer then makes a prediction based on the current parameters in the model (step 5). You compute the cross-entropy loss by comparing the predicted next tokens with the output obtained from step 3. In other words, you compare the model's prediction with the ground truth (step 6). Finally, you will adjust the parameters in the music Transformer so that in the next iteration, the model's predictions move closer to the actual output, minimizing the cross-entropy loss (step 7). The model is essentially performing a multicategory classification problem: it's predicting the next token from all unique music tokens in the vocabulary.

You will repeat steps 3 to 7 through many iterations. After each iteration, the model parameters are adjusted to improve the prediction of the next token. This process will be repeated for 50 epochs.

To generate a new piece of music with the trained model, we obtain a music piece from the test set, tokenize it, and convert it to a long sequence of indexes. We'll use the first, say, 250 indexes as the prompt (200 or 300 will lead to similar results). We then ask the trained music Transformer to generate new indexes until the sequence reaches a certain length (say, 1,000 indexes). We then convert the sequence of indexes back into a MIDI file to be played on your computer.

14.2 *Tokenizing music pieces*

Having grasped the structure of the music Transformer and its training methodology, we'll start with the first step: tokenization and indexing of the musical compositions in our training dataset.

We'll begin with employing a performance-based representation (as explained in the first section) to portray music pieces as musical notes, akin to raw text in NLP. After that, we'll divide these musical notes into a series of events, similar to tokens in NLP. Each unique event will be assigned a different index. Utilizing this mapping, we'll transform all music pieces in the training dataset into sequences of indexes.

Next, we'll standardize these sequences of indexes into a fixed length, specifically sequences with 2,048 indexes, and use them as the feature inputs (x). By shifting the window one index to the right, we'll generate the corresponding output sequences (y). We'll then group pairs of input and output (x, y) into batches, preparing them for training the music Transformer later in the chapter.

As we'll require the `pretty_midi` and `music21` libraries for processing MIDI files, execute the following line of code in a new cell in the Jupyter Notebook application:

```
!pip install pretty_midi music21
```

14.2.1 *Downloading training data*

We'll obtain the piano performances from the MAESTRO dataset, which is made available by Google's Magenta group (https://storage.googleapis.com/magentadata/datasets/maestro/v2.0.0/maestro-v2.0.0-midi.zip) and download the ZIP file. After downloading, unzip it and move the resulting folder, /maestro-v2.0.0/, into the /files/ directory on your computer.

Ensure that the /maestro-v2.0.0/ folder contains 4 files (one of which should be named "maestro-v2.0.0.json") and 10 subfolders. Each subfolder should contain more than 100 MIDI files. To familiarize yourself with the sound of the music pieces in the training data, try opening some of the MIDI files with your preferred music player.

Next, we'll split the MIDI files into train, validation, and test subsets. To start, create three subfolders within /files/maestro-v2.0.0/:

```
import os

os.makedirs("files/maestro-v2.0.0/train", exist_ok=True)
os.makedirs("files/maestro-v2.0.0/val", exist_ok=True)
os.makedirs("files/maestro-v2.0.0/test", exist_ok=True)
```

To facilitate the processing of MIDI files, visit Kevin Yang's GitHub repository at https://github.com/jason9693/midi-neural-processor, download the processor.py file, and place it in the /utils/ folder on your computer. Alternatively, you can obtain the file from the book's GitHub repository: https://github.com/markhliu/DGAI. We'll use this file as a local module to transform a MIDI file into a sequence of indexes and vice versa. This approach allows us to concentrate on developing, training, and utilizing a music Transformer without getting bogged down in the details of music format conversion. At the same time, I'll provide a simple example of how this process works so that you can convert between a MIDI file and a sequence of indexes yourself using the module.

Additionally, you need to download the ch14util.py file from the book's GitHub repository and place it in the /utils/ directory on your computer. We'll use the ch14util.py file as another local module to define the music Transformer model.

The file maestro-v2.0.0.json within the /maestro-v2.0.0/ folder contains the names of all MIDI files and their designated subsets (train, validation, or test). Based on this information, we'll categorize the MIDI files into three corresponding subfolders.

Listing 14.3   Splitting training data into train, validation, and test subsets

```
import json
import pickle
from utils.processor import encode_midi

file="files/maestro-v2.0.0/maestro-v2.0.0.json"

with open(file,"r") as fb:
    maestro_json=json.load(fb)                          ◄─── Loads JSON file
```

```
for x in maestro_json:
    mid=rf'files/maestro-v2.0.0/{x["midi_filename"]}'
    split_type = x["split"]
    f_name = mid.split("/")[-1] + ".pickle"
    if(split_type == "train"):
        o_file = rf'files/maestro-v2.0.0/train/{f_name}'
    elif(split_type == "validation"):
        o_file = rf'files/maestro-v2.0.0/val/{f_name}'
    elif(split_type == "test"):
        o_file = rf'files/maestro-v2.0.0/test/{f_name}'
    prepped = encode_midi(mid)
    with open(o_file,"wb") as f:
        pickle.dump(prepped, f)
```

Iterates through all files in the training data

Places a file in train, validation, or test subfolder based on instructions in the JSON file

The JavaScript object notation (JSON) file you downloaded categorizes each file in the training dataset into one of three subsets: train, validation, and test. After executing the previous code listing, if you explore the /train/, /val/, and /test/ folders on your computer, you should find numerous files in each. To verify the number of files in each of these three folders, you can perform the following checks:

```
train_size=len(os.listdir('files/maestro-v2.0.0/train'))
print(f"there are {train_size} files in the train set")
val_size=len(os.listdir('files/maestro-v2.0.0/val'))
print(f"there are {val_size} files in the validation set")
test_size=len(os.listdir('files/maestro-v2.0.0/test'))
print(f"there are {test_size} files in the test set")
```

The output from the preceding code block is

```
there are 967 files in the train set
there are 137 files in the validation set
there are 178 files in the test set
```

Results show that there are 967, 137, and 178 pieces of music in the train, validation, and test subsets, respectively.

14.2.2 Tokenizing MIDI files

Next, we'll represent each MIDI file as a sequence of musical notes.

Listing 14.4 Converting a MIDI file to a sequence of music notes

```
import pickle
from utils.processor import encode_midi
import pretty_midi
from utils.processor import (_control_preprocess,
    _note_preprocess,_divide_note,
    _make_time_sift_events,_snote2events)

file='MIDI-Unprocessed_Chamber1_MID--AUDIO_07_R3_2018_wav--2'
name=rf'files/maestro-v2.0.0/2018/{file}.midi'

events=[]
notes=[]
```

Selects a MIDI file from the training dataset

```
song=pretty_midi.PrettyMIDI(name)
for inst in song.instruments:
    inst_notes=inst.notes
    ctrls=_control_preprocess([ctrl for ctrl in
        inst.control_changes if ctrl.number == 64])
    notes += _note_preprocess(ctrls, inst_notes)
dnotes = _divide_note(notes)
dnotes.sort(key=lambda x: x.time)
for i in range(5):
    print(dnotes[i])
```

Extracts musical events from the music

Places all musical events in the list dnotes

We have selected one MIDI file from the training dataset and used the processor.py local module to convert it into a sequence of musical notes. The output from the preceding code listing is

```
<[SNote] time: 1.0325520833333333 type: note_on, value: 74, velocity: 86>
<[SNote] time: 1.0442708333333333 type: note_on, value: 38, velocity: 77>
<[SNote] time: 1.2265625 type: note_off, value: 74, velocity: None>
<[SNote] time: 1.2395833333333333 type: note_on, value: 73, velocity: 69>
<[SNote] time: 1.2408854166666665 type: note_on, value: 37, velocity: 64>
```

The output displayed here shows the first five musical notes from the MIDI file. You might have observed that the time representation in the output is continuous. Certain musical notes contain both a note_on and a velocity attribute, complicating the tokenization process due to the vast number of unique musical events resulting from the continuous nature of time representation. Additionally, the combination of different note_on and velocity values is large (each can assume 128 distinct values, ranging from 0 to 127), leading to an excessively large vocabulary size. This, in turn, would render training impractical.

To mitigate this problem and decrease the vocabulary size, we further convert these musical notes into tokenized events:

```
cur_time = 0
cur_vel = 0
for snote in dnotes:
    events += _make_time_sift_events(prev_time=cur_time,
                                     post_time=snote.time)
    events += _snote2events(snote=snote, prev_vel=cur_vel)
    cur_time = snote.time
    cur_vel = snote.velocity
indexes=[e.to_int() for e in events]
for i in range(15):
    print(events[i])
```

Discretizes time to reduce the number of unique events

Converts musical notes to events

Prints out the first 15 events

The output is as follows:

```
<Event type: time_shift, value: 99>
<Event type: time_shift, value: 2>
<Event type: velocity, value: 21>
<Event type: note_on, value: 74>
<Event type: time_shift, value: 0>
<Event type: velocity, value: 19>
<Event type: note_on, value: 38>
<Event type: time_shift, value: 17>
```

```
<Event type: note_off, value: 74>
<Event type: time_shift, value: 0>
<Event type: velocity, value: 17>
<Event type: note_on, value: 73>
<Event type: velocity, value: 16>
<Event type: note_on, value: 37>
<Event type: time_shift, value: 0>
```

The music piece is now represented by four types of events: note-on, note-off, time-shift, and velocity. Each event type includes different values, resulting in a total of 388 unique events, as detailed in table 14.2 earlier. The specifics of converting a MIDI file into a sequence of such unique events are not essential for constructing and training a music Transformer. Therefore, we will not dive deeply into this topic; interested readers can refer to Huang et al (2018) cited earlier. All you need to know is how to use the processor.py module to transform a MIDI file into a sequence of indexes and vice versa. In the following subsection, you'll learn how to accomplish that.

14.2.3 *Preparing the training data*

We've learned how to convert music pieces into tokens and then into indexes. The next step involves preparing the training data so that we can utilize it to train the music Transformer later in this chapter. To achieve this, we define the create_xys() function shown in the following listing.

Listing 14.5 Creating training data

```
import torch,os,pickle

max_seq=2048
def create_xys(folder):
    files=[os.path.join(folder,f) for f in os.listdir(folder)]
    xys=[]
    for f in files:
        with open(f,"rb") as fb:
            music=pickle.load(fb)
        music=torch.LongTensor(music)
        x=torch.full((max_seq,),389, dtype=torch.long)      ◀── Creates (x, y) sequences, with equal lengths of 2,048 indexes and sets index 399 as the padding index
        y=torch.full((max_seq,),389, dtype=torch.long)
        length=len(music)
        if length<=max_seq:
            print(length)
            x[:length]=music                                 ◀── Uses a sequence of up to 2,048 indexes as input
            y[:length-1]=music[1:]                            ◀── Slides the window one index to the right and uses it as the output
            y[length-1]=388                                   ◀── Sets the end index as 388
        else:
            x=music[:max_seq]
            y=music[1:max_seq+1]
        xys.append((x,y))
    return xys
```

As we've seen repeatedly throughout this book, in sequence prediction tasks, we use a sequence x as input. We then shift the sequence one position to the right to create the output sequence. This approach compels the model to predict the next element based on the current element and all preceding elements in the sequence. To prepare training data for our music Transformer, we'll construct pairs (x, y), where x is the input and y is the output. Both x and y contain 2,048 indexes—long enough to capture the long-term relations of music notes in a sequence but not too long to hinder the training process.

We'll iterate through all the music pieces in the training dataset we downloaded. If a music piece exceeds 2,048 indexes in length, we'll use the first 2,048 indexes as input x. For the output y, we'll use indexes from the second position to the 2,049th position. In the rare case where the music piece is less than or equal to 2,048 indexes long, we'll pad the sequence with index 389 to ensure that both x and y are 2,048 indexes long. Additionally, we use index 388 to signal the end of the sequence y.

As mentioned in the first section, there are a total of 388 unique event tokens, indexed from 0 to 387. Since we use 388 to signal the end of the y sequence and 389 to pad sequences, we have a total of 390 unique indexes, ranging from 0 to 389.

We can now apply the `create_xys()` function to the train subset:

```
trainfolder='files/maestro-v2.0.0/train'
train=create_xys(trainfolder)
```

The output is

```
15
5
1643
1771
586
```

This shows that out of the 967 music pieces in the train subset, only 5 are shorter than 2,048 indexes. Their lengths are shown in the previous output.

We also apply the `create_xys()` function to the validation and test subsets:

```
valfolder='files/maestro-v2.0.0/val'
testfolder='files/maestro-v2.0.0/test'
print("processing the validation set")
val=create_xys(valfolder)
print("processing the test set")
test=create_xys(testfolder)
```

The output is

```
processing the validation set
processing the test set
1837
```

This shows that all music pieces in the validation subset are longer than 2,048 indexes. Only one music piece in the test subset is shorter than 2,048 indexes.

Let's print out a file from the validation subset and see what it looks like:

```
val1, _ = val[0]
print(val1.shape)
print(val1)
```

The output is as follows:

```
torch.Size([2048])
tensor([324, 366,  67,  ...,  60, 264, 369])
```

The x sequence from the first pair in the validation set has a length of 2,048 indexes, with values such as 324, 367, and so on. Let's use the module `processor.py` to decode the sequence to a MIDI file so that you can hear what it sounds like:

```
from utils.processor import decode_midi

file_path="files/val1.midi"
decode_midi(val1.cpu().numpy(), file_path=file_path)
```

The `decode_midi()` function converts a sequence of indexes into a MIDI file, playable on your computer. After running the preceding code block, open the file val1.midi with a music player on your computer to hear what it sounds like.

Exercise 14.1

Use the `decode_midi()` function from the processor.py local module to convert the first music piece in the train subset into a MIDI file. Save it as train1.midi on your computer. Open it with a music player on your computer and get a sense of what type of music we use for training data.

Finally, we create a data loader so that the data are in batches for training:

```
from torch.utils.data import DataLoader

batch_size=2
trainloader=DataLoader(train,batch_size=batch_size,
                    shuffle=True)
```

To prevent your GPU from running out of memory, we'll use a batch size of 2, as we've created very long sequences, each comprising 2,048 indexes. If needed, reduce the batch size to one or switch to CPU training.

With that, our training data is prepared. In the next two sections, we'll construct a music Transformer from scratch and then train it using the training data we've just prepared.

14.3 *Building a GPT to generate music*

Now that our training data is prepared, we'll construct a GPT model from scratch for music generation. The architecture of this model will be similar to the GPT-2XL model we developed in chapter 11 and the text generator from chapter 12. However, the size of our music Transformer will differ due to the specific hyperparameters we select.

To conserve space, we'll place the model construction within the local module ch14util.py. Our focus here will be on the hyperparameters chosen for the music Transformer. Specifically, we'll decide the values of `n_layer`, the number of decoder layers in the model; n_head, the number of parallel heads to use to calculate causal self-attention; n_embd, the embedding dimension; and block_size, the number of tokens in the input sequence.

14.3.1 *Hyperparameters in the music Transformer*

Open the file ch14util.py that you downloaded earlier from the book's GitHub repository. Inside, you'll find several functions and classes that are identical to those defined in chapter 12.

As in all GPT models we have seen in this book, the feed-forward network in the decoder block utilizes the Gaussian error linear unit (GELU) activation function. Consequently, we define a GELU class in ch14util.py, exactly as we did in chapter 12.

We employ a Config() class to store all the hyperparameters used in the music Transformer:

```
from torch import nn
class Config():
    def __init__(self):
        sclf.n_layer - 6
        self.n_head = 8
        self.n_embd = 512
        self.vocab_size = 390
        self.block_size = 2048
        self.embd_pdrop = 0.1
        self.resid_pdrop = 0.1
        self.attn_pdrop = 0.1
config=Config()
device="cuda" if torch.cuda.is_available() else "cpu"
```

The attributes within the Config() class serve as hyperparameters for our music Transformer. We assign a value of 6 to the n_layer attribute, indicating that our music Transformer consists of 6 decoder layers. This is more than the number of decoder layers in the GPT model we built in chapter 12. Each decoder layer processes the input sequence and introduces a level of abstraction or representation. As the information traverses through more layers, the model is capable of capturing more complex patterns and relationships in the data. This depth is crucial for our music Transformer to comprehend and generate intricate music pieces.

The n_head attribute is set to 8, signifying that we will divide the query Q, key K, and value V vectors into eight parallel heads during the computation of causal self-attention. The n_embd attribute is set to 512, indicating an embedding dimension of 512: each event token will be represented by a vector of 512 values. The vocab_size attribute is determined by the number of unique tokens in the vocabulary, which is 390. As explained earlier, there are 388 unique event tokens, and we added 1 token to signify the end of the sequence and another token to pad shorter sequences so that all sequences have a length of 2,048. The block_size attribute is set to 2,048, indicating that the input sequence contains a maximum of 2,048 tokens. We set the dropout rates to 0.1, as in chapters 11 and 12.

Like all Transformers, our music Transformer employs self-attention mechanisms to capture relationships among different elements in a sequence. Consequently, we define a `CausalSelfAttention()` class in the local module ch14util, which is identical to the `CausalSelfAttention()` class defined in chapter 12.

14.3.2 *Building a music Transformer*

We combine a feed-forward network with the causal self-attention sublayer to form a decoder block (i.e., a decoder layer). We apply layer normalization and a residual connection to each sublayer for improved stability and performance. To this end, we define a `Block()` class in the local module to create a decoder block, which is identical to the `Block()` class we defined in chapter 12.

We then stack six decoder blocks on top of each other to form the main body of our music Transformer. To achieve this, we define a `Model()` class in the local module. As in all GPT models we have seen in this book, we use learned positional encoding by employing the `Embedding()` class in PyTorch, instead of the fixed positional encoding in the original 2017 paper "Attention Is All You Need." Refer to chapter 11 on the differences between the two positional encoding methods.

The input to the model consists of sequences of indexes corresponding to musical event tokens in the vocabulary. We pass the input through word embedding and positional encoding and add the two to form the input embedding. The input embedding then goes through the six decoder layers. After that, we apply layer normalization to the output and attach a linear head to it so that the number of outputs is 390, the size of the vocabulary. The outputs are the logits corresponding to the 390 tokens in the vocabulary. Later, we'll apply the softmax activation function to the logits to obtain the probability distribution over the unique music tokens in the vocabulary when generating music.

Next, we'll create our music Transformer by instantiating the `Model()` class we defined in the local module:

```
from utils.ch14util import Model

model=Model(config)
model.to(device)
num=sum(p.numel() for p in model.transformer.parameters())
print("number of parameters: %.2fM" % (num/1e6,))
print(model)
```

The output is

```
number of parameters: 20.16M
Model(
  (transformer): ModuleDict(
    (wte): Embedding(390, 512)
    (wpe): Embedding(2048, 512)
    (drop): Dropout(p=0.1, inplace=False)
    (h): ModuleList(
      (0-5): 6 x Block(
        (ln_1): LayerNorm((512,), eps=1e-05, elementwise_affine=True)
```

```
      (attn): CausalSelfAttention(
        (c_attn): Linear(in_features=512, out_features=1536, bias=True)
        (c_proj): Linear(in_features=512, out_features=512, bias=True)
        (attn_dropout): Dropout(p=0.1, inplace=False)
        (resid_dropout): Dropout(p=0.1, inplace=False)
      )
      (ln_2): LayerNorm((512,), eps=1e-05, elementwise_affine=True)
      (mlp): ModuleDict(
        (c_fc): Linear(in_features=512, out_features=2048, bias=True)
        (c_proj): Linear(in_features=2048, out_features=512, bias=True)
        (act): GELU()
        (dropout): Dropout(p=0.1, inplace=False)
      )
    )
  )
  (ln_f): LayerNorm((512,), eps=1e-05, elementwise_affine=True)
 )
 (lm_head): Linear(in_features=512, out_features=390, bias=False)
)
```

Our music Transformer consists of 20.16 million parameters, a figure substantially smaller than the GPT-2XL, which boasts over 1.5 billion parameters. Nonetheless, our music Transformer surpasses the size of the text generator we constructed in chapter 12, which contains only 5.12 million parameters. Despite these differences, all three models are based on the decoder-only Transformer architecture. The variations lie solely in the hyperparameters, such as the embedding dimension, number of decoder layers, vocabulary size, and so on.

14.4 *Training and using the music Transformer*

In this section, you'll train the music Transformer you've just constructed using the batches of training data we prepared earlier in this chapter. To expedite the process, we'll train the model for 100 epochs and then stop the training process. For those interested, you can utilize the validation set to determine when to stop training, based on the performance of the model on the validation set, as we did in chapter 2.

Once the model is trained, we'll provide it with a prompt in the form of a sequence of indexes. We'll then request the trained music Transformer to generate the next index. This new index is appended to the prompt, and the updated prompt is fed back into the model for another prediction. This process is repeated iteratively until the sequence reaches a certain length.

Unlike the music generated in chapter 13, we can control the creativity of the music piece by applying different temperatures.

14.4.1 *Training the music Transformer*

As always, we'll use the Adam optimizer for training. Given that our music Transformer is essentially executing a multicategory classification task, we'll utilize cross-entropy loss as our loss function:

```
lr=0.0001
optimizer = torch.optim.Adam(model.parameters(), lr=lr)
loss_func=torch.nn.CrossEntropyLoss(ignore_index=389)
```

The ignore_index=389 argument in the previous loss function instructs the program to disregard index 389 whenever it occurs in the target sequence (i.e., sequence y), as this index is used solely for padding purposes and does not represent any specific event token in the music piece.

We will then train the model for 100 epochs.

Listing 14.6 Training the music Transformer to generate music

```
model.train()
for i in range(1,101):
    tloss = 0.
    for idx, (x,y) in enumerate(trainloader):        ◀─── Iterates through all
        x,y=x.to(device),y.to(device)                     batches of training data
        output = model(x)
        loss=loss_func(output.view(-1,output.size(-1)),   ◀─── Compares model
                       y.view(-1))                              predictions with
                                                                actual outputs
        optimizer.zero_grad()
        loss.backward()
        nn.utils.clip_grad_norm_(model.parameters(),1)    ◀─── Clips gradient
        optimizer.step()                                       norm to 1
        tloss += loss.item()                           ◀───
    print(f'epoch {i} loss {tloss/(idx+1)}')                Tweaks model
torch.save(model.state_dict(),f'files/musicTrans.pth')  ◀───  parameters to
                                                              minimize loss

                                                         Saves model
                                                         after training
```

During training, we feed all the input sequences x in a batch through the model to obtain predictions. We then compare these predictions with the corresponding output sequences y in the batch and calculate the cross-entropy loss. After that, we adjust the model parameters to minimize this loss. It's important to note that we've clipped the gradient norm to 1 to prevent the potential problem of exploding gradients.

The training process described above takes approximately 3 hours if you have a CUDA-enabled GPU. After training, the trained model weights, musicTrans.pth, are saved on your computer. Alternatively, you can download the trained weights from my website at https://mng.bz/V2pW.

14.4.2 Music generation with the trained Transformer

Now that we have a trained music Transformer, we can proceed with music generation.

Similar to the process in text generation, music generation begins with feeding a sequence of indexes (representing event tokens) to the model as a prompt. We'll select a music piece from the test set and use the first 250 musical events as the prompt:

```
from utils.processor import decode_midi

prompt, _ = test[42]
prompt = prompt.to(device)
```

```
len_prompt=250
file_path = "files/prompt.midi"
decode_midi(prompt[:len_prompt].cpu().numpy(),
            file_path=file_path)
```

We have randomly selected an index (42, in our case) and used it to retrieve a song from the test subset. We keep only the first 250 musical events, which we'll later feed to the trained model to predict the next musical events. For comparison purposes, we'll save the prompt as a MIDI file, prompt.midi, in the local folder.

Exercise 14.2

Use the `decode_midi()` function to convert the first 250 musical events in the second music piece in the test set into a MIDI file. Save it as prompt2.midi on your computer.

To streamline the music generation process, we'll define a `sample()` function. This function accepts a sequence of indexes as input, representing a short piece of music. It then iteratively predicts and appends new indexes to the sequence until a specified length, `seq_length`, is achieved. The implementation is shown in the following listing.

Listing 14.7   A `sample()` function in music generation

```
softmax=torch.nn.Softmax(dim=-1)
def sample(prompt,seq_length=1000,temperature=1):
    gen_seq=torch.full((1,seq_length),389,dtype=torch.long).to(device)
    idx=len(prompt)
    gen_seq[..., :idx]=prompt.type(torch.long).to(device)
    while(idx < seq_length):
        y=softmax(model(gen_seq[..., :idx])/temperature)[...,:388]
        probs=y[:, idx-1, :]
        distrib=torch.distributions.categorical.Categorical(probs=probs)
        next_token=distrib.sample()
        gen_seq[:, idx]=next_token
        idx+=1
    return gen_seq[:, :idx]
```

Generates the new indexes until the sequence reaches a certain length

Divides the prediction by the temperature and then applies the softmax function on logits

Samples from the predicted probability distribution to generate a new index

Outputs the whole sequence

One of the parameters of the `sample()` function is temperature, which regulates the creativity of the generated music. Refer to chapter 8 on how this works if needed. Since we can adjust the originality and diversity of the generated music with the temperature parameter alone, we have omitted `top-K` sampling for simplicity in this instance. As we have discussed `top-K` sampling three times earlier in this book (in chapters 8, 11, and 12), interested readers can experiment with incorporating `top-K` sampling into the `sample()` function here.

Next, we'll load the trained weights into the model:

```
model.load_state_dict(torch.load("files/musicTrans.pth",
    map_location=device))
model.eval()
```

We then call the `sample()` function to generate a piece of music:

```
from utils.processor import encode_midi

file_path = "files/prompt.midi"
prompt = torch.tensor(encode_midi(file_path))
generated_music=sample(prompt, seq_length=1000)
```

First, we utilize the `encode_midi()` function from the processor.py module to convert the MIDI file, prompt.midi, into a sequence of indexes. We then use this sequence as the prompt in the `sample()` function to generate a music piece comprising 1,000 indexes.

Finally, we convert the generated sequence of indexes into the MIDI format:

```
music_data = generated_music[0].cpu().numpy()
file_path = 'files/musicTrans.midi'
decode_midi(music_data, file_path=file_path)
```

We employ the `decode_midi()` function in the processor.py module to transform the generated sequence of indexes into a MIDI file, musicTrans.midi, on your computer. Open both files, prompt.midi and musicTrans.midi, on your computer and listen to them. The music from prompt.midi lasts about 10 seconds. The music from music-Trans.midi lasts about 40 seconds, with the final 30 seconds being new music generated by the music Transformer. The generated music should sound like the music piece on my website: https://mng.bz/x6dg.

The preceding code block may produce output similar to the following:

```
info removed pitch: 52
info removed pitch: 83
info removed pitch: 55
info removed pitch: 68
```

In the generated music, there may be instances where certain notes need to be removed. For example, if the generated music piece attempts to turn off note 52, but note 52 was never turned on initially, then we cannot turn it off. Therefore, we need to remove such notes.

Exercise 14.3

Generate a piece of music consisting of 1,200 notes using the trained Music Transformer model, keeping the temperature parameter at 1. Use the sequence of indexes from the file prompt2.midi you just generated in exercise 14.2 as the prompt. Save the generated music in a file named musicTrans2.midi on your computer.

You can increase the creativity of the music by setting the temperature argument to a value greater than 1, as follows:

```
file_path = "files/prompt.midi"
prompt = torch.tensor(encode_midi(file_path))
generated_music=sample(prompt, seq_length=1000,temperature=1.5)
music_data = generated_music[0].cpu().numpy()
file_path = 'files/musicHiTemp.midi'
decode_midi(music_data, file_path=file_path)
```

We set the temperature to 1.5. The generated music is saved as musicHiTemp.midi on your computer. Open the file and listen to the generated music to see if you can discern any differences compared to the music in the file musicTrans.midi.

Exercise 14.4

Generate a piece of music consisting of 1,000 indexes using the trained Music Transformer model, setting the temperature parameter to 0.7. Use the sequence of indexes in the file prompt.midi as the prompt. Save the generated music in a file named musicLowTemp.midi on your computer. Open this file to listen to the generated music and see if there are any discernible differences between the new piece of music and the music in the file musicTrans.midi.

In this chapter, you've learned how to construct and train a music Transformer from scratch, based on the decoder-only Transformer architecture you used in earlier chapters. In the next chapter, you'll explore diffusion-based models, which are at the heart of text-to-image Transformers such as OpenAI's DALL-E 2 and Google's Imagen.

Summary

- The performance-based representation of music enables us to represent a music piece as a sequence of notes, which include control messages and velocity values. These notes can be further reduced to four kinds of musical events: note-on, note-off, time-shift, and velocity. Each event type can assume various values. Consequently, we can transform a music piece into a sequence of tokens and then into indexes.

- A music Transformer adapts the Transformer architecture, originally designed for NLP tasks, for music generation. This model is designed to generate sequences of musical notes by learning from a large dataset of existing music. It is trained to predict the next note in a sequence based on previous notes, by recognizing patterns, structures, and relationships among various musical elements in the training data.

- Just as in text generation, we can use temperature to regulate the creativity of the generated music.

15

Diffusion models and text-to-image Transformers

This chapter covers

- How forward diffusion and reverse diffusion work
- How to build and train a denoising U-Net model
- Using the trained U-Net to generate flower images
- Concepts behind text-to-image Transformers
- Writing a Python program to generate an image through text with DALL-E 2

In recent years, multimodal large language models (LLMs) have gained significant attention for their ability to handle various content formats, such as text, images, video, audio, and code. A notable example of this is text-to-image Transformers, such as OpenAI's DALL-E 2, Google's Imagen, and Stability AI's Stable Diffusion. These models are capable of generating high-quality images based on textual descriptions.

These text-to-image models comprise three essential components: a text encoder that compresses text into a latent representation, a method to incorporate text information into the image generation process, and a diffusion mechanism to gradually refine an image to produce realistic output. Understanding the diffusion mechanism is particularly crucial for comprehending text-to-image Transformers, as diffusion models form the foundation of all leading text-to-image Transformers. For this reason, you will start by building and training a diffusion model to generate flower images in this chapter. This will provide you with a deep understanding of the forward diffusion process, where noise is incrementally added to images until they become random noise. Subsequently, you will train a model to reverse the diffusion process by gradually removing noise from images until the model can generate a new, clean image from random noise, resembling those in the training dataset.

Diffusion models have become the go-to choice for generating high-resolution images. The success of diffusion models lies in their ability to simulate and reverse a complex noise addition process, which mimics a deep understanding of how images are structured and how to construct them from abstract patterns. This method not only ensures high quality but also maintains a balance between diversity and accuracy in the generated images.

After that, we'll explain how a text-to-image Transformer works conceptually. We'll focus on the contrastive language–image pretraining (CLIP) model developed by OpenAI, which is designed to comprehend and link visual and textual information. CLIP processes two types of inputs: images and text (typically in the form of captions or descriptions). These inputs are handled separately through two encoders in the model.

The image branch of CLIP employs a Vision Transformer (ViT) to encode images into a high-dimensional vector space, extracting visual features in the process. Meanwhile, the text branch uses a Transformer-based language model to encode textual descriptions into the same vector space, capturing semantic features from the text. CLIP has been trained on many pairs of matching images and text descriptions to closely align the representations of matching pairs in the vector space.

OpenAI's text-to-image Transformers, such as DALL-E 2, incorporate CLIP as a core component. In this chapter, you'll learn to obtain an OpenAI API key and write a Python program to generate images using DALL-E 2 based on text descriptions.

15.1   Introduction to denoising diffusion models

The concept of diffusion-based models can be illustrated using the following example. Consider the goal of generating high-resolution flower images using a diffusion-based model. To do that, you first acquire a set of high-quality flower images for training. The model is then instructed to incrementally introduce small amounts of random noise into these images, a process known as forward diffusion. After many steps of adding noise, the training images eventually become random noise. The next phase involves training the model to reverse this process, starting with pure noise images and progressively reducing the noise until the images are indistinguishable from those in the original training set.

Once trained, the model is given random noise images to work with. It systematically eliminates noise from the image over many iterations until it generates a high-resolution flower image that resembles those in the training set. This is the underlying principle of diffusion-based models.[1]

In this section, you will first explore the mathematical foundations of diffusion-based models. Then you will dive into the architecture of U-Nets, the type of model used for denoising images and producing high-resolution flower images. Specifically, the U-Net employs a scaled dot product attention (SDPA) mechanism, similar to what you have seen in Transformer models in chapters 9 to 12. Finally, you will learn the training process of diffusion-based models and the image-generation process of the trained model.

15.1.1 The forward diffusion process

Several papers have proposed diffusion-based models with similar underlying mechanisms.[2] Let's use the flower images as a concrete example to explain the idea behind denoising diffusion models. Figure 15.1 is a diagram of how the forward diffusion process works.

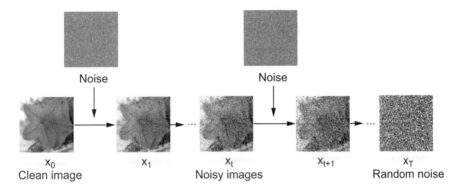

Figure 15.1 **A diagram of the forward diffusion process. We start with a clean image from the training set, x_0, and add noise ϵ_0 to it to form a noisy image $x_1 = \sqrt{(1 - \beta_1)}x_0 + \sqrt{(\beta_1)}\epsilon_0$. We repeat this process for 1,000 time steps until the image x_{1000} becomes random noise.**

Assume that flower images, x_0 (illustrated in the left image in figure 15.1), follow a distribution of $q(x)$. In the forward diffusion process, we'll add small amounts of noise to the images in each of the $T = 1,000$ steps. The noise tensor is normally distributed and has the same shape as the flower images: (3, 64, 64), meaning three color channels, with a height and width of 64 pixels.

[1] Jascha Sohl-Dickstein, Eric A. Weiss, Niru Maheswaranathan, and Surya Ganguli, 2015, "Deep Unsupervised Learning Using Nonequilibrium Thermodynamics." International Conference on Machine Learning, http://arxiv.org/abs/1503.03585.

[2] Sohl-Dickstein et al., 2015, "Deep Unsupervised Learning Using Nonequilibrium Thermodynamics," https://arxiv.org/abs/1503.03585. Yang Song and Stefano Ermon, 2019, "Generative Modeling by Estimating Gradients of the Data Distribution." https://arxiv.org/abs/1907.05600. Jonathan Ho, Ajay Jain, and Pieter Abbeel, 2020, "Denoising Diffusion Probabilistic Models," https://arxiv.org/abs/2006.11239.

Time steps in diffusion models

In diffusion models, time steps refer to the discrete stages during the process of gradually adding noise to data and subsequently reversing this process to generate samples. The forward phase of a diffusion model progressively adds noise over a series of time steps, transforming data from its original, clean state into a noisy distribution. During the reverse phase, the model operates over a similar series of time steps but in a reverse order. It systematically removes noise from the data to reconstruct the original or generate new, high-fidelity samples. Each time step in this reverse process involves predicting the noise that was added in the corresponding forward step and subtracting it, thereby gradually denoising the data until reaching a clean state.

In time step 1, we add noise ϵ_0 to the image x_0, so that we obtain a noisy image x_1:

$$x_1 = \sqrt{1 - \beta_1}x_0 + \sqrt{\beta_1}\epsilon_0 \qquad (15.1)$$

That is, x_1 is a weighted sum of x_0 and ϵ_0, where β_1 measures the weight placed on the noise. The value of β changes in different time steps—hence the subscript in β_1. If we assume x_0 and ϵ_0 are independent of each other and follow a standard normal distribution (i.e., with mean 0 and variance 1), the noisy image x_1 will also follow a standard normal distribution. This is easy to prove since

$$\text{mean}(x_1) = \sqrt{1 - \beta_1}\text{mean}(x_0) + \sqrt{\beta_1}\text{mean}(\epsilon_0) = 0$$

and

$$\text{var}(x_1) = \text{var}\left(\sqrt{1 - \beta_1}x_0\right) + \text{var}\left(\sqrt{\beta_1}\epsilon_0\right)$$
$$= (1 - \beta_1)\text{var}(x_0) + \beta_1\text{var}(\epsilon_0) = 1 - \beta_1 + \beta_1 = 1$$

We can keep adding noise to the image for the next T–1 time steps so that

$$x_{t+1} = \sqrt{1 - \beta_{t+1}}x_t + \sqrt{\beta_{t+1}}\epsilon_t \qquad (15.2)$$

We can use a reparameterization trick and define $\alpha_t = 1 - \beta_t$ and

$$\bar{\alpha}_t = \prod_{k=1}^{t} \alpha_k$$

to allow us to sample x_t at any arbitrary time step t, where t can take any value in [1, 2, ..., T–1, T]. Then we have

$$x_t = \sqrt{\bar{\alpha}_t}x_0 + \sqrt{1 - \bar{\alpha}_t}\,\epsilon \qquad (15.3)$$

Where ϵ is a combination of ϵ_0, ϵ_1, . . ., and ϵ_{t-1}, using the fact that we can add two normal distributions to obtain a new normal distribution. See, for example, the blog of Lilian Weng at https://mng.bz/Aalg for proof.

The farther left of figure 15.1 shows a clean flower, x_0, from the training set. In the first time step, we inject noise ϵ_0 to it to form a noisy image x_1 (second image in figure 15.1). We repeat this process for 1,000 time steps, until the image becomes random noise (the rightmost image).

15.1.2 *Using the U-Net model to denoise images*

Now that you understand the forward diffusion process, let's discuss the reverse diffusion process (i.e., the denoising process). If we can train a model to reverse the forward diffusion process, we can feed the model with random noise and ask it to produce a noisy flower image. We can then feed the noisy image to the trained model again and produce a clearer, though still noisy, image. We can iteratively repeat the process for many time steps until we obtain a clean image, indistinguishable from images from the training set. The use of multiple inference steps in the reverse diffusion process, rather than just a single step, is crucial for gradually reconstructing high-quality data from a noisy distribution. It allows for a more controlled, stable, and high-quality generation of data.

To that end, we'll create a denoising U-Net model. The U-Net architecture, which was originally designed for biomedical image segmentation, is characterized by its symmetric shape, with a contracting path (encoder) and an expansive path (decoder), connected by a bottleneck layer. In the context of denoising, U-Net models are adapted to remove noise from images while preserving important details. U-Nets outperform simple convolutional networks in denoising tasks due to their efficient capturing of local and global features in images.

Figure 15.2 is a diagram of the structure of the denoising U-Net we use in this chapter.

The model takes a noisy image and the time step the noisy image is in (x_t and t in equation 15.3) as input and predicts the noise in the image (i.e., ϵ). Since the noisy image is a weighted sum of the original clean image and noise (see equation 15.3), knowing the noise allows us to deduce and reconstruct the original image.

The contracting path (i.e., the encoder; left side of figure 15.2) consists of multiple convolutional layers and pooling layers. It progressively downsamples the image, extracting and encoding features at different levels of abstraction. This part of the network learns to recognize patterns and features that are relevant for denoising.

The bottleneck layer (bottom of figure 15.2) connects the encoder and decoder paths. It consists of convolutional layers and is responsible for capturing the most abstract representations of the image.

The expansive path (i.e., the decoder; right side of figure 15.2) consists of upsampling layers and convolutional layers. It progressively upsamples the feature maps, reconstructing the image while incorporating features from the encoder through skip connections. Skip connections (denoted by dashed lines in figure 15.2) are crucial in

U-Net models, as they allow the model to retain fine-grained details from the input image by combining low-level and high-level features. Next, I briefly explain how skip connections work.

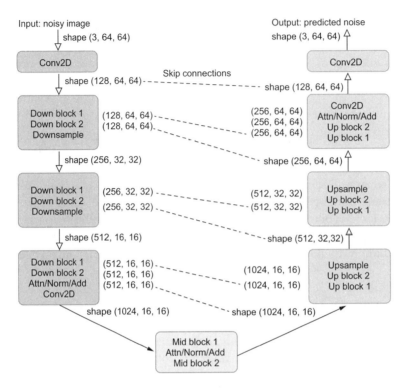

Figure 15.2   The architecture of the denoising U-Net model. The U-Net architecture is characterized by its symmetric shape, with a contracting path (encoder) and an expansive path (decoder), connected by a bottleneck layer. The model is designed to remove noise from images while preserving important details. The input to the model is a noisy image, along with which time step the image is in, and the output is the predicted noise in the image.

In a U-Net model, skip connections are implemented by concatenating feature maps from the encoder path with corresponding feature maps in the decoder path. These feature maps are typically of the same spatial dimensions but may have been processed differently due to the separate paths they have traversed. During the encoding process, the input image is progressively downsampled, and some spatial information (such as edges and textures) may be lost. Skip connections help preserve this information by directly passing feature maps from the encoder to the decoder, bypassing the information bottleneck.

For example, the dashed line at the top of figure 15.2 indicates that the model concatenates the *output* from the Conv2D layer in the encoder, which has a shape of (128, 64, 64), with the *input* to the Conv2D layer in the decoder, which also has a shape of (128, 64, 64). As a result, the final input to the Conv2D layer in the decoder has a shape of (256, 64, 64).

By combining high-level, abstract features from the decoder with low-level, detailed features from the encoder, skip connections enable the model to better reconstruct fine details in the denoised image. This is particularly important in denoising tasks, where retaining subtle image details is crucial.

The scaled dot product attention (SDPA) mechanism is implemented in both the final block of the contracting path and the final block of the expansive path in our denoising U-Net model, accompanied by layer normalization and residual connections (as shown in figure 15.2 with the label Attn/Norm/Add). This SDPA mechanism is essentially the same as the one we developed in chapter 9; the key difference is its application to image pixels rather than text tokens.

The use of skip connections and the model's size lead to redundant feature extractions in our denoising U-Net, ensuring that no important feature is lost during the denoising process. However, the large size of the model also complicates the identification of relevant features, akin to searching for a needle in a haystack. The attention mechanism empowers the model to emphasize significant features while disregarding irrelevant ones, thereby enhancing the effectiveness of the learning process.

15.1.3 A blueprint to train the denoising U-Net model

The output of the denoising U-Net is the noise injected into the noisy image. The model is trained to minimize the difference between the output (predicted noise) and the ground truth (actual noise).

The denoising U-Net model uses the U-Net architecture's ability to capture both local and global context, making it effective for removing noise while preserving important details such as edges and textures. These models are widely used in various applications, including medical image denoising, photographic image restoration, and more. Figure 15.3 is a diagram of the training process of our denoising U-Net model.

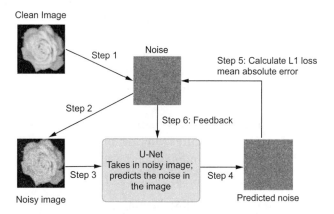

Figure 15.3   The training process of the denoising U-Net model. We first obtain clean flower images as our training set. We add noise to clean flower images and present them to the U-Net model. The model predicts the noise in the noisy images. We compare the predicted noise with the actual noise injected into the flower images and tweak the model weights to minimize the mean absolute error.

The first step is to gather a dataset of flower images. We'll use the Oxford 102 Flower dataset as our training set. We'll resize all images to a fixed resolution of 64 × 64 pixels and normalize pixel values to the range [−1, 1]. For denoising, we need pairs of clean and noisy images. We'll synthetically add noise to the clean flower images to create noisy counterparts (step 2 in figure 15.3) based on the formula specified in equation 15.3.

We'll then build a denoising U-Net model with a structure as outlined in figure 15.2. During each epoch of training, we iterate over the dataset in batches. We add noise to the flower images and present the noisy images to the U-Net model (step 3), along with the time steps the noisy images are in, t. The U-Net model predicts the noise in the noisy images (step 4) based on current parameters in the model.

We compare the predicted noise with the actual noise and calculate the L1 loss (i.e., mean absolute error) at the pixel level (step 5). L1 loss is usually preferred in such situations because it's less sensitive to outliers compared to the L2 loss (mean squared error). We then tweak the model parameters to minimize the L1 loss (step 6) so that in the next iteration, the model makes better predictions. We repeat this process for many iterations until the model parameters converge.

15.2   *Preparing the training data*

We'll use the Oxford 102 Flower dataset, which is freely available on Hugging Face, as our training data. The dataset contains about 8,000 flower images and can be down-loaded directly by using the *datasets* library you installed earlier.

To save space, we'll place most helper functions and classes in two local modules, ch15util.py and unet_util.py. Download these two files from the book's GitHub repos-itory (https://github.com/markhliu/DGAI) and place them in the /utils/ folder on your computer. The Python programs in this chapter are adapted from Hugging Face's GitHub repository (https://github.com/huggingface/diffusers) and Filip Basara's GitHub repository (https://github.com/filipbasara0/simple-diffusion).

You'll use Python to download the dataset to your computer. After that, we'll demon-strate the forward diffusion process by gradually adding noise to clean images in the training dataset until they become random noise. Finally, you'll place the training data in batches so that we can use them to train the denoising U-Net model later in the chapter.

You'll use the following Python libraries in this chapter: datasets, einops, diffusers, and openai. To install these libraries, execute the following line of code in a new cell in your Jupyter Notebook application on your computer:

```
!pip install datasets einops diffusers openai
```

Follow the on-screen instructions to finish the installation.

15.2.1   *Flower images as the training data*

The `load_dataset()` method from the *datasets* library you installed earlier allows you to directly download the Oxford 102 Flower dataset from Hugging Face. We'll then use the *matplotlib* library to show some flower images in the dataset so that we have an idea of what the images in the training dataset look like.

Run the lines of code shown in the following listing in a cell in Jupyter Notebook.

Listing 15.1 Downloading and visualizing flower images

```
from datasets import load_dataset
from utils.ch15util import transforms

dataset = load_dataset("huggan/flowers-102-categories",
    split="train",)
dataset.set_transform(transforms)

import matplotlib.pyplot as plt
from torchvision.utils import make_grid

# Plot all the images of the 1st batch in grid
grid = make_grid(dataset[:16]["input"], 8, 2)
plt.figure(figsize=(8,2),dpi=300)
plt.imshow(grid.numpy().transpose((1,2,0)))
plt.axis("off")
plt.show()
```

◄── Downloads the images from Hugging Face

◄── Plots the first 16 images

After running the preceding code listing, you'll see the first 16 flower images in the dataset, as displayed in figure 15.4. These are high-resolution color images of various types of flowers. We have standardized the size of each image to (3, 64, 64).

Figure 15.4   The first 16 Images from the Oxford 102 Flower dataset.

We place the dataset in batches of 4 so that we can use them to train the denoising U-Net model later. We choose a batch size of 4 to keep the memory size small enough to fit on a GPU during training. Adjust the batch size to 2 or even 1 if your GPU memory is small:

```
import torch

resolution=64
batch_size=4
train_dataloader=torch.utils.data.DataLoader(
    dataset, batch_size=batch_size, shuffle=True)
```

Next, we'll code in and visualize the forward diffusion process.

15.2.2 *Visualizing the forward diffusion process*

We have defined a class `DDIMScheduler()` in the local module ch15util.py you just downloaded. Take a look at the class in the file; we'll use it to add noise to images. We'll also use the class to produce clean images later, along with the trained denoising U-Net model. The `DDIMScheduler()` class manages the step sizes and sequence of denoising steps, enabling deterministic inference that can produce high-quality samples through the denoising process.

We first select four clean images from the training set and generate noise tensors that have the same shape as these images:

```
clean_images=next(iter(train_dataloader))["input"]*2-1   ◄─── Obtains four
print(clean_images.shape)                                      clean images
nums=clean_images.shape[0]
noise=torch.randn(clean_images.shape)   ◄─── Generates a tensor, noise, which has the
print(noise.shape)                           same shape as the clean images; each
                                             value in the noise follows an independent
                                             standard normal distribution.
```

The output from the preceding code block is

```
torch.Size([4, 3, 64, 64])
torch.Size([4, 3, 64, 64])
```

Both the images and the noise tensors have a shape of $(4, 3, 64, 64)$, meaning 4 images in the batch and 3 color channels per image, and the height and width of the images are 64 pixels.

During the forward diffusion process, there are 999 transitional noisy images between the clean images (x_0 as we explained in the first section) and random noise (x_T). The transitional noisy images are a weighted sum of the clean image and the noise. As t goes from 0 to 1,000, the weight on the clean image gradually decreases, and the weight on the noise gradually increases, as specified in equation 15.3.

Next, we generate and visualize some transitional noisy images.

Listing 15.2   Visualizing the forward diffusion process

```
from utils.ch15util import DDIMScheduler                        Instantiates the
                                                                DDIMScheduler() class
noise_scheduler=DDIMScheduler(num_train_timesteps=1000)   ◄──┘  with 1,000 time steps
allimgs=clean_images
for step in range(200,1001,200):                          ◄─┐  Looks at time steps 200,
    timesteps=torch.tensor([step-1]*4).long()               │  400, 600, 800, and 1,000
    noisy_images=noise_scheduler.add_noise(clean_images,
                noise, timesteps)                         ◄─┐  Creates noisy images
    allimgs=torch.cat((allimgs,noisy_images))             ◄─┘  at these time steps

import torchvision
imgs=torchvision.utils.make_grid(allimgs,4,6)                   Concatenates noisy
fig = plt.figure(dpi=300)                                       images with clean images
plt.imshow((imgs.permute(2,1,0)+1)/2)                     ◄───  Displays all images
plt.axis("off")
plt.show()
```

The `add_noise()` method in the `DDIMScheduler()` class takes three arguments: `clean_images`, `noise`, and `timesteps`. It produces a weighted sum of the clean image and the noise, which is a noisy image. Further, the weight is a function of the time step, t. As the time step, t, moves from 0 to 1,000, the weight on the clean image decreases and that on the noise increases. If you run the previous code listing, you'll see an image similar to figure 15.5.

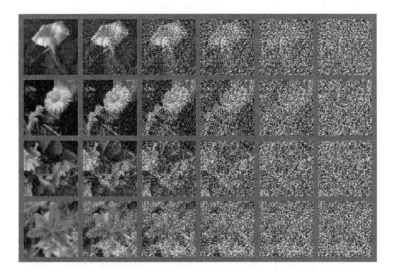

Figure 15.5   The forward diffusion process. The four images in the first column are clean images from the training dataset. We then gradually add noise to these images from time step 1 to time step 1,000. As the time step increases, more and more noise is injected into the images. The four images in the second column are images after 200 time steps. The third column contains images after 400 time steps, and they have more noise than those in the second column. The last column contains images after 1,000 time steps, and they are 100% random noise.

The first column contains the four clean images without noise. As we move to the right, we gradually add more and more noise to the images. The very last column contains pure random noise.

15.3 *Building a denoising U-Net model*

Earlier in this chapter, we discussed the architecture of the denoising U-Net model. In this section, I will guide you through implementing it using Python and PyTorch.

The U-Net model we are going to construct is quite large, containing over 133 million parameters, reflecting the complexity of its intended task. It is engineered to capture both local and global features within an image through a process of downsampling and upsampling the input. The model uses multiple convolutional layers interconnected by skip connections, which combine features from various levels of the network. This architecture helps maintain spatial information, facilitating more effective learning.

Given the substantial size of the denoising U-Net model and its redundant feature extraction, the SDPA attention mechanism is employed to enable the model to concentrate on the most relevant aspects of the input for the task at hand. To compute SDPA attention, we will flatten the image and treat its pixels as a sequence. We will then use SDPA to learn the dependencies among different pixels in the image in a manner akin to how we learned dependencies among different tokens in text in chapter 9.

15.3.1 *The attention mechanism in the denoising U-Net model*

To implement the attention mechanism, we have defined an `Attention()` class in the local module ch15util.py, as shown in the following code listing.

Listing 15.3   The attention mechanism in the denoising U-Net model

```
import torch
from torch import nn, einsum
from einops import rearrange

class Attention(nn.Module):
    def __init__(self, dim, heads=4, dim_head=32):
        super().__init__()
        self.scale = dim_head**-0.5
        self.heads = heads
        hidden_dim = dim_head * heads
        self.to_qkv = nn.Conv2d(dim, hidden_dim * 3, 1, bias=False)
        self.to_out = nn.Conv2d(hidden_dim, dim, 1)
    def forward(self, x):
        b, c, h, w = x.shape
        qkv = self.to_qkv(x).chunk(3, dim=1)           # Passes the input through three linear layers to obtain query, key, and value
        q, k, v = map(
        lambda t: rearrange(t, 'b (h c) x y -> b h c (x y)', h=self.heads),
        qkv)                                            # Splits query, key, and value into four heads
        q = q * self.scale
        sim = einsum('b h d i, b h d j -> b h i j', q, k)   # Calculates attention weights
        attn = sim.softmax(dim=-1)
        out = einsum('b h i j, b h d j -> b h i d', attn, v)   # Calculates the attention vector in each head
        out = rearrange(out, 'b h (x y) d -> b (h d) x y', x=h, y=w)
        return self.to_out(out)                         # Concatenates the four attention vectors into one
attn=Attention(128)
x=torch.rand(1,128,64,64)
out=attn(x)
print(out.shape)
```

The output after running the preceding code listing is

```
torch.Size([1, 128, 64, 64])
```

The attention mechanism used here, SDPA, is the same as the one we utilized in chapter 9, where we applied SDPA to a sequence of indices representing tokens in text. Here, we apply it to pixels in an image. We treat the flattened pixels of an image as a sequence and use SDPA to extract dependencies among different areas of the input image, enhancing the efficiency of the denoising process.

Listing 15.3 demonstrates how SDPA operates in our context. To give you a concrete example, we have created a hypothetical image, x, with dimensions (1, 128, 64, 64), indicating one image in the batch, 128 feature channels, and a size of 64 × 64 pixels in each channel. The input x is then processed through the attention layer. Specifically, each feature channel in the image is flattened into a sequence of 64 × 64 = 4,096 pixels. This sequence is then passed through three distinct neural network layers to produce the query Q, key K, and value V, which are subsequently split into four heads. The attention vector in each head is calculated as follows:

$$\text{Attention } (Q, K, V) = \text{softmax} \left(\frac{Q * K^T}{\sqrt{d_k}} \right) * V$$

where d_k represents the dimension of the key vector K. The attention vectors from the four heads are concatenated back into a single attention vector.

15.3.2 *The denoising U-Net model*

In the local module unet_util.py you just downloaded, we have defined a UNet() class to represent the denoising U-Net model. Take a look at the definition in the file, and I'll provide a brief explanation of how it works later. The following code listing presents a portion of the UNet() class.

Listing 15.4 Defining the UNet() class

```
class UNet(nn.Module):
...
    def forward(self, sample, timesteps):
        if not torch.is_tensor(timesteps):
            timesteps = torch.tensor([timesteps],
                                dtype=torch.long,
                                device=sample.device)
        timesteps = torch.flatten(timesteps)
        timesteps = timesteps.broadcast_to(sample.shape[0])
        t_emb = sinusoidal_embedding(timesteps, self.hidden_dims[0])
        t_emb = self.time_embedding(t_emb)
        x = self.init_conv(sample)
        r = x.clone()
        skips = []
        for block1, block2, attn, downsample in self.down_blocks:
            x = block1(x, t_emb)
            skips.append(x)
            x = block2(x, t_emb)
            x = attn(x)
            skips.append(x)
            x = downsample(x)
        x = self.mid_block1(x, t_emb)
        x = self.mid_attn(x)
        x = self.mid_block2(x, t_emb)
        for block1, block2, attn, upsample in self.up_blocks:
            x = torch.cat((x, skips.pop()), dim=1)
            x = block1(x, t_emb)
            x = torch.cat((x, skips.pop()), dim=1)
```

The model takes a batch of noisy images and the time steps as input.

The embedded time steps are added to the images as inputs in various stages.

Passes the input through the contracting path

Passes the input through the bottleneck path

Passes the input through the expansive path, with skip connections

```
        x = block2(x, t_emb)
        x = attn(x)
        x = upsample(x)
    x = self.out_block(torch.cat((x, r), dim=1), t_emb)
    out = self.conv_out(x)
    return {"sample": out}
```

> **The output is the predicted noise in the input images.**

The job of the denoising U-Net is to predict the noise in the input images based on the time steps these images are in. As described in equation 15.3, a noisy image at any time step t, x_t, can be represented as a weighted sum of the clean image, x_o, and standard normally distributed random noise, ϵ. The weight assigned to the clean image decreases, and the weight assigned to the random noise increases as the time step t progresses from 0 to T. Therefore, to deduce the noise in noisy images, the denoising U-Net needs to know which time step a noisy image is in.

Time steps are embedded using sine and cosine functions in a manner akin to positional encoding in Transformers (discussed in chapters 9 and 10), resulting in a 128-value vector. These embeddings are then expanded to match the dimensions of the image features at various layers within the model. For instance, in the first down block, the time embeddings are broadcasted to a shape of (128, 64, 64) before being added to the image features, which also have dimensions of (128, 64, 64).

Next, we create a denoising U-Net model by instantiating the UNet() class in the local module:

```
from utils.unet_util import UNet

device="cuda" if torch.cuda.is_available() else "cpu"
resolution=64
model=UNet(3,hidden_dims=[128,256,512,1024],
           image_size=resolution).to(device)
num=sum(p.numel() for p in model.parameters())
print("number of parameters: %.2fM" % (num/1e6,))
print(model)
```

The output is

```
number of parameters: 133.42M
```

The model has more than 133 million parameters, as you can see from the previous output. Given the large number of parameters, the training process in this chapter will be time-consuming, requiring approximately 3 to 4 hours of GPU training. However, for those who do not have access to GPU training, the trained weights are also available on my website. The link to these weights will be provided in the following section.

15.4   *Training and using the denoising U-Net model*

Now that we have both the training data and the denoising U-Net model, we're ready to train the model using the training data.

During each training epoch, we'll cycle through all the batches in the training data. For each image, we'll randomly select a time step and add noise to the clean images in the training data based on this time step value, resulting in a noisy image. These noisy images and their corresponding time step values are then fed into the denoising U-Net model to predict the noise in each image. We compare the predicted noise to the ground truth (the actual noise added to the image) and adjust the model parameters to minimize the mean absolute error between the predicted and actual noise.

After training, we'll use the trained model to generate flower images. We'll perform this generation in 50 inference steps (i.e., we'll set time step values to 980, 960, . . ., 20, and 0). Starting with random noise, we'll input it into the trained model to obtain a noisy image. This noisy image is then fed back into the trained model to denoise it. We repeat this process for 50 inference steps, resulting in an image that is indistinguishable from the flowers in the training set.

15.4.1 *Training the denoising U-Net model*

Next, we'll first define the optimizer and the learning rate scheduler for the training process.

We'll use the AdamW optimizer, a variant of the Adam optimizer that we have been using throughout this book. The AdamW optimizer, first proposed by Ilya Loshchilov and Frank Hutter, decouples weight decay (a form of regularization) from the optimization steps.[3] Instead of applying weight decay directly to the gradients, AdamW applies weight decay directly to the parameters (weights) after the optimization step. This modification helps achieve better generalization performance by preventing the decay rate from being adapted along with the learning rates. Interested readers can learn more about the AdamW optimizer in the original paper by Loshchilov and Hutter.

We will also use a learning rate scheduler from the diffusers library to adjust the learning rate during the training process. Initially using a higher learning rate can help the model escape local minima, while gradually lowering the learning rate in later stages of training can help the model converge more steadily and accurately towards a global minimum. The learning rate scheduler is defined as shown in the following listing.

> #### Listing 15.5 Choosing the optimizer and learning rate in training

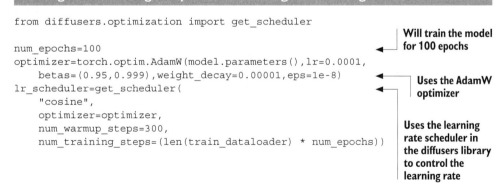

```
from diffusers.optimization import get_scheduler

num_epochs=100                                              ◀─── Will train the model
optimizer=torch.optim.AdamW(model.parameters(),lr=0.0001,        for 100 epochs
    betas=(0.95,0.999),weight_decay=0.00001,eps=1e-8)      ◀───┐ Uses the AdamW
lr_scheduler=get_scheduler(                                 ◀──┘ optimizer
    "cosine",
    optimizer=optimizer,                                        Uses the learning
    num_warmup_steps=300,                                       rate scheduler in
    num_training_steps=(len(train_dataloader) * num_epochs))    the diffusers library
                                                                to control the
                                                                learning rate
```

[3] Ilya Loshchilov and Frank Hutter, 2017, "Decoupled Weight Decay Regularization." https://arxiv.org/abs/1711.05101.

The exact definition of the `get_scheduler()` function is defined on GitHub by Hugging Face: https://mng.bz/ZVo5. In the first 300 training steps (warmup steps), the learning rate increases linearly from 0 to 0.0001 (the learning rate we set in the AdamW optimizer). After 300 steps, the learning rate decreases following the values of the cosine function between 0.0001 and 0. We train the model for 100 epochs in the following listing.

Listing 15.6   Training the denoising U-Net model

```
for epoch in range(num_epochs):
    model.train()
    tloss = 0
    print(f"start epoch {epoch}")
    for step, batch in enumerate(train_dataloader):
        clean_images = batch["input"].to(device)*2-1
        nums = clean_images.shape[0]
        noise = torch.randn(clean_images.shape).to(device)
        timesteps = torch.randint(0,
                noise_scheduler.num_train_timesteps,
                (nums, ),
                device=device).long()
        noisy_images = noise_scheduler.add_noise(clean_images,
                  noise, timesteps)


        noise_pred = model(noisy_images,
                    timesteps)["sample"]
        loss=torch.nn.functional.l1_loss(noise_pred, noise)
        loss.backward()
        optimizer.step()
        lr_scheduler.step()
        optimizer.zero_grad()
        tloss += loss.detach().item()
        if step%100==0:
            print(f"step {step}, average loss {tloss/(step+1)}")
    torch.save(model.state_dict(),'files/diffusion.pth')
```

Adds noise to clean images in the training set

Uses the denoising U-Net to predict noise in noisy images

Compares the predicted noise with the actual noise to calculate the loss

Tweaks model parameters to minimize the mean absolute error

During each epoch, we cycle through all batches of clean flower images in the training set. We introduce noise to these clean images and feed them to the denoising U-Net to predict the noise in these images. We then compare the predicted noise to the actual noise and adjust the model parameters to minimize the mean absolute error (pixelwise) between the two.

The training process described here takes several hours with GPU training. After training, the trained model weights are saved on your computer. Alternatively, you can download the trained weights from my website at https://mng.bz/RNlD. Unzip the file after downloading.

15.4.2 *Using the trained model to generate flower images*

To generate flower images, we'll use 50 inference steps. This means we'll look at 50 equally spaced time steps between t = 0 and t = T, with T = 1,000 in our case. Therefore, the 50 inference time steps are t = 980, 960, 940, . . . , 20, and 0. We'll start with pure random noise, which corresponds to the image at t = 1000. We use the trained denoising U-Net model to denoise it and create a noisy image at t = 980. We then present the noisy image at t = 980 to the trained model to denoise it and obtain the noisy image at t = 960. We repeat the process for many iterations until we obtain an image at t = 0, which is a clean image. This process is implemented through the `generate()` method in the `DDIMScheduler()` class within the local module ch15util.py.

Listing 15.7 Defining a `generate()` method in the `DDIMScheduler()` class

```
@torch.no_grad()
def generate(self,model,device,batch_size=1,generator=None,
     eta=1.0,use_clipped_model_output=True,num_inference_steps=50):
     imgs=[]
     image=torch.randn((batch_size,model.in_channels,model.sample_size,
model.sample_size),
          generator=generator).to(device)          ◀── Uses random noise as the starting
                                                        point (i.e., image at t = 1,000)
     self.set_timesteps(num_inference_steps)         ◀── Uses 50 inference time steps
     for t in tqdm(self.timesteps):                      (t = 980, 960, 940, .., 20, 0)
          model_output = model(image, t)["sample"]   ◀─┐
          image = self.step(model_output,t,image,eta,   Uses the trained
               use_clipped_model_output=\              denoising U-Net model
               use_clipped_model_output)              to predict noise
          img = unnormalize_to_zero_to_one(image)    ◀── Creates an image based
          img = img.cpu().permute(0, 2, 3, 1).numpy()    on predicted noise
          imgs.append(img)                           ◀─┐
     image = unnormalize_to_zero_to_one(image)          Saves intermediate
     image = image.cpu().permute(0, 2, 3, 1).numpy()    images in a list, imgs
     return {"sample": image}, imgs
```

In this `generate()` method, we have also created a list, imgs, to store all intermediate images at time steps t = 980, 960,. . . , 20, and 0. We'll use them to visualize the denoising process later. The `generate()` method returns a dictionary with the generated images and the list, imgs.

Next, we'll use the previous `generate()` method to create 10 clean images.

Listing 15.8 Image generation with the trained denoising U-Net model

```
sd=torch.load('files/diffusion.pth',map_location=device)
model.load_state_dict(sd)
with torch.no_grad():
     generator = torch.manual_seed(1)              ◀── Sets the random seed
     generated_images,imgs = noise_scheduler.generate(   to 1 so results are
          model,device,                                  reproducible
          num_inference_steps=50,
```

```
        generator=generator,
        eta=1.0,
        use_clipped_model_output=True,
        batch_size=10)
imgnp=generated_images["sample"]
import matplotlib.pyplot as plt
plt.figure(figsize=(10,4),dpi=300)
for i in range(10):
    ax = plt.subplot(2,5, i + 1)
    plt.imshow(imgnp[i])
    plt.xticks([])
    plt.yticks([])
    plt.tight_layout()
plt.show()
```

◄────┐ **Uses the defined generate()
     │ method to create 10 clean images**

◄──────── **Plots the generated images**

We set the random seed to 1. As a result, if you use the trained model from my website, you'll get identical results as shown in figure 15.6. We use the generate() method defined earlier to create 10 clean images, using 50 inference steps. We then plot the 10 images in a 2 × 5 grid, as shown in figure 15.6.

Figure 15.6   Flower images created by the trained denoising U-Net model.

As you can see from figure 15.6, the generated flower images look real and resemble those in the training dataset.

Exercise 15.1
Modify code listing 15.8 and change the random seed to 2. Keep the rest of the code the same. Rerun the code listing and see what the generated images look like.

The generate() method also returns a list, imgs, which contains all the images in the 50 intermediate steps. We'll use them to visualize the denoising process.

Listing 15.9   Visualizing the denoising process

```
steps=imgs[9::10]
imgs20=[]
for j in [1,3,6,9]:
    for i in range(5):
```

◄────┐ **Keeps time steps 800,
     │ 600, 400, 200, and 0**

```
        imgs20.append(steps[i][j])
plt.figure(figsize=(10,8),dpi=300)
for i in range(20):
    k=i%5
    ax = plt.subplot(4,5, i + 1)
    plt.imshow(imgs20[i])
    plt.xticks([])
    plt.yticks([])
    plt.tight_layout()
    plt.title(f't={800-200*k}',fontsize=15,c="r")
plt.show()
```

◄───── Selects 4 sets of flowers out of 10

◄───── Plots the 20 images in a 4 × 5 grid

The list, imgs, contains 10 sets of images in all 50 inference steps, t = 980, 960, . . . , 20, 0. So there are a total of 500 images in the list. We select five time steps (t = 800, 600, 400, 200, and 0) for four different flowers (the 2nd, 4th, 7th, and 10th images in figure 15.6). We then plot the 20 images in a 4 × 5 grid, as shown in figure 15.7.

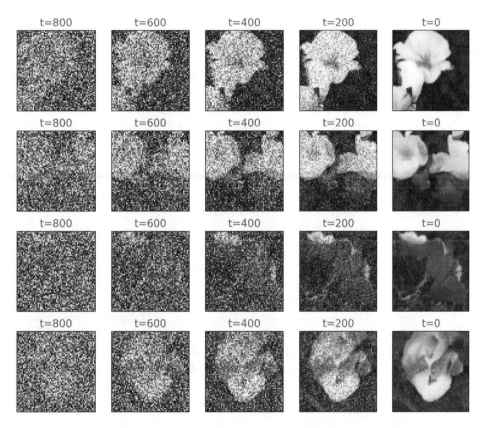

Figure 15.7 **How the trained denoising U-Net model gradually converts random noise into clean flower images. We feed random noise to the trained model to obtain the image at time step 980. We then feed the noisy image at t = 980 to the model to obtain the image at t = 960. We repeat this process 50 inference steps until we obtain the image at t = 0. The first column in this figure shows the four flowers at t = 800; the second column shows the same four flowers at t = 600 . . . ; the last column shows the four flowers at t = 0 (i.e., clean flower images).**

The first column in figure 15.7 shows the four flower images at t = 800. They are close to random noise. The second column shows the flowers at t = 600, and they start to look like flowers. As we move to the right, the images become clearer and clearer. The rightmost column shows the four clean flower images at t = 0.

Now that you understand how diffusion models work, we'll discuss text-to-image generation. The image generation process of text-to-image Transformers such as DALL-E 2, Imagen, and Stable Diffusion is very much like the reverse diffusion process we discussed earlier in the chapter, except that the model takes the text embedding as a conditioning signal when generating an image.

15.5   *Text-to-image Transformers*

Text-to-image Transformers such as OpenAI's DALL-E 2, Google's Imagen, and Stability AI's Stable Diffusion use diffusion models to generate images from textual descriptions. An important component of these text-to-image Transformers is a diffusion model. The process of text-to-image generation involves encoding the text input into a latent representation, which is then used as a conditioning signal for the diffusion model. These Transformers learn to generate lifelike images that correspond to the textual description by iteratively denoising a random noise vector, guided by the encoded text.

The key to all these text-to-image Transformers is a model to understand content in different modalities. In this case, the model must understand the text descriptions and link them to images and vice versa.

In this section, we'll use OpenAI's CLIP model as an example. CLIP is a key component in DALL-E 2. We'll discuss how CLIP was trained to understand the connection between text descriptions and images. We then use a short Python program to generate an image from a text prompt by using OpenAI's DALL-E 2.

15.5.1   *CLIP: A multimodal Transformer*

In recent years, the intersection of computer vision and natural language processing (NLP) has witnessed significant advancements, one of which is the creation of the CLIP model by OpenAI. This innovative model is designed to understand and interpret images in the context of natural language, a capability that holds immense potential for various applications such as image generation and image classification.

The CLIP model is a multimodal Transformer that bridges the gap between visual and textual data. It is trained to understand images by associating them with corresponding textual descriptions. Unlike traditional models that require explicit labeling of images, CLIP uses a vast dataset of images and their natural language descriptions to learn a more generalizable representation of visual concepts.

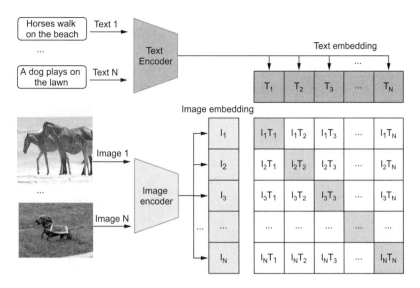

Figure 15.8 **How OpenAI's CLIP model is trained. A large-scale training dataset of text–image pairs is collected. The text encoder of the model compresses the text description into a D-value text embedding. The image encoder converts the corresponding image into an image embedding also with D values. During training, a batch of N text–image pairs are converted to N text embeddings and N image embeddings. CLIP uses a contrastive learning approach to maximize the similarity between paired embeddings (the sum of diagonal values in the figure) while minimizing the similarity between embeddings from nonmatching text–image pairs (the sum of off-diagonal values in the figure).**

The training of the CLIP model, which is illustrated in figure 15.8, begins with the collection of a large-scale dataset comprising images and their associated textual descriptions. OpenAI utilizes a diverse set of sources, including publicly available datasets and web-crawled data, to ensure a wide variety of visual and textual content. The dataset is then preprocessed to standardize the images so they all have the same shape and to tokenize the text, preparing them for input into the model.

CLIP employs a dual-encoder architecture, consisting of an image encoder and a text encoder. The image encoder processes the input images while the text encoder processes the corresponding textual descriptions. These encoders project the images and text into a shared embedding space where they can be compared and aligned.

The core of CLIP's training lies in its contrastive learning approach. For each batch of N image–text pairs in the dataset, the model aims to maximize the similarity between paired embeddings (measured by the sum of diagonal values in figure 15.8) while minimizing the similarity between embeddings from nonmatching text-image pairs (the sum of off-diagonal values). Figure 15.9 is a diagram of how text-to-image Transformers such as DALL-E 2 generate realistic images based on text prompts.

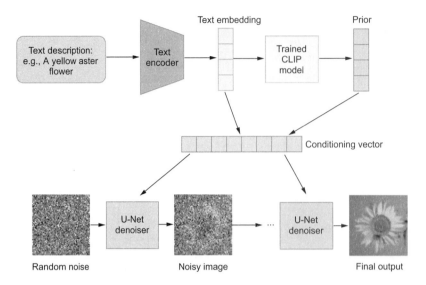

Figure 15.9 How text-to-image Transformers such as DALL-E 2 create images based on text prompts. The text encoder in the trained text-to-image Transformer first converts the text description in the prompt into text embedding. The text embedding is fed to the CLIP model to obtain a prior vector that represents the image in the latent space. The text embedding and the prior are concatenated into a conditioning vector. To generate an image, the U-Net denoiser first takes a random noise vector as input to generate a noisy image using the conditioning vector. It then takes the noisy image and the conditioning vector as input and generates another image, which is less noisy. The process is repeated for many iterations until the final output, a clean image, is generated.

The image generation process of text-to-image Transformers is similar to the reverse diffusion process we discussed earlier in the chapter. Let's take DALL-E 2, for example, which was proposed by OpenAI researchers in 2022.[4] The text encoder in the model first converts the text description in the prompt into a text embedding. The text embedding is fed to the CLIP model to obtain a prior vector that represents the image in the latent space. The text embedding and the prior are concatenated into a conditioning vector. In the first iteration, we feed a random noise vector to the U-Net denoiser in the model and ask it to generate a noisy image based on the conditioning vector. In the second iteration, we feed the noisy image from the previous iteration to the U-Net denoiser and ask it to generate another noisy image based on the conditioning vector. We repeat this process for many iterations, and the final output is a clean image.

15.5.2 *Text-to-image generation with DALL-E 2*

Now that you understand how text-to-image Transformers work, let's write a Python program to interact with DALL-E 2 to create an image based on a text prompt.

---

[4] Aditya Rames, Prafulla Dhariwal, Alex Nichol, Casey Chu, and Mark Chen, 2022, "Hierarchical Text-Conditional Image Generation with CLIP Latents." https://arxiv.org/abs/2204.06125.

First, you need to apply for an OpenAI API key. OpenAI offers various pricing tiers that vary based on the number of tokens processed and the type of models used. Go to https://chat.openai.com/auth/login and click on the Sign up button to create an account. After that, log in to your account, and go to https://platform.openai.com/api-keys to view your API key. Save it in a secure place for later use. We can generate an image by using OpenAI's DALL-E 2.

Listing 15.10 Image generation with DALL-E 2

```
from openai import OpenAI

openai_api_key=your actual OpenAI API key here, in quotes   ◄─┐  Makes sure you
client=OpenAI(api_key=openai_api_key)          ◄──────────────┘  provide your actual
                                                                 OpenAI API key
                                                                 here, in quotes

                                              Instantiates the OpenAI()
                                              class to create an agent
response = client.images.generate(
  model="dall-e-2",
  prompt="an astronaut in a space suit riding a unicorn",
  size="512x512",
  quality="standard",
  n=1,                          Uses the images.generate() method to
)                               generate image based on the text prompt
image_url = response.data[0].url
print(image_url)                                       Prints out the
                                                ◄───── image URL
```

You should place the OpenAI API key you obtained earlier in listing 15.10. We create an agent by instantiating the `OpenAI()` class. To generate an image, we need to specify the model, a text prompt, and the size of the image. We have used "an astronaut in a space suit riding a unicorn" as the prompt, and the code listing provides a URL for us to visualize and download the image. The URL expires in an hour, and the resulting image is shown in figure 15.10.

**Figure 15.10
An image
generated by
DALL-E 2 with
the text prompt
"an astronaut
in a space suit
riding a unicorn"**

Run listing 15.10 yourself and see what image DALLE-2 generates for you. Note that your result will be different since the output from DALLE-2 (and all LLMs) is stochastic rather than deterministic.

Exercise 15.2

Apply for an OpenAI API key. Then modify code listing 15.10 to generate an image using the text prompt "a cat in a suit working on a computer."

In this chapter, you learned the inner workings of diffusion-based models and their significance in text-to-image Transformers, such as OpenAI's CLIP model. You also discovered how to obtain your OpenAI API key and used a brief Python script to generate images from text descriptions with DALL-E 2, which incorporates CLIP.

In the next chapter, you will continue to use the OpenAI API key obtained earlier to use pretrained LLMs for generating diverse content, including text, audio, and images. Additionally, you will integrate the LangChain Python library with other APIs, enabling you to create a know-it-all personal assistant.

Summary

- In forward diffusion, we gradually add small amounts of random noise to clean images until they transform into pure noise. Conversely, in reverse diffusion, we begin with random noise and employ a denoising model to progressively eliminate noise from the images, transforming the noise back into a clean image.

- The U-Net architecture, originally designed for biomedical image segmentation, has a symmetric shape with a contracting encoder path and an expansive decoder path, connected by a bottleneck layer. In denoising, U-Nets are adapted to remove noise while preserving details. Skip connections link encoder and decoder feature maps of the same spatial dimensions, helping to preserve spatial information like edges and textures that may be lost during downsampling in the encoding process.

- Incorporating an attention mechanism into a denoising U-Net model enables it to concentrate on important features and disregard irrelevant ones. By treating image pixels as a sequence, the attention mechanism learns pixel dependencies, similar to how it learns token dependencies in NLP. This enhances the model's ability to identify relevant features effectively.

- Text-to-image Transformers like OpenAI's DALL-E 2, Google's Imagen, and Stability AI's Stable Diffusion use diffusion models to create images from textual descriptions. They encode the text into a latent representation that conditions the diffusion model, which then iteratively denoises a random noise vector, guided by the encoded text, to generate lifelike images matching the textual description.

Pretrained large language models and the LangChain library

This chapter covers

- Using pretrained large language models for text, image, speech, and code generation
- Few-shot, one-shot, and zero-shot prompting techniques
- Creating a zero-shot personal assistant with LangChain
- Limitations and ethical concerns of generative AI

The rise of pretrained large language models (LLMs) has transformed the field of natural language processing (NLP) and generative tasks. OpenAI's GPT series, a notable example, showcases the extensive capabilities of these models in producing life-like text, images, speech, and even code. The effective utilization of these pretrained LLMs is essential for several reasons. It enables us to deploy advanced AI functionalities without the need for vast resources to develop and train these models. Moreover, understanding these LLMs paves the way for innovative applications that leverage NLP and generative AI, fostering progress across various industries.

In a world increasingly influenced by AI, mastering the integration and customization of pretrained LLMs offers a crucial competitive advantage. As AI evolves, leveraging these sophisticated models becomes vital for innovation and success in the digital landscape.

Typically, these models are operated through browser-based interfaces, which vary across different LLMs that function independently of each other. Each model has unique strengths and specialties. Interfacing through a browser limits our ability to fully take advantage of the potential of each specific LLM. Utilizing programming languages like Python, particularly through tools such as the LangChain library, provides substantial benefits for the following reasons.

Python's role in interacting with LLMs enhances the automation of workflows and processes. Python scripts, capable of running autonomously, facilitate uninterrupted operations without the need for manual input. This is especially beneficial for businesses that regularly handle large amounts of data. For instance, a Python script could autonomously generate monthly reports by querying an LLM, synthesizing the data insights, and disseminating these findings via email or into a database. Python offers a greater level of customization and control in managing interactions with LLMs than browser-based interfaces do, enabling us to craft custom code to meet specific operational needs such as implementing conditional logic, processing multiple requests in loops, or managing exceptions. This adaptability is essential for customizing outputs to meet particular business objectives or research inquiries.

Python's extensive collection of libraries makes it ideally suited for integrating LLMs with existing software and systems. A prime example of this is the LangChain library, which extends Python's functionality with LLMs. LangChain enables the combination of multiple LLMs or the integration of LLM capabilities with other services, such as the Wikipedia API or the Wolfram Alpha API, which will be covered later in this chapter. This capability of "chaining" different services allows for the construction of sophisticated, multistep AI systems where tasks are segmented and handled by the best-suited models or services, enhancing both performance and accuracy.

To that end, in this chapter, you'll first learn how to use the OpenAI API to create various content using Python programming: text, images, speech, and Python code. You'll also learn the difference between few-shot, one-shot, and zero-shot content generation. Few-shot prompting means you give the model multiple examples to help it understand the task, while one-shot or zero-shot prompting means one example or no example is provided.

Modern LLMs such as ChatGPT are trained on preexisting knowledge a few months ago so they cannot provide recent or real-time information such as weather conditions, flight status, or stock prices. You'll learn to combine LLMs with Wolfram Alpha and Wikipedia APIs using the LangChain library to create a zero-shot know-it-all personal assistant.

Despite LLMs' impressive capabilities, they do not possess an intrinsic understanding of the content. This can lead to errors in logic, factual inaccuracies, and a failure to grasp complex concepts or nuances. The rapid advancement and widespread application of these models also lead to various ethical concerns such as bias, misinformation, privacy, and copyright. These issues demand careful consideration and proactive measures to ensure that the development and deployment of LLMs align with ethical standards and societal values.

16.1 Content generation with the OpenAI API

While there are other LLMs such as Meta's LLAMA and Google's Gemini, OpenAI's GPT series is the most prominent one. We therefore use OpenAI GPTs as our examples in this chapter.

OpenAI allows you to use LLMs to generate various content such as text, images, audio, and code. You can access their service either through a web browser or an API. We'll focus on content generation with Python programs via an API in this chapter due to the advantages of interacting with LLMs using Python mentioned earlier.

You do need your OpenAI API key for the programs in this chapter to work. I assume you have already obtained your API key in chapter 15. If not, go back to chapter 15 for detailed instructions on how to get one.

I'll focus mainly on text generation in this section but will provide an example for each of the cases of code, image, and speech generation.

This chapter involves the use of several new Python libraries. To install them, run the following lines of code in a new cell in your Jupyter Notebook app on your computer:

```
!pip install --upgrade openai langchain_openai langchain
!pip install wolframalpha langchainhub
!pip install --upgrade --quiet wikipedia
```

Follow the on-screen instructions to finish the installation.

16.1.1 Text generation tasks with OpenAI API

You can generate text for many different purposes, such as question-answering, text summarization, and creative writing.

When you ask OpenAI GPT a question, keep in mind that all LLMs, including OpenAI GPTs, are trained on historical data gathered through automated web crawling. As of this writing, GPT-4 was trained using data up to December 2023, with a three-month lag. GPT-3.5 was trained on data up to September 2021.

Let's first ask GPT a question about historical facts. Enter the lines of code in the following listing in a new cell.

Listing 16.1 Checking historical facts with OpenAI API

```
from openai import OpenAI

openai_api_key=put your actual OpenAI API key here, in quotes    ◄── Provides your OpenAI API key
client=OpenAI(api_key=openai_api_key)    ◄── Creates an OpenAI() class instance and names it client

completion = client.chat.completions.create(
```

```
    model="gpt-3.5-turbo",                                         Defines the role
    messages=[                                                     of the system
      {"role": "system", "content":
        '''You are a helpful assistant, knowledgeable about recent facts.'''},
      {"role": "user", "content":
        '''Who won the Nobel Prize in Economics in 2000?'''}    ◄─── Asks the question
    ]
)
print(completion.choices[0].message.content)
```

Make sure you provide your OpenAI API key in the listing 16.1. We first instantiate the OpenAI() class and call it client. In the chat.completions.create() method, we specify the model as gpt-3.5-turbo. The site https://platform.openai.com/docs/models provides various models available. You can use either gpt-4 or gpt-3.5-turbo for text generation. The former provides better results but also incurs higher expenses. We'll use the latter for most cases since our examples are simple enough, so it provides equally good results.

The messages parameter in the preceding code block consists of several message objects, with each object containing a role (which can be "system," "user," or "assistant") and content. A system message determines the assistant's behavior; absent a system message, the default setting characterizes the assistant as "a helpful assistant." User messages include inquiries or remarks for the assistant to address. For instance, in the previous example, the user message is "Who won the Nobel Prize in Economics in 2000?" The output is

```
The Nobel Prize in Economics in 2000 was awarded to James J. Heckman and
Daniel L. McFadden for their work on microeconometrics and microeconomic
theory.
```

OpenAI has provided the correct answer.

You can also ask the LLM to write an essay on a certain topic. Next, we ask it to write a short essay on the importance of self-motivation:

```
completion = client.chat.completions.create(
    model="gpt-3.5-turbo",
    n=1,
    messages=[
      {"role": "system", "content":
        '''You are a helpful assistant, capable of writing essays.'''},
      {"role": "user", "content":
        '''Write a short essay on the importance of self-motivation.'''}
    ]
)
print(completion.choices[0].message.content)
```

The n=1 argument here tells the assistant to generate one response. If you want multiple responses, you can set n to a different number. The default value for n is 1. The output is

```
Self-motivation is a key factor in achieving success and personal growth in
 various aspects of life. It serves as the driving force behind our
 actions, decisions, and goals, pushing us to overcome obstacles and
 challenges along the way.

One of the primary benefits of self-motivation is that it helps individuals
 take initiative and control of their lives…
```

The output is six paragraphs long, and I have included only the first few sentences. You can go to the book's GitHub repository (https://github.com/markhliu/DGAI) to see the whole essay. As you can see, the writing is coherent, to the point, and without grammatical errors.

You can even ask OpenAI's GPT to write a joke for you:

```
completion = client.chat.completions.create(
  model="gpt-3.5-turbo",
  messages=[
    {"role": "system", "content":
     '''You are a helpful assistant, capable of telling jokes.'''},
    {"role": "user", "content":
     '''Tell me a math joke.'''}
  ]
)
print(completion.choices[0].message.content)
```

We asked it to tell a math joke, and the result is

```
Why was the equal sign so humble? Because he knew he wasn't less than or
greater than anyone else!
```

You can carry out back-and-forth conversations with the assistant. The messages parameter automatically includes conversation history. For example, after running the previous code block, if you run the following:

```
completion = client.chat.completions.create(
  model="gpt-3.5-turbo",
  messages=[
    {"role": "user", "content":
     '''Haha, that's funny! Tell me another one.'''}
  ]
)
print(completion.choices[0].message.content)
```

you'll get a response similar to

```
Sure! Why was the math book sad? Because it had too many problems.
```

The user's query "Haha, that's funny! Tell me another one." only makes sense in the context of the prior messages where you ask the assistant to tell a math joke. Other text generation capabilities include text summarization and classification, and you'll see such examples later in the chapter.

16.1.2 Code generation with OpenAI API

Codex is specifically designed to understand and generate code. It can work with multiple programming languages and can translate natural language descriptions into code. Codex is now an integrated part of OpenAI GPTs.

Next, we ask OpenAI GPT to produce a Python program to plot a sine curve:

```
completion = client.chat.completions.create(
  model="gpt-3.5-turbo",
  messages=[
    {"role": "system", "content":
     '''You are a helpful assistant,
     capable of generating Python programs.'''},
    {"role": "user", "content":
     '''Write a Python program to plot a sine graph.'''}
  ]
)
print(completion.choices[0].message.content)
```

Note that ChatGPT uses GPT-3.5-Turbo to manage both the conversational aspect and the code generation tasks effectively. It does not provide a separate Codex model for code generation only. The output is

```
Sure! Here's a simple Python program using the matplotlib library to plot
a sine graph:

```python
import matplotlib.pyplot as plt
import numpy as np

# Generate x values from 0 to 2*pi
x = np.linspace(0, 2*np.pi, 100)

# Calculate y values using the sine function
y = np.sin(x)

# Plot the sine graph
plt.figure()
plt.plot(x, y)
plt.title('Sine Graph')
plt.xlabel('x')
plt.ylabel('sin(x)')
plt.grid(True)
plt.show()
```

You can run this program in a Python environment with the matplotlib
library installed to visualize the sine graph.
```

If you copy and paste the generated Python program into a cell in Jupyter Notebook and run it, you'll see an image similar to figure 16.1.

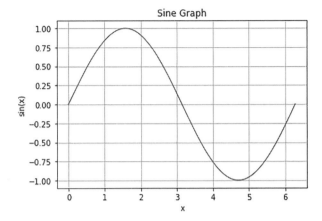

Figure 16.1　Use OpenAI GPT-3.5 to generate Python code to plot a sine curve. We use the text description "Write a Python program to plot a sine graph" to ask it to generate a Python program. We then run the program to create the graph.

The LLM not only provides the Python code, but it also lets you know that you need to run the code in a Python environment with the matplotlib library installed.

16.1.3　Image generation with OpenAI DALL-E 2

DALL-E 2 is an AI model developed by OpenAI, designed to generate images from textual descriptions. It is a successor to the original DALL-E model and represents advancements in the field of generative AI for visual content.

DALL-E 2 uses a diffusion model similar to what we discussed in chapter 15, which starts with a random pattern of pixels and gradually refines it into a coherent image that matches the input text. It has improved upon the original DALL-E by producing higher-quality images with more accurate and detailed representations of the textual descriptions.

Incorporating DALL-E 2 into OpenAI's GPT series allows us to not only generate text but also create images based on text prompts. Next, we ask DALL-E 2 to create an image of someone fishing at the riverbank:

```
response = client.images.generate(
  model="dall-e-2",
  prompt="someone fishing at the river bank",
  size="512x512",
  quality="standard",
  n=1,
)
image_url = response.data[0].url
print(image_url)
```

The code block generates a URL. If you click on the URL, you'll see an image similar to figure 16.2.

Figure 16.2 An image generated by DALL-E 2 with the text prompt "someone fishing at the riverbank"

The URL expires in an hour, so make sure you access it promptly. Furthermore, the image generated by DALL-E 2 is slightly different even if you use the same text prompt because the output is randomly generated.

16.1.4 *Speech generation with OpenAI API*

Text-to-speech (TTS) is a technology that converts written text into spoken words. TTS is trained through multimodal Transformers in which the input is text and the output is in audio format. In the context of ChatGPT, integrating TTS capabilities means that the LLM can not only generate textual responses but can also speak them out loud. Next, we ask OpenAI API to convert a short text into speech:

```
response = client.audio.speech.create(
  model="tts-1-hd",
  voice="shimmer",
  input='''This is an audio file generated by
    OpenAI's text to speech AI model.'''
)
response.stream_to_file("files/speech.mp3")
```

After running the previous code cell, a file, speech.mp3, is saved on your computer, and you can listen to it. The documentation site (https://platform.openai.com/docs/guides/text-to-speech) provides voice options. Here we have chosen the `shimmer` option. Other options include `alloy`, `echo`, and so on.

16.2 *Introduction to LangChain*

LangChain is a Python library designed to facilitate the use of LLMs in various applications. It provides a suite of tools and abstractions that make it easier to build, deploy, and manage applications powered by LLMs like GPT-3, GPT-4, and other similar models.

LangChain abstracts away the complexities of interacting with different LLMs and applications, allowing developers to focus on building their application logic without worrying about the underlying model specifics. It is particularly well suited for building a "know-it-all" agent by chaining together an LLM with applications like Wolfram Alpha and Wikipedia that can provide real-time information or recent facts. LangChain's modular architecture allows for easy integration of different components, enabling the agent to leverage the strengths of various LLMs and applications.

16.2.1 *The need for the LangChain library*

Imagine that your goal is to build a zero-shot know-it-all agent so that it can produce various content, retrieve real-time information, and answer factual questions for us. You want the agent to automatically go to the right source to retrieve the relevant information based on the task at hand without explicitly telling it what to do. The Lang-Chain library is the right tool for this.

In this project, you'll learn to use the LangChain library to combine LLMs with the Wolfram Alpha and Wikipedia APIs to create a zero-shot know-it-all agent. We use Wolfram Alpha API to retrieve real-time information and the Wikipedia API to answer questions about recent facts. LangChain allows us to create an agent to utilize multiple tools to answer a question. The agent first understands the query and then decides which tool in the toolbox to use to answer the question.

To show you that even the most advanced LLMs lack these abilities, let's ask who won the Best Actor Award in the 2024 Academy Awards:

```
completion = client.chat.completions.create(
  model="gpt-4",
  messages=[
    {"role": "system", "content":
    '''You are a helpful assistant, knowledgeable about recent facts.'''},
    {"role": "user", "content":
    '''Who won the Best Actor Award in 2024 Academy Awards?'''}
  ]
)
print(completion.choices[0].message.content)
```

The output is

```
I'm sorry, but I cannot provide real-time information or make predictions
about future events such as the 2024 Academy Awards. For the most accurate
and up-to-date information, I recommend checking reliable sources or news
outlets closer to the date of the awards show.
```

I made this query on March 17, 2024, and GPT-4 was not able to answer the question. It's possible that when you make the same query, you'll get the correct answer because the model has been updated using more recent data. If that's the case, change the question to an event a few days ago, and you should get a similar response.

Therefore, we'll use LangChain to chain together an LLM with the Wolfram Alpha and Wikipedia APIs. Wolfram Alpha is good at scientific computations and retrieving real-time information, while Wikipedia is famous for providing information on both historical and recent events and facts.

16.2.2 Using the OpenAI API in LangChain

The langchain-openai library you installed earlier in this chapter allows you to use OpenAI GPTs with minimal prompt engineering. You only need to explain what you want the LLM to do in plain English.

Here is an example of how we ask it to correct grammar errors in text:

```
from langchain_openai import OpenAI

llm = OpenAI(openai_api_key=openai_api_key)

prompt = """
Correct the grammar errors in the text:

i had went to stor buy phone. No good. returned get new phone.
"""

res=llm.invoke(prompt)
print(res)
```

The output is

```
I went to the store to buy a phone, but it was no good. I returned it and
got a new phone.
```

Note that we didn't use any prompt engineering. We didn't specify which model to use either. LangChain found the best model for the job based on the task requirements and other factors such as cost, latency, and performance. It also automatically formats and structures the queries to be suitable for the model it uses. The preceding prompt simply asks the agent, in plain English, to correct the grammar errors in the text. It returns text with the correct grammar, as shown in the previous output.

Here is another example. We asked the agent to name the capital city of Kentucky:

```
prompt = """
What is the capital city of the state of Kentucky?
"""
res=llm.invoke(prompt)
print(res)
```

The output is

```
The capital city of Kentucky is Frankfort.
```

It tells us the correct answer, which is Frankfort, Kentucky.

16.2.3 Zero-shot, one-shot, and few-shot prompting

Few-shot, one-shot, and zero-shot prompting refer to different ways of providing examples or instructions to LLMs to guide their responses. These techniques are used to help the model understand the task at hand and generate more accurate or relevant outputs.

In zero-shot prompting, the model is given a task or a question without any examples. The prompt typically includes a clear description of what is expected, but the model must generate a response based solely on its preexisting knowledge and understanding. In one-shot prompting, the model is provided with a single example to illustrate the task. In few-shot prompting, the model is given multiple examples to help it understand the task. Few-shot prompting is based on the idea that providing more examples can help the model better grasp the pattern or the rules of the task, leading to more accurate responses.

All your interactions so far with OpenAI GPTs are zero-shot prompting since you haven't provided them with any examples.

Let's try an example of few-shot prompting. Suppose you want the LLM to conduct sentiment analysis: you want it to classify a sentence as positive or negative. You can provide several examples in the prompt:

```
prompt = """
The movie is awesome! // Positive
It is so bad! // Negative
Wow, the movie was incredible! // Positive
How horrible the movie is! //
"""
res=llm.invoke(prompt)
print(res)
```

The output is

```
Negative
```

In the prompt, we provided three examples. Two reviews are classified as positive, while one is classified as negative. We then provided the sentence, "How horrible the movie is!" The LLM classified it correctly as negative.

We used // to separate the sentence and the corresponding sentiment in the previous example. You can use other separators such as ->, so long as you are consistent.

Here is an example of one-shot prompting:

```
prompt = """
Car -> Driver
Plane ->
"""
res=llm.invoke(prompt)
print(res)
```

The output is

```
Pilot
```

By providing one single example, we are effectively asking the LLM, "What is to a plane as a driver is to a car?" The LLM correctly answered `Pilot`.

Exercise 16.1

Suppose you want to ask the LLM, "What is to a garden as a chef is to a kitchen?" Use one-shot prompting to get the answer.

Finally, here is an example of zero-shot prompting:

```
prompt = """
Is the tone in the sentence "Today is a great day for me" positive,
negative, or neutral?
"""
res=llm.invoke(prompt)
print(res)
```

The output is

```
Positive
```

We didn't provide any examples in the prompt. However, we provided instruction in plain English to ask the LLM to classify the tone in the sentence as positive, negative, or neutral.

16.3   *A zero-shot know-it-all agent in LangChain*

You'll learn to create a zero-shot know-it-all agent in LangChain in this section. You'll use OpenAI GPTs to generate various content such as text, images, and code. To compensate for LLM's inability to provide real-time information, you'll learn to add Wolfram Alpha and Wikipedia APIs to the toolbox.

Wolfram Alpha is a computational knowledge engine designed to handle factual queries online, specializing in numerical and computational tasks, particularly in the science and technology fields. By integrating the Wolfram Alpha API, the agent gains the ability to answer virtually any question across various subjects. Should Wolfram Alpha be unable to provide a response, we will use Wikipedia as a secondary source for fact-based questions on specific topics.

Figure 16.3 is a diagram of the steps we'll take to create the zero-shot know-it-all agent in this section.

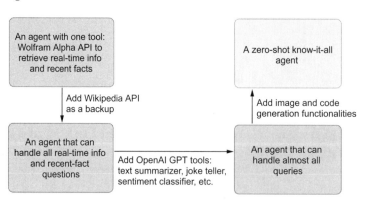

Figure 16.3 Steps to create a zero-shot know-it-all agent with the LangChain library

Specifically, we'll first create an agent in LangChain with just one tool—the Wolfram Alpha API—to answer questions related to real-time information and recent facts. We'll then add the Wikipedia API to the toolbox as a backup on questions related to recent facts. We'll add various tools utilizing the OpenAI API such as text summarizer, joke teller, and sentiment classifier. Finally, we'll add image and code generation functionalities.

16.3.1 Applying for a Wolfram Alpha API Key

Wolfram Alpha gives you up to 2,000 noncommercial API calls per month for free. To obtain an API key, first go to https://account.wolfram.com/login/create/ and complete the steps to create an account.

The Wolfram account itself gives you only browser access; you need to apply for an API key at https://products.wolframalpha.com/api/. Once there, click Get API Access in the bottom left corner. A small dialog should pop up, fill in the fields Name and Description, select Simple API from the dropdown menu, and then click Submit, as shown in figure 16.4.

Figure 16.4 Applying for a Wolfram Alpha AppID

After that, your AppID should appear in a new window. Copy the API key and save it in a file for later use.

Here is how you can use the Wolfram Alpha API to conduct math operations:

```
import os

os.environ['WOLFRAM_ALPHA_APPID'] = "your Wolfram Alpha AppID"

from langchain_community.utilities.wolfram_alpha import \
```

```
WolframAlphaAPIWrapper
wolfram = WolframAlphaAPIWrapper()
res=wolfram.run("how much is 23*55+123?")
print(res)
```

The output is

```
Assumption: 23×55 + 123
Answer: 1388
```

The Wolfram Alpha API provides the correct answer.

We'll also include the Wikipedia API to provide answers to various topics. You don't need to apply for an API key if you have installed the Wikipedia library on your computer. Here is an example of using the Wikipedia API in the LangChain library:

```
from langchain.tools import WikipediaQueryRun
from langchain_community.utilities import WikipediaAPIWrapper

wikipedia = WikipediaQueryRun(api_wrapper=WikipediaAPIWrapper())
res=wikipedia.run("University of Kentucky")
print(res)
```

The output is

```
Page: University of Kentucky
Summary: The University of Kentucky (UK, UKY, or U of K) is a public
land-grant research university in Lexington, Kentucky. Founded in 1865 by
John Bryan Bowman as the Agricultural and Mechanical College of Kentucky,
the university is one of the state's two land-grant universities (the
other being Kentucky State University)…
```

We have omitted most of the output for brevity.

16.3.2 Creating an agent in LangChain

Next, we'll create an agent in LangChain, with only the Wolfram Alpha API in the toolbox. An agent in this context refers to an individual entity designed to handle specific tasks or processes through natural language interactions. We'll then gradually add more tools to the chain so that the agent becomes capable of handling more tasks.

Listing 16.2   Creating an agent in LangChain

```
os.environ['OPENAI_API_KEY'] = openai_api_key
from langchain.agents import load_tools
from langchain_openai import ChatOpenAI
from langchain import hub
from langchain.agents import AgentExecutor, create_react_agent
from langchain_openai import OpenAI

prompt = hub.pull("hwchase17/react")          ◄── Defines which
llm = ChatOpenAI(model_name='gpt-3.5-turbo')       LLM to use
tool_names = ["wolfram-alpha"]
tools = load_tools(tool_names,llm=llm)         ◄── Adds Wolfram Alpha
agent = create_react_agent(llm, tools, prompt)     to the toolbox
agent_executor = AgentExecutor(agent=agent, tools=tools,
```

```
                handle_parsing_errors=True,verbose=True)
```
⟵ **Defines an agent**

```
res=agent_executor.invoke({"input": """
What is the temperature in Lexington, Kentucky now?
"""})
print(res["output"])
```
Asks the agent a question ⟵

The `hwchase17/react` in LangChain refers to a specific type of ReAct agent configuration. ReAct stands for Reactive Action, which is a framework within LangChain designed to optimize the use of language model capabilities in combination with other tools to solve complex tasks effectively. See https://python.langchain.com/docs/modules/agents/agent_types/react/ for more details. When you create an agent in LangChain, you need to specify the tools to be used by the agent. In the previous example, we use only one tool, the Wolfram Alpha API.

As an example, we ask the current temperature in Lexington, Kentucky, and here is the output:

```
> Entering new AgentExecutor chain...
I should use Wolfram Alpha to find the current temperature in Lexington,
Kentucky.
Action: wolfram_alpha
Action Input: temperature in Lexington, KentuckyAssumption: temperature |
Lexington, Kentucky
Answer: 44 °F (wind chill: 41 °F)
(27 minutes ago)I now know the current temperature in Lexington, Kentucky.
Final Answer: The temperature in Lexington, Kentucky is 44 °F with a wind
chill of 41 °F.

> Finished chain.
The temperature in Lexington, Kentucky is 44 °F with a wind chill of 41 °F.
```

The output not only shows the final answer, which says the current temperature in Lexington, Kentucky, is 44 degrees Fahrenheit, but it also shows the chain of thoughts. It uses Wolfram Alpha as the source to obtain the answer.

We can also add Wikipedia to the toolbox:

```
tool_names += ["wikipedia"]
tools = load_tools(tool_names,llm=llm)
agent = create_react_agent(llm, tools, prompt)
agent_executor = AgentExecutor(agent=agent, tools=tools,
        handle_parsing_errors=True,verbose=True)

res=agent_executor.invoke({"input": """
Who won the Best Actor Award in 2024 Academy Awards?
"""})
print(res["output"])
```

I ask who won the Best Actor Award in the 2024 Academy Awards, and the agent uses Wikipedia to get the correct answer:

```
I need to find information about the winner of the Best Actor Award at the
2024 Academy Awards.
Action: wikipedia
```

```
Action Input: 2024 Academy Awards Best Actor
...
Cillian Murphy won the Best Actor Award at the 2024 Academy Awards for his
performance in Oppenheimer.
```

In the preceding output, the agent first decides to use Wikipedia as the tool to solve the problem. After searching through various Wikipedia sources, the agent provides the correct answer.

Next, you'll learn to add various OpenAI GPT tools to the agent's toolbox.

16.3.3 Adding tools by using OpenAI GPTs

We first add a text summarizer so that the agent can summarize text.

Listing 16.3 Adding a text summarizer to the agent's tool box

```
from langchain.agents import Tool
from langchain.prompts import PromptTemplate
from langchain.chains import LLMChain

temp = PromptTemplate(input_variables=["text"],          ◀── Defines a template
template="Write a one sentence summary of the following text: {text}")

summarizer = LLMChain(llm=llm, prompt=temp)              ◀── Defines a summarizer
                                                              function
sum_tool = Tool.from_function(
    func=summarizer.run,
    name="Text Summarizer",
    description="A tool for summarizing texts")          ◀── Adds summarizer as a tool
tools+=[sum_tool]
agent = create_react_agent(llm, tools, prompt)           ◀── Redefines the agent
agent_executor = AgentExecutor(agent=agent, tools=tools,     with the updated
        handle_parsing_errors=True,verbose=True)             toolbox
res=agent_executor.invoke({"input":
'''Write a one sentence summary of the following text:
The University of Kentucky's Master of Science
 in Finance (MSF) degree prepares students for
 a professional career in the finance and banking
 industries. The program is designed to provide
 rigorous and focused training in finance,
 broaden opportunities in your career, and
 sharpened skills for the fast-changing
 and competitive world of modern finance.'''})
print(res["output"])
```

We first provide a template to summarize text. We then define a summarizer function and add it to the toolbox. Finally, we redefine the agent by using the updated toolbox and ask it to summarize the example text with one sentence. Make sure your prompt has the same format as those described in the template so that the agent knows which tool to use.

The output from listing 16.3 is

```
> Entering new AgentExecutor chain...
I need to summarize the text provided.
Action: Summarizer
...
> Finished chain.
The University of Kentucky's MSF program offers specialized training in
finance to prepare students for successful careers in the finance and
banking industries.
```

The agent chooses the summarizer as the tool for the task since the input matches the template described in the summarizer function. We use two long sentences as the text input and the preceding output is a one-sentence summary.

You can add as many tools as you like. For example, you can add a tool to tell a joke on a certain subject:

```
temp = PromptTemplate(input_variables=["text"],
template="Tell a joke on the following subject: {subject}")

joke_teller = LLMChain(llm=llm, prompt=temp)

tools+=[Tool.from_function(name='Joke Teller',
        func=joke_teller.run,
        description='A tool for telling jokes')]
agent = create_react_agent(llm, tools, prompt)
agent_executor = AgentExecutor(agent=agent, tools=tools,
        handle_parsing_errors=True,verbose=True)

res=agent_executor.invoke({"input":
'''Tell a joke on the following subject: coding'''})
print(res["output"])
```

The output is

```
> Entering new AgentExecutor chain...
I should use the Joke Teller tool to find a coding-related joke.
Action: Joke Teller
Action Input: coding
Observation: Why was the JavaScript developer sad?

Because he didn't know how to "null" his feelings.
Thought:That joke was funny!
Final Answer: Why was the JavaScript developer sad? Because he didn't know
how to "null" his feelings.

> Finished chain.
Why was the JavaScript developer sad? Because he didn't know how to "null"
his feelings.
```

We ask the agent to tell a joke on the subject of *coding*. The agent identifies *Joke Teller* as the tool. The joke is indeed related to coding.

> ### Exercise 16.2
>
> Add a tool to the agent's toolbox to conduct sentiment analysis. Name the tool Sentiment Classifier. Then ask the agent to classify the text "this movie is so-so" as positive, negative, or neutral.

16.3.4 *Adding tools to generate code and images*

You can add various tools to the toolbox in LangChain. Interested readers can find more details at https://python.langchain.com/docs/modules/tools/. Next, we add tools to generate other content forms such as code and images.

To add a tool to generate code, you can do the following:

```
temp = PromptTemplate(input_variables=["text"],
template='''Write a Python program based on the
    description in the following text: {text}''')

code_generator = LLMChain(llm=llm, prompt=temp)

tools+=[Tool.from_function(name='Code Generator',
        func=code_generator.run,
        description='A tool to generate code')]
agent = create_react_agent(llm, tools, prompt)
agent_executor = AgentExecutor(agent=agent, tools=tools,
        handle_parsing_errors=True,verbose=True)

res=agent_executor.invoke({"input":
'''Write a Python program based on the
    description in the following text:
write a python program to plot a sine curve and a cosine curve
in the same graph. The sine curve is in solid line and the cosine
curve is in dashed line. Add a legend to the graph. Set the x-axis
range to -5 to 5. The title should be "Comparing sine and cosine curves."
'''})
print(res["output"])
```

The output is

```
> Entering new AgentExecutor chain...
I should use the Code Generator tool to generate the Python program based on
the given description.
Action: Code Generator
Action Input: Write a Python program to plot a sine curve and a cosine
curve in the same graph. The sine curve is in solid line and the cosine
curve is in dashed line. Add a legend to the graph. Set the x-axis range
to -5 to 5. The title should be "Comparing sine and cosine curves."
Observation: import matplotlib.pyplot as plt
import numpy as np

x = np.linspace(-5, 5, 100)
y1 = np.sin(x)
y2 = np.cos(x)
```

```
plt.plot(x, y1, label='Sine Curve', linestyle='solid')
plt.plot(x, y2, label='Cosine Curve', linestyle='dashed')
plt.legend()
plt.title('Comparing Sine and Cosine Curves')
plt.xlim(-5, 5)
plt.show()
Thought:The Python program has been successfully generated to plot the sine
    and cosine curves. I now know the final answer.

Final Answer: The Python program to plot a sine curve and a cosine curve in
    the same graph with the specified requirements has been generated.

> Finished chain.
The Python program to plot a sine curve and a cosine curve in the same
graph with the specified requirements has been generated.
```

If you run the generated code in a cell, you'll see an image as in figure 16.5.

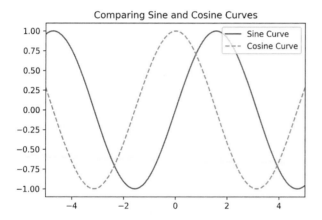

Figure 16.5   Adding a tool in LangChain to generate Python code. The tool then generates code to plot sine and cosine curves in the same graph, with a legend and line styles.

To add an image generator, you can do the following:

```
from langchain_community.utilities.dalle_image_generator import DallEAPIWrapper
temp = PromptTemplate(input_variables=["text"],
template="Create an image base on the following text: {text}")

grapher = LLMChain(llm=llm, prompt=temp)

tools+=[Tool.from_function(name='Text to image',
        func=grapher.run,
        description='A tool for text to image')]
agent = create_react_agent(llm, tools, prompt)
agent_executor = AgentExecutor(agent=agent, tools=tools,
        handle_parsing_errors=True, verbose=True)
image_url = DallEAPIWrapper().run(agent_executor.invoke({"input":
'''Create an image base on the following text:
    a horse grazes on the grassland.'''})["output"])
print(image_url)
```

The output is a URL for you to visualize and download an image. We asked the agent to create an image of a horse grazing on the grassland. The image is shown in figure 16.6.

Figure 16.6   An image generated by a know-it-all agent in LangChain

With that, you have learned how to create a zero-shot know-it-all agent in LangChain. You can add more tools to the toolbox depending on what you want the agent to accomplish.

16.4   *Limitations and ethical concerns of LLMs*

LLMs such as OpenAI's GPT series have made significant strides in the field of NLP and generative AI. Despite their impressive capabilities, these models are not without limitations. Understanding these constraints is crucial for both leveraging their strengths and mitigating their weaknesses.

At the same time, the rapid advancement and widespread application of these models have also given rise to a host of ethical concerns such as bias, inaccuracies, breach of privacy, and copyright infringements. These issues demand careful consideration and proactive measures to ensure that the development and deployment of LLMs align with ethical standards and societal values.

In this section, we'll explore the limitations of LLMs, provide insights into why these issues persist, and present examples of notable failures to underscore the importance of addressing these challenges. We'll also examine the key ethical concerns associated with LLMs and propose pathways for mitigating these concerns.

16.4.1   *Limitations of LLMs*

One of the fundamental limitations of LLMs is their lack of true understanding and reasoning. While they can generate coherent and contextually relevant responses, they do not possess an intrinsic understanding of the content. This can lead to errors in logic, factual inaccuracies, and a failure to grasp complex concepts or nuances.

This manifests in many epic mistakes made by LLMs. The book *Smart Until It's Dumb* provides many entertaining instances of such mistakes made by GPT-3 and ChatGPT.[1] For example, consider this question: Mrs. March gave the mother tea and gruel, while she dressed the little baby as tenderly as if it had been her own. Who's the baby's mother? The answer provided by GPT-3 is Mrs. March.

To be fair, with the rapid advancement of LLMs, many of these mistakes are corrected over time. However, LLMs still make low-level mistakes. A LinkedIn article in June 2023 by David Johnston (https://www.linkedin.com/pulse/intelligence-tests-llms-fail-why -david-johnston/) tests the intelligence of LLMs on a dozen problems that humans can easily solve. LLMs, including GPT-4, struggle with these problems. One of the problems is as follows: name an animal such that the length of the word is equal to the number of legs they have minus the number of tails they have.

This mistake has not been corrected as of this writing. Figure 16.7 is a screenshot of the answer by GPT-4 when I used a browser interface.

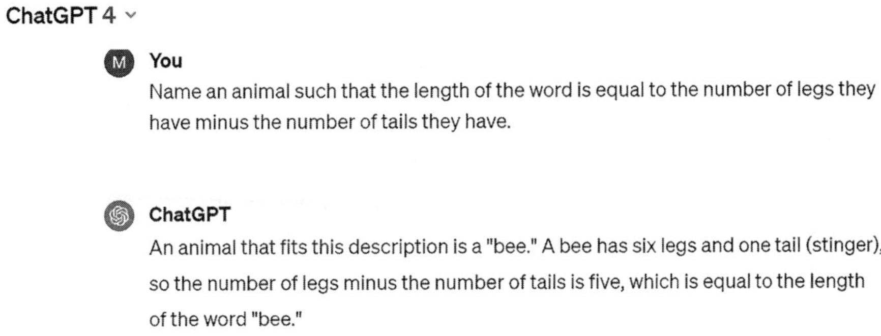

ChatGPT 4 ⌄

You
Name an animal such that the length of the word is equal to the number of legs they have minus the number of tails they have.

ChatGPT
An animal that fits this description is a "bee." A bee has six legs and one tail (stinger), so the number of legs minus the number of tails is five, which is equal to the length of the word "bee."

Figure 16.7 How GPT-4 still makes low-level mistakes

The output in figure 16.7 shows that, according to GPT-4, five is equal to the number of letters in the word "bee."

16.4.2 Ethical concerns for LLMs

One of the most pressing ethical concerns is the potential for LLMs to perpetuate and amplify biases in their training data. Since these models learn from vast datasets often derived from human-generated content, they can inherit biases related to gender, race, ethnicity, and other social factors. This can result in biased outputs that reinforce stereotypes and discrimination.

To mitigate bias, it is essential to adopt diverse and inclusive training datasets, implement bias detection and correction algorithms, and ensure transparency in model

---

[1] Maggiori, Emmanuel, 2023, *Smart Until It's Dumb: Why Artificial Intelligence Keeps Making Epic Mistakes (and Why the AI Bubble Will Burst)*, Applied Maths Ltd. Kindle Edition.

development and evaluation. It's particularly important to establish industry-wide collaboration to set standards for bias mitigation practices and promote responsible AI development.

However, we must keep in mind not to overcorrect. A counterexample is that Google's Gemini overcorrected the stereotypes in image generation by including people of color in groups like Nazi-era German soldiers.[2]

Another concern for LLMs is their potential for misinformation and manipulation. LLMs have the ability to generate realistic and persuasive text, which can be exploited for creating and spreading misinformation, propaganda, or manipulative content. This poses significant risks to public discourse, democracy, and trust in information.

The solution to this concern lies in developing robust content moderation systems. Establishing guidelines for responsible use and fostering collaborations between AI developers, policymakers, and media organizations are crucial steps in combating misinformation.

The third concern is related to privacy. The vast amount of data used to train LLMs raises privacy concerns, as sensitive information can be inadvertently revealed in the model's outputs. Additionally, the potential for LLMs to be used in cyberattacks or to bypass security measures poses significant security risks.

Furthermore, the data used to train LLMs is mostly gathered without authorization. Supporters argue that the way data is used to train LLMs is transformative: the model doesn't merely regurgitate the data but uses it to generate new, original content. This transformation could qualify under the "fair use" doctrine, which allows limited use of copyrighted material without permission if the use adds new expression or meaning. Critics argue that LLMs are trained on vast amounts of copyrighted texts without permission, which goes beyond what might be considered fair use. The scale of data used and the direct ingestion of copyrighted material without transformation during training could be seen as infringing. The debate is ongoing. The current copyright laws were not designed with generative AI in mind, leading to ambiguities about how they apply to technologies like LLMs. It's a debate that likely needs to be resolved by legislative and judicial bodies to provide clear guidelines and ensure that the interests of all parties are fairly represented.

The ethical concerns surrounding LLMs are multifaceted and require a holistic approach. Collaborative efforts among AI researchers, developers, and policymakers are crucial in developing ethical guidelines and frameworks that guide the responsible development and deployment of these powerful models. As we continue to harness the potential of LLMs, ethical considerations must remain at the forefront of our endeavors to ensure that AI advances in harmony with societal values and human well-being.

---

[2]   Adi Robertson, February 21, 2024, "Google Apologizes for 'Missing the Mark' after Gemini Generated Racially Diverse Nazis." The Verge, https://mng.bz/2ga9.

Summary

- Few-shot prompting means you give LLMs multiple examples to help them understand the task, while one-shot or zero-shot prompting means one example or no example is provided.

- LangChain is a Python library designed to facilitate the use of LLMs in various applications. It abstracts away the complexities of interacting with different LLMs and applications. It allows the agent to automatically go to the right tool in the toolbox based on the task at hand without explicitly telling it what to do.

- Modern pretrained LLMs such as OpenAI's GPT series can create various formats of content such as text, images, audio, and code.

- Despite their impressive achievements, LLMs lack a true understanding of the content or the ability to reason. These limitations can lead to errors in logic, factual inaccuracies, and a failure to grasp complex concepts or nuances. Furthermore, the rapid advancement and widespread application of these models have given rise to a host of ethical concerns such as bias, misinformation, breach of privacy, and copyright infringements. These issues demand careful consideration and proactive measures to ensure that the development and deployment of LLMs align with ethical standards and societal values.

appendix A
Installing Python, Jupyter Notebook, and PyTorch

Various ways of installing Python and managing libraries and packages on your computer exist. This book uses Anaconda, an open-source Python distribution, package manager, and environment management tool. Anaconda stands out for its user-friendly nature and capacity to facilitate the effortless installation of numerous libraries and packages, which could be painful or downright impossible to install otherwise.

Specifically, Anaconda allows users to install packages through both 'conda install' and 'pip install,' broadening the spectrum of available resources. This appendix will guide you to create a dedicated Python virtual environment for all projects in this book. This segmentation ensures that the libraries and packages used in this book remain isolated from any libraries utilized in other, unrelated projects, thus eliminating any potential interference.

We will use Jupyter Notebook as our integrated development environment (IDE). I will guide you through the installation of Jupyter Notebook in the Python virtual environment you just created. Finally, I will guide you through the process of installing PyTorch, Torchvision, and Torchaudio, based on whether your computer is equipped with a compute unified device architecture (CUDA)-enabled GPU.

A.1 *Installing Python and setting up a virtual environment*

In this section, I'll guide you through the process of installing Anaconda on your computer based on your operating system. After that, you'll create a Python virtual environment for all projects in this book. Finally, you'll install Jupyter Notebook as your IDE to run Python programs in this book.

A.1.1 *Installing Anaconda*

To install Python through the Anaconda distribution, follow these steps.

First, go to the https://www.anaconda.com/download/success and scroll to the bottom of the webpage. Locate and download the most recent Python 3 version tailored to your specific operating system (be it Windows, macOS, or Linux).

If you are using Windows, download the latest Python 3 graphical installer from this link. Click on the installer and follow the provided instructions to install. To confirm the successful installation of Anaconda on your computer, you can search for the "Anaconda Navigator" application on your computer. If you can launch the application, Anaconda has been successfully installed.

For macOS users, the latest Python 3 graphical installer for Mac is recommended, although a command line installer option is also available. Execute the installer and follow the provided instructions. Verify the successful installation of Anaconda by searching for the "Anaconda Navigator" application on your computer. If you can launch the application, Anaconda has been successfully installed.

The installation process for Linux is more complex than for other operating systems, as there is no graphical installer. Begin by identifying the latest Linux version. Select the appropriate x86 or Power8 and Power9 package. Click to download the latest installer bash script. The installer bash script is typically saved to your computer's Downloads folder by default. Install Anaconda by executing the bash script within a terminal. Upon completing the installation, activate it by running the following command:

```
source ~/.bashrc
```

To access Anaconda Navigator, enter the following command in a terminal:

```
anaconda-navigator
```

If you can successfully launch the Anaconda Navigator on your Linux system, your installation of Anaconda is complete.

> **Exercise A.1**
>
> Install Anaconda on your computer based on your operating system. After that, open the Anaconda Navigator app on your computer to confirm the installation.

A.1.2   *Setting up a Python virtual environment*

It's highly recommended that you create a separate virtual environment for this book. Let's name the virtual environment *dgai*. Execute the following command in the Anaconda prompt (Windows) or a terminal (Mac and Linux):

```
conda create -n dgai
```

After pressing the Enter key on your keyboard, follow the instructions on the screen and press y when the prompt asks you y/n. To activate the virtual environment, run the following command in the same Anaconda prompt (Windows) or terminal (Mac and Linux):

```
conda activate dgai
```

The virtual environment isolates the Python packages and libraries that you use for this book from other packages and libraries that you use for other purposes. This prevents any undesired interference.

> ### Exercise A.2
>
> Create a Python virtual environment *dgai* on your computer. After that, activate the virtual environment.

A.1.3   *Installing Jupyter Notebook*

Now, let's install Jupyter Notebook in the newly created virtual environment on your computer.

First, activate the virtual environment by running the following line of code in the Anaconda prompt (in Windows) or a terminal (in Mac or Linux):

```
conda activate dgai
```

To install Jupyter Notebook in the virtual environment, run the command

```
conda install notebook
```

Follow the on-screen instructions all the way through to install the app.

To launch Jupyter Notebook, execute the following command:

```
jupyter notebook
```

The Jupyter Notebook app will open in your default browser.

> ### Exercise A.3
>
> Install Jupyter Notebook in the Python virtual environment *dgai*. After that, open the Jupter Notebook app on your computer to confirm the installation.

A.2 Installing PyTorch

In this section, I'll guide you through the installation of PyTorch, based on whether you have a CUDA-enabled GPU on your computer. The official PyTorch website, https://pytorch.org/get-started/locally/, provides updates on PyTorch installation with or without CUDA. I encourage you to check the website for any updates.

CUDA is only available on Windows or Linux, not on Mac. To find out if your computer is equipped with a CUDA-enabled GPU, open the Windows PowerShell (in Windows) or a terminal (in Linux) and issue the following command:

```
nvidia-smi
```

If your computer has a CUDA-enabled GPU, you should see an output similar to figure A.1. Further, make a note of the CUDA version as shown at the top right corner of the figure because you'll need this piece of information later when you install PyTorch. Figure A.1 shows that the CUDA version is 11.8 on my computer. The version may be different on your computer.

```
PS C:\Users\mark> nvidia-smi
Sat Nov 18 07:53:08 2023
+-----------------------------------------------------------------------------+
| NVIDIA-SMI 522.06       Driver Version: 522.06       CUDA Version: 11.8     |
|-------------------------------+----------------------+----------------------+
| GPU  Name            TCC/WDDM | Bus-Id        Disp.A | Volatile Uncorr. ECC |
| Fan  Temp  Perf  Pwr:Usage/Cap|         Memory-Usage | GPU-Util  Compute M. |
|                               |                      |               MIG M. |
|===============================+======================+======================|
|   0  NVIDIA GeForce ... WDDM  | 00000000:01:00.0  On |                  N/A |
| 37%   31C    P8    12W / 175W |    614MiB /  8192MiB |      5%      Default |
|                               |                      |                  N/A |
+-------------------------------+----------------------+----------------------+
```

Figure A.1 Checking if your computer has a CUDA-enabled GPU

If you see an error message after running the command `nvidia-smi`, your computer doesn't have a CUDA-enabled GPU.

In the first subsection, I'll discuss how to install PyTorch if you don't have a CUDA-enabled GPU on your computer. You can use the CPU to train all generative AI models in this book. It just takes much longer. However, I'll provide you with the pretrained models so that you can witness generative AI in action.

On the other hand, if you are using a Windows or Linux operating system and you do have a CUDA-enabled GPU on your computer, I'll guide you through the installation of PyTorch with CUDA in the second subsection.

A.2.1 Installing PyTorch without CUDA

To install PyTorch with CPU training, first activate the virtual environment *dgai* by running the following line of code in the Anaconda prompt (in Windows) or a terminal (in Mac or Linux):

```
conda activate dgai
```

You should be able to see *(dgai)* in front of your prompt, which indicates that you are now in the *dgai* virtual environment. To install PyTorch, issue the following line of command:

```
conda install pytorch torchvision torchaudio cpuonly -c pytorch
```

Follow the on-screen instructions to finish the installation. Here, we install three libraries together: PyTorch, Torchaudio, and Torchvision. Torchaudio is a library to process audio and signals, and we need it to generate music in this book. We'll also use the Torchvision library extensively in the book to process images.

If your Mac computer has an Apple silicon or AMD GPU with macOS 12.3 or later, you can potentially use the new Metal Performance Shaders backend for GPU training acceleration. More information is available at https://developer.apple.com/metal/pytorch/ and https://pytorch.org/get-started/locally/.

To check if the three libraries are successfully installed on your computer, run the following lines of code:

```
import torch, torchvision, torchaudio

print(torch.__version__)
print(torchvision.__version__)
print(torchaudio.__version__)
```

The output on my computer says

```
2.0.1
0.15.2
2.0.2
```

If you don't see an error message, you have successfully installed PyTorch on your computer.

A.2.2   *Installing PyTorch with CUDA*

To install PyTorch with CUDA, first find out the CUDA version of your GPU, as shown at the top right corner of figure A.1. My CUDA version is 11.8, so I'll use it as an example in the installation here.

If you go to the PyTorch website at https://pytorch.org/get-started/locally/, you'll see an interactive interface as shown in figure A.2.

Once there, choose your operating system, select Conda as the Package, Python as the Language, and either CUDA 11.8 or CUDA 12.1 as your computer platform (based on what you have found out in the previous step). If the CUDA version on your computer is neither 11.8 nor 12.1, choose the one closest to your version and it will work. For example, if a computer has a CUDA version of 12.4 and someone used CUDA 12.1, the installation would be successful.

The command you need to run will be shown at the bottom panel. For example, I am using the Windows operating system, and I have CUDA 11.8 on my GPU. Therefore, the command for me is shown at the bottom panel of figure A.2.

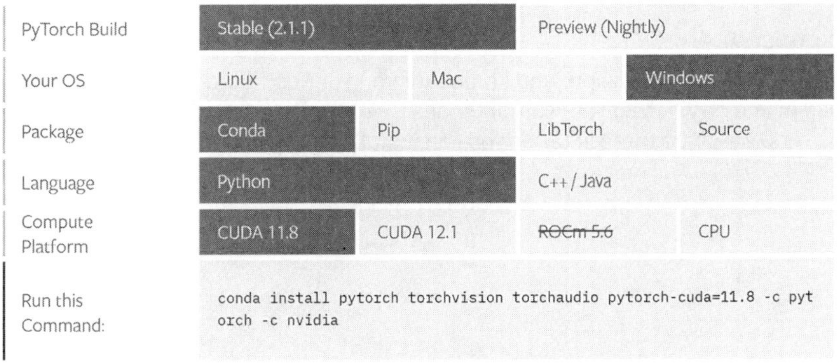

PyTorch Build	Stable (2.1.1)		Preview (Nightly)	
Your OS	Linux	Mac		Windows
Package	Conda	Pip	LibTorch	Source
Language	Python		C++ / Java	
Compute Platform	CUDA 11.8	CUDA 12.1	~~ROCm 5.6~~	CPU
Run this Command:	conda install pytorch torchvision torchaudio pytorch-cuda=11.8 -c pyt orch -c nvidia			

Figure A.2   The interactive interface on how to install PyTorch

Once you know what command to run to install PyTorch with CUDA, activate the virtual environment by running the following line of code in the Anaconda prompt (Windows) or a terminal (Linux):

```
conda activate dgai
```

Then issue the line of command you have found out in the last step. For me, the command line is

```
conda install pytorch torchvision torchaudio pytorch-cuda=11.8 -c pytorch -c
nvidia
```

Follow the on-screen instructions to finish the installation. Here, we install three libraries together: PyTorch, Torchaudio, and Torchvision. Torchaudio is a library to process audio and signals and we need it to generate music in this book. We also use the Torchvision library extensively in the book to process images.

To make sure you have PyTorch correctly installed, run the following lines of code in a new cell in Jupyter Notebook:

```
import torch, torchvision, torchaudio

print(torch.__version__)
print(torchvision.__version__)
print(torchaudio.__version__)
device="cuda" if torch.cuda.is_available() else "cpu"
print(device)
```

The output is as follows on my computer:

```
2.0.1
0.15.2
2.0.2
cuda
```

The last line of the output says `cuda`, indicating that I have installed PyTorch with CUDA. If you have installed PyTorch without CUDA on your computer, the output is `cpu`.

Exercise A.4

Install PyTorch, Torchvision, and Torchaudio on your computer based on your operating system and on whether your computer has GPU training acceleration. After that, print out the versions of the three libraries you just installed.

appendix B
Minimally qualified readers and deep learning basics

This book is intended for machine learning enthusiasts and data scientists across various business fields who possess intermediate Python programming skills and are interested in learning about generative AI. Through this book, readers will learn to create novel and innovative content—such as images, text, numbers, shapes, and audio—that can benefit their employers' businesses and advance their own careers.

This book is designed for those who have a solid grasp of Python. You should be familiar with variable types like integers, floats, strings, and Booleans. You should also be comfortable creating *for* and *while* loops and understand conditional execution and branching (e.g., using *if, elif,* and *else* statements). The book involves frequent use of Python functions and classes, and you should know how to install and import third-party Python libraries and packages. If you need to brush up on these skills, the free online Python tutorial provided by W3Schools is a great resource (https://www.w3schools.com/python/).

Additionally, you should have a basic understanding of machine learning, particularly neural networks and deep learning. In this appendix, we will review key concepts such as loss functions, activation functions, and optimizers, which are essential for developing and training deep neural networks. However, this appendix is not meant to be a comprehensive tutorial on these topics. If you find gaps in your understanding, it is strongly recommended that you address them before proceeding with the projects in this book. A good book for this purpose is *Deep Learning with PyTorch* by Stevens, Antiga, and Viehmann (2020).[1]

No prior experience with PyTorch or generative AI is required. In chapter 2, you will learn the basics of PyTorch, starting with its basic data types. You will also implement an end-to-end deep learning project in PyTorch to get hands-on experience. The goal of chapter 2 is to prepare you to use PyTorch for building and training various generative models in the book.

B.1   Deep learning and deep neural networks

Machine learning (ML) represents a new paradigm in AI. Unlike traditional rule-based AI, which involves programming explicit rules into a computer, ML involves feeding the computer various examples and allowing it to learn the rules on its own. Deep learning is a subset of ML that employs deep neural networks for this learning process.

In this section, you'll learn about neural networks and why some are considered deep neural networks.

B.1.1   Anatomy of a neural network

A neural network aims to mimic the functioning of the human brain. It consists of an input layer, an output layer, and zero, one, or more hidden layers in between. The term "deep neural networks" refers to networks with many hidden layers, which tend to be more powerful.

We'll start with a simpler example featuring two hidden layers, as shown in figure B.1.

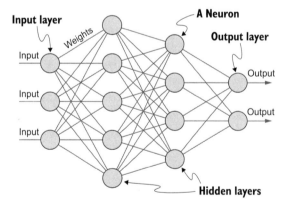

Figure B.1   The structure of a neural network. A neural network is composed of an input layer; zero, one, or more hidden layers; and an output layer. Each layer contains one or more neurons. Neurons in each layer are connected to those in the preceding and subsequent layers, with the strength of these connections represented by weights. In this figure, the neural network features an input layer with three neurons, two hidden layers with six and four neurons, respectively, and an output layer with two neurons.

---

[1] Eli Stevens, Luca Antiga, and Thomas Viehmann, 2020, *Deep Learning with PyTorch*, Manning Publications.

A neural network consists of an input layer, a variable number of hidden layers, and an output layer. Each layer is made up of one or more neurons. Neurons in one layer connect to neurons in the previous and next layers, with the connection strengths measured by weights. In the example illustrated in figure B.1, the neural network features an input layer with three neurons, two hidden layers containing six and four neurons, respectively, and an output layer with two neurons.

B.1.2 *Different types of layers in neural networks*

Within a neural network, various types of layers serve distinct purposes. The most common is the dense layer, where each neuron is connected to every neuron in the next layer. Because of this full connectivity, a dense layer is also referred to as a fully connected layer.

Another frequently used type of neural layer, especially in this book, is the convolutional layer. Convolutional layers treat input as multidimensional data and are adept at extracting patterns from it. In our book, convolutional layers are often employed to extract spatial features from images.

Convolutional layers differ from fully connected (dense) layers in several key ways. First, each neuron in a convolutional layer connects only to a small region of the input. This design is based on the understanding that in image data, local groups of pixels are more likely to be related. This local connectivity significantly reduces the number of parameters, making convolutional neural networks (CNNs) more efficient. Second, CNNs utilize shared weights—the same weights are applied across different regions of the input. This mechanism is similar to sliding a filter across the entire input space. This filter detects specific features (e.g., edges or textures) regardless of their position in the input, which leads to the property of translation invariance. Due to their structure, CNNs are more efficient for image processing, requiring fewer parameters than fully connected networks of similar size. This results in faster training times and lower computational costs. Additionally, CNNs are generally more effective at capturing spatial hierarchies in image data. We discuss CNNs in detail in chapter 4.

The third type of neural network is the recurrent neural network (RNN). Fully connected networks treat each input independently, processing each input separately without considering any relationship or order between different inputs. In contrast, RNNs are specifically designed to handle sequential data. In an RNN, the output at a given time step depends not only on the current input but also on previous inputs. This allows RNNs to maintain a form of memory, capturing information from previous time steps to influence the processing of the current input. See chapter 8 for details on RNNs.

B.1.3 *Activation Functions*

Activation functions are a crucial component of neural networks, functioning as the mechanisms that transform inputs into outputs and determine when a neuron should activate. Some functions are akin to on-off switches, playing a pivotal role in enhancing the power of neural networks. Without activation functions, neural networks would be limited to learning only linear relationships in data. By introducing nonlinearity, activation functions enable the creation of complex, nonlinear relationships between inputs and outputs.

The most commonly-used activation function is the rectified linear unit (ReLU). A ReLU activates the neuron when the input is positive, effectively allowing information to pass through. When the input is negative, the neuron is deactivated. This straightforward on-off behavior facilitates the modeling of nonlinear relationships.

Another commonly used activation function is the sigmoid function, which is particularly suited for binary classification problems. The sigmoid function compresses inputs into a range between 0 and 1, effectively representing the probabilities of a binary outcome.

For multicategory classification tasks, the softmax function is employed. The softmax function transforms a vector of values into a probability distribution, where the values sum to 1. This is ideal for modeling the probabilities of multiple outcomes.

Lastly, the tanh activation function is noteworthy. Similar to the sigmoid function, tanh produces values between −1 and 1. This characteristic is especially useful when working with images, as image data often contains values within this range.

B.2   *Training a deep neural network*

This section provides an overview of the steps involved in training a neural network. A key aspect of this process is dividing your training dataset into a train set, a validation set, and a test set, which is crucial for developing a robust deep neural network. We will also discuss various loss functions and optimizers used in training neural networks.

B.2.1   *The training process*

Once a neural network is built, the next step is to gather a training dataset to train the model. Figure B.2 illustrates the steps in the training process.

On the left side of figure B.2, we see the initial division of the training dataset into three subsets: the train set, the validation set, and the test set. This division is critical for building a robust deep neural network. The training set is the subset of data used to train the model, where the model learns patterns, weights, and biases. The validation set is used to evaluate the model's performance during training and to decide when to stop training. The test set is used to assess the final performance of the model after training is complete, providing an unbiased evaluation of the model's ability to generalize to new, unseen data.

During the training phase, the model is trained on data in the train set. It iteratively adjusts its parameters to minimize the loss function (see the next subsection on different loss functions). After each epoch, the model's performance is evaluated using the validation set. If the performance on the validation set continues to improve, training proceeds. If the performance ceases to improve, training is stopped to prevent overfitting.

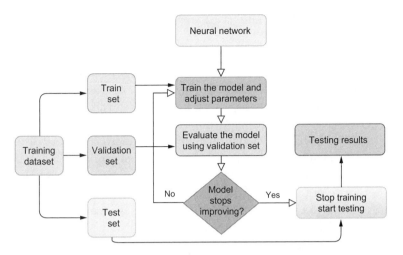

Figure B.2 **Training a neural network. The training dataset is divided into three subsets: the train set, the validation set, and the test set. The process for training a neural network involves the following steps. In the training phase, the train set is used to train the neural network and adjust its parameters to minimize the loss function. During each iteration of training, the model updates its parameters based on data in the train set. In the validation phase of each iteration, the model is evaluated using the validation set. The performance on the validation set helps determine if the model is still improving. If the model's performance on the validation set continues to improve, the next iteration of training proceeds using the train set. If the model's performance on the validation set stops improving, the training process is stopped to prevent overfitting. Once training is complete, the trained model is evaluated on the test set. This evaluation provides the final testing results, giving an estimate of the model's performance on unseen data.**

Once training is complete, the testing phase begins. The model is applied to the test set (unseen data) to assess its final performance and report results.

Dividing the dataset into three different sets is essential for several reasons. The train subset allows the model to learn patterns and features from the data and to adjust its parameters. The validation subset serves as a check against overfitting by enabling performance monitoring during training. The test subset provides an unbiased evaluation of the model's generalization ability, estimating its real-world performance.

By appropriately splitting the data and utilizing each set for its intended purpose, we ensure that the model is well trained and unbiasedly evaluated.

B.2.2 *Loss functions*

Loss functions are essential for measuring the accuracy of our predictions and guiding the optimization process when training deep neural networks.

A commonly used loss function is the mean squared error (MSE or L2 loss). MSE calculates the average squared difference between the model's predictions and the actual values. A closely related loss function is the mean absolute error (MAE or L1 loss). MAE calculates the average absolute difference between predictions and actual values. MAE is often used if the data are noisy and have many outliers since it punishes extreme values less than the L2 loss.

For binary classification tasks, where predictions are binary (0 or 1), the preferred loss function is binary cross-entropy. This function measures the average difference between predicted probabilities and actual binary labels.

In multicategory classification tasks, where predictions can take multiple discrete values, the categorical cross-entropy loss function is employed. This function measures the average difference between predicted probability distributions and actual distributions.

During the training of ML models such as deep neural networks, we adjust the model parameters to minimize the loss function. The adjustment magnitude is proportional to the first derivative of the loss function with respect to the model parameters. The learning rate controls the speed of these adjustments. If the learning rate is too high, the model parameters may oscillate around the optimal values and never converge. Conversely, if the learning rate is too low, the learning process becomes slow, and it takes a long time for the parameters to converge.

B.2.3   *Optimizers*

Optimizers are algorithms used in training deep neural networks to adjust the model's weights to minimize the loss function. They guide the learning process by determining how the model's parameters should be updated at each step, thus enhancing performance over time.

One example of an optimizer is a stochastic gradient descent (SGD). A SGD adjusts weights by moving them in the direction of the negative gradient of the loss function. It updates weights using a subset of the data (mini-batch) at each iteration, which helps speed up the training process and improve generalization.

In this book, the most commonly used optimizer is Adam (Adaptive Moment Estimation). Adam combines the benefits of two other extensions of SGD: AdaGrad and RMSProp. It computes adaptive learning rates for each parameter based on estimates of the first and second moments of the gradients. This adaptability makes Adam particularly suitable for problems involving large datasets and/or numerous parameters.

index